Natural Law and Religious Freedom

Every successive generation finds fresh reasons for the study of natural law. Current interest in the natural law may well be due to a pervasive moral pessimism in the Western cultural context and wider contemporary geopolitical challenges. Those geopolitical challenges result from two significant and worrisome global developments: unprecedented violent persecution of religious minorities on several continents and a growing climate of secular hostility toward religious faith in Western societies. *Natural Law and Religious Freedom* aims to address what is relatively absent from the literature by demonstrating the importance of natural law ethics in both establishing and preserving basic human rights, of which religious freedom has pride of place.

Probing contemporary challenges to natural law thinking that are both internal and external to religious faith, and examining the character and constitution of natural law ethics, *Natural Law and Religious Freedom* will be of interest to theologians, ethicists, and philosophers, as well as policy analysts, politicians, and activists who are concerned to anchor religious freedom and human rights policy considerations in an enduring way.

J. Daryl Charles serves as a contributing editor to *Providence: A Journal of Christianity and American Foreign Policy*; is an affiliated scholar of the John Jay Institute, USA; and is the author, co-author, or editor of 14 books, including (with David D. Corey) *The Just War Tradition: An Introduction* (ISI Books, 2012), *Retrieving the Natural Law: A Return to Moral First Things* (Eerdmans, 2008), *Virtue amidst Vice* (Sheffield Academic Press, 1997), and, most recently, (with Mark David Hall), *America's Wars: A Just War Perspective* (University of Notre Dame Press, forthcoming). Charles has taught at Taylor University and Union University; was a 2013/14 visiting professor in the honors program at Berry College; served as a 2007/8 William B. Simon Visiting Fellow in Religion and Public Life at the James Madison Program, Princeton University; and served as a 2003/4 visiting fellow of the Institute for Faith and Religion, Baylor University. He is a member of the James Madison Society, Princeton University. The focus of Charles's research and writing is the natural law, the ethics of war and peace, criminal justice ethics, and religion and society. Prior to entering the university classroom, Charles did public policy work in criminal justice in Washington, DC.

Natural Law and Religious Freedom

The Role of Moral First Things in Grounding and Protecting the First Freedom

J. Daryl Charles

Routledge
Taylor & Francis Group
LONDON AND NEW YORK

First published 2018
by Routledge

2 Park Square, Milton Park, Abingdon, Oxfordshire OX14 4RN
52 Vanderbilt Avenue, New York, NY 10017

Routledge is an imprint of the Taylor & Francis Group, an informa business

First issued in paperback 2019

British Library Cataloguing-in-Publication Data
A catalogue record for this book is available from the British Library

Library of Congress Cataloging-in-Publication Data
Names: Charles, J. Daryl, 1950– author.
Title: Natural law and religious freedom : the role of moral first things in grounding and protecting the first freedom / J. Daryl Charles.
Description: Abingdon, Oxon ; New York, NY : Routledge is an imprint of the Taylor & Francis Group, an Informa Business, [2018] | Includes bibliographical references and index.
Identifiers: LCCN 2017014519 | ISBN 9781472467775 (hbk : alk. paper) | ISBN 9781315597539 (ebk)
Subjects: LCSH: Freedom of religion. | Religion and law. | Natural law.
Classification: LCC K3258 .C474 2018 | DDC 342.08/52—dc23
LC record available at https://lccn.loc.gov/2017014519

ISBN: 978-1-4724-6777-5 (hbk)
ISBN: 978-0-367-88126-9 (pbk)

Typeset in Sabon
by Apex CoVantage, LLC

Contents

Preface

Two global developments combine in our day to create what may be the most significant story of the twenty-first century. One is the unprecedented violent persecution in many parts of the world of religious minorities – often (though not exclusively) Christian minorities. The second is the "war on religion" that is a primary feature of Western societies. With the latter, I refer to a growing climate of secular hostility toward religious faith; given the religious history of these nations, this hostility unsurprisingly is aimed chiefly at Christianity. Tellingly, neither of these two phenomena, however, is a part of mainstream news reporting. In fact, unless such conflicts are perceived as being "political" in nature, they will go largely unreported. This stunning silence is but one feature of the hostility that characterizes an aggressive, unreflective secularism and serves as an accurate measurement of religious freedom's precarious state.

But it needs to be said that "religious freedom" is not simply an issue for "religious people." In the words of Paul A. Marshall, senior fellow at the Hudson Institute's Center for Religious Freedom, "The persecution of all peoples of any or no religion should be equally as offensive in our eyes as that of believers in any particular religion."[1] That includes atheists and agnostics. It is my hope that those of my readers who would identify themselves as either non-religious or agnostic toward religious belief will be patient in considering my argument in this book: religious freedom is important for *all* people, *whether they confess religious belief or no religious belief*. What's more, since most people in the world profess to be religious believers of one kind or another,[2] our concern for religious freedom "would necessarily include *most of the world's human rights violations* of whatever kind."[3] The matter of religious freedom and persecution is applicable to *all* people groups *the world over* and is not confined to any particular region or continent.[4] Hence, it cannot be viewed solely as a Western concern, even when great responsibilities are lodged with these nations as a result of their cultural history and the influence that they carry – for better or worse – in the world.

There are any number of very helpful books, reports, and surveys in print that since 2000 have called attention to the "war on religion" around the world.[5] And for these resources we can be grateful. Many of these document with great care and precision the status of religious freedom and human rights violations in nations around the globe. What, however, is largely lacking in the literature, at both the academic and popular level, is a defense of the *foundations* of religious freedom.[6] Why is religious freedom of utmost importance? In what view of human nature is it anchored? What is the link between religious freedom and human rights violations? Why is this a perennial issue? On what is religious freedom founded? Why is it universal in scope? And what becomes of a society which fails to safeguard this most fundamental of freedoms for its citizens?

These are the questions that stand behind much of my argument as it unfolds in this volume. My contention is not that we should simply become "activists" for the cause of faith and religious freedom, although responding in humane ways to socio-political atrocity and basic human rights violations both globally and in the West *will* require a measure of activism on our part. But the problem with activism is that it is often not properly guided by a morally serious view of the world, of human nature, and of the common social good. Often it lacks sufficient moral-philosophical *grounding*, even when it might be well intentioned. Permit me to clarify myself. My intent here is not to pit theory against practice, or knowing against doing. Rather, it is to argue that genuine and sustained attempts to safeguard basic human rights, which begin with the "sacred rights of conscience," must both conform with moral reality ("What constitutes just and unjust, good and evil?") and find application with the needy ("Who is my neighbor?"). For this reason, the ethical model of the "Good Samaritan" surfaces in several chapters of this volume, leading to an extended discussion in Chapter 6 of the unity of justice and charity, a unity which underpins natural law ethics. The importance of this unity cannot be overstated given the frequent divorce between justice and charity that characterizes both academic and popular ethical thinking. This divorce derives from the widespread assumption that the two virtues stand in tension or opposition to one another. The fruits of this perceived opposition, however, are disastrous when applied to social ethics and matters of public policy. The Samaritan is "good" because he discerns moral reality, not turning a blind eye toward gross injustice, and because, as a consequence, he acts – despite great inconvenience – justly and charitably toward the "neighbor" in dire need. Stated another way, the "Good Samaritan" embodies a "Golden Rule" ethic – namely, treating others as *we ourselves* would want to be treated. The so-called Golden Rule ethic, it should be noted, has both positive and negative obligations, as I argue in Chapter 5. The negative corollary is that we do not allow others to be treated as we ourselves would not wish to be treated. Chapter 5 contains a specific "test-case" for its application: humanitarian intervention.

Earlier, I noted what is largely lacking in the literature on religious freedom – i.e., any sort of defense of its moral-philosophical *foundations*. Among chroniclers of American religious history, this absence is striking, given the unique character of the nation's founding. Part of the reason for this dearth in the literature has to do with the nature of the conventional narrative as it has developed in the context of American political and legal history. There are, as constitutional lawyer and author Stephen D. Smith observes, the "standard story" and the "revised story" of religious freedom.[7] One of the guiding assumptions of the "standard story" is that Americans "so completely confuse Christianity and freedom in their minds that it is almost impossible to have them conceive of the one without the other."[8] Apologists for a secular view of history prefer to depict a nation's religious past not as a progressive unfolding and development of freedom but as a history of *religious conflict* and *opposition to human rights*. Gradually, according to this narrative, enlightened thinking as a result of the forces of modernism prevailed, and with it, the emergent struggle for human rights as we know it today. The fundamental assumption here is that religion stands in the way of our basic freedoms. Hence, chroniclers of this narrative find it obligatory to require an "either . . . or . . ." reading of American history. As I argue in Chapter 3, this interpretation – an interpretation that is simplistic and dependent on partial truths – does not square with the wider evidence. What makes the American founding unique – an "experiment" in ordered liberty, as the founders understood it – is the blend of the secular *and* the sacred.[9]

A related feature of the "standard story" is an exaggerated fear of "theocracy," an interpretive pattern that warrants a measure of critique in Chapter 4. What is interesting here, however, is that this fear is directed *only toward orthodox Christianity*, not (say) toward Islam, which is theocratic at its heart and considers any "separation" of church and state to be utter blasphemy.[10] While a full-scale critique of this double standard, which fears (or refuses) to criticize theocratic Islam yet is obsessed with removing Christian public presence in society, is beyond the scope of this volume, the double standard itself surely needs exposing, albeit in another venue. For our present purposes, however, this reaction – or overreaction – to American religious and political history, which typically results in a program of "demythologizing," does not serve us well. It fails on several important counts. First, it fully misses, or denies, the importance of religious belief to human beings and human culture. Relatedly, it fails to appreciate, or it intentionally ignores, the wider agreement that was found among the founders and framers on the place of religion in public life, notwithstanding their strongly differing views and considerable diversity. In addition, as noted earlier, it is exaggerated in its criticism of orthodox Christianity while denying, or ignoring, the overtly theocratic assumptions of Islam, with its attempts to implement Islamic law (the Shari'a) in its entirety.[11] These Islamic underpinnings prevent or undermine the very social conditions upon which democratic pluralism and religious freedom are dependent. Finally, it fails to acknowledge the inherently "religious" character of its own philosophical pre-commitments. That the secularist assumptions thought to support "political liberalism," as most people understand it, are in truth "religious"[12] in their very nature is addressed in Chapters 1 and 4. This state of affairs, I maintain, suggests the need for a "post-secular" critique of the assumptions of secularism, parts of which surface in Chapters 1, 4, and 8.

Some advocates of the "standard" narrative call us to get "beyond religious freedom," as one writer and political theorist urges us,[13] as if the concern for basic human freedoms is somehow parochial, anachronistic, or sectarian and tangential to human flourishing. However, neither is it possible nor is it advisable to get "beyond" basic human rights. Alas, we are confronted with a rudimentary question: *are basic human rights and human dignity universal in nature, or are they the product of particular cultures?* Much rides on how we answer that question. What's more, that question has an inescapably religious dimension, as evidenced by most human cultures. If "religious freedom" is central to the health of a "free society," as I maintain in concert with virtually all of the American founders and framers and a sizable number of social commentators today, then it is the very *wellspring* from which *all* – indeed, *all* – other freedoms derive. An important subtheme threading its way throughout this volume is that religious and moral convictions are *pre-political* in their nature and constitution. That is, they are antecedent to the state and to the formulation of law. In probing this "pre-political" character of moral law and religious conviction, the present volume deviates from the focus of much of the established literature, which frequently analyzes the compatibility of various religious traditions in terms of how they bear on political developments, economic issues, discrimination, or human rights.

Furthermore, neither is religious freedom an "impossibility," as one legal theorist insists, based on the questionable assumption that laws protecting the rights of religious believers *cannot be enforced justly*.[14] While there is some truth to this argument in light of current law and political realities, the problem is not with our attempts to protect religious freedom. Rather, it is with the current political and legal climate which fails (or refuses) to protect religious freedom as a "natural right." The solution, then, is not to *give up on the idea* of religious freedom. It is to reform the political and legal system in such a way as to bring it more in line with how the founders and framers envisioned it. While I grant that such change would require time – perhaps several generations – and massive shifts in our understanding, the answer most assuredly is *not* to shoot the messenger, as it were.

From the nation's inception, the founders sought a way of viewing religion and society that was unique to the world. It was conceived as a foremost voluntary and moral arrangement, undergirded by natural law thinking, which aimed – however imperfectly – at religious freedom. It intended as its goal *neither* a non-religious *nor* an anti-religious society. As evidenced by its voluntary approach to the "separation" of church and state, a subject taken up in Chapter 3, it permitted the "free trade of religion," in the words of one historian.[15] The notion that a society could be so "conceived in liberty" derived from a baseline moral assumption of the founders' generation – namely, that there exist certain "self-evident truths" that govern human relations and the affairs of men and nations.[16] This is none other than the natural law.

Full disclosure is necessary at this point. I confess to having become a natural law proponent as a result of my days in Washington, DC, doing public-policy research in criminal justice. As the discussion in Chapter 2 indicates, there is a rich continuum of natural law thinking that stretches over the last two millennia and is to be found among political and moral thinkers of every age. Tragically, in the modern era both religiously minded and secularistic types often have tended to reject natural law moral reasoning. Even among the religiously minded, this suspicion – if not outright rejection – has been very pronounced among Protestants – until of late, that is. While there is no full-scale "revival" of natural law thinking across the board among Protestant types, there has been something of a renewal in some circles.[17] I count myself to be a part of such renewed thinking.

This "renewal" has been enriching in important ways. At the most basic level, it has deepened my own understanding of human nature and human culture, making sense of the "moral impulse" that distinguishes human beings from all of life. It has also forced me to take seriously the study of human history and the history of ideas, something that is quite out of step with the "post-consensus" *Zeitgeist*. After all, if there are no values – if there is no source of moral authority – antecedent to the state and brute political power, then human beings can be manipulated without limit for inhumane purposes, as I argue in Chapter 7. And, in the end, nothing is left in the cosmos that can cry out against the "will to power." We divorce ourselves from our wider cultural history and cultural traditions at our own peril. Correlatively, entering into dialogue with the natural law tradition has developed within me the awareness that periods of social and political upheaval very often are attended by a "renewal" in metaphysics. This is surely no accident. For it is during those periods, in which societies question or throw off foundational elements in their cultural heritage, that renewed thinking about the "permanent things" emerges. I consider the present day to be one such time.

Finally, entering into this centuries-long dialogue has caused me to see the great value in political and cultural engagement. And perhaps here a brief autobiographical note is appropriate. It so happened that I was raised in the Anabaptist tradition. My father was a conscientious objector during the Second World War, performing "alternative service" in a V.A. hospital in light of the draft. From their very beginning in the sixteenth century, the Anabaptists (self-proclaimed "radical reformers") distinguished themselves from fellow Protestant reformers in their confession of absolute separation from the world. This commitment to separation is seen in the 1527 Schleitheim Confession, the earliest document setting forth Anabaptist confessional beliefs (www.anabaptists.org/history/the-schleitheim-confession.html). Even to the present day, in varying degrees, Anabaptists maintain "separation" as a necessary form of social witness. Hence, for example, one will not find Anabaptists in certain vocations that, from their perspective, are thought to mirror an alliance or compromise with surrounding culture. Foremost among these abstentions are service in the military and serving in any political office. But, by extension, Anabaptists will not be found in other vocations of civil service either – for example, in public policy work, government-related service, economics, banking, science and technology, law, and diplomacy, as well as in particular vocations which maintain or protect the common good such as security, law enforcement, and policy analysis.

It goes without saying that my own convictions over the years regarding political participation, public service, law and policy, and the common good have undergone a sizable shift, to say the least. As an adult, my own thinking and experience have been richly broadened by interaction both with people from the wider "Reformed" tradition and with Catholic social thought. Both traditions share important common ground – namely, the conviction that participation in all cultural institutions is to be understood as a matter of *stewardship* and *responsible citizenship*. In many ways, this outlook mirrors a debt to Augustinian thinking about the "two cities"[18] – a theme that is taken up in several chapters of the book. At times, it may be the case that such participation will take the form of moral persuasion and activity to *counter* particular social or cultural currents – currents that are destructive, immoral, or dehumanizing. Nevertheless, this participation, whenever and wherever possible, must always be done as contributing citizens and not in isolation or withdrawal from the culture. "Separation" or "resistance" loses much of its moral authority when it is done in isolation from society or in a sectarian spirit rather than as part of responsible citizenship. Without our active participation, the common good crumbles and "civil society" as we have known it vanishes.

The wider burden of the volume before you is to develop the link between natural law and religious freedom. The latter can be designated the "first freedom" *if and only if* there are moral "first principles." Whether I have succeeded in developing this argument remains to be determined. In any event, I invite the reader to consider this linkage, entering into a timeless – and therefore timely – dialogue.

Notes

1 Paul A. Marshall, ed., *Religious Freedom in the World* (Lanham and London: Rowman & Littlefield, 2008), xiii.
2 According to researchers David B. Barrett and Todd Johnson, "Quantifying Alternate Futures of Religion and Religions," *Futures* 36, no. 9 (2004): 447–60, ca. 80% of the world's population can be classified as belonging to some self-identified religious group.
3 Marshall, *Religious Freedom in the World*, xiii.
4 While this claim is accurate, data taken from the most authoritative studies and surveys indicate that the chief threats to religious freedom are twofold: present or former communist regimes and resurgent/militant Islamist culture.
5 These are identified in Chapter 1. In this regard, see, especially, John L. Allen Jr., *The Global War on Christians: Dispatches from the Front Lines of Anti-Christian Persecution* (New York: Image, 2013); Paul A. Marshall, Lela Gilbert, and Nina Shea, *Persecuted: The Global Assault on Christians* (Nashville: Thomas Nelson, 2013); Rupert Shortt, *Christianophobia: A Faith Under Attack* (Grand Rapids and Cambridge, UK: Eerdmans, 2012); Brian J. Grim and Roger Finke, *The Price of Freedom Denied: Religious Persecution and Conflict in the*

Twenty-First Century (Cambridge and New York: Cambridge University Press, 2011); and Paul A. Marshall and Nina Shea, *Silenced: How Apostasy and Blasphemy Codes Are Choking Religious Freedom Worldwide* (Oxford and New York: Oxford University Press, 2011). To speak of a so-called war on religion is not original to me. It is used by Allen (see the earlier discussion) and is implicit in Shortt (see the earlier discussion) and Marshall/Gilbert/Shea (see the earlier discussion), among others.

6 This is not meant as a criticism; it is simply an observation.

7 Stephen D. Smith, *The Rise and Decline of American Religious Freedom* (Cambridge and London: Harvard University Press, 2014), 1–13.

8 David Sehat, *The Myth of American Religious Freedom* (Oxford and New York: Oxford University Press, 2011), vii.

9 For a helpful corrective to the standard narrative, see John Witte Jr., and Joel A. Nichols, *Religion and the American Constitutional Experiment*, 3rd ed. (Boulder: Westview Press, 2011).

10 In our day, a new term has been invented by those working in the academy – "Islamophobia" – to stifle any criticism of Islam in the Western context. In fact, it would appear to be gaining traction as an academic discipline, as evidenced by the creation of the Islamophobia Research and Documentation Project (IRDP) at the University of California, Berkeley and the *Islamophobia Studies Journal* (http://crg.berkeley.edu/content/islamophobia/islamophobia-studies-journal), and as evidenced by the sheer number of volumes published since 2010 with the word "Islamophobia" in their title. So, for example, Algernon Austin, *America Is Not Post-Racial: Xenophobia, Islamophobia, Racism, and the 44th President* (Santa Barbara: Praeger, 2015); Todd H. Green, *The Fear of Islam: An Introduction to Islamophobia in the West*(Minneapolis: Fortress Press, 2015); Arun, Kundnani, *The Muslims Are Coming! Islamophobia, Extremism, and the Domestic War on Terror* (London and Brooklyn: Verso, 2014); Irene Zempi and Neil Chakraborti, *Islamophobia, Victimisation, and the Veil* (Basinstoke: Palgrave Macmillan, 2014); Carl W. Ernst, ed., *Islamophobia in America: The Anatomy of Intolerance* (New York: Palgrave Macmillan, 2013); Deepa Kumar, *Islamophobia and the Politics of Empire* (Chicago: Haymarket Books, 2012); Nathan Lean, *The Islamophobia Industry: How the Right Manufactures Fear of Muslims* (London: Pluto Press, 2012); Ray Taras, *Xenophobia and Islamophobia in Europe* (Edinburgh: Edinburgh University Press, 2012); John L. Esposito and Ibrahim Kalin, eds., *The Challenge of Pluralism in the 21st Century* (Oxford and New York: Oxford University Press, 2011); Christopher Allen, *Islamophobia* (Surrey, UK, and Burlington: Ashgate, 2010); S. Sayyid and Abdool Karim Vakil, eds., *Thinking Through Islamophobia: Global Perspectives* (New York: Columbia University Press, 2010); and Joe L. Kincheloe, Shirley R. Steinberg, and Christopher Darius Stonebanks, eds., *Teaching Against Islamophobia* (New York: Peter Lang, 2010).The titles themselves are quite telling. Whether fearmongering or deception unites most of these volumes is difficult to say. A fear of truth and a hatred for the West, however, would seem to be a common denominator.

11 Islamists, not all Muslims, constitute the threat to democratic pluralism and religious freedom. For this reason, moderate, anti-Islamist Muslims are a key to lessening religious persecution in many parts of the world. They alone can counter the violent spirit of Islamist thinking.

12 Here I am presupposing the Latin root of the word – *religare*: to bind, bind together, or collect – in order to press this point. All people carry certain assumptions about ultimate reality, even when these are unspoken or implicit.

13 Elizabeth Shakman Hurd, *Beyond Religious Freedom: The New Global Politics of Religion* (Princeton: Princeton University Press, 2015). Resorting to exaggeration in order to make her point, Hurd, too, decries what she believes to be "a *powerful myth* of American exceptionalism that posits the United States as not

only the home of religious freedom but also the place *where both religion and freedom have been perfected*" (17, emphasis added).

14 Winnifred Fallers Sullivan, *The Impossibility of Religious Freedom* (Princeton: Princeton University Press, 2005).

15 So William Lee Miller, *The First Liberty: America's Foundation in Religious Freedom* (Washington, DC: George Washington University Press, 2003), xii.

16 While the amount of literature in this realm is enormous, few works capture the mindset of the founders' generation as thoroughly – and uniquely – as Michael I. Meyerson, *Endowed by Our Creator: The Birth of Religious Freedom in America* (New Haven and London: Yale University Press, 2012); Daniel L. Dreisbach, Mark David Hall, and Jeffry H. Morrison, eds., *The Founders on God and Government* (Lanham and Oxford: Rowman & Littlefield, 2004); and Robert S. Alley, ed., *James Madison on Religious Liberty* (Buffalo: Prometheus Books, 1985).

17 Consider alone those volumes published in the last decade – so, for example: Jesse Covington, Bryan McGraw, and Micah Watson, eds., *Natural Law and Evangelical Political Thought* (Lanham and Plymouth, UK: Lexington Books, 2013); Owen Anderson, *The Natural Moral Law: The Good After Modernity* (Cambridge and New York: Cambridge University Press, 2012); David VanDrunen, *Natural Law and the Two Kingdoms: A Study in the Development of Reformed Social Thought* (Emory University Studies in Law and Religion; Grand Rapids and Cambridge, UK: Eerdmans, 2009); J. Daryl Charles, *Retrieving the Natural Law: A Return to Moral First Things* (Critical Issues in Bioethics; Grand Rapids and Cambridge, UK: Eerdmans, 2008); and Stephen J. Grabill, *Rediscovering the Natural Law in Reformed Theological Ethics* (Grand Rapids and Cambridge, UK: Eerdmans, 2006). These works join other more recent volumes authored by Catholic or non-Protestant authors – among them: Steven J. Jensen, *Knowing the Natural Law: From Precepts and Inclinations to Deriving Oughts* (Washington, DC: The Catholic University of American Press, 2015); Anver M. Emon, Matthew Levering, and David Novak, *Natural Law: A Jewish, Christian, and Muslim Trialogue* (Oxford: Oxford University Press, 2014); J. Budziszewski, *The Line Through the Heart: Natural Law as Fact, Theory, and Sign of Contradiction* (Wilmington: ISI Books, 2011); John Finnis, *Natural Law and Natural Rights*, 2nd ed. (Clarendon Law Series; Oxford and New York: Oxford University Press, 2011); Matthew Levering, *Biblical Natural Law: A Theocentric and Teleological Approach* (Oxford and New York: Oxford University Press, 2008); and Russell Hittinger, *The First Grace: Rediscovering the Natural Law in a Post-Christian World*, 2nd ed. (Wilmington: ISI Books, 2007).

18 Two very readable volumes which develop the implications of Augustine's "city of man" imagery are Michael Gerson and Peter Wehner, *City of Man: Religion and Politics in a New Era* (Chicago: Moody, 2010), and Carl E. Braaten and Robert W. Jenson, eds., *The Two Cities of God: The Church's Responsibility for the Earthly City* (Grand Rapids and Cambridge, UK: Eerdmans, 1997).

1 Introduction – religious freedom as the "first freedom"

What it is and why it matters

That some of the natural rights of mankind are unalienable, and subject to no control but that of the Deity. Such are the sacred rights of conscience. Which in a state of nature, and of civil society, are exactly the same. They can neither be parted with nor controlled, by any human authority whatever.

—Samuel Stillman[1]

There are other branches of knowledge, which will be of great advantage to men in power. It is, at least, desirable that they should have a tolerable acquaintance with natural law – that they understand the natural rights of men, which are the same, under every species of government, and do not owe their origin to the social compact. Such, in a peculiar manner, are the sacred rights of conscience.

—Chandler Robbins[2]

Truth . . . has nothing to fear from conflict, unless by human interposition disarmed of her natural weapons, free argument and debate . . . Truth and reason are eternal. They have prevailed. And they will eternally prevail.

—Thomas Jefferson[3]

The assault on religious freedom

Religious freedom is in trouble. Serious trouble. The very freedom to respond to ultimate convictions – that is, to affirm what is true, definitive, and binding for all time – is under assault, and it is under assault both at home and abroad. Perhaps we have token familiarity with threats to human rights, religious freedom and practice, and public expression of religious beliefs around the world, particularly in communist police states and Islamic nations. However, terrorism and violence will be reported by the broadcast and print media *only* insofar as they are *political* events, not as they bear on religious minorities and religious freedom. Yet the truth is, rarely does a week go by without intimidation and violence against religious minorities in Asia, Africa, and the Middle East. It is a world "marked by persecution, discrimination, terrible acts of violence and religious intolerance."[4]

At present, confessing Christians are the religious group suffering the most severely from persecution on account of their faith, as serious research today indicates and Benedict XVI noted with particular poignancy in 2011:

> It is painful to think that in some areas of the world it is impossible to profess one's religion freely except at the risk of life and personal liberty . . . Many Christians experience daily affronts and often live in fear because of their pursuit of truth, their faith in Jesus Christ and their heartfelt plea for respect for religious freedom. *This situation is unacceptable*, since it represents an insult to God and to human dignity; furthermore, it is a threat to security and peace, and an obstacle to the achievement of authentic and integral human development.[5]

No stranger to inter-religious dialogue, Benedict enunciates what is integral to "human development" and flourishing – namely, *the right to religious freedom*. The absence of religious freedom, he stresses,

> Puts the brakes on authentic development and impedes the evolution of peoples towards greater socio-economic and spiritual well-being. This applies especially to terrorism motivated by [religious] fundamentalism, which generates grief, destruction and death, obstructs dialogue between nations [,] and diverts extensive resources from their peaceful and civil uses.[6]

Benedict is not inattentive, however, to the fact that religious fundamentalism worldwide is not the only challenge to religious freedom. He notes as well that just as religious fanaticism, in particular global contexts, impedes the exercise of the right to religious freedom,

> so too the deliberate promotion of religious indifference or *practical atheism* on the part of many countries obstructs the requirements for the development of peoples, depriving them of spiritual and human resources. *God is the guarantor of man's true development*, inasmuch as, having created him in his image, he also establishes the transcendent dignity of men and women and feeds their innate yearning to "be more." Man is not a lost atom in a random universe . . .: he is God's creature, whom God chose to endow with an immortal soul and whom he has always loved. If man were merely the fruit of either chance or necessity, or if he had to lower his aspirations to the limited horizon of the world in which he lives, if all reality were merely history and culture, and man did not possess a nature destined to transcend itself in a supernatural life, then one could speak of growth, or evolution, but not *development*.[7]

When the state promotes, teaches, or imposes forms of "practical atheism," Benedict concludes, "it deprives its citizens of the moral and spiritual strength that is indispensable for attaining integral human development and it impedes them from moving forward with renewed dynamism as they strive to offer a more generous human response to divine love."[8] Why is that? And how?

In the "Benedictine" spirit, then, both contexts that threaten religious freedom – religious fanaticism and "practical atheism" – deserve examination, insofar as religious fundamentalism and secular fundamentalism *both area* rejection of principled pluralism. Both are an impediment to human flourishing.[9]

Challenges in the global context

Converts from Islam to Christianity, in our day, are subject routinely to surveillance, arrest, interrogation, and imprisonment, torture, destruction of property, displacement, and death. In the words of one authority on religious persecution, " 'Harassment' is much too weak a word" to describe what converts suffer in Middle Eastern countries.[10] It is surely worth noting that for the last 14 centuries, execution has been the prescribed penalty for "apostasy" from Islam. While not all Muslim scholars promote this understanding, most would advocate the death penalty, citing authoritative texts and teachings; in both the Sunni and Shiite schools of Shari'a, the death penalty is prescribed for leaving Islam. In Iran, murdering an apostate falls into the same category as the murder of an adulterer, the murder of a non-Muslim, the murder of a child or grandchild by the father or grandfather, and the murder of a mentally handicapped person. The perpetrator faces no retribution, though he may be required by the courts only to pay "blood money."[11] In Saudi Arabia, religious freedom is non-existent, since all citizens must be Muslim. There the Quran, Shari'a, and the religious traditions of the Prophet Muhammed form the foundation of the nation's laws and constitution; hence, there is no separation of "church and state." Moreover, even for non-Muslims, any public practice of religion other than the officially sanctioned version of Islam is categorically forbidden. These *representative discriminatory* norms, of course, are wholly aside from terrorist attacks in public venues around the world spawned by militant Islamists who draw inspiration from their own sacred texts.[12] In any event, the "Arab Spring" has not led to any sort of "springtime" of religious freedom in the Islamic heartland and beyond, nor can we expect it to do so in the future.[13] Rather, in 2016, by all accounts, it is more accurate to speak of an "Islamic Winter."

In addition to apostasy, consider the centrality in Islam of "blasphemy," which until two decades ago was not taken seriously by most people in the West. Today that has radically changed. As Pope Benedict's 2006 Regensburg speech on reason and violence in religion well illustrated, any perceived insult to the religion of Islam is considered blasphemous, and hence, worthy of recrimination. Thus religious freedom scholar Paul Marshall:

> Twenty years ago, few in the West were concerned with blasphemy restrictions, which, while sometimes still on the statute books, were

> usually thought to be only of historical interest. That began to change when in 1989 the late Ayatollah Khomeini, then head of Iran's government, declared that it was the duty of every Muslim to kill Britain-based writer Salman Rushdie on the grounds that his novel *The Satanic Verses* was deemed blasphemous. Khomeini's edict triggered a wave of violence. Rushdie himself has survived but only at the cost of a hidden and protected life. Others connected with the book were not so fortunate. The novel's Japanese translator was assassinated, its Italian translator was stabbed, its Norwegian publisher was shot, thirty-five guests at a Turkish hotel hosting its Turkish publisher were burned to death in an arson attack. Khomeini's fatwa also inaugurated a worldwide movement to export blasphemy rules already suppressing religious minorities and Muslim dissenters in Muslim majority countries.[14]

The nagging question is why the unspeakable abuse and killing of religious minorities doesn't arouse the same horror and intense public fascination as the celebrated "atrocities" that unfolded at Abu Graib, for instance, or at Guantanamo Bay.[15] Indeed, *why*? Few seem motivated to ask. Something is very wrong with this picture; at the very least, it represents a moral inversion – rather, a moral *perversion* – that calls for a response. Where is our concern for those who are truly suffering?[16]

While a variety of religious groups have demonstrated concern, few policy organizations have performed the service of charting religious persecution worldwide as it exists in our day.[17] This is a persecution that includes, but is not limited to

- Christians and minority religious groups in communist police-states;
- Christians and other religious minorities in the Middle East, where religious freedom is sharply curtailed – when not overtly denied – due to the strictures of Islamic Shari'a law;
- religious minorities in Russia and in former Soviet satellite states of Central Asia;
- Hindu extremism in India;
- religious groups – particularly, the house-church movement – in China;
- Muslim-Christian tensions and violence in significant parts of Africa; and
- disappearance of the Orthodox Church in Syria and Iraq due to genocidal tendencies.

This brief survey and, specifically, the allusion to communist police-states in existence today cannot begin to describe the darkness that characterizes North Korea. There religious faith of any sort conflicts with required worship of the dictator and "supreme leader" (since 2011, Kim Jong-un, son of Kim Jong-il) and hence can result in banishment to prison camps, disappearance, and death. The document *North Korea: A Case to Answer – A Call to Act*, published in 2007 by Christian Solidarity Worldwide,[18] represents the culmination of seven years of research and draws heavily on interviews and consultations with over 80 North Korean defectors. It examines the nature of political repression in the nation, chronicles the brutal oppression of religious believers, and states the urgent need to respond to mass killings, arbitrary torture, and crimes against humanity occurring among religious believers in North Korea. According to one researcher of religion in North Korea who is cited in this document, "All religiously active people have disappeared as a result of the central party's intensive guidance program," with hundreds of thousands of people having been either banished to prison camps or executed if they did not recant their faith.[19] Based on the evidence, this has been the unspeakably tragic plight of many millions of North Koreans since the 1950s.

A number of important efforts have been made in the last decade to document the range of religious freedom and persecution of religious minorities worldwide. For example, the 2011 volume, *The Price of Freedom Denied: Religious Persecution and Conflict in the 21st Century*, authored by Brian J. Grim and Roger Finke and published by Cambridge University Press,[20] is one of the most comprehensive empirical overviews of religious persecution to date. The important volume *Religious Freedom around the World*, published by the Hudson Institute in 2008,[21] examines in meticulous detail the range of religious freedom and of religious persecution in nations around the world – from Afghanistan, Algeria, and Azerbaijan to Turkey, Vietnam, Yemen, and Zimbabwe. Published in 2006, the report "International Religion Indexes" was prepared for coding of the U.S. State Department's international freedom reports.[22] And the annual report *Freedom in the World*, published by Freedom House, evaluates civil liberties and political rights in nations around the globe.

According to Freedom House's 2016 report, which finds "anxious dictators" combined with "wavering democracies" yielding a global freedom index that is part of a strikingly downward trend, the world has been "battered by crises that fueled xenophobic sentiment in democratic countries, undermined the economies of states dependent on the sale of natural resources, and led authoritarian regimes to crack down harder on dissent." These developments, the report concludes, contributed to "the 10th consecutive year of decline in global freedom."[23] Specific findings of the report include the following:

- The number of countries showing a decline in freedom for the year – 72 – was the largest since the ten-year slide began. Just 43 countries made gains.
- Over the past ten years, 105 countries have seen a net decline, and only 61 have experienced a net improvement.[24]
- Ratings for the Middle Eastern and North African regions were the worst in the world in 2015, followed closely by Eurasia.
- Over the last decade, the most significant global reversals have been in freedom of expression and the rule of law.[25]

Based on its own detailed analysis, coupled with U.S. State Department reports and other surveys, in 2008 the Hudson Institute's Center for Religious Freedom concluded that "violations of religious freedom worldwide are massive, widespread, and, in many parts of the world, intensifying." It noted that "attention to and action on religious freedom have been comparatively weak" and that "the important role of religion in conflicts and in political orders has been comparatively neglected."[26]

Finally, it is necessary to cite the 2016 Annual Report published by the U.S. Commission on International Religious Freedom. Created by the International Religious Freedom Act of 1998, this independent and bi-partisan U.S. government advisory body "monitors religious freedom worldwide and makes policy recommendations to the President, Secretary of State, and Congress" based on the standards in the Universal Declaration of Human Rights (UDHR) and other international documents. The 2016 Annual Report *inter alia* documents human rights abuses and makes independent policy recommendations to the U.S. government. In so doing, the report recommends to the U.S. secretary of state that the nations of Burma (Myanmar), Central African Republic, China, Egypt, Eritrea, Iran, Iraq, Nigeria, North Korea, Pakistan, Saudi Arabia, Sudan, Syria, Tajikistan, Turkmenistan, Uzbekistan, and Vietnam be designated "countries of particular concern" at a "Tier 1" level with regard to the violation of human rights. "Tier 2" nations include Afghanistan, Azerbaijan, Cuba, India, Indonesia, Kazakhstan, Laos, Malaysia, Russia, and Turkey.[27]

In the second decade of the twenty-first century, then, violations of religious freedom around the world are indeed "massive," "widespread," and in our day "intensifying" at an alarming rate.[28]

Challenges in the Western context

Despite the relative abundance of civic freedoms and the widespread appropriation of human rights language, Western nations can see a worrying pattern is surfacing as well. This development can be measured not only by broader social trends but also by activity in the courts and policies being enacted by the federal (and, at times, state) government. Religious freedom violations in our day manifest a certain complexity due to the confluence of several factors. These include an increasing hostility toward orthodox religious and moral convictions at the societal level, a concomitant moral pluralism, and the increasing government intrusion into both public and private sectors, to name the most prominent. Surely, it is a sign of things to come that in October of 2011, the U.S. Department of Health and Human Services ended its contract with the U.S. Conference of Catholic Bishops for services to victims of human trafficking. The reason cited was the government's requirement that such services include abortion referral and contraceptives.

Already at various points in the last decade, Catholic Charities has been seeing signs of what is to come. In 2006, one of the nation's oldest adoption agencies (serving for over 100 years), Catholic Charities of Boston (CCB), was faced a very difficult choice: "violate its conscience, or close its doors."[29] CCB, in order to be licensed by the state, would have to obey state laws barring "sexual orientation discrimination." And because of Massachusetts' legal recognition of same-sex marriage in 2004, CCB "could not simply limit its placements to married couples."[30] After the state refused to grant it a religious exemption, CCB was forced to shut down its adoption services. According to U.S. Catholic Conference of Bishops website, Catholic Charities of San Francisco the same year faced "a similar untenable choice" and was forced to end its adoption services as well.[31]

In the nation's capital, Catholic Charities of the Archdiocese of Washington – which, like its sister organization in Boston, provided support to children and families for several generations (eighty-plus years, in fact) – until recently had a partnership with the District of Columbia for its foster care and public adoption program. In 2010, however, a law redefining legal marriage to include same-sex unions took effect in the District. Subsequently, Catholic Charities was informed by the District that it "would no longer be an eligible foster care and adoption partner."[32]

And one year later, Catholic Charities affiliates in Illinois were forced to close down for the same reason. Agencies may not receive state money if they refuse to place children with persons in same-sex relationships as foster or adoptive parents. "In the name of tolerance, we're not being tolerated," declared Bishop Thomas J. Paprocki of the Diocese of Springfield, Illinois, a civil and canon lawyer who represented Catholic Charities in its fight to retain the right to its religious freedom in offering adoptive services.[33]

Is our most cherished freedom truly under threat?, asks the U.S. Conference of Catholic Bishops. Consider its reply:

> Among many current challenges, several state governments have sought to trample on the conscience rights of Catholic charitable service providers. *Religious liberty is more than freedom of worship; it includes our ability to make our contribution to the common good . . . without having to compromise our faith.* Without religious liberty properly understood, all . . . suffer, including the neediest children seeking adoptive and foster families.[34]

And in a joint statement, bishops representing four Catholic dioceses in Massachusetts declared, "If Catholic agencies were required to help same-sex couples adopt children in violation of church teaching prohibiting the practice[,] it would present 'a serious pastoral problem' and threaten religious freedom."[35]

With these signs of hostile government action, we are justified in asking whether the goal of an aggressively secular state is to help families and children or to force the Christian community – in this case, the social welfare arm of the Catholic Church – to violate its beliefs or be forced to terminate its services. It is telling that, in the main, same-sex couples have not established their own adoptive programs. It would appear that they wish to deny religiously based charities the right to religious freedom. This represents a trend that is not benign.[36]

Not surprisingly, in 2013 the Pew Research Center published a report chronicling a sharp rise in restrictions on religion in the United States, from both government action and the wider culture.[37] In much of the Western world, and increasingly in North America, to give public witness to religious conviction and to affirm standards of "right and wrong," acceptable and unacceptable, good and evil is to be labeled "hate-filled," "bigoted," and "intolerant." As one social commentator put it, we have moved from "culture wars" to "conscience wars."[38] Notably the last two generations have been witness to the evaporation of anything deemed an American "public philosophy" or consensus on "the common good." Any sort of religious or moral consensus is today impossible, given the character of "pluralism" that has taken root – a pluralism that has moved from principled to perverse – that is, devoid of moral principle and indifferent to the possibility of truth.[39]

In both North America and Europe, threats to religious liberty and conscience are not only faced by pastors who promote biblical morality or by religious groups and organizations that have particular hiring conditions and preferences but also confront a wide array of vocations and institutions. Many are in the health care field, as a result of "non-discrimination" laws or policies enacted by the state or pressure from the authorities to provide services that are morally objectionable. They entail counseling agencies, welfare agencies, charities, and social service agencies offering services such as adoption and foster care, many of which are faced with "non-discrimination" restrictions designed to thwart a traditional Christian understanding of sexuality. And they extend to businesses, which are forced increasingly to comply with "non-discrimination"/"diversity" hiring policies, as well as educational institutions, which must comply with federal or regional accrediting and federal funding regulations.

Consider, by way of example, the intrusion of an increasingly invasive and discriminatory state into the public realm of health care. As I write, the General Pharmaceutical Council (GPC) in Great Britain has just launched a consultation on "religion, personal values and beliefs" on the part of pharmacy professionals as it affects the delivery of "person-centred care" in pharmacy.[40] The GPC proposes to change the expectations of pharmacy professionals when their religious beliefs impact "their ability to provide services" to clients. The changes would "shift the balance in favour of the needs and rights of the person in their care" and "reflect the relevant legal framework of human rights and equality law."

As recently as March of 2010, revised code of conduct from the regulator allowed pharmacists to opt out of providing items such as the morning-after pill and contraception.[41] Britain's National Secular Society had wanted the GPC to scrap the so-called conscience clause. Under the new code (as of 2010), pharmacists with strong religious principles are be able to continue to refuse to sell or prescribe products if they believe that doing so would contradict their religious or moral convictions. At the same time, the GPC indicated that pharmacists who refuse services could be obliged to tell patients where they can access those products.

A mere seven years later, all that could change. The moral implications of the change would be massive. Note the rationale here: shifting the moral balance "in favour of the needs and rights" of the patient and reflecting "the relevant framework of human rights and equality law." It is surely significant that the GPC mentions *not one word* about *the ethical character* of such potential changes. That is, whatever the contemporary and "relevant legal framework" dictates is to be forced upon pharmacists, in spite of the religious and moral convictions that might inform their work as health-care professionals. The GPC proposes to make changes to the current wording of "Standard 1" from

- recognize their own values and beliefs but do not impose them on other people
- tell relevant health professionals, employers or others if their own values or beliefs prevent them from providing care, and refer people to other providers

To the following:

- recognize their own values and beliefs but do not impose them on other people [unchanged]
- take responsibility for ensuring that person-centered care is not compromised because of personal values and beliefs (of the care-giver) [revised]

What is being communicated here is striking: pharmaceutical professionals may not discriminate against someone under their care based on *the professionals' own religious and moral principles*. The care or advice must be given to the client even if it is for the care-giver morally objectionable. The wording of the GPC's proposal makes it clear that the most appropriate action to be taken depends not on the moral guidance of the professional but the "needs" and circumstances of patient. Thus, for example, in some situations referring the patient to another provider would not be permissible, since "person-centered care" might be "compromised." Chief executive of the GPC, Duncan Rudkin explains,

> People who use pharmacy services have a right to safe and effective care. The changes we are proposing to our standards and guidance emphasise that pharmacy professionals are responsible for ensuring the person-centred care is not compromised because of their religion, personal values or beliefs . . . We understand the importance of a pharmacy professional's religion, personal values or beliefs but we want to make sure people can access the advice, care and services they need from a pharmacy, when they need them. We recognize that this represents a

> significant change and through this consultation we want to hear as many views as possible about our proposals and what impact they could have on patients and the public, pharmacy professionals and employers.[42]

Chris Whitehouse, Education Spokesman of the Conservative Group on the Isle of Wight Council, points out one of the crucial implications of the GPC proposal, should it become law.

Defending the right to conscientious objection to participation in abortion has been an important alternative for health care professionals ever since abortion was legalized in Great Britain in 1967. But that right could be taken away. "The body that oversees pharmacists and pharmacy technicians [the GPC] looks set to deny those professionals the right to act according to their conscience when it comes to issuing the abortifacient morning after pill, in a move that could see careers in pharmacy being a non-starter for those who hold pro-life or strong religious views."[43]

Consider the attendant moral burden. How could a Roman Catholic, an evangelical Christian, or those of the Muslim and Orthodox Jewish traditions conform with a requirement to provide abortifacients? The consultation would appear to raise the threat of criminal sanctions for those who do express conscientious objection, insofar as it warns, "Pharmacy professionals should not put themselves in a position where refusal to provide services would 'result in a person not receiving the care or advice they need, or breach human rights or equality legislation.'"[44]

Should the change be enacted and conscientious objection be denied pharmaceutical professionals *and their respective employers*, it stands to reason that in the future people of traditional religious faith – whether Christian, Jewish, or Muslim – would be prevented even from entering the profession in the first place. This would likely be on a far greater scale than, say, those who have chosen not to enter obstetrics and gynecology because of their refusal to practicing abortion. Such is none other than an issue of religious freedom.

As in the previous example of CCB, San Francisco and Washington, DC, illustrates, at a very basic level, the *most fundamental* of all institutions in society, marriage, is under assault, as states are being pressured to recognize same-sex unions. Regardless of whether you the reader affirm my position, consider the logic involved here. The flip side of this social and moral inversion is the question of whether individuals and institutions which believe that marriage is between one man and one woman – in accordance with the norms of human social and cultural history – will face civil liability and loss of access to government programs and benefits in their refusal to acknowledge this radical re-definition. It needs emphasizing that in states where there have been legislative attempts to re-define marriage religious freedom protections for individuals or groups opposing the legalization of same-sex unions have not arisen. In this regard, we are only beginning to feel the consequences unleashed by the *Obergefell vs. Hodges* U.S. Supreme

Court case in June of 2015, in which five justices decreed that all 50 states must license same-sex marriage. Even merely to offer commentary on this development – a development in which common sense, human nature, and human history have been turned upside down – is to incur the wrath of our contemporaries (at least, those who shape public opinion).

In this vein, 2016 has not been a particularly good year for the citizens of the People's Republic of California. And were the events in that state not indicative of trends that filter down to other states in the Union, they would strike us as utterly laughable. Writing recently in the *Orange County Register*, one journalist laments that the state is "in the grip of an incipient state religion."[45] That religion, he notes, is secular fundamentalism, which, we are learning, is no less tolerant or dogmatic than – and "increasingly resembles" – the former Soviet Union, present-day Iran, and Saudi Arabia.[46] Two pieces of state legislation well illustrate not only that common sense and moral sobriety have been jettisoned but also that a new, infinitely rigid orthodoxy is in place. One is Senate Bill 1146, which seeks to curtail historically broad exemptions by which the state and the federal government have permitted religious schools to be, yes, *religious*. Under the guise of "tolerance," Bill 1146 would include the promotion of transgender bathrooms and a restriction of expressions of faith by both students and faculty, which traditionally have been normative for those institutions. The bottom line is that many schools believe the bill would jeopardize both their mission and their funding in order to "'solve' gender and social equity problems" on their campuses – "problems" that, in truth, do not exist.[47] California evidently "cannot tolerate the autonomy of religious institutions if they refuse to embrace the secularist ideology that dominates the state."[48] Surely, it is only a matter of time before religious institutions in California will be required to celebrate "Lesbian-Bisexual-Gay-Transsexual-Queer-and-Undecided Month" as mandated by the state. At that point, it would be illegal to practice a cardinal tenet of religious faith – in this case a foundational tenet of Christianity, Judaism, and Islam – out of deference to the homosexual "other." So, whether it is a Washington state florist, an Oregon baker, a New Mexico photographer, subpoenaed pastors in Houston, or a recently fired fire chief of Atlanta, religious believers are being harassed for their beliefs and are losing their religious freedom.[49]

The second piece of legislation, Senate Bill 1161, which (as I write) mercifully has been temporarily tabled, is the "Orwellian-named 'California Climate Science Truth and Accountability Act of 2016,'" which would attempt to "prosecute anyone who dared challenge the climate orthodoxy" and would seek "redress for unfair competition practices committed by entities that have deceived, confused or misled the public on the risks of climate change or financially supported activities that have deceived, confused or misled the public on those risks."[50] Thus, the emerging attack on anyone questioning climate change orthodoxy indeed represents "another kind of religion, one that gives officially sanctioned science something close to papal infallibility."[51] By no means confined to the state of California, these and like expressions of the cult of political correctness have reached such ridiculous and irrational levels that the University of California system considers it a "microaggression" to assert that "America is a land of opportunity" or to dare to criticize race-based affirmative action.[52]

It needs emphasizing that the aforementioned *Orange County Register* journalist, no self-professing religious believer, does not exaggerate:

> The new progressive intolerance now represents, in many ways, as great, if not more pervasive, a threat to the republic than that posed by either religious fundamentalists or even the most fervent climate change denier. It violates the Madisonian principle that assumed that religious and moral ideas "must be left to the conviction and conscience of every man; and it is the right of every man to exercise it as these may dictate." To revoke that principle is to reduce the United States to just another authoritarian state, even if the official ideology is couched in scientific research or estimable embrace of racial or gender differences.[53]

In the end, regarding basic moral issues – for example, on how to define marriage or using taxpayer money to pay for abortifacient services – government cannot avoid taking a moral stance; there is, simply put, *no such thing* as "moral neutrality." In fact, the illusory assumption that moral relativism (often in the guise of "political liberalism") provides the key to peaceful co-existence is, in fact, a cause of social divisions and a denial of the dignity of human beings.[54] For this reason then, as analyst Thomas Messner rightly observes, "government overreach raises the stakes of moral discourse and encourages intolerance."[55] Moreover, when civil liability or access to government programs or benefits is contingent on embracing the "official" position of the state on controversial moral matters, "the potential for infringement of religious liberty and rights of conscience is clear. As the diversity of moral viewpoints in society increases, the number of social conflicts will only rise."[56]

Given its intolerant and authoritarian nature, the jihad against dissent and common sense – and let it be said that these dissenters might be religious or non-religious citizens – invites the possibility of persecution at the formal level. In their groundbreaking work *The Price of Freedom Denied* noted earlier, authors Brian J. Grim and Roger Finke observe the various patterns of religious persecution today to be "pervasive" and "pernicious."[57] While their commentary is directed chiefly at religious persecution around the world, their conclusion – that it is "pervasive" and "pernicious" – could be applied to Western nations as well. At first glance, one might conclude that there is no larger pattern here. After all, one is international, and one is peculiarly Western. Yet, a common bond can indeed be detected, as Allen D. Hertzke, the David Ross Boyd Professor of Political Science and Faculty Fellow in Religious Freedom with the Institute for the American Constitutional Heritage at the University of Oklahoma, has perceptively noted.[58] Hertzke is convinced that what Grim and Finke worry about in the international context is applicable to Western nations. The common bond between Western and non-Western nations is the failure to acknowledge or take seriously religious claims, religious beliefs, and contributions of religion to the wider cultural fabric.

Confirmation of Hertzke's argument – that Western/North American and international violations of religious liberty are linked – is found in a fascinating and thoroughly illuminating volume by Thomas Farr, who served as the U.S. State Department's first director of the Office of International Religious Freedom. In *World of Faith and Freedom: Why International Religious Liberty Is Vital to American Security* (2008), Farr depicts the religious nature of most of the politically "hot spots" around the world while offering, from the inside, an almost painful description of diplomats' inability to understand the sphere of religion. This, of course, is as we might expect, given their secular training and the low priority that religious freedom traditionally has had in terms of foreign policy matters.

In Western societies, the problem can be identified as an erosion of awareness – and appreciation for – religious freedom in our past.[59] This amnesia is compounded by two notable and related factors: the growth of the state as an all-encompassing – and intrusive – regulatory vehicle and an aggressive secular fundamentalism that masquerades as (or is mistaken for) "liberalism."[60] One is reminded of the observation of George Orwell, penned in the late 1930s, before the Nazification of Europe was in full bloom and before we in the West had full comprehension of the atrocities of Stalinism. It is quite possible, Orwell wrote, "We are descending into an age in which two and two will make five if the leader says so."[61]

The troubling global pattern in our day that Grim and Finke observe causes them to revisit lessons learned from the "grand experiment" of the American founding. The founders and framers, through toil and travail, sought to eliminate religious establishments and assure religious freedoms for all. Citing Jefferson's autobiographical reflections late in life, Grim and Finke note that the establishing of religious freedom "was meant to be universal" and that to be included "within the mantle of its protection" were "the Jew and the Gentile, the Christian and the Mahometan [sic], the Hindoo [sic], and the Infidel of every denomination."[62] Madison's reflections, as well, taken from his important "Memorial and Remonstrance against Religious Assessments," are further evidence to Grim and Finke of the dangers of both *coercion and exclusion*. Madison saw this not only as a weakening of religion but also, more fundamentally, an undermining the "sacred rights" of conscience.[63]

***

That matters of conscience can be called "sacred rights" may strike us as self-obvious, especially for a culture whose understanding of liberty has been etched in its conscience from the beginning. When and where, however, society's structures and ethos either actively deny or conspire in complicity against the "first freedom," it is time to revisit moral first principles. On what basis can we declare – if we in fact can – that human beings are "free?" What constitutes the "first freedom?" And on what moral-philosophical grounds can religious freedom be secured?

What I am proposing in the present volume is that there exists a lack of adequate moral-philosophical grounding for religious freedom. Part of our task, then, among other priorities, is to re-visit the founders' vision, wherein a robust justification for the rights of conscience and religious freedom is to be found – justification that is consensual and broad-based, even when it was continually evolving and subject to profound disagreement and debate. This we shall attempt to do in Chapter 3. The issue at hand, it needs to be emphasized, is *not* arriving with ultimate precision at the "correct" interpretation of early American history – regardless of whether our bias is secular or more religiously inclined. Alas, in the founders' generation we find *both* the secular and the religious – indeed, a blend of the best of both. The two overlap, yet without denying or canceling out one another, unlike modern interpretations are inclined to require. For this reason, religious freedom was foundational to the "experiment" that we call American constitutional order.

Moreover, "religious freedom" should be understood not merely as a foremost *private* right to worship but rather as "the right to act on the highest obligations, the deepest human aspirations."[64] That means that it is a *fundamental right* that is deserving of *generous accommodation*.[65] To the extent that religious liberty is neglected or suffers, all civil liberties suffer. In my argument I will be assuming that because religious freedom is the "first freedom," it is ontologically prior to one's obligations to the state; hence. It should be a "reliable lodestar" for properly construing the First Amendment and constitutional law.[66] And because the United States, for better or worse, will continue to play a pivotal role in international affairs, a proper construal of religious freedom and its moral-philosophical basis will necessarily inform international norms of "human rights."

The essence of the "first freedom"

The present volume proceeds from the conviction that, as stated earlier, religious freedom is in serious trouble. However, it is also rooted in the conviction that one reason for this dilemma is the misunderstanding – if not a supreme neglect – of its moral-philosophical underpinnings.[67] To speak of religious liberty as the "first freedom," as the present volume proposes to do, is to begin by hearkening back to the vision, struggles, and "public philosophy" of the American founders (and I write in the American context). They were responding, ever so tentatively, to the European experience and the tragic history of both religious coercion and social anarchy. This task, of course, will not be easy, given our reticence to listen and learn from the past and the moral obtuseness that characterizes our age. For the founders, government *per se* has no religious identity, but that is not to contend that government has no religious *significance* or that it plays no role helping to preserve religious freedom. These distinctions, however, will need to be revisited in our later discussion of church and state.

The essence of human freedom

But how is moral freedom to be conceptualized? In a totalitarian scheme, whether ancient or modern, secular or religious in justification, the options are twofold: live according to the dictates of the state (and live a meager life) or live according to the dictates of conscience (and live in prison or die). But human history and the occasional in-breaking of human wisdom suggest a non-totalitarian alternative. This alternative is anchored in religious freedom. At the same time, according to the American founders and framers, insofar as government is "of . . ., by. . ., and for the people," there is no such entity as a "Christian state." The non-establishment assumptions undergirding this nation's charter documents denude and limit the powers of the state just as they prevent religious coercion. Practically speaking, this means that at times government will recognize religious beliefs and the place of religion in the public sphere – as the free exercise clause suggests – and at other times it will be discretionary or "non-establishment" in its posture. Authentic freedom for the founders – and by this we mean religious freedom, i.e., the freedom to obey one's conscience – was understood to be neither coercive nor exclusionary. Authentic freedom would suggest that a healthy dialogue between civil and religious institutions is possible,[68] even when this dialogue will be messy and contentious at times. Significantly, Tocqueville was given a vivid (and enduring) impression upon visiting the United States two generations after its founding, causing him to write, "From the beginning, politics and religion were in accord, and they have not ceased to be so since."[69] It is noteworthy that, only 30 years after Thomas Jefferson had served as a foreign minister in France, Tocqueville, in his visit to the new Republic, does not describe the relationship between religion and the state as a "wall" – much less a "high" or "impregnable" wall that was the adopted metaphor of the Supreme Court's ruling in the twentieth century. Rather, his report, as we have it in *Democracy in America*, understands this relationship to be interactive and protective, insofar as religious freedom *supports* rather than undermines republican democracy.

This posture, of course, is in some respects consonant with St. Augustine's vision of the "earthly city." As the "city of man," it was understood to be a place co-mingling with the "city of God" – and hence a constant reminder that as citizens we have dual allegiances. The implication is twofold, and patent: because we have ultimate allegiances – allegiances that are "pre-political" – neither should one think that the state is ultimate, nor should one conclude that one's earthly citizenship is unimportant. Our dual citizenship matters. *But can an atheist be a good citizen as well?*, the reader is likely to ask with justified suspicion. At the risk of seeming evasive, I would maintain that it hinges on what we mean by "citizen" and "good." Certainly, it is true that an atheist can be a virtuous, morally serious person and affirm a communal good, even when that person will strain philosophically to anchor his or her morality and sense of "goodness" in something that transcends self-interest (or our genes).[70] John Locke, as is well known, thought it not possible. His rationale, in the end, was that an atheist cannot be trusted with covenants, oaths, and promise-keeping. This, of course, will strike us as quaint and exceedingly parochial. But *is* it? Locke, after all, is still celebrated, even by atheists, as a champion of tolerance – and he well should be. James Madison, certainly no rigid theist, also thought it not possible, under the assumption that to be a "good citizen" one must be subject to the "Governor of the Universe."[71] Yes, we may readily grant, it is true that the U.S. Constitution is "secular" to the extent that it does not make direct or formal reference to God. At the same time, the founders, in representative charter documents, utilize the language of "self-evident truths," the "law of nature" and "nature's God" – for them, contemporary parlance for moral law and an assumed, broadly theistic framework – to anchor responsible citizenship.[72]

The essence of "civil society"

Religious freedom, it needs to be emphasized, is not merely the immunity from coercion (which it is). More fundamentally, it is "an ability to order one's own choices in accordance with truth."[73]At bottom, religious freedom is *the condition for the pursuit of truth*. Truth does not impose itself by force or violence but rather "*by the force of its own truth*."[74] One of the chief findings of *The Price of Freedom Denied*, the Grim-Finke volume noted earlier, is that the attempt to restrict religious expression and activity – whether within a culture or across cultures, whether induced by the state or by a religious monopoly – *inevitably* leads to conflict and persecution.[75] The founders and framers, of which Madison and Jefferson were partially representative, surely recognized this reality as well. And, to some extent, so did Tocqueville, given his astute observations about a tyranny of either the minority or the majority. Tocqueville took note of the fact that "freedom of association has become a necessary guarantee against the tyranny of the majority."[76] The influence of the majority, as he understood it, was "a great peril" for the American republic, if in fact the majority – rooted in "the sovereignty of the people"[77] – was in denial of basic moral principle in its thinking and practice. In the end, the greatest danger of the American republic, in Tocqueville's view, came from "the omnipotence of the majority."[78]

What tempers the tyrannical tendency for Tocqueville in democratic republics is the combined effect of several important elements. One is the absence of "administrative centralization," coupled with the legal "counterweight" of the courts and law, wherein the jury – which represents "the minds of all citizens" – whose "habits are precisely those that best prepare the people to be free."[79] Another is the importance of religion in public affairs, which Tocqueville observes, is not hostile toward democratic and republican institutions.[80] Yet another element consists of "habits of the heart and mind"[81] which produce self-government – what Tocqueville, in common with the founders, understood as the moral impulse that prevents "freedom" and "equality" from degenerating into democratic despotism.[82]

At bottom, threats to religious freedom guarantee potential threats to other civil liberties as well, and because of connection, it is accurate to classify religious freedom as the "first freedom," the *fons et origo* of all other freedoms and rights.[83] The denial of religious freedom, given enough time, will usually result in harassment, physical abuse and violence, and eventual displacement, as many crisis spots around the world today tragically illustrate; in some instances, genocide and war are the result.

Religious freedom is a fundamental good – in fact, the *most basic* of human goods – which gives meaning to all others. For this reason, one might argue that how a society approaches religious freedom is in fact a barometer of how it will handle social conflict. Not surprisingly, religion serves as an important (and necessary) buffer between citizens and a potentially oppressive state. The deepest beliefs of human beings are freely embraced and cannot be coerced. Coercion dishonors a person's dignity as a free, rational, moral agent.[84] And, of course, coercion can operate in two directions: it can force conformity to religious belief on the one hand and it can force the exclusion or denial of religious belief on the other.[85] In any event, citizens and political authorities in a relatively free society will need to distinguish between just and unjust laws, regardless of how that process is adjudicated. It goes without saying, then, that religious freedom, as is the case with any civil liberty, is fragile and inconvenient. Fragile because the rights of minorities are fragile, requiring the utmost in social sensitivity, and thus in need of being protected. Inconvenient because it requires the sustained effort of those in power and the garnering of public support. In the words of two veteran human rights observers, "Enforcing this liberty comes with a price, but the price of denying the freedom may be far higher."[86] It is the argument of the present volume that the price of denial is *always and everywhere* "far higher."

The foundations of a decent society require a commitment to common moral principles and to supporting institutions that embody that commitment. Among the most basic of these principles area respect for human life, protection of the family and marriage as bedrock institutions of society, and just laws enacted by a (relatively) just government. Each of these reinforces the other, helping to create a social environment in which human beings can flourish. Not surprisingly, as constitutional scholar Robert P. George has rightly argued, all three of these elements have been seriously weakened in our day, with consequences that are dire.[87]

Stated in different words, a "just society" requires just individuals who as citizens comprise that social environment. At the most basic level, this begins with a view of human personhood that fosters human dignity,[88] the sanctity of human life, and the cultivation of virtuous attitudes that esteem the common social good. At the same time, society requires not only virtuous people but also external constraints as well, since human nature is flawed[89] and the common good (wherein people can flourish) must be preserved.[90] Just laws are necessary for the establishment and maintenance of what St. Augustine described as the *tranquillitas ordinis*, a justly ordered peace. Were this not the case, "totalitarian" and "despotic" regimes would never appear on the stage of human history. The American founders, of course, well understood the human tendency toward both dignity and depravity as they attempted to craft a democratic polity in which the best of human nature might be encouraged and the worst restrained.

One of the "self-evident truths" on which the founders and framers constructed their understanding of a "good society" was the conviction that *all men are created equal* and that *all men are endowed by their Creator with certain inalienable rights*. This they knew, based on "nature and nature's God" – which is to say, the natural moral law. As "natural lawyers," the founders acknowledged a broad and exceedingly rich tradition of reflecting on moral truth as it applied to the social and political order. This tradition, it needs emphasizing, is not some "medieval" construct as is often assumed by our contemporaries, but rather a tradition that, in various ways, united people as richly diverse as Aristotle, Aquinas, Hugo Grotius, Francisco de Vitoria, the Protestant reformers, and John Locke.

Chief among the foundational principles of a decent society – *any* decent society – is its fundamental commitment to respect the human person. For where there is no presumed human dignity, there can be no justice. In truth, human dignity serves as the basis for all other freedom's and "rights." This would explain the language of Article 1 of the UDHR, adopted and proclaimed on December 10, 1948 by the General Assembly of the United Nations, which states: "All human beings are born free and equal in dignity and rights. They are endowed with reason and conscience and should act towards one another in a spirit of brotherhood." In its preamble, the UDHR refers to "the inherent dignity" of "all members of the human family."[91] The implications of this affirmation are spelled out in Article 18:

> Everyone has the right to freedom of thought, conscience and religion; this right includes freedom to change his religion or belief, and freedom, either alone or in community with others and in public or private, to manifest his religion or belief in teaching, practice, worship and observance.[92]

Most of the founders were part of this tradition, which acknowledged "self-evident truths" and drank from its resources. They understood that human goods, based on human nature, need protecting. And protecting those human goods lies at the heart of justice. Thus, the primary role of government, as we have suggested, is to protect and preserve the foundations of civil society. Human abuses by government and political authority, in the end, lead to tyranny and totalitarianism, of the type that we have witnessed with great sadness in the twentieth and twenty-first centuries.[93] Threats to human sanctity, at bottom, become threats to religious freedom and the very existence of religion itself.

Confronting (and purging) the post-consensus Zeitgeist

What in our day is disconcerting – indeed, frightening – is the fact that it is supremely difficult for people, in the Western context, to engage in moral discourse of any type. While the language of "justice" is found on the lips of virtually all our contemporaries, there is a virtual ban on speaking in the public sphere of moral absolutes, upon which justice – if it is truly "just" – is predicated. When and where people do attempt moral discourse, the frequent (and immediate) charge is "religious fundamentalism," behind which supposedly stand people who are "hate-filled," "bigoted," and "intolerant." Such broad-based intolerance creates an environment in which moral reasoning and discourse are well-nigh impossible, and the social climate seems to be growing less and less tolerant of dialogue on moral matters. This development is infinitely tragic, since *human beings are moral agents by nature*.

This cultural intractability notwithstanding, I wish to argue that even the most ardent "postmodern" theorist and the most entrenched moral skeptic, many of whom have made their living and advanced their careers at the academic level by denying moral normativity, are forced to concede, in the end, that relativism is impossible to live out and utterly self-contradictory.[94] For as soon as we begin using the language of "should" and "should not" – which we all do on a daily basis in virtually all spheres of living – we expose our real (i.e., moral) nature. As moral agents, all human beings draw the line between "just" and "unjust," between "right" and "wrong," between acceptable and unacceptable. Those who use such language, moreover, do not believe *really* that all moral positions are acceptable in the public sphere and that our differences are merely differences in *personal preference*. Our contemporaries who disagree with us on contentious ethical issues *really do* believe that we are "wrong" and that we *really should* agree with their position. The question, then, is not whether we are moral in our constitutive nature and whether there is moral truth; it is, rather, *where we draw the line* in relation to moral truth and *whether our decisions accord with moral reality*.[95] For this reason, the matter of "tolerance" in moral matters – and specifically the question of moral "neutrality" – will need to be revisited in a later chapter.

Thus far, my argument has taken the position that religious freedom is the equivalent of freedom of conscience. In doing so, it is necessary to make the critical distinction, as Michael Sandel has done, between "freedom of conscience" and "freedom of choice."[96] This need is owing to the dominant strain of thinking about the public sphere of our day. Two cardinal tenets of secular liberalism needing re-consideration are the assumption that government must remain "neutral" regarding competing moral visions as they impinge on public life, and that individual rights and autonomy, rather than the common social good, must be guarded at all costs. As Sandel and others have shown, government *cannot* be neutral in this sense, since competing moral visions are precisely that – moral visions that are informed by moral assumptions of reality. Alas, there is *no such thing* as moral neutrality.[97] Moreover, the tragedy of the "unencumbered self" in the end is that it has no obligations to others and to the common good, since the self becomes sovereign – a social development that the founders (and Tocqueville) greatly feared. In the process, "choices" become "lifestyle" preferences, not deep metaphysical convictions that correspond with reality, while duties tend to be trumped by a newer (and supremely elastic) version of "rights" – a version that loses sight of the common good.

As it concerns religious liberty, the founders understood "freedom of conscience" to mean "the freedom to exercise *religious liberty* – to worship or not, to support a church or not, to profess belief or disbelief – *without suffering civil penalties* or incapacities."[98] As Sandel notes, this had nothing to do with "a right to choose one's beliefs."[99] In fact, the founders' argument for religious liberty "relies heavily on the assumption that beliefs are not a matter of choice,"[100] as suggested by Thomas Jefferson in the preamble to the Virginia Statute of Religious Freedom, wherein he observes, "The opinions and belief of men depend not on their own will, but *follow involuntarily the evidence* proposed to their own minds."[101]

At bottom, freedom of conscience – that is, what constitutes our deepest beliefs about life, our ultimate convictions about reality – is inherently "religious"[102] in nature, whether we are theistic or a-theistic in self-identification; these beliefs are thus "inalienable." For this reason, and because threats to religious freedom inevitably impinge upon other civil liberties, the great challenge is to ensure protection for religious freedom, the "first freedom." The right of every person to live according to the dictates of his or her conscience – which is also a duty toward the Creator who gave us such freedom[103] – is unassailable; as an "inalienable" right, it precedes the state. The just state recognizes this human right and protects it through law. In so doing,

> The state recognizes the limits of its own capacity: it cannot coerce consciences; it cannot compel belief. For the state that recognizes and protects religious freedom is not an omnicompetent state, but rather a state that acknowledges the rights of conscience and prerogatives of the institutions that men and women freely sustain to express and passion religious convictions. It recognizes its duty to serve, and not to impede, those communities of civil society. Thus there cognition of religious freedom in full is a crucial barrier to the totalitarian temptation that seems to exist in all forms of political modernity.[104]

While protecting the "inalienable" perhaps requires no cost at the theoretical or "academic" level, it is supremely difficult to undertake where majoritarian opinion – which may metastasize into *majoritarian tyranny* –

is resistant at the social-cultural level. A commitment to uphold religious freedom, therefore, forces us to reflect with sobriety not only on the nature of religious belief and expression but also on the essence of political power and, hence, the role and nature of the state. To recognize the place of religious freedom is to recognize the limits of the state; it is to acknowledge that transcendence accords not with government or political power but with the "wholly other." The inversion and perversion of the two – the political and the transcendent – is far-reaching and critically important, having resulted in the gruesome and terrifying totalitarian projects of the twentieth century.[105]

Undergirding the basic argument set forth in this volume is the premise that where and when religious liberty is neglected or suffers, all civil liberties suffer. At bottom, the task of protecting religious freedom confronts us with our most fundamental moral obligations, which are issues that are pre-political and of a *metaphysical* nature.

Religious freedom and natural law

Religious freedom as pursuit of truth

On what basis, it is fitting to ask, could the founders of the American experiment – indeed, on what basis can *anyone* –speak of "self-evident truths?" Such language, to be sure, strikes us two centuries removed as outmoded and quaint, when not downright offensive. After all, the dominant *Zeitgeist*, at least in Western societies, insists that liberal democracy is best maintained by eschewing – if not renouncing – public reliance on any sort of "first principle" that claims to embody any sort of objective truth.[106] Evidently, that there are *no* self-evident truths is self-evidently true for many in our day, or so it would seem.

And yet it is a curiosity that even the most ardent theoretical defenders of this outlook – *There is no absolute truth!*– tend to live out their lives on a daily basis as if certain truths *were* in fact self-evident. At bottom, the language of "self-evident truths" suggests a moral universe and moral norms that are common to all of humanity, regardless of social and cultural location. Important distinctions, however, are in order. The notion of "self-evident truths" does not refer to that which is "instantly apprehensible" without thinking, reflecting and reasoning. Neither does it denote objectivized feelings. Nor does it correspond to contemporary notions of personal autonomy. Rather, it refers to rational axioms and values that, upon reflection, are self-evidently good and hence worthy of being pursued.[107] Because society must be ordered – and recall that the founders conceived of the American project as an experiment in "ordered liberty" – every successive generation of citizens must wrestle with the complicated task of working out how those moral realities bear upon the ordering of society and civic life. What's more, every successive generation must decide *if* "civil society" as we have known is to remain "civil" and on what basis.

Although the United States was not simply the *outcome* of religious belief, it is undeniable that religious belief was important at its founding. As William Lee Miller has noted, the distinctive – and normative – feature of the American beginning was neither its religious underpinnings nor its emancipation from them, but rather the intersection and blending of religious conviction and "secular" common sense that manifested itself in moral principle and self-government.[108] Thus, the acknowledgment of – and reliance upon – religiously grounded morality, it needs emphasizing in our day, is *not* a violation of the so-called establishment clause, constitutionally speaking. As the founders well knew and believed, religion is a necessary source of morality and should be welcomed. Religion is not a "conversation-stopper" in the sense that Richard Rorty and others have argued with considerable sophistication.[109] The problem, as Michael Perry rightly insists, is not *that* religious arguments are used in the public sphere but rather *how* they are used.[110] But the fact *that* religion infuses every dimension of life for the religious person demonstrates personal wholeness and integrity, something which should be encouraged and praised, as voices as diverse as Nicholas Wolterstorff and Benedict XVI have argued:

> It belongs to the *religious convictions* of a good many religious people in our society that *they ought to base* their decisions concerning fundamental issues of justice on their religious convictions. They do not view as an option whether or not to do so. It is their conviction that they ought to strive for wholeness, integrity, integration in their lives: that they ought to allow the Word of God, the teachings of the Torah, the command and example of Jesus, or whatever, to shape their existence as a whole, including, then, their social and political existence. Their religion is not, for them, about *something other* than their social and political existence; it is *also* about their social and political existence. Accordingly, to require of them that they not base their decisions and discussions concerning political issues on their religion is to infringe, inequitably, on the free exercise of their religion.[111]
>
> [I]t is inconceivable that believers should have to suppress a part of themselves – their faith – in order to be active citizens. It should never be necessary to deny God in order to enjoy one's rights.[112]

But what does this mean when the vast majority of the citizenry is no longer "religious" in the formal sense? When references to a Judeo-Christian tradition are in our day chiefly a source of divisiveness rather than cohesion? For those of us living in the United States, this question has special significance, given (a) the very self-conscious and deliberate manner in which the founders and framers conceived the American republic, contrasted with (b) the aggressive manner in which secular liberalism would bracket God and religion today and increasingly make religion a private affair, not to be tolerated in the public sphere. The tragedy of viewing religion *in sic* as inimical to a "free society" was stated with clarity by John Paul II in comments delivered at the appointment of the U.S. ambassador to the Vatican in 1997. His observations, made as an "outsider," are worth pondering:

> It would truly be a sad thing if the religious and moral convictions upon which the American experiment was founded could now some how be considered a danger to free society, such that those who would bring these convictions to bear upon your nation's public life would be denied a voice in debating and resolving issues of public policy. The original separation of church and state in the United States was certainly not an effort to ban all religious conviction from the public sphere, a kind of banishment of God from civil society. Indeed, the vast majority of Americans regardless of the irreligious persuasion, are convinced that religious conviction and religiously informed moral argument have a vital role in public life.[113]

The thrust of John Paul's remarks deserves reiteration: *religious conviction and religiously informed moral argument have a vital role to play in public life.*[114] In his comments to the U.S. ambassador, John Paul reminded his audience that the American founders maintained their claims to freedom on the basis of certain "self-evident truths" about the human person – truths that could be discerned rationally about human nature which was owing to "nature's God."

Natural law as mirror of basic truth

The most basic of such "self-evident" truths – namely, that "all men are created equal" and that "all men are endowed with certain inalienable rights," allow citizens to fulfill their obligations not only toward their own but also toward the common good of the community. Without such moral responsibilities and a sense of mutual accountability, there can be no authentic freedom insofar as people live their lives in community and thus have a responsibility to the common social good. An awareness of these moral-social realities, if we are honest about the empirical evidence, would not seem to originate in biology or in our incremental research-and-discovery of genetic transfer. Nor does it seem plausible, as some proponents of "sociobiology" and evolutionary psychology would maintain, that they issue forth from our supposed pre-human history, notwithstanding the amount of research being done by scientists on altruistic tendencies among apes.

"Self-evident truths" point, at bottom, to "nature and nature's God," to use the language of the founders and enlightened theists. This presumption – and I have no qualms about acknowledging that this is a "worldview" assumption that informs all of life – has eminent social and political consequences. At the very least, it means that there are human "goods" – goods that determine human "flourishing" – which must be protected and preserved. If this were not the case, then there is no such thing as "civil" society; consequently, any manipulation of human beings, by those in power, would be justifiable. It also means that certain classes or categories of humans – be they the unborn, the infirm, the elderly, or even *religious minorities*– because of human dignity must not be excluded from civic and legal protection. Again, John Paul's exhortation is worth bearing in mind:

> The moral history of your country [the United States] is a story of your people's efforts to widen the circle of inclusion in society, so that all Americans might enjoy the protection of law, participate in the responsibilities of citizenship, and have the opportunity to make a contribution to the common good.[115]

Protecting these human "goods" which encourage human flourishing, then, is the goal of any decent society, and this we call "justice."

But how, we may ask, do humans intuit justice? After all, the great apes do not wrestle with issues of justice, indignity, or the problem of evil. How does one arrive at an awareness of moral principle? Whence comes the human "moral sense?"

While this matter will surface again in later discussions in the book, we may sketch out some conceptual starting-point ever so tentatively by considering those capacities that distinguish human beings from other life forms. What are these? While human behavior is surely complex and thus a composite, it is foremost rational, perceiving, intuiting, and conceiving. Thus it is that we concern ourselves not merely with our rawest physical needs, as all animals do, but with our soulish or moral-spiritual as well as mental and intellectual needs. In fact, it is accurate to say that, with some exceptions, human beings are inclined to prioritize the latter (the moral-spiritual) over the former (the physical). Philosophers tend to speak of this tendency in terms of human flourishing.

As proponents of human flourishing, natural law theorists set themselves apart from metaphysical materialists and non-theists in critically important ways. They are *natural* lawyers because of their essential view of human nature, whereby they understand human beings to be moral-spiritual and not merely physical-material in their constitution. And they are natural *lawyers* insofar as they affirm the reality of moral principles–"laws," if you will – which govern the actions of all human beings – laws that are uniform and normative for all humanity, regardless of time, culture, and location. The natural lawyer is less taken by the differences in moral codes that are to be found among diverse peoples and cultures than by *what is shared in common* among these diverse people-groups. *Why* is it that murder and thievery and fraud and incest and disrespect toward elders are unacceptable, and *universally* so? Why is it that both Plato and Jesus, in addition to other cultural versions, teach a moral truth, a "Golden Rule," that is universally recognized and universally admired – namely, *Do unto others as you would have them do unto you*, with its corollary, *Don't do unto others what you would not want them to do unto you*?

Different people and different cultures, of course, have used different means to describe what we call "the natural moral law." What the Chinese wisdom tradition calls the *Tao*, what has been depicted in Plato and Jesus as the "Golden Rule," what is embodied in the Ten Commandments as well as in the wisdom literature of the Old Testament, what St. Paul described as the "law written on the heart," and what the founders of the American republic referred to as the "laws of nature" (mirroring "nature's God") and "self-evident truths" – one could identify (at least, until recently) a consensus among human beings as to what constitutes good and evil, right and wrong, just and unjust. And this, notwithstanding human beings' seemingly eternal propensity for excuse-making.

In theological terms, historic Christian belief distinguishes between special or particular revelation and that which is general in character. As distinct from special revelation mediated through "salvation-history," that which is common to all of human bears witness to "necessary truths" – moral first principles – as evidenced by the natural law. Deep within the human consciousness is found a "law" that we did not construct or create yet which we feel compelled to observe. Because this "law" is rooted in human "nature" – which is to say, in theological terms, the *imago Dei* – the conscience of all human beings bears witness to moral reality, with their thoughts accusing (or excusing) them. This is none other than the language of the natural law. It is "nature" because it describes human *design* and *the way things are*. The fact that not everyone gives assent to the natural law does not assail it universal reality. It is "law" because *nothing can change our essential nature*. The potential in humans for moral depravity, devastating as it may be, neither eliminates our ability to choose to do good (freedom) nor releases us from the sense of moral obligation (culpability) before the Creator (righteousness) or other human beings (the common good).

The truth of human dignity

Most voices in the mainstream of the Christian moral tradition (wherein I stand) would understand human dignity to be anchored in the *imago Dei*. This uniqueness, which sets human creation *apart* from all other life forms, is mirrored *inter alia* in human reason (rationality), in the yearning for justice (righteousness), in the capacity for stewardship and accountability (rulership), and in the capacity for fellowship and communion, both with the Creator and with fellow-humans (relationship).These capacities are moral-spiritual and immaterial in their essence. In the words of Benedict XVI, human dignity can be understood as the "capacity to transcend one's own materiality and to seek truth."[116]

Religious freedom, it needs emphasizing, is not the exclusive reserve of religious believers. It should be the concern of *all* people, since, as a foundational element of a constitutional state, its denial has the effect of encroaching on all fundamental freedoms and rights.[117] Natural law and human dignity, one might argue, go together like love and marriage, to the extent that the natural law – which moves the human spirit to do good and avoid doing evil[118] – protects human nature from both self-destruction and despoiling others. Natural law ethics furnishes human beings with the "first principles" of morality.[119] As self-evident principles, they correspond with the time-worn and tested adage, "What is just is to be done, and what is unjust is to be avoided." And as self-evident principles, they express themselves in the universal prescriptions such as one finds in the Ten Commandments. That is, they are unchanging and binding for all at all times and in all places; there is no situation or set of circumstance in which they are not obligatory. At the most basic level, the natural law inhibits human beings from moral choices that would negate human flourishing at least and destroy human life at worst.[120] We choose properly when we choose the good, which exists prior to human existence. We are thus *not* free to define what is "good" or "bad," thereby constructing our own independent morality. In the same vein, practical moral truths concern not what *is* but rather what *should be* – that is to say, what *is to be chosen* upon deliberation and moral reflection.

Robert P. George has helpfully expressed the importance of natural law ethics as it bears on the most basic of human needs:

> A natural-law theory is a critical reflective account of the constitutive aspects of well-being and fulfillment of human persons and the communities they form. Such a theory will propose to identify principles of right action–moral principles–specifying the first and most general principle of morality: namely, that one should choose and act in ways that are compatible with a will toward integral human fulfillment. Among these principles are respect for rights people possess imply by virtue of their humanity–rights that, as a matter of justice, others are bound to respect, and governments are bound not only to respect but also, to the extent possible, to protect.[121]

George's burden can be summarized in this way: there are irreducible dimensions of human existence and flourishing, and the moral-spiritual component is central to this constitution.

Given this commitment to protecting basic human "goods" on the basis of *intrinsic* worth, natural law thinking is essential to the promotion and preservation of justice and human rights – and hence, religious freedom. It will create within us a sense of obligation to respond to attempts to remove these basic "rights" where and when they are found. Such fundamental "rights," then, are not predicated on being identified with a particular ethnicity, race, culture, class, or gender; they inhere in our being *human*. Human "rights," therefore, arise out of human *dignity*. If, in fact, a human "right" has been identified, its universality and the basic terms of its application are patent. As George insists, "governments have a moral obligation to respect and protect that right and, correspondingly, to enforce the obligation."[122] Even where governments do *not* sense this moral obligation to protect, human beings themselves do. These rights, once again, are *pre-political*, anchored in an awareness of the natural moral law – a "law" which humans do not construct but rather discover.[123]

Natural law, reason, and religious freedom: what is at stake?

Qualifying the "natural" in natural law

I conclude the opening chapter with reflections on how natural law thinking is intrinsic to religious freedom and why it matters how we ground the "first freedom." These reflections begin with the observation, based on human experience and sociological fact, that all human beings acknowledge and make moral judgments. They assume that there is a difference between right and wrong, between just and unjust, between good and bad in the realm of human activity and actions. Moreover, all human beings intuitively assign a moral and social value to these actions. Actions that are judged to be "right," "good," or "just" are deemed worthy of approval, praise, and emulation. Actions that are judged to be "bad," "wrong," or "unjust" are deemed unacceptable, blameworthy, and condemnable. Moreover, all human beings *expect* that others think and judge in this way; they *expect* others to treat them as they wish to be treated. The same can be said for any and all people-groups. This is in keeping with human "nature"; we are moral beings and moral agents, and every thought, decision and action – whether consciously or unconsciously – is inclined in this direction. It is, quite simply, the nature of our design.

Perhaps it needs emphasizing in the twenty-first century that despite the prominence of metaphysical materialism (a term which I use interchangeably throughout the volume with naturalism and atheism), throughout human history most people have affirmed some form of religious belief. In fact, I would even contend that so-called non-religious people, such as self-professing "atheists" and agnostics, in fact have ultimate beliefs about the cosmos and human nature that qualify as "religious" (from the Latin *religare*: to bind, to connect, to form a whole). All have basic assumptions about ultimate reality. These assumptions, furthermore, are taken on "faith," sometimes *because of* and sometimes *in spite of* the evidence available. Thus, any claims by proponents of a belief system that promotes itself as morally "neutral" will need debunking.

A further qualification is necessary on matters of vocabulary. "Religion" can denote anything from animism, polytheism, and pantheism to "traditional" forms of religion found the world over such as Judaism, Christianity, Buddhism, Hinduism, and Islam. Thus, as natural law proponent Christopher Wolfe has suggested, we can either dispense with the notion of "religion" altogether or we can adopt an understanding of "religion" which grants that certain tenets of a belief system comport with reality as people perceive them.[124] I prefer the latter option. In fact, it is reasonable to distinguish between "natural" and "revealed" religion in order to accommodate *both* naturalists *and* supernaturalists to facilitate our discussion of "religious freedom."[125]

This distinction is by no means arbitrary. One reason for this is that advocates of natural law thinking traditionally have assumed that epistemology rests on two sources: reason and divine revelation. While not all natural lawyers share this baseline assumption, some – notably those advocates of "new natural law theory" such as Germain Grisez, John Finnis, and Robert P. George – argue that the natural law is not part of "revealed religion" in the narrow sense. They hold that it is anchored in practical reason as a basic human good.[126] How, then, it needs asking, do human beings reason toward "the good?"

Whether or not one agrees with the "new natural lawyers," most proponents of the natural law take their cues to some extent from Thomas Aquinas, particularly in their understanding of anthropology and metaphysics. Aquinas's conceptualization of the natural law begins, of course, with his presupposition that human beings "participate" in the eternal or divine law.[127]However, it does not end there. His appeal is to reason as well – and notably, "right reason."[128] By means of our rational capabilities, all humans "participate" in moral activity, moral discernment, and moral action. It should be emphasized that reason and revelation are not mutually exclusive; they do not cancel one another out. Theists simply acknowledge that knowledge can transcend the limits of pure reason, even when this knowledge accords with human reason. They presume that a moral law in the universe is not reasonable without a lawgiver. This awareness, then, is a source of knowledge about the Creator, about the self, and about moral reality. Reason, Aquinas maintains, and not merely "divine revelation," can lead human beings to a lawgiver as the source of *law* insofar as he is the source of human *nature*. "Natural" knowledge of moral reality, consequently, can be illustrated by our imperfect awareness of "good" and "evil," and the ability at the most basic level to distinguish between the two. Take murder, for example. Most people may have difficulty apart from purely utilitarian reasons articulating *why they themselves* consider it evil or *why society* should consider it such, yet they intuit its wrongness at the deepest level. And notice that this is a universal intuition; it does not vary with Kansans, Cambodians, Canadians, or Kazakhstanis. Why is that? Indeed, human beings "discover" a law that they did not create yet which they are bound to recognize and obey. This correlation – between moral law and human nature – remains a constant and unites natural law thinkers of any age, whether Aquinas, Suárez, Grotius, Locke, or more contemporary voices. In fact, this fusion – what might be described as "natural theology"[129] – is evident among the founders and framers of the American experiment, as we have already suggested and as will be argued in Chapter 4.[130]

We refer to the metaphysical reality of *natural* law because it corresponds to our fundamental *nature* – that is, to human design and the manner in which we are created to function as moral agents. But what do we mean by "nature?" Natural law does not refer to mere biology, inasmuch as human instincts and desires may or may not be beneficial, serving the "good," and morally sound. In fact, very often the moral sense will necessarily *counter* the biological instinct. Nor does it refer to mere habit or inclination or custom, all of which can be molded, ignored, or compromised, for the purposes of good or ill. Neither is the natural law some rationalistically deduced set of rules that are immediately evident and automatically applicable to every concrete historical situation. What's more, we call it natural *law* because it is *universally binding* and a common fund that serves as a *guide* for all human beings in moral matters. In truth, as moral creatures we should perhaps be bothered more by the common moral ground shared by diverse cultures around the globe than by their differences. In brief, then, natural law points toward the aim or goal of human nature, and it nudges us to inquire how laws – civil law and positive law – can assist humans in fulfilling that end.[131]

Qualifying the "rational" in religion and natural law

I am well aware that many of my readers may not grant some of the operational assumptions that I am making. My account of the natural law, which in turn informs my understanding of religious freedom, is admittedly a theistic account, and I am a Christian believer who affirms the unity and harmony of reason and revelation. A theistic starting-point need not jeopardize reason as a mode of discernment and discretion, and in a "post-secular" cultural moment – if we may use this term cautiously – a fresh awareness of the importance of the religious viewpoint is to be welcomed. (I take up this point later in the book).[132]

I am also well aware of that some of my readers assume that belief in God is not rational. It is widely thought that philosophical endeavor, whether it is moral or political in nature, must theism appeal solely to reason, with support and confirmation coming from a consensus of supposedly "rational" people, all of whom tend to be aggressively secular. Therefore, the injection of theistic considerations into public and political discussions is an imposition of the irrational. But in spite of false stereotypes that are perpetuated *ad infinitum*, I must stress in the opening chapter of this book that the mainstream of the historic Christian tradition has always affirmed the *rationality* of faith. This epistemological awareness that reason and faith work in symbiosis facilitates, especially in our "post-secular" day, a rich dialogue that is very much needed. It is a dialogue, for example, that was illustrated by discussions between Jürgen Habermas and Benedict XVI in the last decade, and that promises to be fruitful. And because of the interwoven nature of reason and faith, matters of religious freedom, regardless of cultural location, are understood to be of enormous import. Few have articulated the symbiosis of reason and religious faith more forcefully than Benedict's predecessor, John Paul II, in his final encyclical *Fides et Ratio* (1998). Tellingly, the first line of this important document reads, "Faith and reason are like two wings on which the human spirit rises to the contemplation of truth."[133]

Despite the grossly inflated skepticism characterizing our time, *Fides* insists that "it *is* possible to discern a core of philosophical insight within the history of thought as a whole," without throwing to the wind the principles of non-contradiction, finality, and cause, as well as the concept of the person as a free and intelligent subject."[134] Modern philosophy, however, makes this project more problematic: "Rather than make use of the human capacity to know the truth, modern philosophy has preferred to accentuate the ways in which this capacity is limited and conditioned."[135] This has given rise to various forms of agnosticism and relativism that "have led philosophical research to lose its way in the shifting sands of widespread skepticism."[136] A legitimate plurality of views, however, has yielded "an undifferentiated pluralism," based on the assumption that "all positions are equally valid, which is one of today's most widespread symptoms of the lack of confidence in truth."[137] Philosophical thinking in our time, tragically, has "tended to pursue issues – existential, hermeneutical, or linguistic – which ignore the radical question of the truth about personal existence, about being and about God."[138] But manifesting "a false modesty," people are content with "partial and provisional truths, no longer seeking to ask radical questions about the meaning and ultimate foundation of human, personal and social existence."[139]

As evidence of the harmony between "the knowledge conferred by faith" and "the knowledge conferred by reason," John Paul points the existence of "wisdom literature." What is striking about the writings associated with this literary genre embedded in the Hebrew scriptures is that *inter alia* "they embody not only the faith of Israel but also the treasury of cultures and civilizations which have long vanished."[140] The "wise" person, moreover, is one who *desires* knowledge of and *pursues* the truth. In wisdom literature, what is conspicuous is the conviction that "there is a profound and indissoluble unity between the knowledge of reason and the knowledge of faith."[141] John Paul gives clarity to this symbiotic relationship: "The world and all that happens within it, including history and the fate of peoples, are realities to be observed, analyzed and assessed with all the resources of reason, but without faith ever being foreign to the process."[142] Faith's role, John Paul insists, is "not to abolish reason's autonomy nor to reduce its scope of action."[143] Summarizing their unity, he maintains,

> Reason and faith cannot be separated without diminishing the capacity of men and women to know themselves, the world and God in an appropriate way . . . There is thus no reason for competition of any kind between reason and faith: each contains the other, and each has its own scope for action.[144]

The Second Vatican Council declaration on religious freedom *Dignitatis Humanae*, which will be analyzed in Chapter 5, accords with John Paul's burden in *Fides et Ratio*. In its introduction, it declares, "The human person has a right to religious freedom."[145] This freedom means that all persons

> are to be immune from coercion on the part of individuals or of social groups and of any human power, in such wise that no one is to be forced to act in a manner contrary to his own beliefs, whether privately or publicly, whether alone or in association with others, within due limits.[146]

The right to religious freedom, the document insists, has its foundation in "the very dignity of the human person" as this dignity is known through reason and revelation.[147] This right of the human person to religious freedom, moreover, is "to be recognized in the constitutional law whereby society is governed and thus it is to become a civil right."[148]

It is in accordance with their dignity as persons that human beings are endowed with reason and moral agency. Because of these endowments, humans therefore bear *personal moral responsibility*; that is to say, they are "impelled by nature and also bound by a moral obligation to seek the truth, especially religious truth."[149] Moreover, "They are also bound to adhere to the truth, once it is known, and to order their whole lives in accord with the demands of truth."[150] However, a caveat is in order: "Men cannot discharge these obligations in a manner in keeping with their own nature unless they enjoy immunity from external coercion as well as psychological freedom."[151] Therefore, *Dignitatis* asserts, "The right to religious freedom has its foundation not in the subjective disposition of the person, but in his very nature."[152] In consequence, the right to this immunity continues to exist even in those who do not live up to their obligation of seeking the truth and adhering to it and the exercise of this right is not to be impeded, provided that just public order be observed.

Qualifying religious freedom

Religious freedom, as I am representing it, possesses both positive and negative elements. It entails a freedom *toward* belief and practice and as well as a freedom *from* coercion as it affects belief and practice. How are these elements that constitutive of religious freedom best safeguarded? Any belief system that gives prominence to virtues such as charity and justice would seem best suited to – we might even argue, be a necessary *pre-condition* for – religious liberty.[153] And from the standpoint of natural law thinking, a society which honors religious freedom will exhibit a public philosophy that is built on several non-negotiable tenets. These include legitimate and constrained governmental powers; affirmation of moral law, which informs civil law; a commitment to guarding the common good; and perhaps most importantly, a respect for the dignity of the human person. Each of these components will need revisiting in later chapters.

At this point, I am well aware that my reader may be questioning – or perhaps objecting to – my approach to religious freedom. A most basic and controversial question presents itself. Should the religious viewpoint be allowed *at all* in the public sphere? Shouldn't the public sphere remain free of religious arguments, as many of our social philosophers have argued with considerable force? The answer to this question, one that vexes moderns and their post-modern children, typically yields an all-or-none response. At least for the committed secularist, such is the case. To permit one expression of religious sentiment in the public sphere is to allow the camel's nose inside the tent.

I have noted and welcomed the "post-secular" shift and will assume in my overall argument that presenting religiously grounded moral arguments in the public sphere runs afoul *neither* of democratic norms *nor* of constitutional norms.[154] Simply because *political controversy* is owing to *moral controversy*, it *does not follow* that law and politics should ban the source of that moral controversy, which often is religious conviction. What's more, it is often the case that some moral positions (which inevitably become political positions and law) are supported by *both* religious and "secular" premises. Where or not particular "religious beliefs" invite legal censure fundamentally depends (or should depend) on whether the common social good is being undermined. I grant here that people will have differing understandings of what constitutes the "good," but at that point, civil law must be informed by moral law, and, more fundamentally, moral law must be informed and supported by moral discourse.

But what precisely is *morality*? What is the nature of *public morality*? And what does liberal democracy assume about the *moral commitments* of its citizens? Foundational to any relatively free society is a commitment to the freedom of every person to be true to his or her ultimate convictions. (Such assumes that these convictions do not undermine the common good.) This freedom – let us call it "religious freedom" – gives rise to other related freedoms, freedoms that we take for granted. The sort of environment I am describing we generally call a "liberal democracy."[155] Of course, in the Western context we are accustomed to hearing arguments for keeping religiously ground beliefs out of the public sphere, arguments that have been fashionably, and at times persuasively, made. But when competing claims are jostling in the public sphere, there is *nothing* in liberal democracy, properly construed, that forbids religiously grounded arguments from assuming their place in public. There is *nothing* therein that is incompatible with liberal democracy. There are *no grounds* for formal censorship thereof in a liberal democracy.[156] Even where a *majority* of its citizens are intent on excluding the religiously informed moral viewpoint from the public sphere, it is possible, as the founders and framers of the American experiment well intuited, that majoritarian thinking can be misguided, even fundamentally immoral. I will focus, in later discussion, on the *possibility* of what Tocqueville calls a "tyranny of the majority."

In their important 2013 volume *Persecuted: The Global Assault on Christians*,[157] Paul Marshall, Lela Gilbert, and Nina Shea survey the current configuration of global attitudes toward religious freedom. The authors examine the former Soviet satellite states of Central Asia, the region of Southeast Asia, the Muslim world of the Middle East, and Muslim nations in central, northern, and eastern Africa.[158] For those of us who live in Western societies, religious freedom has been largely taken for granted and government intrusion or interference, at least up to now, has not been repressive. This, however, is beginning to change. Meanwhile, many are either blissfully ignorant of or indifferent to the sufferings of religious believers around the world – a state of affairs, as we have argued, that is worsening. The old adage "To whom much has been given, much will be required" is apropos as we consider our responsibilities to those who are experiencing intense persecution due to their religious convictions. Those inhabiting the mainstream media, whether electronic or print, are tone-deaf to the reality of outright persecution around the globe and its attendant suffering. The plight of many who are suffering outrageously is routinely ignored, when it is not under-reported.

Data from organizations like the Pew Research Center indicate that the world is becoming increasingly religious.[159] At the same time, it is becoming increasingly intolerant of religious believers. The argument set forth in this volume is not that we in the West should feel guilty for the freedoms that we take for granted. Rather, it is that an adequate grounding for religious freedom – the "first freedom" – is needed in order to establish and safeguard religious freedom, both at home and abroad. This grounding should contribute to sound social and foreign policy.

In the penultimate chapter of this volume, I argue that significant shifts in social and cultural attitudes regarding what a society is willing or unwilling to tolerate need "preparation." This social-cultural process is verified again and again by historical experience. Sometimes this preparation is slow, and sometimes it proceeds at an alarming pace. In the face of a changing and increasingly dangerous world, it behooves those of us living in the twenty-first century to "bear the burden" of those who are suffering for their faith, and to consider the very roots from which the "first freedom" – a tender shoot – derives.

Notes

1 Samuel Stillman, *A Sermon Preached Before the Honorable Council, and the Honorable House of Representatives of the State* (Boston: T. and J. Fleet, 1779), 11.
2 Chandler Robbins, *A Sermon. Preached Before His Excellency John Hancock Esq.: His Honor Samuel Adams Esq. Lieutenant Governour: The Honourable the Council and the Honourable Senate and House of Representatives, If the Commonwealth of Massachusetts, May 25, 1791, Being the Day of General Elections* (Boston: Thomas Adams, 1791).
3 Thomas Jefferson, *Light and Liberty: Reflections on the Pursuit of Happiness*, ed. Eric S. Petersen (New York: The Modern Library, 2004), 114.
4 Benedict XVI, *Religious Freedom, the Path to Peace* no. 1, accessible at http://w2.vatican.va/content/benedict-xvi/en/messages/peace/documents/hf_ben-xvi_mes_20101208_xliv-world-day-peace.html.
5 Ibid., emphasis added.
6 Benedict XVI, encyclical *Caritas in Veritate* no. 29, accessible at http://w2.vatican.va/content/benedict-xvi/en/encyclicals/documents/hf_ben-xvi_enc_20090629_caritas-in-veritate.html.

7 Ibid., emphasis added.

8 Ibid.

9 Both religious fundamentalism and secular fundamentalism (what Benedict calls "practical atheism") have the effect of absolutizing a partial, reductionistic, and, thus, truncated vision of the human person, as Benedict is careful to highlight (*Religious Freedom* no. 8).

10 Paul A. Marshall, "The Range of Religious Freedom," in Paul A. Marshall, ed., *Religious Freedom in the World* (Lanham and Plymouth, UK: Rowman & Littlefield, 2008), 10.

11 This would not merely explain why Muslims who do convert do so secretly; it would also offer justification for so-called honor killings. The options, in Islamic thought, are twofold: total submission to Allah or treason, worthy of death.

12 While Islamic terrorists are not representative of Islam's millions of adherents, they nevertheless draw inspiration from particular often long-standing traditions and interpretations of shared Islamic faith. This morning as I write, I read of an elderly French priest who yesterday was murdered in a hostage situation in a church south of Rouen, Normandy, in northern France by Islamist attackers. As reported in France's *Le Figaro*, one of the "executioners" gave "an Arabic sermon from the altar" while the priest, Father Jacques Hamel, was forced to kneel before having his throat slit (Edouard de Mareschal, "EN DIRECT – Saint-Etienne-du-Rouvray: l'un des assassins était connu des services antiterrorists," *Le Figaro*(June 27, 2016), accessible at www.lefigaro.fr/actualite-france/2016/07/26/01016-20160726LIVWWW00086-prise-d-otage-en-cours-dans-une-eglise-de-saint-etienne-du-rouvray-pres-de-rouen.php. Yesterday the news concerned Christian churches being burned to the ground by Muslims in Tanzania. And the day before it concerned a group of Christian families being attacked by a mob of 300 Muslims in Egypt. Tomorrow the terror will take yet another form. Whether it expresses itself in mainstream persecution of minorities domestically in Islamic cultures or in violent attacks and the murder of innocents in both Islamic and non-Islamic cultures, the "jihadist" spirit is very much alive worldwide. Despite the unwillingness of the mainstream (Western) media to acknowledge such, violent manifestations of Islamic radicalism have been *the* defining feature of the twenty-first century thus far, and the resurgence of Islamic fundamentalism has fostered among many Muslims – even among many residing in the West – the belief that a religious war (*jihad*) is necessary because of the Christian religion.

13 This is the position of the authors of "In Defense of Religious Freedom: A Statement by Evangelicals and Catholics Together," *First Things* (March 2012), accessible at www.firstthings.com/article/2012/03/in-defense-of-religious-freedom. It is difficult to disagree.

14 Paul A. Marshall, "Why Religious Freedom Must Be a Top Priority," *Cardus* (November 24, 2011), accessible at www.cardus.ca/policy/article/2992/.

15 To his credit, John L. Allen Jr., *The Global War Christians: Dispatches from the Front Lines of Anti-Christian Persecution* (New York: Image, 2013), 3, is one of the few to have raised this question.

16 Those who have obsessed over Abu Graib and Guantanamo Bay – both religious and secular – do so not because of any concern for religious freedom or persecuted religious minorities worldwide, even when the norm in Islamic cultures around the world is infinitely worse. Their indignation, rather, arises from political opposition to U.S. foreign policy.

17 Representative organizations that exist for the express purpose of serving the "persecuted church" include, for example, Open Doors, Voice of the Martyrs, International Christian Concern, Christian Solidarity International, and Barnabas Aid, among others. Not insignificantly, all of these organizations were founded in the West, even when their burden is to alleviate suffering in

non-western nations and people-groups, and most all of them were birthed in the United States or the United Kingdom.

18 Christian Solidarity Worldwide, "North Korea: A Case to Answer – A Call to Act," accessible at file:///C:/Users/owner/Downloads/north-korea-a-case-to-answer-a-call-to-act.pdf.

19 Ibid., 65.

20 Brian J. Grim and Roger Finke, *The Price of Freedom Denied: Religious Persecution and Conflict in the 21st Century* (Cambridge Studies in Social Theory, Religion, and Politics; Cambridge and New York: Cambridge University Press, 2011).

21 See n. 10.

22 Brian J. Grim and Roger Finke, "International Religion Indexes: Government Regulation, Government Favoritism, and Social Regulation of Religion," *Interdisciplinary Journal of Research on Religion* 2 (2006), accessible at www.religjournal.com/pdf/ijrr02001.pdf.

23 Freedom House, "Freedom in the World 2016 – Anxious Dictators, Wavering Democracies: Global Freedom under Pressures," accessible at https://freedomhouse.org/report/freedom-world/freedom-world-2016.

24 Todd Johnson, director of the Center for the Study of Global Christianity at Gordon-Conwell Seminary, has estimated that in the ten-year period of 2000–2010 approximately one million people worldwide were martyred, which averages about 1000,000 per year. See his "Christian Martyrdom: A Global Demographic Assessment," accessible at https://icl.nd.edu/assets/84231/the_demographics_of_christian_martyrdom_todd_johnson.pdf.

25 In this regard, works such as John L. Allen Jr.'s *The Global War on Christians* (see n. 15) are invaluable in helping to mediate to the wider public the extraordinary anti-Christian sentiment that is found worldwide in our day – whether in Africa, Asia, Latin America, the Middle East, or Eastern Europe.

26 Marshall, *Religious Freedom in the World*, 11.

27 The report was written prior to the so-called coup attempt in Turkey in 2016, which many observers believe to have been staged by the Turkish dictator, who in the months since has purged Turkish society by totalitarian means. What is remarkable is the silence of European nations to this outrage, if for no other reason Turkey is a member of the EU.

28 From a journalistic perspective, two works need citing for their painstaking attempts to raise the profile of persecuted religious minorities worldwide. One is the 2013 volume by senior Vatican analyst for CNN John L. Allen Jr., *The Global War on Christians* (see n. 15); the other is Rupert Shortt's 2012 volume *Christianophobia: A Faith Under Attack* (Grand Rapids and Cambridge, UK: Eerdmans, 2012). Both of these works, despite their somewhat misleading titles, chronicle for the reader the plight of persecuted religious minorities worldwide, though with a particular focus on Christians.

29 "Discrimination Against Catholic Adoption Services," accessible at www.usccb.org/issues-and-action/religious-liberty/discrimination-against-catholic-adoption-services.cfm.

30 Ibid.

31 Ibid.

32 Ibid.

33 Ibid.

34 Ibid., emphasis added.

35 Michael Terheyden, "Catholic Charities Forced to Shut Down Services Around the Country," accessible at www.catholic.org/news/national/story.php?id=41680.

36 On adoption, child services and religious freedom, see Sarah Torre and Ryan T. Anderson, "Adoption, Foster Care, and Conscience Protection," *Backgrounder* no. 2869, accessible at www.heritage.org/research/reports/2014/01/

adoption-foster-care-and-conscience-protection#_ftn25. The authors write, "Foster care and adoption policy should put the best interests of children first. Public policy therefore should seek to increase the likelihood of adoption by removing barriers to families that are seeking to adopt and providers that are seeking to place children in need of a home. Achieving this goal requires a public policy that provides freedom to the diverse groups that serve the needs of children. Provided these agencies meet basic requirements protecting the welfare of children, they should be free to operate according to their values, especially their religiously informed beliefs about marriage."

37 "Rising Tide of Restrictions on Religion," Pew Research Center Religion and Public Life Project (September 2013), accessible at www.pewforum.org/2012/09/20/rising-tide-of-restrictions-on-religion-findings.

38 Thomas Messner, "From Culture Wars to Conscience Wars: Emerging Threats to Conscience," *Backgrounder* no. 2543 (April 13, 2011), accessible at www.heritage.org/research/reports/2011/04/from-culture-wars-to-conscience-wars-emerging-threats-to-conscience.

39 That a consensus regarding moral values has evaporated in North America is not to argue that it should not be desired or sought; it only means that citizens will need to engage creatively and faithfully in moral persuasion in the public sphere, at least to the extent that cultural authorities and institutional realities permit. Whether cultural conflict can lead to consensus is a matter yet to be determined.

40 General Pharmaceutical Council, "We Are Consulting on Religion, Personal Values and Beliefs in Pharmacy Practice," (12 December 2016), accessibleatwww.pharmacyregulation.org/news/gphc-consults-religion-personal-values-and-beliefs-pharmacy-practice.

41 BBC News, "New Pharmacy Code Continues Opt-Outs over Beliefs," (25 March 2010), accessible at http://news.bbc.co.uk/2/hi/uk/8586344.stm.

42 "We Are Consulting."

43 Chris Whitehouse, "Pharmacy Workers – and a New Threat to Religious Freedom from Equality Laws Meant to Protect It," (February 13, 2017), accessible at www.conservativehome.com/platform/2017/02/chris-whitehouse-pharmancy-workers-and-a-new-threat-to-religious-freedom-from-equality-laws-meant-to-protect-it.html.

44 Ibid.

45 See Joel Kotkin, "California's State Religion," *The Orange County Register* (June 19, 2016), accessible at www.ocregister.com/articles/state-719782-climate-religious.html.

46 Ibid.

47 Ibid.

48 Apparently, even religious clubs and organizations on the various campuses of the California State University system can no longer restrict their leadership to individuals who actually are believers and embody their group's beliefs.

49 The issue is *not* whether men and women may have emotionally close or enduring relationships with members of the same sex. The issue, rather, as Allen Hertzke ("Introduction: A Madisonian Framework for Applying Constitutional Principles on Religion," in Allen Hertzke, ed., *Religious Freedom in America: Constitutional Roots and Contemporary Challenges* [Norman: University of Oklahoma Press, 2015], 20) rightly insists, is whether there is any legitimate rationale for the state to privilege – or undermine – the traditional and conventional understanding of marriage, which has been a sociological, societal, and pre-political norm for millennia. Indeed, the debate over same-sex marriage, at the most profound philosophical level, concerns the very definition of marriage itself. Hertzke does not exaggerate one bit: "Once same-sex marriage is deemed a fundamental right, then dissenters can be subject to the full weight of this anti-discrimination infrastructure [of government and law]" (ibid., 21).

50 Ibid. The designation "California's State Religion" derives from the bill itself, not the journalist I am quoting, who concludes with a bit of drama: "So, fellow Californians, sign onto Gov. Torquemada's program or face possible prosecution and the fires of hell."
51 Ibid.
52 Ibid.
53 Ibid.
54 Benedict XVI, *Religious Freedom* no. 3 (see n. 4), has pressed this point with supreme clarity.
55 Messner, "From Culture Wars to Conscience Wars."
56 Ibid.
57 Grim and Finke, *The Price of Freedom Denied* (see n. 17), 1–24. Of course, to describe religious persecution as "pervasive" and "pernicious" does not tell us the reasons why it is occurring around the world in a variety of cultural settings.
58 Hertzke, "Introduction," 3–10.
59 Hertzke argues persuasively that this amnesia, or indifference to our past, is at the root of much contemporary misunderstanding about religious freedom and church-state relations.
60 Here we might identify two sources of bias – one that is less strident yet quite influential (for example, the arguments of John Rawls on "reasonableness" and the public sphere) and one that is more shrill (for example Brian Leiter's *Why Tolerate Religion?* (Princeton: Princeton University Press, 2013). Both of these prejudices, one eminently "reasonable" and one more vehement, exert an inordinate influence on the thinking of the academy.
61 Sonia Orwell and Ian Angus, eds., *Collected Essays, Journalism and Letters of George Orwell – Vol. 1: An Age Like This, 1920–1940* (New York: Penguin, 1970), 413–14.
62 Grim and Finke, *The Price of Freedom Denied*, 5. See Paul Leicester Ford, ed., *The Autobiography of Thomas Jefferson, 1743–1790* (Philadelphia: University of Pennsylvania Press, 2005), 71.
63 Ibid., 5–6.
64 Hertzke, "Introduction," 10.
65 Ibid.
66 Ibid.
67 Here we stand in agreement with one social critic, who recently set forth this argument while contrasting two competing versions of "religious liberty" in America's founding. See Matthew J. Franck, "Two Tales of Freedom: Getting the Origins of Religious Liberty Right Matters," *Touchstone*(July/August 2016): 19–26.
68 Hence, as I shall argue later, the preferred metaphor here for "church and state" is less a "wall" than it is a fence with gates.
69 Alexis de Tocquville, *Democracy in America*, trans. and ed. Harvey C. Mansfield and Delba Winthrop (Chicago and London: University of Chicago Press, 2000), I.2.9, p. 275.
70 I am not much persuaded by the arguments of the "new biology" – with its tributaries in evolutionary psychology and the social sciences – that genetics can explain the "moral sense."
71 See, especially, his *Memorial and Remonstrance*.
72 The religious beliefs of the founders cover a very broad spectrum. In the words of Richard B. Morris, "In the main the Founding Fathers would hardly have labeled themselves orthodox Christian thinkers, but they were Christian, dues-paying, if not orthodox" ("The Judeo-Christian Foundation of the American Political System," in Robert S. Alley, ed., *James Madison on Religious Liberty* [Buffalo: Prometheus, 1985], 110). Tellingly, however, individual states at our nation's founding did exclude atheists from public office. On whether atheists

can be good citizens, see Richard John Neuhaus's stimulating response in *American Babylon: Notes of a Christian Exile* (New York: Basic Books, 2009), Chapter 4. Neuhaus concludes that, notwithstanding the diversity of opinion and worldviews of the founders, the American experiment was not conceived in and dedicated to atheism, even when it was tolerated (117–18). Notice the tension yet priority in Neuhaus's summary; this is as it should be, and as it was to the founders.

73 Benedict XVI, *Religious Freedom* no. 3.

74 *Dignitatis Humanae* no. 1 (Declaration on Religious Freedom of the Second Vatican Ecumenical Council). The encyclical is accessible at www.vatican.va/archive/hist_councils/ii_vatican_council/documents/vat-ii_decl_19651207_dignitatis-humanae_en.html.

75 Grim and Finke, *The Price of Freedom Denied*, 62, 71, 212–13.

76 Tocqueville, *Democracy in America* I.2.4., p. 183.

77 Ibid. I.2.7, pp. 239–64.

78 Tocqueville, *Democracy in America* I.2.7. See "On the Omnipotence of the Majority in the United States and Its Effects," esp. pp. 248–9.

79 Ibid. I.2.8., p. 262.

80 Ibid.

81 Ibid. I.2.9, p. 275.

82 Ibid. II.4.6–8, pp. 661–76. See, especially, Chapter 6: "What Kind of Despotism Democratic Nations Have to Fear." In the concluding statement of *Democracy*, Tocqueville writes that it is left to citizens to decide whether they will choose "servitude or freedom," "enlightenment or barbarism," "prosperity or misery" (II.4.8, p. 676).

83 Although the phrase "first freedom," in contemporary parlance, is typically used in association with *religious* freedom, some (particularly in the American context) would apply it to freedom of speech, freedom of the press, and issues of "censorship." Thus, for example, Robert B. Downs and Ralph E. McCoy, eds., *The First Freedom Today Critical Issues Relating to Censorship and to Intellectual Freedom* (Chicago: American Library Association, 1984). I would argue, however, that freedom of speech and press are derivative, owing their existence to a freedom that is more basic – namely, religious freedom, from which all other freedoms flow. In any case, this was the view of the founders and framers.

84 As Benedict XVI observes, while human dignity is an essential of Judeo-Christian wisdom, it is nevertheless recognized by – and accessible to – all, made known through reason.

85 For a deeply insightful discussion of religious freedom as a necessary buffer between the human person and the omnipotent state, see Robert P. George, "Why Moral Truths Matter" and "Religious Liberty: A Fundamental Human Right," Chapters 9 and 11 of *Conscience and Its Enemies: Confronting the Dogmas of Liberal Secularism* (Wilmington: ISI Books, 2013), 91–105 and 115–25.

86 Grim and Finke, *The Price of Freedom Denied*, 213.

87 George, *Conscience and Its Enemies*, 3–6.

88 Benedict XVI writes, "Each person is endowed with the sacred right to a full life . . . Without the acknowledgement of his spiritual being, without openness to the transcendent, the human person withdraws within himself, fails to find answers to the heart's deepest questions about life's meaning, fails to appropriate lasting ethical values, and fails even to experience authentic freedom and to build a just society" (*Religious Freedom* no. 2, emphasis present).

89 This acknowledgement is not simply the domain of Christian theology, which understands human nature as "sinful" and "fallen" (that is, capable of both good and evil). It has implications for non-theists as well, for whom biology and basic "instincts" – frequently in our day understood in chemical and physiological terms – explain the mechanisms of human behavior.

90 This sense of the *tranquillitas ordinis* is presupposed in the teaching of the Apostle Paul in the New Testament as well; cf. Rom. 13:4.

91 The Second World War was a turning point insofar as up to that point, most governments around the world assumed that international law did not remove their sovereignty, and hence, their prevent what later were viewed as massive human rights violations.

92 United Nations, "Universal Declaration of Human Rights," accessible at www.ohchr.org/EN/UDHR/Documents/UDHR_Translations/eng.pdf.

93 For this reason, Benedict XVI has challenged his fellow Europeans: "May Europe . . . be reconciled to its own Christian roots, which are fundamental for understanding its past, present and future role in history; in this way it will come to experience justice, concord and peace by cultivating a sincere dialogue with all peoples" (*Religious Freedom* no. 14).

94 The sort of self-contradictory nihilism that insists on the relativity of knowledge, rejects the possibility of objective truth, and holds many different "truths" to be equally valid, strangely, does not translate into diversity of opinion at the university and within our various academic departments. There the atmosphere is one of rigidity, disdain for authentic diversity, and intolerance. Certain viewpoints, in fact, are *not* to be tolerated.

95 Of his own discipline, anthropologist Philip Carl Salzman observes with considerable prescience: "anthropology . . . has jettisoned the objective, scientifically-grounded study of humankind's cultures in favor of advocating for selected 'victims' of supposed Western perfidy. The outcome of this abandonment of the search for Truth is not a plethora of 'truths,' but a regnant false Truth that reduces scholarship to advocacy and demands blind adherence to approved yet false narratives. If anthropologists hope to restore the integrity of their field, they must abandon their intellectually flaccid, morally corrupt habits and readopt the scientific objectivity toward their subjects that marked their discipline from its inception"(http://dailycaller.com/2016/07/19/anthropology-abandon-all-truth-ye-who-enter/).

96 Michael J. Sandel, "Freedom of Conscience or Freedom of Choice?" in James Davison Hunter and Os Guinness, eds., *Articles of Faith, Articles of Peace: The Religious Liberty Clauses and the American Public Philosophy* (Washington, DC: Brookings Institution, 1990), 74–92.

97 That government is required to be "neutral" on religious matters needs severe qualification. Only in the 1947 Supreme Court case *Everson vs. Board of Education* was it first ruled that "neutrality" should be mandated, but such a conclusion this was not the intent of the First Amendment, whose language permits the "free exercise" of religion and protects individual states from federal intrusion.

98 Ibid., 87, emphasis added.

99 Ibid., 87–8.

100 Ibid., 88.

101 Thomas Jefferson, "A Bill for Establishing Religious Freedom," sec. 1, in Merrill D. Peterson, ed., *Thomas Jefferson: Writings* (New York: Library of America, 1984), 346.

102 From the Latin *religare*: to bind, to connect, to tie together.

103 So argues James Madison in *Memorial and Remonstrance.*

104 "In Defense of Religious Freedom" (see n. 13).

105 Peter Berger argues that affirmations of religious freedom are grounded in the refusal to participate in the "flight into fanaticism" which constitutes the social psychology of all fundamentalisms – religious or secular. See his "Afterword," in James Davison Hunter and Os Guinness, eds., *Articles of Faith, Articles of Peace: The Religious Liberty Clauses and the American Public Philosophy* (Washington, DC: Brookings Institution, 1990), 114–21.

106 James W. Ceaser helpfully addresses the political implications of this outlook in "The Doctrine of Political Nonfoundationalism" in James W. Ceaser, ed., *Designing a Polity: America's Constitution in Theory and Practice* (Lanham and Plymouth, UK: Rowman & Littlefield, 2011), 3–21 (= Chapter 1). Ceaser notes that what variously goes by "anti-foundationalism," "political deconstruction," "deliberative democracy," "public reason," etc. is a product of the recent past. In any case, non-foundationalists, whatever their stripe or feather, find common ground in "seeking to erect a high wall of separation between [moral] foundations and politics" (4).

107 So David F. Forte, "The Natural Law Moment," in David F. Forte, ed., *Natural Law and Public Policy* (Washington, DC: Georgetown University, 1998), 6.

108 William Lee Miller, "The Moral Project of the American Founders," in James Davison Hunter and Os Guinness, eds., *Articles of Faith, Articles of Peace: The Religious Liberty Clauses and the American Public Philosophy* (Washington, DC: Brookings Institution, 1990), 37. Miller is correct to note the wisdom of this intersection and blending, for unlike Europe, the United States over time would not divide politically and systematically along religious fault-lines. There were no two Americas – a Catholic one and a Protestant one – and neither were there religious conservatives who were anti-republican or political radicals who were anti-religious. This, then, would contribute in important ways to the creation and preservation of a "principled pluralism."

109 Thus, for example, Richard Rorty, "Religion as Conversation-Stopper," *Common Knowledge*3, no. 1 (1994): 1–6.

110 Michael J. Perry, *Under God? Religious Faith and Liberal Democracy* (Cambridge and New York: Cambridge University Press, 2003), 44.

111 Robert Audi and Nicholas Wolterstorff, *Religion in the Public Square: The Place of Religious Convictions in Public Debate* (Point/Counterpoint; Lanham: Rowman & Littlefield, 1997), 105, emphasis present.

112 Benedict XVI, *Address to the General Assembly of the United Nations* (April 18, 2008), accessible at http://w2.vatican.va/content/benedict-xvi/en/speeches/2008/april/documents/hf_ben-xvi_spe_20080418_un-visit.html.

113 The editors, "John Paul II on the American Experiment," *First Things* 82 (April 1998): 37.

114 This burden has also been forcefully articulated by Benedict XVI: "Religion should not be marginalized or prohibited, but seen as making an effective contribution to the promotion of the common good. In this context, mention should be made of the religious dimension of culture, built up over centuries thanks to the social and especially ethical contributions of religion. This dimension is in no way discriminatory towards those who do not share its belief, but instead reinforces social cohesion, integration and solidarity" (*Religious Freedom* no.6).

115 "John Paul II on the American Experiment," 36.

116 Benedict XVI, *Religious Freedom* no. 2.

117 Thus, Benedict XVI, in the encyclical *Caritas in Veritate* no. 11.

118 This formulation of the *esse* of the natural law – doing good and avoid doing evil – is owing to Thomas Aquinas, for whom all moral principles derive from this baseline conviction (*Summa Theologica* [hereafter *S.T.*] I–II Q. 94, a. 2).

119 See Chapter 2.

120 The natural law theorist does not deny the reality of one's practical and incremental learning – typically in a social unit called the family – of moral principle. In this sense, then, knowledge of the natural law is not "innate." At the same time, the human being is rational from earliest childhood – ask any parent! – and hence "intuits" the "rightness" or "wrongness" of what he or she is taught. In this sense, knowledge of the natural *is* "innate." Were this not the case, people could not consistently and normatively be taught that murder is

in sic wrong, for if it would be purely learned in a social setting (and not truly *known*), then roughly half of all people would murder with joy while the other half would restrain their moral impulses. And in this sense, "criminal justice" would be a mere crap shoot.

121 George, *Conscience and Its Enemies*, 76.

122 Ibid., 78.

123 Hence the wrongheaded nature of Jonathan Glover's argument in *Humanity: A Moral History of the Twentieth Century* (New Haven: Yale University Press, 2000). Glover points to Friedrich Nietzsche who viewed the idea of moral law as being almost extinct. In essay one of *The Genealogy of Morals* (published in 1887 with the subtitle "A Polemic"), Nietzsche wrote: "morality will gradually perish now" – a spectacle that Nietzsche predicted would last "for the next two centuries in Europe" (Friedrich Nietzsche, *On the Genealogy of Morals*, trans. Walter Kaufmann and R.J. Hollingdale [New York: Vintage, 1989], 161). Glover seems to be applauding Nietzsche's desire to move "beyond good and evil" when he writes, "The collapse of the external authority of morality removes one of the main obstacles to conscious projects of self-creation" (11). In the place of the old "external authority," Glover's solution is to promote the fruits of "rational self-interest" which, he is convinced, lead toward altruistic tendencies (18). Glover does not "connect the dots," however, in observing what moving "beyond good and evil" did to Nietzsche's own people – and the rest of the world.

124 Christopher Wolfe, *Natural Law Liberalism* (Cambridge and New York: Cambridge University Press, 2006), 220.

125 Ibid., 220–6 chooses to adopt this distinction.

126 I do not wish to diminish the levels of disagreements among various natural law theorists on this score, and it is probably fair to say that most natural lawyers follow Aquinas in viewing the natural law as "participation" in the divinely instituted moral law by means of human reason.

127 *S.T.* I-II Q. 91, a. 2. This is a recurring subtheme in the encyclicals of John Paul; see esp. *Veritatis Splendor*.

128 "Right reason" does not mean that all people agree. Rather, it suggests that the development and use of reason will vary among people. In his writings, Aquinas identifies several categories of anomaly or variation that give rise to moral contradiction of disagreement – among these, the nature and influence of the passions, self-interest, diversity of conditions and circumstances, and uneven or unequal development of moral faculties.

129 So Wolfe, *Natural Law Liberalism*, 222–3, following Aquinas and others.

130 Again, recall the frequent references to the "laws of nature," "nature's God," "the Creator," "Providence," "Governor of the universe," and so forth.

131 So, David F. Forte, "Family, Nurture, and Liberty," in David F. Forte, ed., *Natural Law and Public Policy* (Washington, DC: Georgetown University Press, 1998), 84.

132 Here the natural lawyer takes exception to the widely embraced Rawlsian understanding of justice, the common good and the public sphere that is predicated on a utilitarian scheme supported by "mutual disinterestedness," "fairness," "efficiency," "average utility," "freestanding views," a "veil of ignorance," and definitions of "reason" and "reasonable consensus" which effectively bleach the public sphere of any religious viewpoint ("comprehensive doctrine"). The Rawlsian conception of society and political life dons a mantle of "moral neutrality" which in fact is anything but "neutral," as the natural lawyer well intuits. See John Rawls, *A Theory of Justice* (Cambridge: Belknap Press, 1971); John Rawls, *Political Liberalism* (New York: Columbia University Press, 1993); and John Rawls, *Justice as Fairness: A Restatement*, ed. Erin Kelly (Cambridge: Belknap Press, 2001). According to the editor of *Justice as*

Fairness, the latter volume addresses questions not taken up in *A Theory of Justice* and "corrected what Rawls' had come to see as mistakes in some of *Theory*'s arguments" (xii). From the standpoint of the natural law, religious freedom, and principled pluralism, however, any shifts in Rawls' thinking do not alter his basic premises about justice, about the nature of political liberalism, and about the participation of religious viewpoints in the public sphere.

Although any extended discussion of Rawls' ideas is well beyond the scope of this volume, several qualifications are necessary, given the version of "political liberalism" and the public sphere set forth by Rawls as well as his remarkable influence. The "political liberalism" that Rawls formulates is by all measurements a *comprehensive* view, and yet it is a view that excludes "comprehensive doctrines" (his term) from political life. While numerous elements in Rawls' thinking are problematic, several need identifying. One that needs particular scrutinizing is his idea of "public reason" or "reasonable pluralism." This understanding of pluralism and a "public consensus" among "reasonable" people assumes that the "truth" of a secularized political regime is greater than or more "reasonable" than truths that issue out of religious beliefs ("comprehensive doctrines"). Rawlsian political liberalism, in the end, reduces religious belief and conviction to the *private sphere*, where it cannot intrude and create controversy on ethically sensitive matters (for example, abortion). This view perpetuates the false, "irrational" stereotype of religion that secularists, with considerable success, have advanced. Thus, a "liberal public reason" that Rawls promotes is inadequate to the true nature of civil society and the public sphere. And for the "natural lawyer," it is deficient to the extent that neutrality on moral matters is neither possible nor desirable. For useful – and in many ways penetrating – critiques of Rawls' thought, see Wolfe, *Natural Law Liberalism*; Christopher Wolfe and Robert P. George, eds., *Natural Law and Public Reason* (Washington, DC: Georgetown University Press, 2000); and Robert P. George, ed., *Natural Law, Liberalism, and Morality* (Oxford: Clarendon, 1996).

133 *Fides et Ratio*, introduction. The encyclical is accessible at https://w2.vatican.va/content/john-paul-ii/en/encyclicals/documents/hf_jp-ii_enc_14091998_fides-et-ratio.html.
134 Ibid., no. 4.
135 Ibid., no. 5.
136 Ibid.
137 Ibid.
138 Ibid.
139 Ibid.
140 Ibid. no. 16.
141 Ibid.
142 Ibid.
143 Ibid.
144 Ibid., nos. 16–17.
145 *Dignitatis Humanae* no. 1. The encyclical is accessible at www.vatican.va/archive/hist_councils/ii_vatican_council/documents/vat-ii_decl_19651207_dignitatis-humanae_en.html.
146 Ibid., no. 2.
147 Ibid.
148 Ibid.
149 Ibid.
150 Ibid.
151 Ibid.
152 Ibid.
153 So Wolfe, *Natural Law Liberalism*, 231–2.

154 Here I broadly follow Michael J. Perry, "Why Political Reliance on Religiously Grounded Morality Does Not Violate the Establishment Clause" and "Why Political Reliance on Religiously Grounded Is Not Illegitimate in a Liberal Democracy" (Chapters 2 and 3, respectively), in *Under God? Religious Faith and Liberal Democracy* (Cambridge: Cambridge University Press, 2003), 20–52, even when I disagree with some his conclusions.

155 Here I am using the term "liberal" in its classical expression, not in the standard political-ideological sense of our day by which we distinguish between "liberals" and "conservatives."

156 So, for example, Brendan Sweetman, *Why Politics Needs Religion: The Place of Religious Arguments in the Public Square* (Downers Grove: IVP Academic, 2006); Perry, *Under God? Religious Faith and Liberal Democracy*, 38–46; and Nicholas Wolterstorff, "The Role of Religion in Decision and Discussions of Political Issues" and "Audi on Religion, Politics, and Liberal Democracy," in Robert Audi and Nicholas Wolterstorff, eds., *Religion in the Public Square: The Place of Religious Convictions in Political Debate* (Lanham: Rowman & Littlefield, 1997), 67–120 and 145–65, respectively.

157 Paul Marshall, Lela Gilbert and Nina Shea, *Persecuted: The Global Assault on Christians* (Nashville: Thomas Nelson, 2013).

158 It is the conviction of the authors that most persecution worldwide springs from three causes: totalitarian political control (such as is found in Communist and post-Communist nations), attempts to preservation of Hindu or Buddhist culture (such as one finds in Southeast Asia), and resurgent Islam (which is "generating an expanding global crisis" [ibid., 9]).

159 For data that is both global in scope and specific to North America, see www.pewforum.org/data/.

2 Natural law and our cultural and religious traditions

Ethics and the permanent: contending for the moral impulse

The last two decades have been witness to a revival of sorts – not a new movement *per se* but a renewal, it is accurate to say – in the way in which we think about the moral life. Characterized by a concern for "the permanent things," this renewal finds its roots in the deepest and most cherished traditions of our wider cultural heritage. Perhaps some will understand this "movement" as a reaction to the overreach of both modern and postmodern philosophical assumptions, and there is surely some truth to this. In our own cultural history, not surprisingly it has been during times of pronounced social upheaval that a "renewal" of natural law thinking has emerged – or shall we say, re-emerged.

Thus, natural law reasoning has to do with moral "first principles." In the words of one legal scholar and natural law theorist, "On the day when humanity was first gifted with reason, the natural law moment truly began. On the day that man first felt the ego-tug of his passions, the natural law moment was in danger of passing. The ambivalence of that first day is with us still."[1] And indeed it is. *How do we* identify what is moral? And *on what basis* can we – and will we – make moral judgments? Where individuals and societies have ignored or rejected natural with its moral first principles, humanity has been degraded in unspeakably tragic ways, to which the twentieth and early twenty-first centuries bear gruesome testimony.[2]

The realm of natural law is important because it is a realm bounded by reason. And while the natural law – the "law written on the heart" – is not faith *per se*, it unites faith and reason, in accordance with our fundamental nature and moral tuitions. We call it "natural" law because it accords with shared human *nature*, and we call it natural "law" because it witnesses to moral principles that are universally shared among all people. Much in contrast to the persistent nihilism of our day, in which "choice," autonomy, and the untrammeled self tend to trump all moral considerations, natural law theorists insist that "morality is not so much to be defined as to be discovered; reality is not created but apprehended."[3]

First things first. While the "Ten Commandments" are understood to be divine revelation of an ethical standard to ancient Israel, the "covenant people" of the Old Testament, they are more. Their origin 3,300 years ago constitutes a major moral marker in the history of human civilization. Given the fact that the twentieth century was one of the bloodiest, inhumane, and barbaric in human history, it is reasonable to question how "civilized" human civilization has become over those 33 centuries. Those recent horrors notwithstanding, what sets humans apart from lower forms of biological life is their ability to reflect on their actions, to consider alternatives *before* they act, and to be consciously aware of the consequences that accompany their chosen actions.[4] This moral capacity is in fact the very hallmark of civilized humanity. We do not expect animals to offer excuses or justifications for their behavior. To employ a language of "morality" is to possess moral agency – the freedom to choose particular types of actions over others, which can be deemed praiseworthy or blameworthy. The question, then, is whether human beings will acknowledge the moral impulse that makes them truly "human."

The late Allan Bloom began his best-seller *The Closing of the American Mind* a generation ago with the now famous – and almost quaint – observation that there is "one thing a professor can be absolutely certain of: almost every student entering the university believes, or says he believes, that truth is relative."[5] The debauched nihilism that Bloom was decrying in its nascent form 30 years ago is a given today, only in a more "mature" form. Anyone, inside or outside of the academy, who clings to some form of moral normativity in our day faces the scorn of the entire culture. But the more interesting question might be how we got to this point. How did we as a society move from affirming universal moral givens ("We hold these truths to be self-evident") to the radical relativizing and denial of all moral judgments ("There can be no givens")?[6] The answer surely does not lie merely in epistemic humanity.

Let us be frank: moral relativism, if followed to its logical conclusion, is self-refuting, since the proposition "There are no absolutes"/"There can be no givens" itself cannot be an absolutely *true* statement. Political philosopher Hadley Arkes puts the matter in proper focus:

> Anyone who makes it his vocation these days to teach in the "moral sciences" will soon encounter a primate who protests that, after, "there is no truth." The stock response of the philosopher, of course, is to ask whether that proposition is itself true . . . If it is, then people will no doubt be pleased to discover that there *is* truth after all.[7]

And yet with stunning creativity relativism continues to don a new appearance with each successive generation. Not surprisingly, frequently at the root of such strategies in our time is the "virtue" of individual autonomy. Now, autonomous choice, as few would deny, is a marvelous function of human existence – within certain limits, that is. Individual liberty is only meaningful in the context of an ordered society, and political liberty – that rare treasure sought the world over – is rendered impossible when moral-social order collapses. Political philosophy is predicated on moral philosophy and moral realities, and therefore, on a particular view of human nature. If there is nothing that is universal – i.e., shared – in the moral nature of humankind, and if personal autonomy (= "choice") trumps moral principle at every turn, then political activity truly becomes "war by other means" and "culture wars" are no mere metaphor.

To a society which previously understood itself – rightly or wrongly – as indebted to Christian influence, it can be disorienting to encounter diverse aspects of radical pluralism that are presently regnant. How might people of good will respond? The late Lesslie Newbigin helpfully distinguished in his writings between two senses of "pluralism."[8] The first variety, pluralism as part of the created world in which we live – that is, the phenomenological reality of different social, cultural, ethnic, and linguistic spheres – is to be celebrated as a fact of life.[9] The second variety, ideological pluralism, by contrast, calls into question any claims to certainty or to the normativity and universality of "truth." Such claims, we are told *ad nauseum*, are narrow, reductionistic, bigoted, imperialistic, and intolerant. Thus to defend – let alone, advance – Christianity or moral principle is hereby viewed as an intrusion, and thus offensive and intolerable in a pluralistic society.

Newbigin's distinction between social-cultural and ideological pluralism allows us to appreciate and recognize the diversity of beliefs and practices among cultures of the world. At the same time, it permits us to acknowledge that certain types of human behavior – e.g., murder, incest, theft, torture, disrespect for parents, defrauding one's neighbor, child molestation, and the like – are proscribed universally. Why? If morality were merely a convenient way of describing social consensus, then culturally conditioned practices such as burning widows, female genital mutilation, slavery, torture, castration, or genocide – to name but a few examples – escape any moral censoring whatsoever. They must be permitted to stand as morally acceptable because of intrasocial, culture-specific approval.[10] Were ethical relativism a logically consistent and thus morally tenable position, it would be impossible to criticize cultures or eras, past or present, on moral grounds. Hence, the abolition of slavery cannot be viewed as a *moral victory*, only as *political change*. And the Nuremberg Code, a response by the universal community to German political and medical horrors that occurred during the Third Reich, represents at most a kangaroo court, possessing no universal authority by which to sanction "crimes against humanity."[11] Moreover, if ethical beliefs and practice cannot be assessed or scrutinized based on abiding and enduring moral standards, any notion of moral progress (whether conceived of in religious or non-religious terms) is incoherent and delusory. As the nations learned at the end of the Second World War, and as cultures tend to do following cataclysmic events, renewed contact with traditions and voices from the past provide much needed wisdom for the present, as well as for the future task. And, as well, they remind us that ideological pluralism indeed is nothing new.

Evidence of the universality of practical moral norms is found among diverse cultures themselves, not merely in the Western cultural tradition. The relevance of moral wisdom can be measured by the fact that many of the peoples of the ancient Near East, including the Israelites, developed particular insights into living – proverbial wisdom – and enshrined them in a corpus of "wisdom literature," examples of which come to us in the Old Testament canonical books of Job, Proverbs, and Ecclesiastes. Wisdom proceeds from observations and moral reflection on physical as well as human nature. Wisdom is not confined to any one people; it is the possession of all who seek it and is part of what distinguishes being "human." Consider these intuitions collected from African proverbial wisdom:

- No polecat ever smelled his own stink.
- When it rains, the roof always drips the same way.
- He has the kindness of a witch.
- It is patience that gets you out of a net.
- A butterfly that flies among the thorns will tear its wings.
- The strength of a crocodile is in the water.
- When you marry a beautiful woman, you marry problems.
- The sons of a king do not need to be taught about power.

These insights, it goes without saying, would be regarded as universally true by anyone at any time in any cultural context. None of the aforementioned, in terms of meaning and implication, would escape the non-African reader. Wisdom, then, can be seen as constituting a common mode of discourse for all people, the world over. In a very practical sense, wisdom shows itself to be a necessary and universally accessible foundation for ethics. The manner in which proverbial wisdom bridges morality and social dealings in all cultures and eras is on display in the fascinatingly relevant wisdom sayings of the Old Testament book of Proverbs. Consider several examples:

- Hatred stirs up dissension, but love covers over all wrongs.
- As vinegar to the teeth and smoke to the eyes, so is a sluggard to those who send him.
- When pride comes, then comes disgrace, but with humility comes wisdom.
- A kind man benefits himself, but a cruel man brings himself harm.
- He who scorns instruction will pay for it, but he who respects a command is rewarded.
- Better a dry crust of bread with peace and quiet than a house full of feasting with strife.
- Starting a quarrel is like breaching a dam; so drop the matter before a dispute breaks out.
- A king's rage is like the roar of a lion, but his favor is like dew on the grass.
- Even a child is known by his actions, by whether his conduct is pure and right.
- Like a bad tooth or a lame foot is reliance on the unfaithful in times of trouble.[12]

The same wisdom that bridges moral truth and social setting expresses itself in different literary genres. Ponder, just for the moment, the manner in which the complexities of life are addressed in the book of Ecclesiastes. Several important themes in the book are recurring, calling for a measure of moral reflection on the part of the reader. One is that "there is nothing new under the sun." Patterns of human behavior and human questions concerning the meaning of life are recurring, inter-generational, and trans-cultural) in nature. Another is that there is a time and place – a proper "season" – for everything that occurs in life, including suffering, misfortune, making moral judgments, grieving, and death. The end product of Qoheleth's philosophical musings – the "conclusion to the matter" and the "whole duty of man" (12:13) – is twofold: nothing in life has meaning and purpose outside of a theistic outlook, and there is a moral accounting for all human deeds, whether good or evil. The philosophical bottom line is intended to express universal truth and have universal application. For that reason, Ecclesiastes remains an invaluable, though exceedingly neglected, part of the biblical canon. In neglecting this writing, we rob ourselves of much needed insight into the complexities and vicissitudes of life as we navigate our way among competing world- and life views in pluralistic culture.

Identifying ultimate values: the role of presuppositions

Anyone who accepts the joys and tribulations of building a house knows how utterly critical the laying of the house's foundations is. Some years ago, my wife and I decided to have a house built for the family. Though wholly (and blissfully) unfamiliar with the mind-numbing detail that is part of the home-building ordeal, I shall never forget my nervousness as the house's foundation was laid. This was magnified by the fact that 45 truck-loads of dirt were needed to help raise the building site that was among the lowest in the neighborhood (and what seemed like the lowest on the East Coast). I distinctly recall my deep anxiety upon arriving at the building lot to inspect the foundation that had been poured the morning before. Holding my breath, I walked around the perimeter of fresh concrete and steel in which the entire structure was to rest. Why the anxiety? Instinctively I knew that *everything* structurally was dependent on the quality of that slab. Any blemishes or cracks would affect the total structure, and if not discovered these defects would render the house permanently flawed. The reality was unsettling: the foundation *is* the house.

World- and life-views – i.e., frameworks for interpreting ultimate reality – are supported at the foundation level by certain governing assumptions – assumptions about God (= theology), the cosmos (cosmology), knowledge (epistemology), human nature (anthropology and psychology), society (sociology), and, of course, ethics. Even when most people do not consciously work through these foundations, their lives are expressions of certain deeply held convictions. One might compare the function of presuppositions to the function of the tracks on which a train runs and which determine the train's direction and destination. A person's commitment – or should we say, *pre-commitment* – to a set of assumptions about life, whether consciously or unconsciously, leads to inevitable and ineluctable results. It goes without saying that this has profound implications for ethics, since one's convictions are formed out of one's views of ultimate reality.

For the pantheist, for whom creation and God are indistinguishable, there is no transcendent reality in which humans order their lives and before which they give account; the universe and the divine are one. Similarly, the a-theist or metaphysical materialist conforms to no ultimate transcendent norm or standard. The reason for this is the Darwinian assumption of natural selection, the guiding "law" of "nature." Implied is that for humans to evolve further, natural selection must continue. Such, in turn, assumes "the struggle" and *inter alia* the elimination of the weak. It was only "logical," then, that Social Darwinists of the late-nineteenth and early twentieth centuries would propose the need for eugenics and selective breeding. The poor, the infirm, the weak, and the criminal elements of society – in short, the unwanted – were to recede and disappear in favor of the stronger and fitter of the human species, contributing over time to a "better" society. Where this naturalistic ethic flourished in the century past, incomparable harm and horror followed.[13] And despite our recoil and revulsion at these atrocities, it is important to recognize that the philosophical foundations of naturalism, in various forms, are still intact in much of Western culture. Left unaddressed, they make possible the dehumanization of the human race at both ends of the life spectrum – at birth and at death – as well as in between, in terms of "life-enhancement." G.K. Chesterton was surely correct: when people stop believing in God, they don't merely believe in nothing; they will believe anything.

Certain presuppositions, it needs emphasizing, die hard, particularly those governing one's understanding of human nature and the moral impulse. Consider, for example, the work of Frans de Waal, the C. H. Candler Professor in the Psychology Department of Emory University, Director of the Living Links Center at the Yerkes National Primate Research Center, in Atlanta, GA. According to his website, de Waal's books – translated into 20 languages – have made him one of the world's most visible "primatologists." His books include *Are We Smart Enough to Know How Smart Animals Are?* (2016); *The Bonobo and the Atheist: In Search of Humanism among the Primates* (2013); *The Age of Empathy: Nature's Lessons for a Kinder Society* (2009); *Our Inner Ape: A Leading Primatologist Explains Why We Are Who We Are* (2006); *Primates and Philosophers: How Morality Evolved* (2006); *Tree of Origin: What Primate Behavior Can Tell Us about Human Social Evolution* (2002); *Good Natured: The Origins of Right and Wrong in Humans and Other Animals* (1997); as well as two edited volumes, *Evolved Morality* (2014) and *The Primate Mind* (2012). As the aforementioned titles suggest, much of de Waal's work is devoted to applying evolutionary assumptions about human behavior to the concepts of justice and morality. De Waal contends that human moral intuitions – and notably our sense of "justice" – are evident in higher primates and other social animals.[14] While he stops short of calling animals moral creatures, he does argue for the presence in animals of emotional and psychological mechanisms that are involved in human morality.[15] In fact, de Waal employs the image of a high-rise to illustrate his assumptions about the moral impulse. The lower stories are said to comprise the moral impulses in animals, while the upper stories denote the human moral impulse; all, however, belong to *one building*. Hence, he argues, it is illogical not to view human morality as extended forms of the "moral impulses" of certain primates. Tellingly, de Waal has stated his belief that we are now reaching a point at which biology may finally be able to "wrest morality from the hands of philosophers."[16] This posture is reminiscent of sociobiologist E.O. Wilson's rather remarkable claim a generation ago that "the time has come for ethics to be removed temporarily from the hands of the philosophers and biologicized."[17] Such calls, however widespread, should give us pause.

Consider for the moment what de Waal is saying: science – or perhaps, more accurately, pseudo-science – is capable of explaining morality, i.e., what historically has been the domain of philosophy and theology. What evolutionary theorists, however, fail to acknowledge – and de Waal is simply representative, even when he is one of the more highly visible theorists out there – is the possibility that human reasoning is *distorted* by biological instincts. In truth, more often than not, moral reasoning and moral principle will go *against* natural instincts (as most parents know), and thankfully so. At bottom, the question of the human moral impulse is much more a *philosophical* matter than it is a scientific one. Hence, it is not only unrealistic to expect science to "settle" the moral question but also pure hubris to think in such terms. Science properly understood will not – indeed, it *cannot* – speak to the question of whether there are moral truths, what distinguishes human beings as moral creatures, or whether (and to what degree) human beings are to be held accountable for their behavior.[18]

To the extent that human beings deny the moral-spiritual – which is to say, non-material – component of human nature and suppress the moral law with its wisdom, they do so at their own peril. This very burden constitutes the heart of what may be one of the most important literary works of the twentieth century, *The Abolition of Man*. Its author, C.S. Lewis, was observing already in his day (three generations ago) the trend in the West to reduce – and, in time, eliminate – the essence of what it means to be human, and this by means of misapplied "science." Humans reduce themselves, as he saw it, when they belittle the significance of the natural law (what he called "the Tao") and claim that there are no normative moral truths. Such elimination of humans' ability to judge between right and wrong abolishes the very essence of humanity – hence the title of Lewis's work.

Retrieving the natural law

Wisdom from the not-too-distant past

In addition to Lewis, writers such as G.K. Chesterton, T.S. Eliot, Dorothy Sayers, Evelyn Waugh, and J.R.R. Tolkien, despite being generations removed, retain immense popularity among Americans, and particularly among American religious, due to their extraordinarily fecund imaginations, lucid defense of common sense, and literary dexterity.[19] But they also have in common the knack for stressing "the permanent things." Consider in this regard Lewis, who is not foremost known for his writings on political themes. Nevertheless, in addition to his wildly popular nonfiction writing, we find him addressing topics as wide-ranging as capital punishment, crime, statism, socialism, welfare, the atom bomb, censorship, ethics, and more. What is striking about the undercurrent of Lewis's thinking, regardless of the literary genre being employed, is that he consistently seeks to emphasize *the permanent*; hence, his views have lasting value generations later.

In several of his works – notably, in *Mere Christianity* and *The Abolition of Man* – Lewis speaks of "the Tao" to denote a universal moral code that speaks to the individual conscience. To the Chinese, moral reality is the *Tao* (literally, "the way"),[20] which accords with other universal descriptions; to Asian Indians, it is *dharma*; to Westerners, it is "nature"; to the American founders, it was "self-evident truths"; to political philosophers and political historians, it is the natural law; and to the apostle Paul, it is "the law written on their hearts" (Rom. 2:14–15). In "Right and Wrong as a Clue to Meaning in the Universe," the first of the essays that comprise *Mere Christianity*, Lewis seeks to probe the moral impulse in human beings – evidence of which he believes seems to point toward the existence of a Creator – and contends that every person is born with a moral sense to distinguish between right and wrong. If there is no such thing as "right and wrong," no "law of nature," then what, Lewis asks, is the difference between fair and unfair treatment? Whence comes the distinction between "just" and "unjust?"

> Whenever you find a man who says he does not believe in a real Right and Wrong, you will find the same man going back on this a moment later. He may break his promise to you, but if you try breaking one to him he will be complaining "It's not fair" before you can say Jack Robinson.[21]

If "just" and "unjust" are not fluid, Lewis concludes, we are "forced" to believe in a transcending concept of right and wrong. For despite our intellectual justifications to the contrary, we expect to be treated with human decency by others, so much so that one is justified in calling this expectation a moral "law." Moral first principles, then, though anterior to human experiments and thus unable to be "proven," are nevertheless *evidenced* by daily living, as one political philosopher has pointed out:

> The person who seeks to deny the existence of morals will spend most of his days trying to flee from the perils of contradiction and the tangle of his own argument. He will discover, again, that for the man of reason the existence of morals must hold the place of a necessary assumption or a first principle in the ground of his understanding.[22]

What Lewis refers to as the "law of nature" or the "law of oughtness" – namely, the awareness and expectation within all people to be treated fairly, justly, and decently – is what philosophers and theologians refer to as "judicial sentiment." Conscience, which both accuses and excuses the individual, is fickle and can be ignored, violated, or hardened. And whereas our conscience sometimes lets us off the hook when we behave badly toward others, our judicial sentiment *refuses to let others* off the hook when they behave badly toward us. The latter moral intuition seems to be unswerving, wholly consistent, and virtually unerring. Why is that?

Those who object to such a universal moral phenomenon, notes Lewis, perhaps will attempt to argue that morality is a social or cultural convention or that conventional morality is little more than a herd instinct. To the latter objection it can be said that our varied instincts will, at some point, be in conflict with each other. How to adjudicate between and prioritize these? Such is the function of the natural law. While the moral impulse, for the metaphysical materialist, is random and evolutionary in nature (though supposedly "guided" by the interaction of genetic and social-cultural factors), and at bottom the result of chemical processes, such extrapolation, for Lewis, does not offer an adequate account of mind, reason, reflection, and morality. To the former objection, Lewis reminds us of the simple fact that although conventions are passed on from generation to generation, this does not automatically render them mere cultural constructs. Why is it that most societies, over millennia, transmit moral standards that are remarkably similar? Why are murder, incest, theft, torture, disrespect for parents, and defrauding others – among other proscriptions – *universally* decried by diverse cultures? Moreover, they were decried multiple millennia ago, in the earliest expressions of recorded human civilization, and are not a mere recent development. Such is not the result of "democratic" consensus, as the mafia, terrorists, pirates, and bandits since time immemorial well illustrate; rather, it is evidence of a moral law at work.

Natural law, then, may be understood as a "non-democratic" consensus that spans the centuries about notions of right and wrong. The "natural" aspect, as we have argued, reminds us that evidence exists all around as to how nature – our *composite human nature* – operates. The "law" reminds us of the consistency and uniformity of things as they should be. The existence of natural law, it must be emphasized, is independent of faith, which is not to argue that it is not confirmed by faith. This means that religious as well as non-religious people can reach conclusions about moral reality, and consequently, together can arrive at what is acceptable and unacceptable in society. Part of that consensus will express itself in the establishment of laws that protect society and impugn murderers, molesters, thieves, the morally reprobate, and those who undermine the common social good. This universal moral code, what Lewis variously calls "the Tao," the "law of oughtness," and "the law of [human] nature," is inescapable and accessible to all people, independent of their social upbringing, cultural background, or private experience.

Wisdom from the ancients

We find the idea of universal moral realities to be already present well before the Christian advent – and conspicuously so in thinkers such as Heraclitus, Socrates, and Aristotle. Despite the observation that all things are in a constant state of flux, Heraclitus (ca. 536–470 BC) believes that wisdom points to a wider "law" of the universe, a transcending *logos*, or reason, to which human nature and human ethical striving are ordered. Such, Heraclitus taught, was intuited through wisdom: "Wisdom is the foremost virtue, and wisdom consists in *speaking the truth*, and in *lending an ear to nature* and *acting according to her*. Wisdom is common to all."[23] Significantly, Heraclitus's attempt to posit a "natural moral law" as unchangeable stands in noted contrast both to the demagoguery of the Sophists and to the capriciousness of the population. The Sophists of his day, as the Sophists of any era, refused to venerate the "natural moral law," since they viewed laws as artificial constructs that merely served the interests of those in power. It is in this light that we best understand Socrates's and Plato's veneration of the *nomoi*, the "laws"; thus, legal historian Heinrich Rommen states,

> The philosophers spoke of the . . . laws with great respect: the peoples who had no polis were to them barbarians. Hence, it happened, too, that Socrates, despite his distinction between what is naturally right and legally right, pronounced the laws of Athens to be "right" without qualification.[24]

Both Plato and Aristotle reject a subjectivism about what is "good." The good, for Plato, consists, for example, in knowledge and beauty and is self-evident, independent of a human reference point. Aristotle, while essentially agreeing, differs on one point. He holds the good to stand in association with human nature, for which an analogy is necessary. An acorn derives from the genus oak *by nature*, from which all oaks are identified, regardless of their maturation point or variety. Yet, in spite of their differences on what constitutes the "good," one observes in both Plato and Aristotle a care to preserve the social order. Consequently, both place a strong emphasis on the ethical, what is just, and how human laws might reflect transcending moral norms. And both recognize that what is *legally* just may or may not be what is *morally* just.[25]

In Aristotle, we find what is perhaps the high point of the development of a pagan ethical theory, and certainly one that furnishes a stepping-stone to natural law reasoning,[26] even when it is incomplete. "What is by nature just," writes Aristotle, "has the same force everywhere, and does not depend on what we regard or do not regard as just."[27] This law, he observes, is "universal."[28] In fact, because of this Aristotle believes in and defends the "legislating" of morality. The reason for this is that laws, whether *written or unwritten*, help shape character, since men are not born virtuous.[29] Aristotle believes that everything occurring in life has a purpose or proper place – an end (*telos*) – which results in a "natural" order of all things.[30] Nature, then, serves as an ethical guide for citizens, for politicians, and for statesmen.[31] Ethics accords with our fundamental nature, and illuminated by right reason, guides human beings in distinguishing between virtue and vice. In *Nichomachean Ethics*, Aristotle acknowledges certain human behaviors that are intrinsically wrong – for example, murder, theft, and adultery.[32] In addition, he distinguishes between "conventional justice" and "natural" justice, as well as between conventional or positive law and natural law.[33] What is legal is not inevitably moral, and Aristotle is not inattentive to the difference.[34]

Something in the classical philosophers' understanding and observations about human nature was enduring, for Heraclitus's presentation of the "natural law" and the Aristotelian understanding of ethics would serve as a precursor to the Stoic notion of the *Logos* that pervades and unifies all the cosmos while placing upon all humans certain ethical obligations. Writing in the first century BC, Cicero is considered the primary interpreter and transmitter of the Stoic understanding of natural law. He speaks of the *lex nata*, the law within, which he regards as the foundation of law in general. This law of right and wrong, he observes, is universally valid and unbending. It is born within us, not learned and received by tradition. Perhaps the most important early Roman treatise on the natural law is his *De Republica*:

> True law is right reason in agreement with nature; it is of universal application, unchanging and everlasting; it summons to duty by its commands, and averts from wrong doing by its prohibitions . . . It is a sin to try to alter this law, nor is it allowable to attempt to repeal any part it, and it is impossible to abolish it entirely. We cannot be freed from its obligations by senate or people, and . . . there will not be different laws at Rome and at Athens, or different laws now and in the future, but one eternal and unchangeable law will be valid for all nations and all times.[35]

For Cicero, the *lax nata* allows human beings to distinguish between good and bad human ordinances, between just and unjust laws, and between what is honorable and what is dishonorable. Only a "madman," he notes, "would conclude that these judgments are matters of opinion, and not fixed by Nature."[36] Civil laws must find their roots in the deeper principles of enduring moral law. Cicero was able to look past legal forms to the moral substance of legislation. There is a marked difference between expediency and moral rectitude.[37]

With the advent of the Christian era, the New Testament presupposes, rather than negates (as some biblical commentators would suggest), the natural law – a natural law that expressed itself in the particular contours of the Ten Commandments.[38] The apostle Paul, the chief theologian of the New Testament, writes to those living in the imperial seat, "Ever since the creation of the world his eternal power and divine nature, invisible though they are, have been understood and seen through the things he has made. So they are without excuse" (Rom. 1:20). This awareness, he reminds his readers, is true for Jew or Gentile, believer or non-believer. Even the non-believing Gentiles, when they "by nature" do what the moral law requires, show that the requirements of the law are "written on their hearts" (2:14–15).

One of the more lucid demonstrations of early Christian interaction with the Stoic worldview is provided by Paul himself while working in the city of Athens. It comes to us through Luke's brief but tantalizing portrait of Paul in Athens, recorded in Acts 17:16–34. Here, in the Socratic mold, Paul is seen "dialoguing" with the philosophers in the agora, the marketplace, prior to addressing the Council of the Areopagus. It is perhaps no coincidence that Luke depicts the "apostle to the Gentiles" as being in line with other noted philosophers of the past who came and "disputed" (*dialegomai*, 17:17) in the marketplace – among these, Anaxagoras and Protagoras (both mid-fifth century BC). Moreover, Luke may well have in mind the tradition surrounding Socrates, who was accused in Athens of introducing "foreign deities," the charge raised by some Epicurean and Stoic philosophers against Paul (17:18).[39] Indeed, not only Socrates but also Anaxagoros and Protagoras were accused of this "crime."

Significantly, in the Areopagus address (vv. 22–32) Paul appeals to "nature" – both the nature of the cosmos and human nature – in contending for the God who has made himself known. He does this while exploiting important Stoic philosophical assumptions such as cosmic unity, kinship, divine offspring, and human knowing. It is rhetorically significant that Paul utilizes a word-play on "knowledge," not incidental in light of the Stoic primacy of knowledge and knowing as the foundation of the moral life (cf. esp. 17:18 and 17:22–31). To observe that Paul is "accommodating" himself by employing moral categories that Stoics and Christians have in common is not to deny the radical difference between the two. It is only to point out that the Christian message will look for common ground in bridge building to the non-believing mind. In the Areopagus speech, "general revelation" and "natural law" give way – that is, they serve as an introduction – to "special revelation" in Christ the God-man (v. 31). The truth of the gospel is disclosed by the "apostle to the Gentiles": God has made himself known to all, through a variety of means, all of which point to God's ultimate revelation in his Son.

In line with Paul's use of natural law reasoning in the Areopagus address, several rhetorical strategies are conspicuously on display in the apostle's presentation – among them are the following:

- He addresses core philosophical assumptions of both Stoics and Epicureans (cf. 17:18) that need adjustment – for example (a) what can be "known" (17:23, 30), the cosmos as independent or contingent (17:24–25), (c) the universe as solely material (17:24, 25, 31), (d) the "divine" as impersonal reason, and (e) kinship with the "divine."
- The occurrence of the verb "to know" and cognate forms in the Greek text – e.g., "unknown" (*agnostos*) in 17:23 and "ignorance" (*agnoia*) in 17:30, from which forms the English "agnostic" derives – suggests a word-play being used by Paul.
- Relatedly, he exploits an element of irony by developing the important sub-theme of "ignorance" (17:23b, 30) over against the Athenians's (and particularly the Stoics's) great learning and erudition.
- He appeals to "general revelation" (17:24–28) – what can be known from both the cosmos and the human conscience – for the purposes of establishing a bridge with the audience.
- He attempts to expose the fallacy of materialism – i.e., metaphysical naturalism (17:24–25, 29) – and with it, the Stoic view of universal continuum, which denies that history as we know it will terminate and that an afterlife, which follows a day of moral reckoning, exists (17:31).

Undergirding the apostle's work is the assumption of universal moral norms – norms that are rationally perceived. Whether he is writing to believers living in the imperial seat of Rome or addressing academics sitting on the Council of the Areopagus, Paul's purpose is to stress that all people are morally accountable. This is because moral norms are known to all. Natural law reasoning furnishes a necessary starting-point in understanding and advancing moral goodness and social norms.

Wisdom from medieval and early modern voices

The notion of natural law, part of the ebb and flow of early and later patristic writings as the fathers interact with the surrounding culture,[40] was central to the Church's social teaching during the medieval period. In most discussions of the natural law, it is assumed that Aquinas, in the thirteenth century, best represents the tradition both in its theological grounding and in its application to virtuous character and Christian social ethics. Aquinas concerns himself with the perennial questions that affect the moral life, and for this reason, in his last major encyclical, *Fides et Ratio* (1998), John Paul II praises Aquinas, whose thought scales "heights unthinkable to human intelligence."[41] John Paul commends Aquinas to all who seek truth, since in his integrated thinking the demands of reason and the power of faith "find the most elevated synthesis ever attained by human thought" without demeaning the distinctiveness of either.[42] For this reason among others, any study of the natural law must be conversant with Aquinas.

Aquinas's work can be understood *inter alia* as a response to challenges to the faith arising from Aristotelian thought as it re-emerged in the thirteenth century as well as from Muslim influences. Many commentators tend to view Aquinas's system as a fusion or synthesis of Aristotelian, Stoic, and Christian thought. While this is not inaccurate as far as it goes, it needs qualification. Thomas does not merely wish to view reason as some vague source of "natural law"; rather, he attempts to identify and underscore the manner in which human "nature" fulfills the divinely intended purpose for which it was created. In parlance familiar to some contemporary readers, he understood that "all truth is God's truth."

By way of "natural reason," human beings "discern what is good and what is evil." As Aquinas sees it, this is a self-evident premise and "habit" of all people; it is "nothing else than an imprint on us of divine light." In this light it is "evident," he concludes, that the natural law is "nothing else than the rational creature's participation" in the eternal law.[43] For Aquinas, the natural law mirrors the very order and structure of creation, and notwithstanding the ravages of sin and human fallenness, this order and structure remained self-evident through revelation *and* reason:

> So it is clear that as far as the general principles of reason are concerned, whether speculative or practical, there is one standard of truth or rightness for everybody . . . So we must conclude that the law of nature, as far as first principles are concerned, is the same for all as the norm of right conductis equally well known to all.[44]

Where humans depart from or reject right use of reason, "it has the quality not of a law but of an act of violence," which is to be viewed as "unnatural."[45] In fact, Aquinas believes that human reason *cannot fail* to grasp *some* knowledge of the truth; basic moral principles, he insists, are knowable, "inscribed on the human heart."[46]

What is significant is that Aquinas does not insist that our awareness of the natural law is dependent on religion *per se*, even when as a Christian he acknowledges Christ to be the fullest expression of divine revelation. "We cannot know the things that are of God as they are in themselves," he insists; rather, these things come to us on the basis of what is revealed to all people through general revelation.[47] Human rationality is *by nature* directed toward the good of man and the good of society. This permits every human act to be measured as right or wrong, morally acceptable or unacceptable, to the extent that it *fulfills or undermines* human nature and the divine intention. Reason is the chief means by which we determine the moral quality of our actions, and reason operates to apply this moral standard – pursue the good, avoid doing evil – in specific situations as it affects the common good of all.[48]

The Protestant reformers, without systematically treating the subject in their writings, presuppose the notion of the natural law and maintain continuity with their Catholic counterparts therein. This is the case even when they believed that reason has been effaced due to human fallenness.[49] Martin Luther describes the innate awareness of right and wrong behavior in two ways. He speaks both of *Naturrecht* (natural justice) and *natuerliches Recht* (natural law), noting of the latter:

> Thus, "Thou shalt not kill, commit adultery, steal, etc." are not Mosaic laws only, but also the natural law [*natuerliches Recht*] written on each man's heart, as St. Paul teaches (Rom. 2). Also Christ himself (Matt. 7) includes all of the law and the prophets in this natural law.[50]

Referring to the awareness of the so-called Golden Rule in all people, Luther writes, "By nature they judge that one should do to others what one wants done to oneself." Luther is well aware of the misperception among the religiously minded that the natural law is the common fund only of Christian societies. To the contrary, he insists, it is demonstrated by human experience that all nations, all cultures, and all people-groups possess this rudimentary knowledge. The natural law "is written in the depth of the heart and cannot be erased."[51] Luther believes that the natural law exists as a moral standard among non-Christian people-groups:

> Natural law [*natuerliches Recht*] is a practical first principle on the sphere of morality; it forbids evil and commands good. The basis of natural law is God, who has created this light, but the basis of positive law is civil authority.[52]

Philip Melanchthon, the "quiet reformer," and John Calvin understand natural law in much the same way as Luther. Melanchthon's defense of the natural law appears to be based on Romans 2:15: "A natural law is a common judgment to which all men alike assent, and therefore one which God has inscribed upon the soul of each man."[53] Calvin's description is almost identical: "The things contained in the two tables [of the law] are, in a manner, dictated to us by that inner law, which, as has already been said, is in a manner written and stamped on every heart."[54] Calvin also writes, "The activity and insights of conscience are the language in which the law of nature is couched."[55] An "unchangeable rule of right living," the natural law for Calvin is "a living law," since it is "the common law of nations."[56]

Three "early modern" theorists who appeal to the natural law in the context of social and political upheaval in their day deserve mention. By the year 1510, disquieting reports had reached Spain that Native Americans were being denied basic liberties and property. The immediate challenge confronting Francisco de Vitoria (1480–1546) was the Spanish vision to colonize the new peoples of the Americas. Spain was prepared to justify war with Native Americans to possess their land and seek their "conversion" to the Christian faith. Vitoria's task was to challenge the Spanish king on the basis of the unjust treatment of these peoples. Against conventional thinking, his argument was nothing short of scandalous: neither the king nor the pope, for that matter, could authorize war against the Indians. Neither religious nor economic nor political reasoning *per se* could justify coercion and warfare, Vitoria argues in *Reflections on the Indians and the Law of War*; Indians and Spaniards have equal rights. The only cause for war is just is a wrong that is intuited and confirmed through the natural moral law, a wrong that is discernable to all people everywhere through reason. Aggression based on religious differences or "the spirit of discovery" is not justifiable. No aggression is just that inflicts upon a population unprovoked injustice. And even were the Indians to attack the Spanish, a just response would be only a defensive response that sought to minimize loss.

In Vitoria are to be found the beginnings of international law – that is, of principles governing all nations that are anchored in natural moral law. Vitoria's argument is significant because it acknowledges an international community of independent states or people-groups having certain rights, territorial sovereignty, and reciprocal duties as to conduct outside their own borders. Unlike thinkers before him, Vitoria grounds the notion of "just war" not in Christian theology per se, but in moral obligation that is known through natural law reasoning. What natural reason has established among the nations is that certain rights and privileges, rooted in justice, are inviolable. Nature establishes a bond between all men. If the principles of "just war" are applicable to non-Christian peoples, then the rationale – the very basis – for justice and peace could not be narrowly "Christian." Human rights violations are the same for all people everywhere; they are anchored in moral realities that are unchanging and universally applicable.

Central to the work of Francisco Suárez (1548–1617) are the emphasis on natural law and the matter of how states are to conduct themselves. Whereas civil law is alterable, based on customs and usage, the law of nature is universal and unchanging, governing how human beings as well as nations deal with one another. All aspects of justice flow from this reality. Under the rubric of charity, Suárez scrutinizes the role of the state in both defensive and offensive postures: "A required mode and uniformity as to it [warfare] must be observed at its beginning, during its prosecution and after victory." This mode of moral continuity, Suárez is careful to insist, is founded upon the natural law and is common to religious and non-religious alike.[57]

Considered the father of modern international law, Hugo Grotius (1583–1645) confronts the dilemma of just limits to war and aggression in much the same way as Vitoria and Suárez. The results of his work would be foundational for "just war" thinking in the modern era. In his important work *The Law of War and Peace* (1625), Grotius argues that how nations relate to one another is governed by universally binding moral principles. These are "binding on all kings" and "known through reason."[58] This argument has important implications for both the Church and the state, for it places limitations on both. It also places limitations on whether nations may go to war justly and how warfare is to be conducted. Given the reality of the natural law, such rules of military engagement are valid for all people. The importance of Grotius's work can scarcely be understated, for it contributes to the normalization of international law, a law grounded in the "laws of humanity" that govern international relations, and it advocates universal moral laws that impose legal restrictions on nations.

Vitoria, Suárez, and Grotius understand justice to have deeper roots than mere religious confession. Justice is known through nature and is intuited universally as binding upon all people everywhere. Thus, the "law of nature" becomes a "law to the nations" (*jus gentium*), holding people-groups accountable to the unchanging demands of justice, which orders right relations.

In his work *Of the Laws of Ecclesiastical Polity*, penned in 1594, Richard Hooker observes of the law of nature: "Her seat is the bosom of God, her voice the harmony of the world."[59] Similarly, Nathaniel Culverwell writes in 1652, "By this great and glorious Law every good action was commanded, and all evil was discountenanc'd, and forbidden from everlasting." Culverwell, significantly, would exercise direct influence on the thinking of an important political philosopher of the next generation, John Locke.

In the late seventeenth century, a notable shift in emphasis away from the moral authority of the Church and Scripture and toward reason can be detected. The writings of John Locke, as it turns out, would undergird the American experiment and the founders' appeal to natural law in order to ground the new nation's establishment.[60] Locke and the framers of America's charter documents would speak of human beings possessing certain "self-evident truths" and "inalienable" rights that issue from the "Laws of Nature and Nature's God." For Locke, the natural law is distinct from (though not unrelated to) natural right (*jus natural*) in that the latter "consists in the fact that we have free use of something." The former, by contrast, is "that which either commands or prohibits some action" and indicates "what is and what is not consonant with a rational nature."[61] Reason, he insists, is not "the maker of this law," but rather "its Interpreter."[62] And to the objection that *no such universal moral exists*, since evidence suggests that most people live without it or do not recognize it, Locke answers, "as in civic affairs, [simply] because a blind man cannot read a notice displayed publicly, it does not follow that a law does not exist or is not promulgated."[63] Nor should "private interest" be confused with the natural law, inasmuch as the former, which is not binding, fails to be "protective of the safety and security of men's possessions" as is the latter.[64] The natural law, Locke is at pains to emphasize, is "binding on all men, and by its own force," "perpetual," and "universal."[65] To abolish or negate the natural law, Locke warns, is to "overturn at one blow all government among men, [all] authority, rank, and society."[66] This law "will never be abrogated, since men cannot alter this law."[67]

The framers of the late-eighteenth-century American experiment in republican democracy show themselves to be heirs of Lockean thinking, embarking on a rather novel project that synthesized broadly theistic thinking, classical political theory, and natural law reasoning. The result, according to one student of the natural law tradition, was a polity that was "complex, balanced, and elegant."[68] Because all discussions and debates concerning religious freedom are informed by history, we shall need to return in the next chapter to the synthesis that the founders and framers of the American experiment conceived. Suffice it to say here that this synthesis, which was at times painful in its emergence and did not spring up all at once, nonetheless resulted from a mindset that wished to guarantee neither religion nor secularism *per se*, but *liberty* in the sense of self-government.

Wisdom from modern voices

Despite the very Protestant cast of the American founding, with its debt to Lockean thinking, the concept of natural law has long been associated with Catholic social thought, and for good reason. Where a "renewal" of natural law thinking during the twentieth century has occurred, it has been chiefly due to the influence of Catholic thinkers. This pattern has remained for the most part, with some exceptions, up to the present. Contemporary Protestantism, by contrast, has "no comparable coherent framework for grounding its social thought." This was the conviction voiced 25 years ago by theologian and founding director of the Center for Catholic and Evangelical Theology Carl Braaten in his provocative essay "Protestants and Natural Law."[69] Braaten was not the first Protestant to make this observation, however. A similar conviction was expressed a century before by the Dutch Reformed theologian (and former prime minster) Abraham Kuyper, whom Braaten cites."[70] In 1891, on the occasion of the publication of Pope Leo XIII's encyclical *Rerum Novarum*, Kuyper conceded:

> It must be admitted to our shame that the Roman Catholics are far ahead of us in their study of the social question. Indeed, very far ahead . . . The Encyclical of Leo XIII gives the principles which are common to all Christians, and which we share with our Roman Catholic compatriots.[71]

Kuyper's appreciation of Roman Catholicism on matters moral and social, to which Braaten called attention, finds further confirmation seven years later, in the 1898 Stone Lectures that Kuyper delivered at Princeton University. Kuyper praises "the marvelous energy displayed in the latter half of this century by Rome" and "Rome's successful efforts in social life."[72] He also calls fellow Protestants to acknowledge,

> What we have in common with Rome concerns precisely those fundamentals of our Christian creed now most fiercely assaulted by the

> modern spirit . . . Now, in this conflict Rome is not an antagonist, but stands on our side.[73]

In both his 1891 and his 1898 remarks Kuyper is addressing two broader tendencies among fellow Protestants. First, relatively speaking, is a sectarian spirit that is unable – or unwilling – to acknowledge Roman Catholics as fellow Christians who confess the same creedal realities in the face of a hostile cultural environment.[74] The second is the Protestant inability to learn from Catholic social teaching. The "principles . . . common to all" used by Leo and noted by Kuyper relate *inter alia* to natural law – a concept that, in Braaten's words, "serves as a bridge category on ethical and social questions between church and world, between those with a priori commitment to sacred Scripture and the Christian creed and those outside the community of faith."[75] Braaten's call, then, was for Protestants to re-appropriate the natural law tradition – a tradition that was part of the framework of the magisterial Protestant reformers' thinking, even when they challenged Rome on matters soteriological and ecclesial.

If Braaten's challenge was timely in 1992, it is all the more relevant today, given the vacuous and splintered nature (not to mention the theological bankruptcy) of American Protestantism in the twenty-first century as well as the moral collapse of social institutions around us. Braaten concluded his essay with the following challenge:

> Moral relativism joins political activism to sabotage the rules and standards needed to implement a societal system ordered by principles of justice and truth. When the normlessness and the nihilistic effects of the deconstructionist mindset are no longer confined to academic, but invade the wider public [as they have done], the way is prepared for the moral collapse of social institutions or for the enthronement of the totalitarian state . . . Perhaps it is time to expose current relativist and nihilist theories as the underside of totalitarian ideologies and political authoritarianism. A revival of natural law can be of use in that project."[76]

I am inclined to agree with Braaten. And I would say that his comments a quarter-century later are all the more prescient. The normlessness and nihilism that Braaten decried have hardened in our day and have "invaded the wider public" sphere with a peculiar ferocity. In the second decade of the twenty-first century, as I write, the moral collapse of social institutions around us as well as the moral impoverishment of much of the Christian Church is nothing short of breathtaking. But I can anticipate the response of the reader, who will surely object that, with Braaten, I am exaggerating and being alarmist in speaking of "the moral collapse of social institutions" and "the enthronement of the totalitarian state." To which I reply, to speak in such a way is not "alarmism." Rather, it is to be a *moral realist*, in much the same way that John Paul II called for vigilance in the

West against the wedding of moral relativism and democratic pluralism. To wed these two elements, he worried, is to breed a brand of "civil barbarism" that results in socio-political tyranny because it undermines human personhood.[77]

But to use the word "barbarism" – and I can hear the protestations among some of my readers – is to appreciate the manner in which the Roman Catholic theologian John Courtney Murray used it two generations ago. Barbarism, Murray wrote, is not merely primitive savagery. Rather, it is also "the lack of reasonable conversation according to reasonable laws."[78] And in using the word "conversation," Murray means living together and talking together. Society becomes barbarous, he believed,

> when men huddle together under the rule of force and fear; when economic interests assume the primacy over higher values; when material standards of mass and quantity crush out the values of quality and excellence; when technology assumes an autonomous existence and embarks on a course of unlimited self-exploitation without purposeful guidance from higher disciplines of politics and morals . . . when the state reaches the paradoxical point of being everywhere intrusive and also impotent; when the ways of men come under the sway of the instinctual, the impulsive, the compulsive.[79]

These symptoms, described with considerable precision by Murray, suggest when and where barbarism is afoot. For Murray, when men cease talking together according to "reasonable laws," then *civility dies with the death of ethical dialogue*. Outmoded as it may strike the contemporary reader, the commonly shared vocabulary that allowed (and continues to allow) Americans – indeed, any "free" society – to have "conversation" is the language of natural law.[80] Tellingly, the difference between the French and American revolutions, writes Murray, was "less a revolution than a conversation"[81] – an observation that should give us pause.

The German legal scholar Heinrich Rommen, whose name is relatively unknown,[82] understood well the symbiotic relationship between the moral and political spheres. Rommen's work began to emerge at the time of the dissolution of the Weimar Republic in the 1930s, when Nazi ideology was ascendant. For his legal and political views Rommen was imprisoned by the Nazis, and then in 1938, he fled Germany for the United States. Nazi ideology, as Rommen saw it, aimed "not at a revolution" so much as "a legal grasp of power according to formal democratic processes."[83] Every generation, perhaps the historian will conclude, finds a new reason for the study of natural law. For those like Rommen, totalitarianism provided the impetus. Wrote Rommen, "Man is stirred to free himself from the pessimistic resignation that characterizes these relativist theories and to return to his principles."[84] Evidence of what Rommen argues is damning. Already in 1935, Nazi jurist Hans Frank had written, "Formerly we were in the habit of saying: 'This is right or wrong.' Today we ask the question: 'What would the Fuehrer say?' "[85] Frank conceded that devotion to Hitler "has become a concept of law."[86]

The question, then, is unavoidable, when discomfiting or off-putting. Apart from the natural law, what argument and protection do we have – does *any society* have – against evil when it manifests itself?[87] On what basis can it be declared, post-Nuremberg, that there exist universal human rights? Surely many contemporaries – both non-religious *and* religious – would consider the claim made earlier as exaggerated – namely, that moral degeneration truly *does* prepare the soil for the enthronement of at least a "softer" form of totalitarianism. And yet, history confirms this pattern. In a period of crumbling moral foundations, not only can a revival of natural law thinking be "of use" in the prognosis, as Braaten writes, but also *absolutely critical* to the health of the American republic, given the advanced state of the decomposition of its institutions.

Elsewhere I have voiced hearty and unqualified agreement with Braaten's challenge to Protestants. Along the way, I have found it necessary to examine the nature of the strong prejudice against natural law thinking that is found among Protestants (both orthodox and revisionist). Identifying influential theological voices, especially recent generations of those voices, which have stood in opposition to natural law ethics might be useful as we attempt to argue for a "revival" of natural law thinking in the twenty-first century. And to these voices we shall now turn.

The "problem" of natural law: an anatomy of protestant opposition

Karl Barth

To his credit, the teaching of the Swiss theologian Karl Barth in the decade before Hitler's rise to power helped pave the way for the resistance that took the form of the "Confessing Church." This group, emergent within the official state (Lutheran) church, "confessed with fresh devotion historic commitments in the light of their immediate political situation."[88] One year after Hitler's accession to power, a conference of confessional church leaders, meeting in Barmen,[89] drew up the brief declaration consisting of six points that became the theological foundation for resistance to Nazi hegemony. Barth would play a key role in drafting the "Barmen Declaration."[90]

Barth does not deny the function of the state in the divine economy – namely, the maintenance of justice and order over injustice and chaos. Rather, the state fails in its duty to the extent that it falls short of protecting what is right in the face of evil. The enthronement of National Socialism effectively constitutes a "fundamental dissolution of the just State."[91] Moreover, Western civilization as a whole has failed to confront National Socialism firmly "because the realization of the Christian revelation among the civilized people of the West (not only among the Germans!) had become dim."[92] Barth believes that an "artificial structure" of German Christianity had characterized the period preceding Hitler's ascendancy, and, consequently, the German church had little resistance to offer since German political parties, German jurisprudence, science, art, and philosophy had already capitulated.[93]However, Barth insists, "the far better equipped Roman Catholic Church has done no better" than the Protestant church. Both had drunk too deeply from the eighteenth and nineteenth centuries in order "to be equal to the [present] crisis."[94]

Barth's own examination of the prior two centuries leads him to conclude that a romanticized view of "nature," coupled with Europe's increasing secularism, had serious implications for German thought.[95] At bottom, any theological or philosophical concept rooted in "nature" is not merely deficient but rather heretical for Barth, inasmuch it undermines "Christ-centered" faith. Likewise, any moral framework that attempts "to deny or obscure its derivation from God's command" and "set up independent principles" is to be rejected, for it is a "replacement" for the grace of God.[96] To Barth, "natural theology" functions as a sort of Trojan horse inside the walls of Christendom. The God of "natural law" cannot be the God of the Bible, in which grace, not barbarism, is the norm. Natural law theory, Barth worries, creates a realm of autonomy separated from God's revelation in Jesus Christ. On the surface, this burden seems plausible and even commendable, given the character of political and cultural fascism of his day. Any claim to another authority other than or alongside Jesus Christ and the word of God are to be rejected.

But there is a conundrum that Christians of another era must face, and that is how to communicate the faith to non-believers, whose worldview and language are shaped by images, constructs, and assumptions that are devoid of biblical and Christological understanding. How do Christians communicate meaningfully in a non-Christian world, in a cultural environment in which the Bible and Jesus Christ or foreign? That point of contact or reference point with the non-believer is what we call "general revelation." And natural law constitutes the moral aspect of the penetrating arrow of general revelation, as one political philosopher has suggested.[97] With the natural law, there is no common ground, no point of connection, no meaningful engagement between Christians and non-believers.

Barth, it should be remembered, was not the only one who grappled with the dilemma of National Socialism and the totalitarian state. Heinrich Rommen, Yves Simon, Jacques Maritain, and Eric Voegelin were among European émigrés of note who arrived in the United States during the 1930s and 40s and contributed to a renewal of natural law thinking. And not coincidentally, most of the leading thinkers in this renewal were Catholic. What they shared in common, in contrast to Barth, was the conviction that a traditional metaphysics of natural law, consistent with traditional Christian moral philosophy, might be advanced without capitulating to the modernist, secularist, positivist, or fascist *Zeitgeist*. And at the theological level, they did not pit "nature" against grace, as Barth was wont to do.

One must note in this context the heated exchange that Barth had with Emil Brunner during the 1940s that centered on the natural law. At the heart of their disagreement was whether fallen human beings possess a basic knowledge of God and of moral truth. Brunner represented the position that "nature" indeed instructs us, and that because this moral sense is embedded in the human heart, all people can recognize it (even when they can reject it). As Brunner saw it, the reality of sin and our fallenness does not eradicate reason and conscience as constituents of the *imago Dei*. Barth's response was adamant. Knowledge about God might be "a possibility in principle but not . . . in fact."[98] Sin has in fact obliterated *any possibility* of natural theology, and therefore any utility of "natural law." No second "independent" category of moral knowledge, for Barth, could exist in the aftermath of the fall. Reason simply could not regain the pristine status that it had before humans sinned.

The difference between Barth and Brunner is instructive, for it captures the fundamental disagreement between Protestants and Catholics over natural law to the present day.[99] Ever since the Barth-Brunner controversy, Protestant theology has been riddled with suspicion and skepticism vis-à-vis the natural law, and it would appear that Barth's influence has been dominant. The crucial question is whether human reasoning and human apprehension of basic moral truth are universal, present, and operative within human beings by nature, and thus, whether humans can be held accountable for their actions. The historic Christian tradition, without equivocation, answers affirmatively to both questions. Moreover, the mainstream of that tradition holds to the conviction that although moral depravity is actual and pervasive in terms of its scope, it is limited in degree; that is, it neither eradicates our ability to choose the good (freedom) nor releases us from the sense of moral obligation (culpability, the common good).The orders of creation, of which natural law is a part, are part of biblical theology. They do not exist independent of – or separate from – salvation made known through Christ. Both the "creational" and the "salvific" belong to the divine economy; both, contra Barth, are confessed by Christians creedally. They are simply, to use Luther's apt metaphor, the left and right hands of God.

Jacques Ellul

An extremely eclectic thinker, Jacques Ellul is not particularly known for his theological writings. His more important writings concern technology, sociology, political philosophy, and social critique. Ellul nonetheless warrants a brief critique, given his adamant rejection of natural law on expressly theological grounds. In a brief but significant volume appearing in 1946 and subsequently translated under the English title *The Theological Foundation of Law*, the French social and legal critic concedes the renewal of natural law thinking in his day, and he grants the "disastrous consequences" of positivism as a legal alternative to totalitarianism. At the same time, given the state of modern culture and the social challenges it poses, the natural law is incapable of addressing these, in his view.

At the most fundamental level, Ellul shares Barth's suspicion of any attempt by theologians or natural lawyers to find common ground between Christians and non-Christians, since it ignores the difference, as he understands it, between "nature" and grace. To posit, a universal "law" is in effect to undermine grace. Ellul's bias against the natural law is not merely the fear of rationalist autonomy; it is also undergirded by two other important factors: the context of redemption as seen through the cross of Christ and an understanding of the human predicament (sin) that is anchored in a peculiar reading of Genesis. On the one hand, a Christocentric understanding of justice "radically destroys the ideas of objective law and of eternal justice."[100] On the other hand, through the fall, man loses any resemblance to Adam that he may have otherwise had, and because humans' perversion by sin is radical, "we cannot admit the idea of the *imago Dei* being preserved in man as the foundation of natural law."[101] "If one adopts a strictly biblical view," Ellul insists, "then it would seem that one could hardly do otherwise than to follow Karl Barth on the subject of the impossibility of the natural knowledge of God by man, which leads to the same impossibility for the knowledge of the good."[102]

On this point, Ellul waxes emphatic: "In scripture, there is no possible knowledge of the good apart from a living and personal relationship with Jesus Christ."[103] Ellul does not offer an account of how Noah or Abraham or Melchizedek knew right from wrong. For him, there is no normative ethics of the good, only an "ethics of grace." At bottom, any *natural knowledge* of the good does not derive from "the will of God" but rather stands in competition with it, producing a "double standard of morality."[104] And in the end, Ellul is forced to reject the notion of the natural law as a mistaken "medieval presupposition."[105]

Our interest in Ellul is due not to his broader influence but chiefly the manner in which he is representative of the "Protestant error" of ethical discontinuity not only between the Old and New Testaments but also between "creational" and "salvific" orders, to use theological language. While he is partly correct to argue for the "the impossibility of the Christian ethic" apart from divine grace,[106] he is mistaken to deny the *imago Dei* within all human beings and the "moral sense" that attends being created in the divine image. This view, it goes without saying, has profound theological and ethical implications. For this reason, his commentary on the "error" of John Calvin, who affirmed the natural law alongside a deep belief in divine grace, well illustrates the mistaken understanding that is adopted by many Protestants:

> In the degree in which he [Calvin] was living within Christianity, or in which he shared the philosophic ideas of his ages, especially concerning the nature of man, he was prevented from drawing from his theology the logical consequences in the field of natural morality and of natural

> law. But today, Christians who have based themselves on the existence of a permanent human nature which they used as a point of departure for the doctrine of a partial fall, of the possibility of a natural knowledge of the good on the part of man, etc., and who have imposed this interpretation on the biblical texts, should be embarrassed by the fact that scientific investigations tend to deny the existence of this "nature," unless it be in a sociological sense. In looking at the biblical texts, we are obliged to set aside these natural premises, which in the present situation do not appear to be confirmed.[107]

In his appeal to modern "science" as disproof of the "natural morality" and "natural law" mistakenly affirmed by Calvin, Ellul fails to interact with fellow magisterial Protestant reformers such as Luther, Melanchthon, Zwingli, and Bullinger. They, too, embrace Calvin's "error" and are in ethical continuity with their Catholic counter-parts by affirming the natural law without equivocation. Nor does Ellul acknowledge that the natural law is affirmed by the fathers of the Church from the beginning.

Helmut Thielicke

Animating the thinking of this important German Lutheran theologian, whose views are on display most forcefully in his magisterial 1966 work *Theological Ethics*, is the conviction that God "relativizes" law as expressed in the Old Covenant in the New Covenant. This "relativizing" is grounded chiefly in two pieces of evidence: the so-called Sermon on the Mount and "Paul's relating the law to transgressions."[108] It would be "quite erroneous," Thielicke argues, to ascribe to "law" a kind of "timeless validity"; "the moment we do this the Decalogue becomes 'natural law,' " and hence, "abstract" and "ahistorical."[109] Divine law, as Thielicke understands it, has significance *only* "for a particular historical epoch within salvation history"; law cannot stretch as a moral-legal norm from "creation across this [present] interim to the eschaton."[110] Divine law only corresponds to humans in a fallen world and thus is *not part of the created order*.

Thielicke worries that Roman Catholic moral theology, because it affirms an objective component of our nature as human beings, skews our understanding of grace and justification. Given Protestant's strong accent on sin's pervasiveness, he criticizes the natural law as a "doubtful concept" insofar as it represents "not an order which for man is something given" but rather "an order which *man has himself brought into being*."[111] Given Luther's doctrine of justification, there can be logically no cooperation of human reason in furnishing moral knowledge. Luther, Thielicke is convinced, was "inconsistent" and not clearly seeing the consequences of his own doctrine of justification – an inconsistency that in time gave rise to secularism.[112] This critique extends not only forward to us but also backward to Thomas Aquinas, whose view of "nature" is "invalidated" due to "the structural form of *fallen* existence."[113]

In his important chapter "The Negativity of the Commandments and Natural 'Lawlessness,'" Thielicke insists, "The Decalogue cannot be understood in terms of natural law. In fact, he reasons, the Decalogue does not mirror natural law but 'natural law-lessness.'" That is to say, it characterizes human sinfulness and rebellion, leaving "no intact [moral] order in human existence.[114] Therefore, natural law "can no longer be described as . . . meaningful"; "[i]n no case can natural law have the rank of an 'order of creation.'"[115]

Thielicke is adamant that Roman Catholicism errs insofar as it believes that "sin does not permeate all things" and that a sphere of "nature" remains, fundamentally unaffected and intact (hence its affirmation of the natural law).[116] Relatedly, it does not take seriously the *sola fide* of the Protestant reformers; consequently, it embraces a "false security" that humans can satisfy the law, which in turn undermines the Gospel of Christ.[117]

Thielicke's perception of law as possessing a wholly negative function is instructive, allowing us more fully to discern his theological bias. "The law," he insists, "establishes itself on a soil composed of facts created by the fall of man."[118] Moreover, "The Law itself tells us what we had previously been forbidden to know."[119] For Thielicke, then, law is an accommodation to human beings in the sense of *compromise*, not creation. In the end, we must conclude that, given how adamant Thielicke is in his rejection of the natural law, it is striking how utterly "un-Lutheran" – and unbiblical – this Lutheran theologian's view is. What is also remarkable is that in Thielicke's important work *Nihilism*, published in 1951 – that is, scarcely a couple of years after the United Nations Declaration on Human Rights was published, any discussion of natural law is all but absent.

Paul Lehmann

Roughly contemporary to Ellul and Thielicke, Paul Lehmann was in many ways an unorthodox theological ethicist. Best known for his *Ethics in a Christian Context* (1963), he shared with Barth and Ellul, and to a lesser extent Thielicke, the "Christological" starting point in thinking about ethics. In answering the question *What is the Protestant approach to ethics?*, he argued that we can understand "the good" only through the lens of faith in Christ and, specifically, only in light of the Pauline and Reformational emphasis on justification. Justification, he insisted, "redefines" all ethical categories: "The presuppositions and implications of justification offer a more adequate account of ethical motivation, achievement, and failure than alternative philosophical, theological, and religious ethical analyses."[120] And because "the good" is grounded in God, recognizing the good and doing good are governed by this, with the consequence that virtues and duties are no longer "self-evident norms"; now they are meaningful only because of redemption in Christ.[121]

But we have a problem, according to Lehmann: "The whole history of Christian ethics has been overshadowed by the Stoic doctrine of the *lex naturae.*" And when "the correspondence between divine reason and human reason is accepted as law and when this correspondence is 'Christianized' by grounding it in the biblical doctrines of creation and providence," the way is open for "the perpetration of things *as they are* over against things as they *ought to be.*"[122] Thus, perpetuating the analogy between the Decalogue, natural law, and moral law represents none other than the "infiltration" of the world's ethic into Christian ethics, "as had been the case for the whole patristic and medieval ethics."[123] Lehmann laments the purported result: the "radical love ethics" of Christ disappears behind a "morality of obedience."[124]

Not unlike Barth and Ellul, Lehmann insists that the starting point for social ethics is not "general revelation" or a body of objective moral truths but the relationship of the moral agent to Christ through faith. It is, then, "Christocentric" rather than anthropocentric. There can be no knowledge of the good apart from faith in Christ, neither can any knowledge of the good be defined abstractly in terms of moral laws or principles. Nothing is good in and of itself; what's more, the good is not self-evident, Lehmann believes.[125] Only God is good; hence, the good cannot be reduced to law, which "obscures rather than discloses God's love."[126] Otherwise, "nature" reduces to biology or sociology.[127] Law, Lehmann insists, "is neither the fundamental nor the final will of God."[128]

Lehmann's resultant "koinonia ethic" does not concern itself, from an epistemological standpoint, with what is good but rather what I as a believer in Christ, in the context of Christian fellowship or *koinonia*, am to do. Only in the context of Christian fellowship can one "mature" ethically. In the end, this wrong "starting point" prevents Lehmann from engaging consistently and coherently in important policy issues such as war, race, violence, etc., which have wider cultural significance and are justice related. Because his "koinonia ethic" fails to (a) discern the biblical basis for certain anthropological and moral realities (independent of faith) and (b) take seriously social-cultural and political aspects of society, it fails to facilitate responsible dialogue on conflicting moral claims and moral choices in the public arena. This, in turn, undercuts the need for strong moral analysis and ethical decision-making in the social, political, and economic spheres.

John Howard Yoder and Stanley Hauerwas

What passes as "Protestant" (from "protest") is wide-ranging, and other voices demand inclusion, particularly in their construal of "law." Yet another species of opposition to natural law thinking grounds itself in what it believes to be "radical obedience" to the biblical witness of Jesus. Perhaps the most persuasive representative of this view is Anabaptist theologian John Howard Yoder, whose well-known work *The Politics of Jesus* sets forth the argument that the authentic Christian social ethic is rooted in a radical – and "non-violent" – understanding of Jesus's teaching, and in a particular reading of the so-called Sermon on the Mount.

In seeking to understand the political order theologically, Yoder laments that two dominant interpretations have clouded our thinking. One rests on the "catholic" concept of natural law, which is questionable because it presumes an optimistic view of human nature and human capacity for divine revelation.[129] A second is equally regrettable – namely, the "Augustinian-reformed" version of "necessary compromise or order of preservation." Both of these interpretations, Yoder insists, are "unacceptable."[130]

In all of his writings there is a baseline assumption that pervades Yoder's thought. It is the belief that the early Church, in time, wrongly absorbed pagan philosophical influence – for example, the Stoic emphasis on reason and the law of nature – which played a significant role in permitting it, by Ambrose's and Augustine's day, to be "compromised" by the political powers. Christian social ethics, according to Yoder, evolved in such a way as to justify Christian presence and participation in Roman *imperium*; hence, Yoder's unrelenting "radical critique of Constantinianism." The history of the Church, for Yoder, is one long, continuing road of apostasy and cultural idolatry – that is, until the period of the "radical Reformation" in the sixteenth century. Christian social ethics, as Yoder conceives it, is located neither in human "nature" nor in rational notions of justice or the common good. Rather, it subsists in our radical obedience to what Yoder understands as Jesus's ethics of non-violent resistance to political and social oppression.

As it concerns ethical decision-making, Yoder advances what he understands to be Jesus's "prophetic" stance over against other models – models that he believes have "distracted" us over the last several centuries. One "distraction" is that Roman Catholics keep reminding us that nature and grace do not stand in opposition. The Catholic emphasis, Yoder believes, has "foreshortened" the vision of the Kingdom of God by its focus on "the nature of things" in this fallen world.[131] The result, he worries, is national idolatry and patriarchy. Yoder is supremely pessimistic about any moral education that predates the "radical Anabaptism" to which he belongs. In all fairness, given the genesis of Anabaptism in the sixteenth century, with persecution coming from both the Catholic and Protestant sides, this pessimism might seem warranted. In the end, Yoder is unwilling to submit his notion of moral formation to the collective wisdom of the historic Christian tradition. While he is fluent in his critique of twentieth-century idolatries, he is simplistic, when not silent, in his understanding of Christian ethics as the cumulative wisdom of a wider Christian – indeed, Judeo-Christian – tradition. As might be expected, his reading of history is remarkably selective, and given his overarching commitment to ideological pacifism, Yoder's rejection of natural law might therefore be viewed as a by-product, not a cause, of his pacifist ethics.[132]

In assorted writings, the Methodist theologian Stanley Hauerwas confesses his debt to Yoderian Anabaptism, wishing to advance Yoder's vision of Christian social ethics. That one newsmagazine in 2001, rightly or wrongly, described Hauerwas as the most influential theologian in America is some indication not only of his celebrity but also his influence in molding

Protestant ethical thought. A prolific writer, Hauerwas has been explicit in his rejection of natural law thinking – notably in *The Peaceable Kingdom* and in *Truthfulness and Tragedy*. As with Yoder, the deep-seated distrust of natural law thinking in ethics is, for Hauerwas, related to the Church's purported compromise with "Constantinianism." Thus, it is argued, "the alleged transparency of the natural law norms reflects more the consensus within the Church than the universality of the natural law itself."[133] The power of natural law as a systematic idea, Hauerwas believes, "was developed in and for the Roman imperium and then for 'Christendom.'" Natural law, hence, became the means of codifying a particular "imperial" moral tradition.[134]

Consequently, as interpreted by Hauerwas, rather than offering an account of moral principles that are "the same for all, both as to rectitude and as to knowledge" (so Thomas Aquinas) and universally intuited so that all are without excuse (thus St. Paul in Romans 1 and 2), the natural law tradition is a "culturally assimilationist" attempt at Christian ethics that mirrors the Church's "cultural captivity" rather than the practice of Christian virtue.[135] Although Hauerwas does acknowledge points of contact between Christian ethics and "other forms of moral life," he is unable to identify these with any amount of usefulness and concludes that these "are not sufficient to provide a basis for a 'universal' ethic grounded in human nature *per se*."[136] He writes, "While the way of life taught by Christ is meant to be an ethic for all people, it does not follow that we can know what such an ethic involves objectively by looking at the human."[137]

Anticipating objections to the absence of any natural law and creational considerations in his understanding of ethics, and responding specifically to ethicist James Gustafson's charge that his ethical approach is sectarian, Hauerwas reasons in a manner that has typified Protestant thinking – namely, by arguing that nature and grace, natural morality and Christ's lordship, creation and Christology, are diametrically opposed. He mistakenly presumes that a common morality, based on a common human nature, is somehow "autonomous" from divine revelation and grace.[138]

Ultimately, Hauerwas believes that "Christian ethics theologically does not have a stake in 'natural law.'" Numerous "difficulties" are adduced to support such a claim. In addition to "confusing" nature and grace, natural law ethics fails to acknowledge that there is no such thing as a universal morality, only many moralities. Also, it fails to inhibit violence in the world; in fact, it tempts us to coerce those who disagree with us. Furthermore, it fails to acknowledge that reason is insufficient to lead people to a basic awareness of moral principle. And mirroring the argument of John Howard Yoder, natural law thinking and "natural theology" are alleged to represent a sort of "primitive metaphysics" and reflection of the Constantinian era which well nigh "perverts" the nature of Christian ethics.[139] In the end, natural law ethics is alleged to be insufficiently "christological."

Like most fellow Protestants, Hauerwas believes that the nature-and-grace "abstraction" has "distorted how ethics has been undertaken in the

Catholic tradition."[140] But this widespread assumption of "autonomy," whereby Protestants presuppose that nature and grace stand in opposition, is to erect a false dichotomy that finds no place in historic Christian theology, as theologian Oliver O'Donovan has reminded us.[141] Some of Hauerwas's concerns, as the reader will recognize, issue out of his ideological pre-commitment to pacifism, and the shrillness of his insistence is highly instructive:

> [P]ut as contentiously as I can, you cannot rightly read the Sermon on the Mount unless you are a pacifist . . . The Sermon does not generate an ethic of nonviolence, but rather a community of nonviolence is necessary if the Sermon is be read rightly.[142]

What is relevant in light of Hauerwas's objection is the fact that, far from preparing society for violence, the natural law *preserves* social bonds and *guards* basic freedoms rather than threatening them. If there were no human nature that is common to all, if there were no ethical "Golden Rule," if justice were not uniform the world over, then this could not be so. (Curiously, in this regard Hauerwas fails to interact with the magisterial Protestant reformers, who assume the natural law as foundational to their ethical understanding and thereby demonstrate full continuity with their Catholic counter-parts, even when they lodge vigorous protest along theological and ecclesial lines.) Moreover, ideological pacifists such as Hauerwas fail to make the fundamental distinction between force and violence. This distinction is critically important and, in the end, renders the pacifist position untenable). In the words of John Courtney Murray, force is "the measure of power necessary and sufficient to uphold . . . law and politics. What exceeds this measure is violence, which destroys the order of both law and politics."[143] As an instrument of responsible public policy, then, force is morally neutral and absolutely necessary for guarding the common social good.

Mainstream Christian moral thinking stands in stark contrast to the Yoderian-Hauerwasian approach to social ethics, an approach that is exceedingly popular in our day, doubtless due to the "prophetic" mantle that it tends to don. Consistent with the wider Judeo-Christian moral tradition, it understands that public morality must rest upon publicly accessible principles – principles that are recognizable and rooted in human nature. For this reason, natural law thinking has been lodged at the heart of the Christian moral tradition from the beginning. The general tone of Protestant resistance to natural law thinking would strike the Church fathers *of any era* as remarkable, wrong-headed, and theologically untenable. Christian moral thinkers from Aquinas to Luther to C.S. Lewis to John Paul II and Benedict XVI in our own day have argued for the application of natural law reasoning in the realm of public discourse, and this for eminently *public and universal* reasons. All exhibit recognition of the need to contend for moral first principles on the basis of our shared human nature. To do so in a pluralistic cultural environment is *not* to capitulate to the culture or to "independent" reasoning, as opponents of natural law ethics would have us believe.

Further reflections on natural law, public discourse, and public persuasion

As the previous discussion indicates, a frequent argument adduced by opponents of natural law thinking is that it wrongly accords to human reason powers and moral intuition that simply are not warranted – at least, in terms of Christian theology. This stance can take two forms. One is to argue that natural law incorporates "pagan" or "worldly" philosophical elements into its framework – elements that are foreign to the Christian scriptures themselves and insufficiently "Christocentric." The other is to argue that human reason has been so debilitated by our sinfulness that it is impossible, or next to impossible, for human beings to recognize "right" from "wrong." Hence, natural law thinking allegedly elevates reason to a false level of moral awareness, given its fundamental impotence as a result of the fall. Both of these arguments, as we have suggested, tend to be aimed at Catholic exponents of natural law theory by Protestants.

I shall not rehearse the varied responses of mainstream Christian thinking to each of these distortions. Nevertheless, several remarks are in order. It is surely true that Protestant theologians of the Reformation era belittled scholasticism, fearing an idolatry of reason – and of human works – that might undermine what they understood to be the biblical teaching on theological justification. Luther's disparaging of Aristotle is to be seen in precisely this light. Yet they did not reject the natural law. However deeply entrenched the neglect of – or opposition to – natural law might be among Protestants today, it cannot be attributed to the reformers of the sixteenth century. While it is decidedly true that they championed a particular understanding of faith and grace, this was *not* to the exclusion of other vehicles of divine agency. It is accurate to insist that in nature the Reformation controversies within the Catholic Church were foremost theological and ecclesiastical, not ethical.[144]

It has been the voice of mainstream Christian thinking through the ages to insist that "all truth is God's truth." The quaintness of this saying should not obscure its truth. If ancient philosophers – be they Stoic, Aristotelian, or Platonic – grasped *in part*, ever so dimly, the reality that reason and revelation are *not* two incommensurate, discontinuous, and unrelated realms, it is surely the case that Christian theology through the ages has grasped this reality. By maintaining such, I am not denying the difference in substance of Stoic versus Christian concepts of the divine, nor am I am denying that one is far less precise in its conceptualization than the other. It is only to emphasize the fact that natural law theory, at least in its classical formulation, exhibits some correlation between reason and revelation. This perhaps is the underlying significance of Hugo Grotius's claim, frequently cited, that natural law exists independently of whether we affirm *the existence of God* or not. "The law of nature is so unalterable," Grotius adds, "God himself cannot change it."[145]

What is Grotius arguing? The context of this claim indicates that his burden is *the intrinsic nature* of things. Good cannot be changed to evil, he notes, and neither can what is intrinsically evil be made good. God cannot act in contradiction to this moral reality, since he is the author of that nature.[146] Natural law, according to Grotius's line of reasoning, does not depend on human will or pleasure or passions; rather, it is the "dictate of right reason, which shows the moral deformity or moral necessity of any act."[147] The very notion of "necessity" implies that human action cannot be guided, at bottom, by pleasure or pain, self-interest or self-abandonment. Justice, then, well illustrates *the importance of reason*, rightly informed and directed, moving in the direction of *what is necessary*. When Aristotle, no theist by any stretch of the imagination, can contend that justice has a universal quality, he intuits a moral reality that is shared by the Christian theologian. It is no less true that a non-theist has declared it to be so. This, I think, is what Grotius might have in mind.

What further irritates many Protestant theologians of our day is the perception that natural law is somehow independent of ("autonomous" seems to be the preferred term among critics) the moral theology of Christianity or Judaism. This, quite simply, is not true. Rather, the Judeo-Christian moral tradition affirms the complementary categories of "general" and "special" revelation to describe the varied, though interwoven, mechanisms by which the Creator reveals himself to human creatures. The moral norms that inhere in a moral universe are recognized – "intuited," if you like – in part *by reason*. Revelation presupposes creation and a particular order or "nature" as a necessary, though not sufficient, condition.[148] And how are these "conditions" recognized by human beings? By general reflection on the nature of things. In this regard, natural law theorist David Novak properly observes:

> Indeed, for theologians as otherwise diverse as Maimonides, Aquinas, and Calvin, natural law is the most immediately intelligible part of the larger divine law . . . It is no accident, then, that virtually all contemporary natural law theorists are adherents of some religion of revelation such as Judaism or Christianity.[149]

The reason for belaboring the fact of Protestant opposition to the natural law, however, should not be construed as purely academic or strictly theological; it expresses itself in a very public manner, resulting in a *truncated social ethics*. As such, natural law critics fail to discern the role that our common human nature plays not only in moral theory but also in moral discourse. This deficiency undermines any attempts to enter the public sphere and engage meaningfully in ethical discoursed with non-likeminded people when and where critical social, political, and ethical issues are at stake. At best, perhaps we convince ourselves that in our "radical" commitment to "the ethics of Jesus," or in our "radical separation and denunciation of "the powers" ("speaking truth to power" is the parlance of many self-styled contemporary "prophets"), or in our radical apocalypticism (whereby we check out of the world in terms of meaningful engagement), we most faithfully embody Christian responsibility in the world. At worst, we delude ourselves by being severed not only from the mainstream of historic Christian thought but also from the wisdom of the ages that previous generations were forced to glean. In practice, this posture prevents us – and those falling under our influence – from entering into heartfelt, honest dialogue with fellow citizens in the public sphere. Alas, there remains for those who are so predisposed no language of ethical "transmission" which is intelligible to both religious believer and non-believer. In the end, apart from the natural law, we appear to lose any basis upon which to morally persuade and to preserve "civil society." For this reason, the *Catechism of the Catholic Church* declares, "In defending the ability of human reason to know God, the Church is expressing her confidence in the possibility of speaking about him to all men and with all men, and therefore of dialogue with other religions, with philosophy and science, as well as with unbelievers and atheists."[150]

An abiding task, then, for most citizens – and especially religious communities – is to understand natural law in relationship to public discourse. Because of the inherent tension between religious faith and the culture, we are naturally prone toward multiple distortions in our thinking and in discourse to which we need to be sensitized. These errors range from the secular hope of finding "neutral" common moral ground in the public sphere to the religious tendencies either to develop more theocratic, quasi-imperialist visions of society or to embody the more existentialist and pietistic error, by which we retreat from the culture and aim to be raptured away from our responsibilities in the world. It is for this reason, then, given the many competing tensions between religious conviction and an increasingly "bleached" public sphere, that any "ecumenical" dialogue regarding the natural law is to be welcomed. In the words of John Courtney Murray, "[a]s a metaphysical idea . . . natural law is timeless, and for that reason timely."[151]

At bottom, the alliance of faith and reason – in their proper relationship – that characterizes the mainstream of the historic Christian tradition should be viewed as precisely that – mainstream Christian thinking. This remains true even when the divorce of the two, a conspicuous human tendency, has been a constant challenge in our own cultural tradition, to both the secular and the religious, resulting in fideism on the one hand and rationalism on the other.[152] In what some view as "the most astounding synthesis of all,"[153] the framers of the American constitutional experiment melded classical political theory, natural law theory, belief in a providential Creator, and liberal conception of human rights into a mix that was remarkable – and unprecedented. A particular consequence of this mix was that the founders and framers thought and spoke in terms of "self-evident truths." And it is to these thinkers, with the assumptions they bore, that we must now turn.

Notes

1 David F. Forte, "The Natural Law Moment," in David F. Forte, ed., *Natural Law and Contemporary Public Policy* (Washington, DC: Georgetown University Press, 1998), 3.

2 For contrasting estimates of the number people killed for political-ideological reasons in the twentieth century, see, for example, Stéphane Courtois, Nicolas Werth, Jean-Louis Panné, Andrzej Paczkowski, Karel Bartošek, and Jean-Louis Margolin, *The Black Book of Communism: Crimes, Terror, Repression*, trans. Jonathan Murphy and Mark Kramer (Cambridge: Harvard University Press, 1999), and Robert Conquest, *Reflections on a Ravaged Century* (New York: W.W. Norton, 2000). Courtois et al. locate the number of deaths at around 100 million. Conquest's estimate is in the vicinity of 170 million. By any measure, the stench of death is simply mind-boggling.

3 So Forte, "The Natural Law Moment," 8.

4 This remains uncontroversial despite undaunted attempts by some theorists in our day to explain away free will and moral agency.

5 Allan Bloom, *The Closing of the American Mind: How Higher Education Has Failed Democracy and Impoverished the Souls of Today's Students* (New York: Simon & Schuster, 1987), 25.

6 To critique moral relativism is not to deny the fact of moral complexity or the complex nature of certain types of moral decision-making. It is only emphasize that in denying moral absolutes we thereby render all moral issues subjective, in the end preparing the soil for moral atrocity and terror.

7 Hadley Arkes, *First Things: An Inquiry into the First Principles of Morals and Justice* (Princeton: Princeton University Press, 1986), 51. See, in particular, Chapter 4 of Arkes' important volume ("On Necessary Truths and the Existence of Morals"). The logic of moral "laws," Arkes argues, is simply that, given moral agency and moral freedom among human beings, they made necessary in order to have access to any moral understanding.

8 See, for example, Lesslie Newbigin, *The Gospel in a Pluralist Society* (Grand Rapids: Eerdmans, 1989).

9 I avoid using the term "multiculturalism" in this context insofar as the term becomes something of a Trojan horse for those who wish to undermine established (Western) culture and traditional Judeo-Christian moral authority. In this sense, "multiculturalism" becomes a means to *multimorality*, whereby objective moral norms are denied or negated.

10 While the literature on ethical and cultural relativism is virtually endless, a very useful test-case that exposes its illogic and inconsistency *in practice* can be found in Loretta M. Kopelman, "Female Circumcision/Genital Mutilation and Ethical Relativism," in Paul K. Moser and Thomas L. Carson, eds., *Moral Relativism: A Reader* (New York: Oxford University Press, 2001), 307–25.

11 It is significant that in the Nuremberg trials, arguments in defense of those accused of "crimes against humanity" were repeatedly and consistently relativist. Consider this one bit of testimony: "Experiments that time and again have been described in the international literature without meeting any opposition do not constitute a crime from the medical point of view . . . In view of the complete lack of *written* legal norms, the physician, who generally knows only little about the law, has to rely on and refer to the admissibility of what is generally recognized to be admissible all over the world" (emphasis in the original). This is an extract from the Closing Brief for the Defendant [Dr.] Ruff, *Military Tribunal* I, vol. 1, p. 92, cited by Ruth Macklin in "Universality of the Nuremberg Code," in George J. Annas and Michael A. Grodin, eds., *The Nazi Doctors and the Nuremberg Code: Human Rights in Human Experimentation* (New York: Oxford University Press, 1992), 247.

12 Prov. 10:12, 26; 11:2, 17; 13:13; 17:1, 14; 19:12; 20:1; 25:19.
13 Elsewhere I discuss the link between social Darwinism and ethics in pre-Nazi Germany in the epilogue to *The Unformed Conscience of Evangelicalism: Recovering the Church's Moral Vision* (Downers Grove: InterVarsity Press, 2002), 246–62.
14 Constitutive elements of "justice" for de Waal are hierarchy, reciprocity, and mutual obligation. A fundamental weakness of de Waal's work is his inability to give an account of moral agency, rationality, and "free will," much less the "problem of evil." Thus, de Waal's use of the term "justice" – which entails hierarchy, reciprocity, and mutuality – requires severe qualification.
15 See especially his work *Good Natured: The Origins of Right and Wrong in Humans and Other Animals* (Cambridge: Harvard University Press, 1996).
16 Cited in Kim A. McDonald, "A Primatologist Examines the Biological Basis for Ethical Behavior in Humans," *Chronicle of Higher Education* (March 15, 1996): A10–11.
17 Edward O. Wilson, *Sociobiology: The New Synthesis* (Cambridge: Harvard University Press, 1975), 562.
18 The issue, let us be clear, is not whether human behavior is complex or whether the human is a composite being; it is rather, that we are moral-spiritual beings – and hence unique in the cosmos.
19 Already by the late 1980s, more than 70 million copies of Lewis' books had been sold. In the early 2000s, HarperCollins announced the purchase rights to Lewis' works, which should guarantee that Lewis is the best-selling author of all time.
20 In appropriating this term, Lewis is not intending to import Confucian philosophical or metaphysical assumptions, and in some respects, he is susceptible to legitimate criticism for this usage.
21 C.S. Lewis, *Mere Christianity*, rev. ed. (New York: Palgrave Macmillan, 1960), 19.
22 Arkes, *First Things*, 84.
23 Heraclitus, *Fragments*, 112–14, reproduced in Charles M. Bakewell, *Source Book in Ancient Philosophy* (New York: Scribner, 1907), 34, emphasis added.
24 Heinrich A. Rommen, *The Natural Law: A Study in Legal and Social History and Philosophy*, trans. T.R. Hanley (Indianapolis: Liberty Fund, 1998), 7.
25 Plato, *Laws*, 889–90. Even when direct appeals to nature as the foundation of unchanging ethical norms are not developed explicitly in Plato, the basic argument found in his *Republic* is that there exists an order both in physical nature and in human nature that is objective and universal.
26 For this reason, Aquinas devotes significant attention to "the Philosopher" and his ethical categories.
27 Aristotle, *Ethica nichomachea* 5.7 (1134b); I am relying on Aristotle, *Nichomachean Ethics*, 3rd ed., trans. Martin Ostwald (New York: Palgrave Macmillan, 1986), 131.
28 Ibid. (1135a).
29 Ibid. 10.9 (1179b–1180b).
30 Aristotle, of course is a naturalist and not a theist; the cosmos is to be understood as self-existing.
31 It should be noted, however, that Aristotle used "nature" to justify the inferiority of women, children, and slaves (*Politics* 1254–1255).
32 See in particular Book 2 of *Nichomachean Ethics*.
33 See in particular Book 5 of ibid.
34 Ibid 5.7 (1097a–1135a).
35 Cicero, *On the Republic*, trans. Clinton W. Keyes (Loeb Classical Library; Cambridge: Harvard University Press, 1928), 3.22 (79).
36 Cicero, *De Legibus*, trans. Clinton W. Keyes (Loeb Classical Library; Cambridge: Harvard University Press, 1928), 1.16.45 (347).
37 Cicero, *De officiis*, 401.

38 Jesus affirms the moral law (Matt. 5:17–48), as does Paul (Rom. 7:22; 10:4 [Christ as *telos* – the *goal*, not the "end," of the law, as some translations have improperly translated it – of the law]; 13:8–10), and James (2:10–11).
39 For this accusation against Socrates, we are dependent on the testimony of Xenophon: "Socrates does wrongly, for he does not acknowledge the gods which the state acknowledges; rather, he introduces other newly-fashioned gods" (*Memorabilia* 1.1.1).
40 Elsewhere I offer an overview of representative fathers – from Justin, Tertullian, and Clement of Alexandria to John Chrysostom, Ambrose, and Augustine. See J. Daryl Charles, *Retrieving the Natural Law: A Return to Moral First Things* (Critical Issues in Bioethics; Grand Rapids and Cambridge, UK: Eerdmans, 2008), 85–90, and J. Daryl Charles, "Pacifists, Patriots, or Both? Second Thoughts on Pre-Constantinian Attitudes Toward Soldiering and War," *Logos: A Journal of Catholic Thought and Culture* 13, no. 2 (2010): 17–55.
41 *Fides et Ratio* no. 44.
42 Ibid. no. 98.
43 Thomas Aquinas, *Summa Theologica* I-II Q. 91., a. 2.
44 Ibid. Q. 94.
45 Ibid. Q. 6, a. 4–5, and Q. 92, a. 1–2.
46 In this context, Aquinas observes, "All inclinations of human nature, to whatever part they belong . . ., all come under natural law so far as they can be charged with intelligence" (ibid. Q. 94, a. 2).
47 Ibid. Q. 93, a. 2.
48 Ibid. Q. 90.
49 The Protestant reformers, while affirming the "total depravity" of human nature, did not mean thereby that humans are always as bad as they can possibly be, nor did they understand the problem of sin and fallenness to eliminate the image of God.
50 *Luther's Works*, vol. 40, ed. Conrad Bergendoff (Philadelphia: Fortress Press, 1958), 97.
51 Ibid.
52 *Luther's Works*, vol. 54, ed. T.G. Tappert (Philadelphia: Fortress Press, 1967), 293.
53 *The "Loci Communes" of Philip Melanchthon*, ed. and trans. Charles L. Hill (Boston: Meador, 1944), 112.
54 John Calvin, *Institutes of the Christian Religion* 2.8.1; I am utilizing the translation if *Institutes* by H. Beveridge (Grand Rapids: Eerdmans, 1957).
55 Ibid. 2.2.22.
56 Ibid. 2.2.22 and 4.10.16.
57 Francisco Suárez, *Three Theological Virtues* 3.8.1–2. We are dependent on the English translation of James B. Scott, *The Spanish Origin of International Law: Lectures on Francisco de Vitoria (1480–1546) and Francisco Suárez (1548–1617)* (Washington, DC: Georgetown University Press 1929), 77.
58 Hugo Grotius, *The Law of War and Peace* 1.1.10 and 1.3.16.
59 Richard Hooker, *Of the Laws of Ecclesiastical Polity*, 3 vols., ed. John Keble, R.W. Church and Francis Paget (Oxford: Clarendon, 1888), 1:285.
60 See in particular Locke's *Questions concerning the Law of Nature*, ed. Robert H. Horwitz, Jenny Strauss Clay, and Diskin Clay (Ithaca and London: Cornell University Press, 1990), and *Two Treatises of Government*, ed. Peter Laslett (New York: Cambridge University Press, 1960), and especially the second treatise, sections 6 and 12.
61 Locke, *Questions*, 101.
62 Ibid. Locke distinguishes "right reason" from "natural appetites"/"the natural inclination of mankind"; the former facilitates knowledge of the natural law, but the latter cannot, given its tendency toward all manner of vice.

63 Ibid., 109.
64 Ibid., 235, 239.
65 Ibid., 211, 217.
66 Ibid., 213.
67 Ibid., 229.
68 Forte, "The Natural Law Moment," 4.
69 Carl E. Braaten, "Protestants and Natural Law," *First Things* 19 (January 1992): 20–6.
70 Tireless in his efforts to apply Christianity to every realm of life, Kuyper was the founder of the Free (Reformed) University of Amsterdam in 1880, and from 1901 to 1905, he served as prime minster of the Netherlands.
71 Kuyper, quoted in Braaten," Protestants," 20.
72 Abraham Kuyper, *Lectures on Calvinism*, rev. ed. (Grand Rapids: Eerdmans, 1987), 183.
73 Ibid.
74 Kuyper is by no means oblivious to the fact that "the Reformation has established a fundamental antithesis between Rome and ourselves." But he does state winsomely, "I for my part am not ashamed to confess that on many points my views have been clarified through my study of the Romish theologians" (ibid., 183–4).
75 Braaten, "Protestants," 25.
76 Ibid.
77 This is a particular emphasis of John Paul's 1995 encyclical *Evangelium Vitae*, wherein the relationship between moral law and civil law is accented.
78 John Courtney Murray, *We Hold These Truths: Catholic Reflections on the American Proposition* (New York: Sheed and Ward, 1960), 13.
79 Ibid., 13–14.
80 Murray's discussion of natural law in *We Hold These Truths* (ibid.) belongs chiefly to two chapters – "The Origins and Authority of the Public Consensus" and "The Doctrine Lives: The Eternal Return of Natural Law."
81 Ibid., 31.
82 I offer further reflections on Rommen's thought in the concluding chapter.
83 Heinrich Rommen, *The State in Catholic Thought* (St. Louis: Herder, 1945), 48, 212.
84 Ibid., 48.
85 Hans Frank, cited in Robert Conot, *Justice at Nuremberg* (New York: Palgrave Macmillan, 1983), 79.
86 Ibid.
87 Although this volume does not attempt to be an excursus on the problem of evil, the question is unavoidable: How *does* a society regulate what is ethical and unethical, just and unjust, acceptable and unacceptable, without recourse to the language of "good" and "evil?" Without such, the strategies tend to be four in number: (1) we can deny that evil exists (which typically is the ploy of the metaphysical materialist); (2) short of denying it, we can "regulate" it (which is to say, redefine it – biologically or therapeutically – and reduce it to manageable proportions; (3) we can engage in moral equivalence, such that all actions are as bad (or as good) as the next, rendering "good" and "evil" virtually indistinguishable; or (4) we can accuse those who identify "good" and "evil" as "intolerant" and "judgmental." Employing any or all of these strategies, we find that good and evil disappear.
88 Karl Barth, *The Church and the War* (New York: Palgrave Macmillan, 1944), v.
89 Barmen is part of present-day Wuppertal, Germany. The "confessing" synod of the German Evangelical Church met there on May 29–31, 1934, following Hitler's moves to muzzle the state church and create a *Reichskirche*.

90 One gets an accurate sense of the trajectory of the Barmen Declaration through the confession's preamble: "The Confessional Synod of the German Evangelical Church met in Barmen, May 29–31, 1934. Here representatives from all the German Confessional Churches met with one accord in a confession of the one Lord of the one, holy, apostolic Church. In fidelity to their Confession of Faith, members of Lutheran, Reformed, and United Churches sought a common message for the need and temptation of the Church in our day. With gratitude to God, they are convinced that they have been given a common word to utter. It was not their intention to found a new Church or to form a union. For nothing was farther from their minds than the abolition of the confessional status of our Churches. Their intention was, rather, to withstand in faith and unanimity the destruction of the Confession of Faith, and thus of the Evangelical Church in Germany. In opposition to attempts to establish the unity of the German Evangelical Church by means of false doctrine, by the use of force and insincere practices, the Confessional Synod insists that the unity of the Evangelical Churches in Germany can come only from the Word of God in faith through the Holy Spirit. Thus alone is the Church renewed." The text of the Declaration is accessible at www.sacred-texts.com/chr/barmen.htm.

91 Barth, *The Church and the War*, viii.

92 Ibid., 5.

93 Ibid., 7–8.

94 Ibid., 8.

95 See Karl Barth, *Protestant Theology in the Nineteenth Century: Its Background and History*, rev. ed. (London: SCM, 2001).

96 Karl Barth, *Church DogmaticsII/1*, trans. Geoffrey W. Bromiley (Edinburgh: T. & T. Clark, 1961), 527.

97 J. Budziszewski, *Written on the Heart: The Case for Natural Law* (Downers Grove: InterVarsity Press, 1997), 185.

98 Emil Brunner and Karl Barth, *Natural Theology*, trans. Peter Fraenkel (London: Jeffrey Bless/Centenary Press, 1946), 106.

99 Stephen J. Grabill's lucid account of the Barth-Brunner rift captures the sense in which Barthian thought, to the present day, has exerted its influence in predisposing Protestant theologians negatively toward natural law thinking. See his *Rediscovering the Natural Law in Reformed Theological Ethics* (Grand Rapids and Cambridge, UK: Eerdmans, 2006), 21–53 (Chapter 1: "Karl Barth and the Displacement of Natural Law in Contemporary Protestant Theology"), esp. 21–9.

100 Jacques Ellul, *The Theological Foundation of Law*, trans. Marguerite Wieser (London: SCM, 1961), 49.

101 Ibid., 61.

102 Jacques Ellul, *To Will and to Do*, trans. C. Edward Hopkin (Philadelphia and Boston: Pilgrim Press, 1969), 16. See as well Grabill's very helpful tracing of the Barthian cast of Ellul's presuppositions in *Rediscovering the Natural Law*, 40–3.

103 Ibid., 16.

104 Ibid., 73–110 (Chapter 5, "The Double Morality").

105 Ibid., 118.

106 Ibid., 201–24 (Chapter 12, "The Impossibility of a Christian Ethics").

107 Ibid. 269–70, n. 4.

108 Helmut Thielicke, *Theological Ethics – Vol. 1: Foundations* (Philadelphia: Fortress, 1966), 149.

109 Ibid., 149–50.

110 Ibid., 150.

111 Ibid., 269, emphasis added.

112 Ibid., 326.
113 Ibid., 440.
114 Ibid., 447.
115 Ibid.
116 Ibid.,501–2.
117 Ibid., 505.
118 Ibid., 569.
119 Ibid.
120 Paul Lehmann, "Toward a Protestant Analysis of the Ethical Problem," *Journal of Religion* 24, no. 1 (January 1944): 1.
121 Ibid.
122 Ibid.
123 Ibid. Here Lehmann is citing with approval observations made by German theologian Ernst Troeltsch, in *Gesammelte Schriften*, I (Tübingen: Mohr, 1912), 442.
124 Ibid., 2.
125 Ibid., 5.
126 Ibid., 7.
127 Ibid., 5–6.
128 Ibid., 7.
129 John Howard Yoder, *Karl Barth and the Problem of War*, ed. Mark Thiessen Nation (Portland: Wipf & Stock, 2003), 120.
130 Ibid.
131 Donald E. Miller and John H. Yoder, "Does Natural Law Provide a Basis for Christian Witness to the State? A Symposium," *Brethren Life and Thought* 7 (1962): 8–22.
132 Elsewhere I devote fuller attention to Yoder's thinking in *Retrieving the Natural Law* (see n. 40), pp. 137–41, and "Burying the Wrong Corpse: Evangelicals and Natural Law," in Jesse Covington, Bryan McGraw, and Micah Watson, eds., *Natural Law and Evangelical Political Thought* (Lanham and Plymouth, UK: Lexington Books, 2013), 3–34.
133 Stanley Hauerwas, *The Peaceable Kingdom: A Primer in Christian Ethics* (Notre Dame: University of Notre Dame Press, 1983), 51.
134 Ibid.
135 Ibid.
136 Ibid., 60–1.
137 Ibid., 58.
138 Stanley Hauerwas, "Why the 'Sectarian Temptation' Is a Misrepresentation: A Response to James Gustafson (1988)," in John Berman and Michael Cartwright, eds., *The Hauerwas Reader* (Durham: Duke University Press, 2001), 107–8.
139 Hauerwas, *The Peaceable Kingdom*, 51–64. Elsewhere Hauerwas mistakenly writes that "natural law functions ideologically to justify the assumption that Christians have a responsibility to fulfill the demands of the state and institutions associated with it. It is no accident, therefore, the 'natural law' as a doctrine flourished during the Constantinian era of the church" (*Truthfulness and Tragedy: Further Investigations in Christian Ethics* [Notre Dame and London: University of Notre Dame Press, 1977], 214, n. 5). Natural lawyers would find this claim most remarkable. Hauerwas might consider the fact that many of the thinkers who contributed to a renewal of natural law thinking in the twentieth century were in truth European emigrées who had suffered the effects of totalitarianism, whose chief responsibility was to *oppose* – rather than "fulfill" – "the demands of the state," as Hauerwas somewhat carelessly claims.
140 Ibid., 55–7.

141 Oliver O'Donovan, *Resurrection and Moral Order: An Outline for Evangelical Ethics* (Grand Rapids: Eerdmans, 1986), 15.
142 Stanley Hauerwas, *Unleashing the Scripture: Freeing the Bible from Captivity to America* (Nashville: Abingdon, 1993), 64, 72.
143 Murray, *We Hold These Truths*, 288.
144 Elsewhere I have examined the place of natural law thinking in the magisterial reformers – viz. Luther, Melanchthon, Calvin, Zwingli, and Bullinger – wherein it is firmly ensconced. See J. Daryl Charles, "Burying the Wrong Corpse: Evangelicals and Natural Law," in Jesse Covington, Bryan McGraw and Micah Watson, eds., *Natural Law and Evangelical Political Thought* (see n. 132), 3–34, and J. Daryl Charles, "Natural Law and the Protestant Prejudice," *Retrieving the Natural Law*, 111–55 (Chapter 4). See as well Stephen J. Grabill's important work *Rediscovering the Natural Law in Reformed Theological Ethics*, noted previously, which, inclusive of Calvin, profiles representative thinking in Protestant orthodoxy up to the mid-eighteenth century. It needs emphasizing that the reformers are clear and unequivocal in their affirmation of the natural law, even when it is not a major theme in their writings collectively.
145 Hugo Grotius, *The Rights of War and Peace*, 3 vols., ed. and trans. Richard Tuck and Jean Barbeyrac (Indianapolis: Liberty Fund, 2005) 1.10.
146 Ibid.
147 Ibid.
148 So David Novak, "Privacy," in David F. Forte, ed., *Natural Law and Contemporary Public Policy* (Washington, DC: Georgetown University Press, 1998), 21.
149 Ibid.
150 *Catechism of the Catholic Church* no. 9.
151 Murray, *We Hold These Truths*, 320.
152 Perhaps the most thorough examination of the symbiosis between faith and reason can be found in the final encyclical of John Paul II, *Fides et Ratio*, published in 1998. See https://w2.vatican.va/content/john-paul-ii/en/encyclicals/documents/hf_jp-ii_enc_14091998_fides-et-ratio.html.
153 So Forte, "The Natural Law Moment," 4.

3 Religious freedom, natural law, and the American experiment

In their important anthology *The Forgotten Fathers on Religion and Public Life*, Daniel L. Dreisbach, Mark David Hall, and Jeffry H. Morrison the editors observe two general deficits when one surveys the almost boundless scholarship devoted to America's founding.[1] First, there is the inclination of scholars to focus on the elite and more prominent figures, usually a cast of five characters – Washington, Franklin, Madison, (John) Adams, and Jefferson. The flip side of this presentation is the neglect of other important, though less prominent, figures – individuals such as John Witherspoon, James Wilson, George Mason, Samuel Adams, John Jay, Edmund Randolph, Benjamin Rush, and Roger Sherman. While the reasons for this prioritizing are understandable, they invite important questions.

Second, one detects the scholarly tendency to discount or downplay the role of religion in the founders' and framers' political thought and in the world of which they were a part. In the words of one cultural historian,

> It would seem wildly implausible that American historical scholarship over the years has largely neglected the study of religion. Yet it is sadly true. Aside from a handful of moments in American history . . ., precious little in the story of American history that survives in our standard text books even hints at the strong and abiding religiosity of the American people.[2]

This neglect is perhaps as we might expect, given the increasing secularization of American society that has characterized the last 125 years. Where historical scholarship has in fact acknowledged the role of religion, the focus of discussion and debate has typically been the nature of the founders' religious belief – orthodox versus heterodox, deist versus Christian, Calvinist versus non-Calvinist – or the character of their *privately* held religious views. What is often missing, whether this omission is witting or unwitting, is the power and depth of these beliefs and the very *public expressions* of those beliefs to the extent that they influenced the political culture of the day and helped safeguard the institutions that guaranteed religious freedom.[3] It is accurate to maintain that several generations of scholarship have "thoroughly misconstrued the high achievements of the founding generation with respect to religious liberty." Many political and legal historians are seemingly "bewildered by . . . the extensive practical accommodations between religion and state" that the founders strained to realize.[4]

A further, related tendency has characterized conventional scholarship of the founding era. That is its relative failure to grasp the unique manner, among religions of the world, in which both Judaism and Christianity presuppose the importance of freedom of conscience. In fact, it is accurate to argue that Christianity introduced – if it did not strengthen in Hebrew religion –certain dimensions of social and cultural life not found in the classical pagan world. Among these were monotheism, a concern for truth, two jurisdictions (religion as distinguished from the state), and the complement of interior and exterior virtue ("faith and works"). Together these elements would contain the seeds of freedom of conscience and religious freedom.[5] When contrasted with Islam (whether in its early, medieval, or contemporary expression), its differences are telling. These dissimilarities are profound, notably as they concern (a) the very notion of human dignity, (b) the manner in which divine freedom and human responsibility interact via moral agency), and (c) how religion and state co-exist in a non-theocratic arrangement so as to create "civil society" as we have come to understand it.

Let us pause for a moment to consider the differences. For example, Muslims do not – and in fact are *not permitted* to – speak of human beings as "made in the image of God"; such, for them, would be blasphemous, since *nothing* is the express image of God. Nor do Muslims speak conceptually of human freedom, inasmuch as they understand humans to be subordinated to God and his greatness. Correlatively, in Islam people do not "reason" their way to the truth; rather, they *submit* to it and are ostracized – even condemned to death – for "refusing" to submit to it.[6] In this sense, then, "natural law" as it is developed and understood in the Christian moral tradition, does not exist in Islam, since divine revelation is thought to account for everything that is morally required of the Muslim. And, in Islam, although Muslims do speak of justice, it is significant that they do *not* speak of the *love* of God. In the Christian tradition, by contrast, love of God and love of one's neighbor are united by human response and an act of the will, which suggests the importance of moral freedom.[7]

A final – and very crucial – example is sufficient to illustrate the two radically disparate conceptualizations of society. Consider the well-known saying from Jesus: "Render to Caesar the things that are Caesar's, and to God the things that are God's" (Matt. 22:15–22; Mark 12:13–17). The two realms represented hereby seem to co-exist, even when Jesus's words constitute an important barrier to the totalitarian state. According to Jesus, particular "service" with accompanying obligations, in a qualified way, is to be rendered to both spheres – a distinction that is impermissible, indeed unthinkable, in theocratic Islam. Here in Christ's teaching we have a partial rationale for the autonomy of church and state. Neither does religious belief deny the functions and role of the political authorities, nor does the state have the authority to coerce or restrict religious belief and religiously grounded practice.[8] The two realms intermingle, as the "two cities" imagery developed by St. Augustine in *Civitatis Dei* is meant to signify. In the words of one social historian,

> One can see in the American founding . . . the workings of a God who wishes to be worshiped in spirit and truth, in the honesty of conscience within, and in uncoerced exercise in the public square of daily life, among men and women who are free, independent, self-reliant, cooperative with one another in civil society, and responsible for their own destiny.[9]

Yet another curiosity – and lacunae in traditional scholarship – needs explanation. In standard accounts of the founders' political thinking, there seems a supreme reticence to acknowledge one of the most conspicuous features of the founders' understanding of human nature. I refer here to their *overwhelming* conviction that political power must be constrained and limited, and this due to the fact that human beings, in theological language, are "fallen" and "sinful." While evidence is plentiful to support the founders' broader thinking, two illustrations serve to make the point. One is a series of reflections offered by George Washington to John Jay – a neglected if not "forgotten" father – in August of 1786 ("Deficiencies of the Confederation") in which Washington expresses concerns about the need to balance coercive power and human freedom:

> We have probably had too good an opinion of human nature in forming our confederation. Experience has taught us, that men will not adopt and carry into execution, measures the best calculated for their own good without the intervention of a coercive power.

Commenting on human nature, he concludes, "Perfection falls not to the share of mortals."[10] The combined experience of leading American troops in the revolutionary war and an American presidency would surely inculcate this moral realism in Washington.

A second example of the founders' view of human nature lies with James Madison. A curious fact often overlooked in scholarly treatments of Madison is that his mentor was John Witherspoon,[11] the only clergyman among the signers of the Declaration of Independence. A delegate to the Second Continental Congress and an important thinker and statesman in his own right, Witherspoon served as the sixth President of the College of New Jersey (to become Princeton University) from 1768 until 1794 and, significantly, was against an established church for reasons of private judgment.[12]

Madison appears to have shared Witherspoon's thinking regarding both the disestablishment of religion and the perils of unrestrained authority due to human nature. Some historical commentators insist that Madison's anti-establishment sentiments stemmed from a similar source as those of

Jefferson – namely, a deistic tendency and rejection of Christian orthodoxy.[13] However, a serious reading of Madison suggests something quite different: his anti-establishment sentiments were rooted in the virtue of religious freedom and the "sacred rights" of conscience.[14] Indeed, Madison appears to have been as much an heir to the Christian tradition, with deep sensitivities to religious tolerance, as he was a son of the Enlightenment.[15] Unquestionably, this realm of shared understanding between Madison and Witherspoon – a belief in human fallenness – has received far less scholarly attention than their anti-establishment sentiments. Yet, it is fundamental to understanding Madison. Take, for example, his oft-cited observation, recorded in Federalist #51, that "if men were angels, no government would be necessary." As the context indicates, Madison was concerned about balance:

> If angels were to govern men, neither external nor internal controls on government would be necessary. In framing a government which is to be administered by men over men, the great difficulty lies in this: you must first enable the government to control the governed; and in the next place oblige it to control itself. A dependence on the people is, no doubt, the primary control on the government; but experience has taught mankind the necessity of auxiliary precautions.[16]

Strangely, in the American context such an understanding of human nature would even be shared by deists and (purported) atheists in their midst. Mirroring this consensual thinking of the founders, the U.S. Constitution is meticulous in its delineation of powers and specifying of checks and balances, even when it is couched in non-theological language. But we need to pause and ask, *Whence comes this mode of thinking?* What is the source of this sort of moral "realism?" Such is by no means the fruit of "Enlightenment rationalism," the assumption of which undergirds most scholarly treatments of this era. This anthropological wisdom, coupled with the founders' and framers' reflection on (and reaction to) European excesses, caused the founding generation to think and act, politically, with a moral realism that *commends itself to every successive generation.* And it calls for our engagement as well.

More recent literature has demonstrated a greater willingness to address several of the aforementioned deficiencies, and particularly the role that religion played in the political thinking of the founders and framers.[17] This is as it should be. Two things are striking about the panorama of this wider religious landscape. Recent scholarship has pointed not only toward the remarkable diversity that existed at the nation's founding – a diversity, it goes without saying, that was conspicuously Protestant in character[18] – but also toward notable areas of agreement among religious groups – agreement that would inform matters of polity in important ways. So much so, in fact, that Jefferson could later observe that the authority of Declaration of Independence rested on "the harmonizing sentiments of the day."[19]

Notwithstanding Maryland's founding in 1632 by Lord Baltimore and other Roman Catholics, Catholics became a minority in their own colony. Yet, even this minority "continued to benefit from the religious toleration that they had legislated."[20] All in all, religious diversity in colonial America was notable, even when some colonies and states had established religious identification. It is true that the development and growth of religious diversity was in many respects slow and painful; disestablishment was neither acknowledged nor welcomed by all. Nevertheless, one may speak of legitimate diversity – a diversity that included Anglicans and Episcopalians, Presbyterians, Congregationalists, Quakers, Lutherans, Baptists and Anabaptists, Moravians, Catholics, independents, Jews,[21] and, of course, deists and atheists as well.

The agreement that did exist among various religious groups, it needs emphasizing, is often clouded by the tendency among scholars and jurists to give disproportionate weight to founders who were unrepresentative.[22] Moreover, this "agreement" was shaped by the fact that most religious groups in early America were motivated by particular compelling images or visions as they applied to the nation's beginning, and these visions had an "integrating" effect on the nation. As a wide array of early American writings indicate, references to "covenant," "chosenness," "mission," "a city upon a hill," and even allusions to Moses stretching his hand toward the Red Sea and Israel in the wilderness were present from the earliest years among religiously diverse groups.[23] And these continued even up to the mid-nineteenth century.[24]

The fruit of recent historical scholarship suggests an important question for our consideration. Does it really matter that traditional scholarship has tended to focus on the "famous five"[25] and ignore or discount views of the more pious founders because they failed to leave much of a "paper trail" or, perhaps more importantly, because their ideas and actions were shaped by deeply held religious convictions? After all, most scholars have been trained, for better or for worse, to discount or overlook these elements, since they might offend our modern sensibilities. According to constitutional and legal historian Daniel L. Dreisbach, indeed it matters greatly, and for both symbolic as well as substantive reasons.[26]

To limit our vantage point to the "few and famous" is potentially to distort our understanding, to the extent that these individuals may not be representative of their peers. What's more, it is to slight the legacies of those founders who are not as famous. One's legacy, after all, depends chiefly on a paper trail that has been left behind for posterity, causing one political historian to wryly note, "Fame has not smiled on founders of few words."[27] This would indeed appear to be the case. Relatedly, this inattention obscures the founders' diverse backgrounds, perspectives, and biases, yielding an incomplete picture inasmuch as the contributions of the less famous were considerable. The resultant incomplete picture might suggest that the founders were more heterodox than they really were. More importantly, and of immense practical concern, the resultant distortions are not infrequently translated into modern law and policy, and as Dreisbach points out, judicial interpretations of the First Amendment well illustrate the problem. Consider, for example, the near exclusive reliance by the Supreme Court of the United States on the views of Jefferson and Madison.[28] But this interpretative practice might well be questioned, since (a) Jefferson was serving as foreign minister in France when the First Amendment was being framed (thereby relegating his influence to be indirect at best) and (b) Madison had suffered "decisive defeats" in his efforts to mold the actual content of the Amendment's religion provisions.[29]

In his important 2012 volume *The Religious Roots of the First Amendment: Dissenting Protestants and the Separation of Church and State*, Nicholas P. Miller argues that the Protestant theological commitment – particularly among dissenting Protestants – to the right of private judgment in matters of biblical interpretation (a corollary to the Protestant doctrine of the priesthood of all believers) led to a respect for individual conscience that propelled the ideas of religious liberty and disestablishment in the early modern era.[30] The burden of Miller's argument is to show religion's ideological contribution to the political culture of the day and to insist that the notion of religious freedom is owing to *religion* and *not* the Enlightenment, even when the two intertwine and are overlapping in their effects.

The typical story line, as summarized by Miller, is that in the eighteenth century, reason triumphed over faith. But this is mistaken, Miller insists. Rather, a more accurate telling of the American founding is that faith and reason work in symbiosis, not mutual exclusion. In early America, the disestablishment impulse was decidedly religious in nature, not secular – or even narrowly political, for that matter.[31] Religious groups exerted the greatest influence in the shaping and evolving of this impulse. Even the more "theocratic" and establishment-minded colonies of New England, in time, would adopt a more moderate position – a position that was displayed in Virginia in particular and then among the other states over time.[32]

But what contributes to these two very different tellings of the founding narrative? On what assumptions do they proceed? And why has the "secularist"[33] version been so compelling, not only among social, political, and legal historians but also at the popular level as well? At this point, we shall need to consider these two narratives more closely, if we hope to acquire a more accurate understanding of the roots of religious freedom in our own cultural history.

A tale of two narratives: religious freedom in America's founding

The conventional narrative

The present volume began by noting that religious freedom, both around the world and in Western nations, is in trouble – serious trouble. Most assuredly, one of the reasons for this dilemma is that its intellectual underpinnings are misunderstood or greatly neglected. More recently, Matthew J. Franck, Director of the William E. and Carol G. Simon Center on Religion and the Constitution at the Witherspoon Institute, in a most telling fashion has contrasted two narratives of America's founding,[34] not unlike what Nicholas Miller has attempted to demonstrate. One origin narrative Franck calls "The Myth of the Secular Enlightenment," while the second is devoted to "The Religious Basis of Religious Freedom." A re-telling of the basic contours of these two narratives, as Franck views it, is instructive.

The standard account that is widely disseminated today is that religious freedom was the creation of the secular Enlightenment.[35] On this understanding, it was a phenomenon that sprang "fully grown from the brow of Thomas Jefferson,"[36] even when its genesis might be traced to earlier reformers such as Pierre Bayle and John Locke. Here we find religious liberty to be fruit of reflection on religious violence that had ravaged Europe during episodes such as the Thirty Years' War. According to this narrative, those thinkers who gave birth to the notion of religious freedom were notably secular, deist, or irreligious individuals "who preached a rigorously secular politics of radical individualism, in which religion is essentially privatized."[37] Since such is a common component in the conventional re-telling of the narrative and since this legacy is frequently associated – in one way or another – with the "famous five," it behooves us to consider the evidence.

Many historians of the early American era proceed on the belief that the American regime was founded on ideological pre-commitments of Enlightenment rationalism. This particular view rests *inter alia* on certain assumptions about the "wall" of separation between church and state, on the absence of any religious affirmations or biblical citations in the framers' charter documents, and on the purported "deistic" references to the divine in the nation's charter documents.[38] What makes the debate, to the present day, so interesting and compelling is that it serves as a mirror of ongoing division to the present day among scholars of America's founding.[39] Was the American founding based on a publicly shared sense of religious conviction that had its roots in Christian belief, or was it, rather, a far more "secular affair" – one that was grounded in the principles and assumptions of enlightened deism?[40]

While it is supremely difficult to identify the "doctrinal core" of deism as a metaphysical framework, what can be said of its constitution, in very general terms, is that it is a philosophical orientation that rejects revelatory authority as a source of religious knowledge. It fashions itself according to a particular understanding of reason, whereby human rational powers concerning the cosmos are sufficient to understand the nature of the Creator. What it rejects is the supernatural element of revealed religion such as one finds in the Christian scriptures. The rise of this moderating and freethinking orientation in eighteenth-century England would find a peculiar form in early America, where it often manifested itself in a mix of providential deistic assumptions about a transcendent Creator and revealed Christianity. In early American history, those individuals who embraced a deistic framework were "decidedly not anti-Christian," much in contrast to their English counterparts.[41]

In the end, the "militant deism" of individuals such as Thomas Paine "never really threatened mainstream Protestantism in early American."[42] The presence and influence of deist founders would appear not to have been sufficient enough to support the claim by some scholars that the founding was a "secular affair." We may grant that if the "famous five" described earlier were in fact deists of a more militant type, then the argument that Christianity played a major role in the political thinking of the founders is undermined. The evidence suggests, however, quite the opposite. Moreover, the evidence of the "forgotten fathers" points overwhelmingly in the direction of Christianity's influence in the political thinking of most. In the words of one political historian,

> The Christianity that served as a founding creed in the new nation was a remarkably "big tent" affair, including Calvinists and Quakers, evangelicals and Universalists, and Unitarians and fundamentalists. Evidently, the tent was so capacious as to even comfortably accommodate the odd Deist.[43]

At bottom, commentators tend to prefer either a "secular" interpretation of the Republic or a "providentialist" interpretation. But this is an oversimplification; it is more accurate to speak of a blending of the two elements in the thinking of the founders.

But we have digressed somewhat. A chief assumption – and major implication – tied to the conventional story is that religion is a source of controversy, conflict, and division in society and that it impinges upon a pluralism of beliefs that is necessary for political purposes. The options, then, thus seen, are twofold in terms of polity. One is to recognize an officially established church that receives its sanction from the state. The other is to ensure that religion is isolated and insulated from political life. This second option appears to be the only "reasonable" alternative, at least by the assumptions of secular liberalism.

Taking their cues from this wider narrative, most historians of U.S. history and judicial theorists would argue that the establishment clause of the First Amendment mirrors this second solution, removing religion and religious beliefs from the public sphere and keeping the public sphere "neutral" – which is to say, *bleached* of divisive positions and viewpoints that might intrude into political life. Strengthened by the observation that the U.S. Constitution *per se* does not reference religion, this interpretation understands "separation" of church and state as absolute and inviolable rather than restrictive and allowing citizens in a pluralistic society to rub against one another, agree or disagree, and contend in the public sphere. Again, the underlying assumption here is that religious belief is divisive and corrosive in its effects, given its purported "irrational" constitution. In fact, this narrative ends up pitting reason and faith against one another, which has the consequence of making society religiously indifferent and relegating religion to the private sphere, where it does not interfere with political matters and cannot do harm to "civil society." So construed, the state becomes the guarantor of basic "freedoms," with "the Church," churches, and religious belief in general being viewed as that which *undermines* rather than fortifies the "common good."

Retelling the narrative

A second American "origins" narrative proceeds under different assumptions. The heart of its telling is that "the principles of religious freedom grew, not without pain and struggle, out of Jewish and Christian reflection on the human person as a being endowed with dignity that is stamped on its nature as *imago Dei*, made in the image of God."[44] While this rehearsal of early American history does not deny or negate the contributions of people like Locke, and while it resists the temptation to "christianize" the influential founders, it understands the roots of religious freedom to be much deeper than the seventeenth century (or even the Protestant Reformation of the sixteenth century, for that matter). It anchors the notion of religious freedom in the wider Judeo-Christian tradition, wherein it is understood that faith and conviction can never be coerced but rather are the fruit of moral freedom and the "sacred" rights of conscience.

This re-telling of the story of religious freedom in America restores to their pride of place an almost endless cavalcade of religious heroes in our own national history. These include Roger Williams and William Penn, as well as the Quakers, the Baptists, and the Methodists of the two Great Awakenings in the eighteenth and nineteenth centuries, the Anabaptists, Bishop John Carroll, Mormons, and Jews. And in this re-telling we encounter, once again, the distinctively Western contribution to human rights and human flourishing, "and thus, inescapably, a Christian contribution" to it as well.[45] Barry Alan Shain, in probing whether the founders' generation was chiefly "Enlightened" or "Protestant," criticizes what he calls "unreliable historical accounting" not only because it has "falsely reified Enlightenment secularism into America's chosen political ideology" but also because "a long, rich, and authentic tradition of American political thought has been rendered falsely illegitimate and 'un-America.' "[46] "America's democratic and localist Reformed Protestant inheritance," he insists, "is its most enduring political tradition." This is true even when American intellectual historians and "intolerant secularists" tend to give it short shrift.[47]

Frequently overlooked by the first "origins" narrative, as Franck argues, is the development of "American constitutionalism," which, he insists, "owes much its success and longevity to the religious impulses of the American people."[48] That is to say, what has been praiseworthy and advantageous to American civil polity came about *not in spite of but because of* Americans' religious faith. One may argue, then, that our charter documents, which declare all to be "created equal" with "inalienable rights" that have been "endowed by the Creator" and assert that these truths that are anchored in the "law of nature and nature's God," are in fact a mirror of those religious convictions. A belief in the intrinsic dignity of every person turns out to anchor the most important aspects of civil polity and public policy that a democratic regime might enact. In theological terms, this understanding of "religious freedom" proceeds from an awareness of human beings as the *imago Dei*. At bottom, justice needs such a foundation in which to inhere; equality and justice are "rootless human preferences" apart from something that transcends human experience.[49] Without this understanding, "inalienable rights" become "alienable" and shift according to trends, the social climate, or a person's functionality and social utility. It is the religious impulse which acknowledges the source of our most basic rights to be transcendent; only in this way can we insist that human rights are *pre-political*, and hence cannot be adjudicated by government or competing claims in the public sphere.[50]

Another corrective to the first narrative is in order. It concerns the place of religious faith in Locke's political thought, given the founders' debt to Lockean presuppositions about moral law, human nature, political governance, and non-coercion in religious matters. Not infrequently, Locke's views are bleached of their Christian influence in the recounting of the tale as told by narrators of secular liberalism. We may surely grant that tracing ideological influences and roots, be they political or theological, can be a notoriously complicated task. After all, most people are eclectic in their "belief system." More importantly, all people go through particular stages in the development of their thinking; to say that people "evolve" in their thinking is simply to state the obvious. And not infrequently these stages seem to be diametrically opposed to one another, as Locke himself well illustrates, given the shift in his understanding of the magistrate's role in regulating religion.

It is well known that Locke grew up in an environment shaped by Calvinist theological thinking. Not a few historians and scholars proceed on the assumption that John Locke was at odds with this tradition. The result is that in noting the influence of Lockean thinking on the founders, their scholarship assumes a conspicuously secular cast, with a coloring of individual rights, government by consent, the right to resist tyranny, and religious tolerance that is interpreted by the lens of "secular liberalism."[51] One of the tendencies of much historical scholarship is that it minimizes the religious voice – at times the Reformed or Calvinist voice, at times the dissenting Protestant voice – to be found in Locke.[52] Rarely is it acknowledged that Locke gives expression to both.[53]

Based on the literary evidence from the founders, political historian Mark David Hall concludes, "By the 1760s, American leaders were familiar with Locke, but *few thought [that] his political philosophy was at odds with traditional Christian or Calvinist political ideas.*"[54] A principal piece of evidence for this, as adduced by Hall, is the Reformed clergy's willingness to cite Locke in public contexts such as sermons and pamphlets. To the objection that the clergy's use of Locke is evidence of a "Lockean conquest" or Lockean *repudiation* of Puritan political thought,[55] Hall responds that most Reformed-minded ministers to this time, in addition to being well educated,[56] in fact had promoted political ideas that were consonant to those of Locke. Why is it, Hall asks, that virtually no Reformed ministers were objecting to the use of Locke by fellow Calvinists?[57] The issue here is not to deny points of tension between Locke and Calvinism; clearly, they exist. It is only to emphasize what is often neglected (if not dismissed) in historical scholarship.[58] In addition to the use of theological language, one of those neglects is the clear emphasis in Lockean thought on natural moral law.

It is fair to maintain, as Nicholas P. Miller argues, that most Americans, both before and after the 1760s, "absorbed" Locke's political ideas along with Christian influence.[59] Which is to say that "natural rights" and "liberty" go hand in hand with the gospel; the two spheres need not be relegated purely and solely to either "enlightenment rationalism" or Christianity.[60] Baptists and Quakers in particular showed this to be case, as the work of Isaac Backus – author of *A Seasonable Plea for Liberty of Conscience* (1770) and *An Appeal to the Public for Religious Liberty, Against the Oppressions of the Present Day* (1773) – and Locke's direct connection to William Penn[61] and Quaker interests in the 1670s and 80s well illustrate. In *A Seasonable Plea* we find Backus directly alluding to Locke's *Letter on Toleration* as he sets forth his understanding of the role of governing authorities and the "right" of religious freedom.[62] Following Roger Williams, Baptists sought shelter from Puritan excesses in New England and were an enthusiastic minority wherever they were planted in early America. The same can be argued of Quakers as well. Although we have no official record of Penn and Locke interacting, it is "quite likely" that Penn would have been tutored by Locke at Oxford.[63] While Locke may be called the theoretician of religion freedom, others sought to implement it in early America.

Locke's views, to be sure, were radically progressive for his time, and yet it is not uncommon for social and political historians to either ignore – or at least downplay – his assumptions about religious faith or to assume that Locke moved away from the theistic assumptions of his religious upbringing. Undeniably, his views on the civil magistrate evolved, permitting us to distinguish between an "earlier" Locke (seen, for example, in *Two Tracts of Government* and Locke's willingness to allow the magistrate to impose restrictions on religious freedom out of fear that people will not know where to stop[64]) and a "later" Locke (seen, for example, in *Essay on Human Understanding* and *Letter on Toleration*). It is likely that this evolution was the fruit of Locke's contact and interaction with religious dissenters of his day.[65] In *Letter*, Locke is more resolute in his insistence that the magistrate can neither legislate nor coerce on religious matters.

Reading Locke, one encounters ample evidence of his theological precommitments, which frequently go unnoticed or are ignored by tellers of the "first" narrative of the American founding. Consider one example, taken from Locke's argument in *Second Treatise of Government*, Chapter 2:

> The state of nature has a law of nature to govern it, which obliges every one: and reason, which is that law, teaches all mankind, who will but consult it, that being all equal and independent, no one ought to harm another in his life, health, liberty, or possessions: for *men being all the workmanship of one omnipotent, and infinitely wise maker; all the servants of one sovereign master, sent into the world by his order, and about his business; they are his property, whose workmanship they are, made to last during his, not one another's pleasure.*[66]

Yet another adjustment to the secular narrative of the American founding, already intimated at the beginning of this chapter, needs our attention. It concerns the founders' collective view both of human dignity and human depravity. Consider once more the language of the Declaration of Independence – that "all men are created equal"; that "they are endowed by their Creator with certain unalienable rights"; that, to secure these rights, "governments are instituted among men, deriving their just powers from the consent of the governed"; and that "whenever any form of government becomes destructive of these ends, it is the right of the people to alter or abolish it." Take note, for the moment, of the important undergirding themes: human dignity, human rights that are unalienable, and limited government. What view of human nature is lodged behind these assertions? And what did the founders perhaps fear the most?

Social visions, whether for better or for worse, differ in their basic conceptions of human nature. In his important – though very much neglected – work *A Conflict of Visions: Ideological Origins of Political Struggles*,[67] Thomas Sowell contrasts two competing understandings of human nature that animate the public sphere. He calls these the "constrained" and "unconstrained" visions.[68] On Sowell's telling, the "unconstrained" vision found fertile soil in which to grow during the "age of reason" and continues to endure, expressing itself in countless ways in human society. Characteristic of this mode of thinking is the belief in unlimited (and untapped) human potential – an anthropological optimism, if you will. As such, human nature is viewed as "unconstrained" in that this view does not presuppose egocentrism as constitutive, and hence a fundamental flaw, of human psychology. Rather, human nature is improvable, and in fact, "perfectible" to an unlimited degree. And where self-interest does manifest itself, it is to be understood as the result of circumstances and not an invariable law of human nature.

The "constrained" vision of human nature, for Sowell, stands in stubborn contrast. Thereby it is understood that the moral limitations of man and his egocentricity in particular are "inherent facts of life,"[69] facts which necessarily "constrain" our vision of what comprises "civil society" and what should be expected from government in its essence. Therefore, the main social challenge is to make the best of this arrangement, based on a moral realism, rather than "dissipate [our] energies in an attempt to change human nature."[70] Sowell cites Edmund Burke, roughly contemporary to the founding era, who perhaps best summarized the "constrained" vision from a political vantage point when he spoke of the presence of "a radical infirmity in all human contrivances."[71] Consequently, prudence, or practical wisdom, is of utmost importance for those embracing the "constrained" vision – indeed, for Burke, it was "the first of all virtues."[72]

As Sowell observes, the great evils of the world such as war, poverty, and crime for starters – are viewed in completely different terms by those with "unconstrained" and "constrained" visions. If human options are not inherently constrained, "then the presence of such repugnant and disastrous phenomena virtually cries out for explanation – and for solutions."[73] Because in the unconstrained vision of human nature there are no intractable causes of social evils, there is no reason why they cannot be solved.[74]

What view of human nature undergirded the founders' and framers' thinking? The evidence is overwhelming that what they feared the most was a view of government and society that either discounted or understated the human propensity for self-interest and the abuse power. Presupposing human fallenness, they were convinced of the perils of concentrated political power. It is for this reason that the Constitution is detailed and exacting in its delineation of lines of authority as well as of checks and balances to those authorities that have been established. Similarly, the authors of *The Federalist Papers* were supremely conscious of the need for checks and balances. "It may be a reflection on human nature that such devices should be necessary to control the abuses of government," one reads in Federalist #51. "But *what is government itself but the greatest of all reflections on human nature*?"[75] Not "perfectibility," but *imperfection* is the *esse* of what it means to be human. "Why has govern been instituted at all?" the *Federalist* asks rhetorically. "Because the passions of men will not conform to the dictates of reason and justice *without constraint*," is the answer.[76]

The "constrained" vision, alas, is a "tragic" vision of the human condition. It is "tragic" not in the sense of something to be avoided or denied but rather in the sense of moral and political realism. It is tragic insofar as it is *true*; therefore, public policy should mirror its reality. Sowell, I would argue, is correct: "how human nature is conceived at the outset is highly correlated with the whole conception of knowledge, morality, power, time, rationality, war, freedom and law which defines a social vision."[77]

What insights or lessons, then, might be gleaned from our acknowledgment of the second "origins" narrative? In what ways might it serve as a necessary corrective? Several invite our consideration. One, as the preceding discussion sought to make clear, is a "moral realism" that must inform our understanding of human nature, human institutions, human government in particular, and public policy. It follows from this that both human dignity, with its commitment to protect basic human "rights" or freedoms, and human fallenness, with its propensity for denying those fundamental rights, are to be reckoned with in the affairs of men and nation. Another is that religion and the religious viewpoint are to be both reasonably understood and welcomed in the public sphere. In the American context, this has been so from the beginning, and exclusion of the religious viewpoint is only a product of the recent past. This acceptance, of course, does not mean (or require) that there has been in the past or must be in the future a uniformity of religious viewpoints. But the fact that many chose, and continue to choose, to live as one society – *E pluribus unum* – is itself evidence that religious belief has always been a part of public life in this nation. This foundation furnishes an authentic pluralism, what we may rightly call a "principled" pluralism. Contrary to secular fundamentalism, principled pluralism facilitates genuine plurality. The founders offer us an important reminder: plurality and commonality are not mutually exclusive.

Churches and religious groups, unless and until they violate the public order,[78] become, in the words of Franck, "the paradigm case of voluntary association, with none preferred over others."[79] At the same time, churches are not just *any* voluntary association, and hence they deserve a unique constitutional protection – that is, a certain measure of autonomy without exclusion. But why? Why a "unique protection?" Before my response, which proceeds in the following section, permit me to suggest a fundamental distinction between "unique protection" and "government support." I thus concur with Madisonian thinking in maintaining "separation" of religion and the state – *if*, that is, we qualify the nature of this separation so that it does not equate to exclusion or hostility toward religion and religious institutions.

Just as the first American Revolution marked a break from traditional monarchy in political-philosophical terms, the second – as it concerned religious freedom – would mirror a new way of thinking about the relationship of government and religion. In this light, then, we must re-visit the fundamental notion of "separation," as it was debated then and is disputed now. Such, it is hoped, will bring a bit of clarity to an exceedingly controversial, and exceedingly misunderstood, idea.

Revisiting the "wall of separation"

Rethinking church-state relations

In his important book *Designing a Polity: America's Constitution in Theory and Practice*, political philosopher James W. Ceaser argues that one of the greatest threats to American society today is what might be called "political non-foundationalism." Advocates of this outlook – and they are legion, including celebrated thinkers such as John Rawls, Richard Rorty, Jacques Derrida, and Jürgen Habermas – hold that "liberal democracy is best maintained by renouncing public reliance on any kind of first principle (or 'foundation') that claims to embody an objective truth – something, for example, like the 'laws of nature' invoked in the Declaration of Independence."[80] Regardless of their differences, Ceaser points out, these influential theorists stand united in rejecting metaphysical notions – or "comprehensive doctrines," to use Rawls's term – and joining together with tenacity in "seeking to erect a high wall of separation between foundations and politics."[81] Moreover, for such theorists, this "high wall" cannot be high enough in their understanding of church-state relations.[82]

But this "non-foundational" posture, as Ceaser reminds us, is a creation of the recent past and departs from the vision of the founders and framers. William Lee Miller agrees, noting a significant feature of church-state relations in *The First Liberty: America's Foundations in Religious Freedom*:

> The separating of church and state certainly has not meant – despite some shrill cries that it should – the separating of religion from politics. Far from it. Churches and church-goers have been active in American politics and social policy on explicit religious grounds from the American Revolution through . . . the Civil Rights movements.[83]

The First Amendment to the U.S. Constitution reads, "Congress shall make no law respecting an establishment of religion, or prohibiting the free exercise thereof." More familiar to most Americans than First Amendment language, however, is the language of "separation of church and state." "No phrase in American letters has more profoundly influenced discourse and policy on church-state relations than Jefferson's 'wall of separation,'" writes Daniel L. Dreisbach, author of *Thomas Jefferson and the Wall of Separation between Church and State*.[84] But if "separation of church and state" indeed does not mean a separation (and exclusion) of religion from politics and public life (which it clearly did not mean to the founders), then what *does* it mean?[85] How is it to be construed rightly? What if the Amendment, in fact, differs in its trajectory from Jefferson's image, or from the conventional understanding of that image (which has become far more recognizable to the American public than the Amendment itself)? What if the "wall" constructed by the modern courts and legal commentators is different from the "wall" described by Jefferson, and a wrong construal of the First Amendment?[86] What, then, *were* the views of the founders and framers? And, despite their vehement disagreements, in what specifically were their unified?

A judicious reading of the founders makes it quite clear that, in the late eighteenth century, there was *no single model* of understanding relations between church and state. Americans of the founding era were divided about separating church and state, with some strongly favoring state-supported religion and others opposed to it. The founders, writes Kurt Lash, "had been anything but unanimous about the dangers of a union between church and state and had not intended to express any such nonestablishment value."[87] As Dreisbach notes, by the time of independence, "there was growing disagreement as to what constituted an 'establishment of religion,' and church-state arrangements in the former colonies were in transition."[88] In fact, the very definition of "establishment" varied from region to region and even denomination to denomination.[89] Madison, Washington, and Jefferson themselves, for all the profundity of their thought and their status, disagreed about the proper relationship of church and state. And while they agreed that religious freedom was a "natural right" and that the state must safeguard religious liberty, they disagreed about what those rights consisted of and how they ought to be protected constitutionally.[90] After all, each of the colonies possessed its own particular religious character and history, and thus, its own understanding of how church and state should interact. Madison, by way of illustration, supported religious freedom for different reasons than did Jefferson. For the latter, a free people are guided by science and reason. For the former, freedom is important because of the potential for encroachment by both religion and the state and because of the "sacred" character of private judgment.[91]

Attitudes, however, would be shifting in the decades to come, and the last holdout – Massachusetts – would abandon its established church in 1833. What the founders *did* share in common, despite their disagreements, was the consensual view that moral and political foundations are just that – underpinnings that are *foundational* to the health and vibrancy of American polity. "Laws of nature," "self-evident truths," "inalienable rights," and "endowment by the Creator," alas, are not mere theoretical constructs invented by the more analytical of the founders and framers and detached from the practical workings of a regime. To the contrary, they express metaphysical realities that bear on the very essence of an ordered republic. Hence, religion could never be anything but foundational to the American experiment.[92] And here one might trace Locke's influence again, particularly his *natural law* "metaphysic," which the founders readily affirm but which much modern scholarship has tended to ignore.

In reflecting further on what the founders and framers held in common, we find among them a general consensus that valued qualified individual autonomy, resulting in their opposing the restriction of personal religious belief. At the same time, this opposition was qualified. That is, while they favored the protection of religious beliefs, even those of a dissenting nature, they also understood the need to regulate the expression of those beliefs if and where they impeded the public order. What had history taught them? An important – and often painful – lesson was to avoid one dominant religious voice that suppressed or oppressed others. This meant, in the end, stretching the limits of toleration as the founders understood them, tolerating "the Jew and the Gentile, the Christian and the Mahometan, the Hindoo, and infidel of every denomination."[93] On the other hand, one could argue, as one commentator has done, this was "no empty ceremonial deism"[94] inasmuch as this was an experiment in "ordered liberty," by which the *plural* needed to be regulated if it was to be *one*.

One may therefore agree with Thomas S. Kidd that the First Amendment was a triumph for *both* dissenting evangelical types and the "enlightenment rationalists." That is to say, both groups did their part in preventing the national government from giving preferences to one religious group at the expense of others, on the one hand, and excluding the religious voice or practicing religious persecution, on the other. In the words of Kidd, "More liberal champions of religious freedom, such as Madison, played essential roles as political leader, but the popular momentum for religious freedom and disestablishment came primarily from rank-and-file evangelicals, especially Baptist."[95] This "both . . . and . . ." understanding of religious freedom in the founding era is underscored by Mark David Hall, who writes that even when James Madison was a "driving force" behind the Bill of Rights, the document was, in the end, "a product of community" – a community that included members of Reformed[96] and evangelically minded churches, including Roger Sherman, Oliver Ellsworth, Fisher Ames, Benjamin Huntington, Elias Boudinot, William Paterson, and Fisher Ames. All of these individuals, Hall reminds us, played important roles in serving on committees and participating in debates.[97] What's more, as Hall points out, none of these men advocated anything approximating a strict (or "impenetrable") "wall of separation" between church and state; all were convinced, in fact, that states and local municipalities should encourage religion.[98]

Rethinking the notion of "separation"

The founders' and framers' declarations expressed in the First Amendment – disestablishment and free exercise of religion – in important ways defied centuries of assumptions regarding church and state that were inherited from the European tradition.[99] Their wisdom can be seen in their refusal to either *pre*scribe or *pro*scribe religion. In the words of one constitutional scholar, '[t]he cumbersome and inelegant answer, it seems, is that the clauses [of the First Amendment] came to reflect and express acceptance of these commitments as a result of two complicated changes that have taken place over the course of American history."[100] Of this consensus constitutional scholar Stephen D. Smith, author of *The Rise and Decline of American Religious Freedom*, writes,

> What we can say with confidence is that both notions – freedom of the church and separation of church and state – resonate with the classical and Christian idea of dual jurisdictions . . . [and of] the independence of spiritual and secular authorities.

The two clauses and jurisdictions are "of one piece."[101]

As reiterated by the 1988 Williamsburg Charter, the establishment clause and the free exercise clause are "mutually reinforcing provisions that act as a double guarantee of religious liberty."[102] But given the varied interpretations in our day of the First Amendment and the meaning of the two clauses, it is useful to rehearse the assumptions that informed this dual perspective:

- The duties and obligations we owe the Creator can be directed only by reason and conviction, not coercion; this conviction must be left to every individual and as such is a right that is "unalienable" and "sacred."

- If society cannot regulate this conviction in individuals, much less can – and should – a legislative body; such would amount to "tyranny."
- All human beings are equal. Therefore, all possess equal rights, even minorities, and to violate these rights constitutes political oppression.[103]
- The "establishment" of religion by the state is not needed for support,[104] as Christianity itself teaches.[105] It flourishes on its own.
- Almost 15 centuries of Western history, quarrelsome and controversy-laden to say the very least, have provided evidence of two realms or "offices" – whether depicted as the "two cities," "two powers," "two swords," or "two kingdoms" – which co-mingle yet are distinct.[106]
- Just government protects the rights of conscience in its citizenry; it does not "establish" what is "sacred" and a "natural right."
- "Establishment" alienates the citizenry and disturbs social harmony,[107] and it tends to undermine the vibrancy of religious faith itself.[108]
- "Disestablishment" not only denotes non-coercion but also signifies, on the one hand, government not meddling with religious institutions and religious beliefs, and on the other hand, clerics not serving as politicians.[109]
- "Free exercise" is a gift of "nature and nature's God," and hence, a sacred right. Because conscience is ordered to the truth, it is "sacred" and hence to be respected.
- The founders wished to protect the free exercise of religion in the various states, and to that end, they insisted that the federal government could neither establish one religion nor abolish established religions in the states. Never did they imagine *excluding* religion from *public life*; indeed, quite the opposite.
- "Tolerance" as it was understood in the eighteenth century was a foremost political virtue. "Tolerance" was *not* taken to be the belief that any proposition is as true as another; it acknowledged the fact that truth and error (co)exist. But because most people embrace partial truth and because we respect human dignity, we "tolerate" this mixture, even error itself when and where its effects do not undermine public life and the common good.
- Human nature is a mixture of dignity and depravity. Therefore, to concentrate too much power in the hands of too few is dangerous.
- Just laws and just relations proceed from an awareness of the natural moral law.
- Moral law is foundational to a virtuous and "self-governed" people.
- Democracy cannot survive without virtuous and self-governed citizens.

It is not uncommon for political and legal scholars to assume and argue that the establishment clause of the First Amendment was agnostic in its fundamental orientation toward religion when it was adopted. But this perspective tends to ignore the history leading up to the drafting and ratification of the First Amendment. In truth, neither the Constitution nor the First

Amendment *per se* was responsible for creating the American understanding of freedom of religion. Rather, both simply express a vision – a collective wisdom – that had evolved from a shared national experience at the time of America's founding.[110] The degree to which Washington, as the first president, sensed the sobriety of operating within this collective wisdom and tradition finds expression in his letter to Madison: "As the first of everything, in our situation will serve to establish a Precedent, it is devoutly wished on my part that these precedents may be fixed on true principles."[111]

A wall, a line, or a fence?

Much is made in conventional scholarship of Jefferson's famous letter to the Danbury Baptists in 1802, in which Jefferson utilizes the "wall" metaphor to encourage these Baptists in the state of Connecticut, where the Congregational Church was established. Several observations here are in order. One is that Jefferson was not the first to use the "wall" metaphor. The Baptist Roger Williams, 150 years earlier in the year 1643, had spoken of a "wall of separation" in a somewhat different manner than Jefferson – namely, as a means of protecting the integrity of religion. "Cultivating God's garden" is the language employed by Williams to denote corrupting influences of the world."[112] In fact, Williams was not even the first to employ the "wall" image. It appears already three generations after the Protestant Reformation in the work of Anglican apologist and political theorist Richard Hooker.[113] Jefferson's use of the "wall" metaphor was intended to reassure Baptists in Connecticut – and those like them – that the First Amendment prohibited the federal government from interfering with their religious exercise. Thus, it is inaccurate to contend or suggest that the "wall" metaphor was intended to remove religion from the public sphere – in *any* sense – or that the Danbury letter introduced a new concept into American constitutional understanding. Rather, the metaphor is best understood as a summary of the president's understanding of what the U.S. Constitution already had declared and accomplished.[114] In the words of Daniel Dreisbach, the "wall" was intended to underscore a "jurisdictional" or "structural" understanding of the First Amendment and separated "the federal regime on one side and ecclesiastical institutions and state governments on the other."[115] That is, the founders and framers were concerned, first and foremost, with preventing a national religious uniformity that might be dictated by the encroachment and intrusion of federal government, on the one hand, or the federal establishment of one particular church, on the other.

Following his own presidency two decades after Jefferson penned the Danbury letter, Madison himself wrote a letter that intended to summarize church-state relations, in a manner not wholly unlike Jefferson. Addressed to a clergyman, the letter cited no less than Martin Luther as an authority and is remarkable for its clarity and its judicious tone. Acknowledging the legitimacy and co-existence of both "offices" – the apparatus of the state and one's duties to God – Madison wrote that distinguishing between "what is due Caesar and what is due God," in the end,

> *best promotes* the discharge of *both* obligations. The experience of the United States is a happy disproof of the error so long rooted in the unenlightened minds of well-meaning Christians, as well as the corrupt hearts of persecuting usurpers, that without a legal *incorporation* of religious and civil policy, neither could be supported. A *mutual* independence is found most friendly to practical Religion, to social *harmony*, and to political prosperity.[116]

Madison's perspective on "separation" should be understood neither as exclusion, nor as alienation, nor as removal from protection. This can be seen in the language used – "best promotes," "incorporation," "mutual independence," "social harmony." The founders and framers feared divisiveness and sectarian violence, it is true. At the same time, they viewed religion as the source of virtue, without which a republic could not survive. Regardless of their strong disagreements about the precise nature of "religious freedom" and the state's role in facilitating such, they believed that government has a duty to help foster a healthy moral environment and consensus among a presumably "self-governed" people. This "protection," if you will, does not negate the "thinner" version of separation, by which the *relative* autonomy of church and state are affirmed. At the same time, neither does a "wall" capture with precision what the founders envisioned in terms of interaction between church and state. Here we concur with voices such as Daniel Dreisbach,[117] Mark David Hall,[118] and Michael I. Meyerson[119] that a "line" or a "fence" – another metaphor used by Jefferson[120] – might be a more apt metaphor for the relationship between church and state insofar as "relationships" do presuppose some form of interaction.[121] For these scholars, this conclusion finds confirmation *inter alia* in Madison's observations after 50 years of evidence that the American experiment was working, albeit with tentativeness: "I must admit," Madison adds with caution,

> That it may not be easy, in every possible case, to trace the *line of separation*, between the rights of Religion & the Civil authority, with such distinctness, as to avoid collusions & doubts on unessential points. The tendency to a usurpation on one side, or the other, or to a corrupting coalition or alliance between them, will be best guarded against by an entire abstinence of the Government from interference, in any way whatever, beyond the necessity of preserving public order, & protecting each sect against trespasses on its legal rights by others."[122]

The proper "relationship," then, as the founders and framers conceived of it – what Madison refers to as a "line of separation" – is achieved not by *excluding* churches and religious influence from the culture but by maintaining a *mutually understood independence*. This has the effect of "protecting" them; otherwise, government becomes hostile toward religion. This is, after all, the *other side* of the disestablishment coin as declared in the First Amendment.[123] The First Amendment "wall," hence, is permeable and not "impregnable,"[124] as is indicated by (a) precursors to Jefferson's use of the metaphor, (b) Jefferson's Danbury letter, and (c) the language and two-fold function of the First Amendment.[125] Chief Justice Warren Burger, representing the majority opinion in *Lynch v. Donnelly* (1984), that is, 37 years after Justice Hugo Black's majority opinion of *Everson v. Board of Education* (1947), offered the proper adjustment to Black's overreaching conclusion:

> The concept of a "wall" of separation between church and state is a useful metaphor but *is not an accurate description* of the practical aspects of the relationship that in fact exists. The Constitution does not require complete separation of church and state; it affirmatively mandates accommodation, not merely tolerance, of all religions, and forbids hostility toward any. Anything less would require the "callous indifference" that was never intended by the Establishment Clause.[126]

My own interpretation of the founders is that, in sharp contrast to the entrenched opinion of our own day, their world- and life-view understood religious belief to extend into all realms of human life and existence, and *most assuredly* into politics and civil society. They did not misconstrue the *institutional* separation between church and state in such a way as to create the false dichotomy between religion and so-called secular life. Unmistakably they viewed religion and religious belief as nothing short of all encompassing, exerting a necessary impact on all of public life.[127]

Religion and the state

Through its actions and laws and because of its fundamental nature, the state cannot ground freedom of conscience, freedom of religion, human rights, and the like. These are, as we have sought argue, *pre-political* in their constitution; they arise from the natural law and are propounded – and encouraged – by churches, voluntary groups ("mediating structures"), and society's religious impulse. This leaves us, logically, with three possibilities in terms of the interaction and church and state. One alternative is establishment, by which the state not only favors religion but also one particular expression of religion. And in the end it operates on the basis of coercion.[128] This option, notwithstanding various "establishment" sentiments in some colonies, the founders and framers, in the end, wished to reject. Another alternative is its polar opposite – i.e., alienation and exclusion. Thereby the state's official position is not merely not "protective"; it is one of open hostility toward religion in general and individual churches in particular. In the words of John Courtney Murray, "If the laws bear so heavily on a religious group as effectively to inhibit freedom of exercise," then "it may be shown that the state is hostile and thus breaching the principle of separation."[129]

The third option – qualified separation – seeks to avoid the excesses of both extremes and yet be attentive to the important distinction between exclusion and "neutrality" rightly construed – a distinction that today is often obscured or denied.[130] While an establishment of religion cannot adequately serve a nation dedicated to religious pluralism, the response of our courts and legal commentators – namely, that a complete or absolute disestablishment of religion is necessary – also cannot serve a people "so widely devoted to a public religion and a religious public."[131]

The wisdom of the founders can be parsed in very practical ways, and even in their wild disagreements, they embodied a collective insight and wisdom in their day. They had learned from the European experience – with its establishment of religion and frequently ensuing religious wars – and they were attentive to the lessons of wider history, by which the "offices" of religion and state are to be kept distinct. In embracing a "separation" between church and state the founders, in their own unique way, were "recovering and implementing" an ancient Christian ideal.[132] They understood that government does not – indeed *cannot* – form consciences or teach virtue. They understood the need for voluntary, mediating structures and authorities. And they well understood that people and institutions cannot be entrusted with too much power.

At bottom, religion serves to remind society and the magistrate that the state is not absolute and strictly autonomous; rather, the state exists *instrumentally* to serve society, and not vice versa. In addition, religious communities foster a wide array of voluntary associations and groups – other "mediating structures" – that constitute a healthy, vibrant civil society. And notwithstanding the shrill objections of our secularist friends, religion is the primary source for morality, whether we have in mind public virtue or private self-governance.[133] Religion exists *inter alia* to foster the common good.[134] Rehearsing and re-stating the wisdom of the founders is particularly critical in our day, given the "liberal monism"[135] by which seemingly all institutions – especially *religious* institutions – must conform to one single authority and according to which religion must be kept privatized and marginalized, since it is perceived to be "unreasonable." The founders, by contrast, were convinced that religion helped protect society against the mindlessness of the mob on the one hand and the oppressiveness of the state on the other.[136]

But surely some will object that religion should have *any* sort of special status in political life. Other reasons might be adduced in support of this claim. Among the most basic is the fact that religious freedom is the "first freedom" – it is *the guarantor of all other human freedoms* and inalienable rights. Religious belief, as someone has observed, "cannot be compelled because it is compelled already," that is to say, compelled "by our own best grasp of the truth." Viewed thusly, "religion is not so much chosen as it is accepted, as a truth one has discovered or has learned."[137] At bottom, human beings have a duty – an *ultimate* duty – to follow truth wherever it might lead, in recognition of "an authority that is higher than any that men and women can assert."[138] These duties "to the Creator," as Madison insists in his *Memorial and Remonstrance*, have "precedent" over all others, "both in time and in degree of obligation."[139] Madison's rationale is this: "Before any man can be considered as a member of Civil Society, he must be considered as a subject of the Governour of the Universe."[140] Madison, not unlike his mentor John Witherspoon, and not unlike many of the founding era, could speak of "Providence," "Creator," or "Maker" interchangeably. This pattern represents neither a sermonizing tendency on their part nor a designation bleached of theological substance. Rather, it mirrors the conviction – an eminently religious conviction – that God is involved in the affairs of men and nations.[141]

In sum, it is accurate to say that the pattern for church-state relations was never static in the Western cultural tradition. Yet, it has generally recognized two realms or spheres of authority that intersect in our common life – an intersection of dual jurisdictions that mirrored an ancient Christian, indeed Judeo-Christian, ideal. That age-old dialogue, often clashing and exceedingly controversial in nature, was enriched by the American experiment, which was the beneficiary of diverse and important philosophical and religious threads. At bottom, these diverse strands represented the conviction that outward coercion can never produce inner, genuine faith. This conviction, moreover, united a wide array of actors, including those who came to the New World, religious liberty dissidents like Roger Williams, William Penn, or Isaac Backus, as well as figures such as John Locke and James Madison. In the end, as Madison noted in his *Memorial and Remonstrance*, a qualified "separation" – let us call it a "wall" with gates, windows, and fences – was necessary both for the vitality of religion and for the tranquility of society. Without a proper understanding of the intersection between church and state, we fail to make sense of – and appreciate – religious freedom as an inalienable right and a protection against religious persecution. Church-state relations, as conceived by the founders and framers, *welcomed and protected the role of religion in public life*, allowing for the toleration of differing points of view that were uncoerced by state. The founders did not envision, nor would they have approved of, the bleaching or marginalizing of religion from the public sphere that has proceeded in our day.[142] Institutions cannot survive, much less operate effectively, where there are found no shared ethical convictions. The founders and framers surely would agree with Benedict XVI: "A culture and a nation that cuts itself off from the great ethical and religious forces of its own history commits suicide." Benedict reminds us of the public task of Christian churches in the world today:

> It is an essential aspect of the Church that it is neither the state nor a part of the state but a *fellowship based on conviction*. But it is also essentially aware of its responsibility for the totality: it cannot accept a limitation to its own affairs. On the basis of its own freedom, it must address the freedom of all human beings so that moral forces of history may remain forces in the present. This permits people, in continually

> changing circumstances, to grasp the evidential character of those values without which a shared freedom is impossible.[143]

Given the character of contemporary pluralism and the challenges to religious freedom, the arguments and consensual thinking of the founders remain exceedingly relevant. They challenge us to recalibrate our understanding of the role of the state and the role of religion in the public sphere. They remind us that it is possible to balance individual freedoms with wider religious expression, so long as neither has the effect of undermining the social order. In our time, they remind us of the ever-present tendency of the state to encroach on matters of religious conviction. And they remind us that, in periods of social upheaval and political mistrust, religion is a fundamental and eminently public value, shared by many. Our great diversity and pluralism today are owing to the founders; it therefore behooves us to resist the tendency toward cultural amnesia and reflect with sobriety on the founders' vision. My hunch – a very unscientific one, to be sure – is that the very questions that vexed Madison et al. perplex most Americans today.

Revisiting Tocqueville: reflections on religion and majoritarian tyranny

Religious expression and religious freedom, it is accurate to say, flourished in the early American republic. The reason for this is not hard to grasp: from the start, religion and democracy were not co-belligerents; they were, rather, close friends. In fact, religious groups in America thought that, to a large degree, a new republican government was *their creation*.[144] And so it was. It is surely not insignificant that Madison himself, late in his career, can testify on multiple occasions not only that religion had been thriving since the revolution ("with an increase in religious instruction") but also that religious freedom had proven itself to be the fruit of non-establishment and non-coercive tendencies of the state. As we observed in the previous section, Madison's 1833 correspondence to a Rev. Adams mirrors what Madison believed to be "fifty years" of evidence that the American experiment was working, at least reasonably well.

It is at this time – in May of 1831, to be exact – that a young Frenchman with interests in history and political theory journeyed to America, which was barely two generations old as an "experiment." He traveled in the company of a friend, Gustave de Beaumont, to observe firsthand a "great democratic revolution," with its "almost complete equality of conditions" that was taking place in America, and to chronicle those observations.[145] This visit would last just over nine months, with an itinerary beginning in New York. From there they went northward to Buffalo and on to the Great Lakes region and the frontier territory of Michigan and Wisconsin. Following two weeks in Canada, they traveled to Boston, Philadelphia, and Baltimore, then westward to Pittsburgh and Cincinnati, and then southward to Nashville, Memphis, and New Orleans, returning through the southern states to Washington and New York, from whence they had departed. Along the way, according to historian George W. Pierson, among the many and varied people Alexis de Tocqueville would meet were John Quincy Adams, Andrew Jackson, Albert Gallatin, Francis Lieber, Daniel Webster, Sam Houston, Roger Taney, and Charles Carroll.[146]

What is noteworthy about Tocqueville is the fact that his reporting takes account of two significant "foundings" in the American story, not merely the formal, constitutional founding.[147] The other was the *religious* founding that had its beginnings in the New England colonies and, though it needed pruning and purging through disestablishment sentiment, in many ways animated the second "founding." Tocqueville is careful to take note of the cultural and social "mores" as well as mental habits that are distinct among the Americans and contribute to the development of American republic government. "From the beginning," he writes, "politics and religion were in accord, and they have not ceased to be so since."[148] In this light, then, we can see that Tocqueville shares with the founders a "foundational" metaphysical assumption: individual self-government and public virtue derive from sound mores, and these are best accounted for by religion. Because of this, Tocqueville concludes tellingly, "Religion, which among Americans, never mixes directly in the government of society, should therefore be considered as *the first of their political institutions*."[149]

Among the more significant reflections in Tocquesville's "report" – published under the title *Democracy in America* – was to inquire into the nature of American democracy and ask what the prospects might be for this unique experiment to degenerate into either one of two forms of "tyranny." While despotism can present itself through a single person or a multitude, as Tocqueville saw it, the American inducement would be a "tyranny of the majority," given Americans' obsession with freedom and equality.[150] "The moral empire of the majority" in America, Tocqueville notes, is founded on "the principle that the interests of the greatest number ought to be preferred to those of the few."[151] Hence, if the "democratic majority" wills something, the minority will be vulnerable and helpless to resist, given not only the reality of "representative" government but also the utter pressure that majoritarian opinion places on the rest of society. For when the majority "has irrevocably pronounced, everyone becomes silent and friends and enemies alike seem to hitch themselves together to its wagon."[152] The consequence, wryly noted by Tocqueville, should give us pause:

> Chains and executioners are the coarse instruments that tyranny formerly employed; but in our day civilization has perfected even despotism itself, which seemed, indeed, to have nothing more to learn . . . . Under the absolute government of one alone, despotism struck the body the body crudely, so as to reach the soul; and the soul, escaping from those blows, rose gloriously above it; but in democratic republics, tyranny does not proceed in this way; it leaves the body and goes straight for the soul.[153]

Perhaps unlike most aristocrats of his day, Tocqueville was not scornful of democracy *per se*, even when he feared majoritarian tyranny and saw it at work in the form of public opinion. At the same time, he found it remarkable that the American revolution, unlike its French counterpart, did not respond in violent rejection of religion and the Church, as was the French experience; hence his remark, "On my arrival in the United States it was the religious aspect of the country that first struck my eye."[154] By contrast, religion was *the* identifying feature that characterized the American project. Numbered among the benefits to this project, as Tocqueville saw it, were *inter alia* public virtue and the curbing of selfishness, uncoerced religious belief, a belief in divine providence, and the equality of human beings. And his conclusion was telling: "Despotism can do without faith, but freedom cannot."[155] Freedom rightly understood views religion as a companion, not competition.[156]

While Tocqueville's observations about religious expression in the public sphere and about the dangers of egalitarianism in a republican democracy may strike readers in our day as quaint, they are worth contemplating. At the center of these concerns is the place of religion as it informs the moral impulses of a culture. In America, as Tocqueville saw it, not only did religion contribute to a healthy and vibrant society, but it also contributed to a people's understanding of self-government and character. The ability to focus on future consequences, rather than on the fulfillment of "a thousand little passing desires," to use his words, helped explain why religious peoples have had such lasting accomplishments.[157] For in having their lives anchored in transcendent values they experience the secret of succeeding in this world by bringing about meaningful change.

Either human beings will be "governed" or they will be self-governed. And while the U.S. Constitution, though couched in non-religious language, delineates the need for political checks and balances, Tocqueville seemed to be inquiring, as the founders and framers had done, into *internal* checks and balances. Again, we sense in an important thinker a profound sensitivity to the flaws of human nature – a moral realism, if you will.

Tocqueville's observations about the political consequences of religious belief[158] and the dangers of majoritarian "tyranny" are surely worth pondering. He was struck by the sense that churches in America, despite the fact that they are neither established nor supported by the state, nevertheless exerted far more influence in social life than the state-sponsored churches in Europe. This caused him to identify religion as "the first" among America's political institutions. From a logical standpoint, it would appear, at least in Tocqueville's thinking, that the place of religion and the inclination toward majoritarian tyranny are, in some respects, related. Not insignificantly, Tocqueville's final reflections as recorded in *Democracy* concern the possibility of an American form of despotism. "Despotism . . . appears to me particularly to be dreaded in democratic ages," he writes.[159] At the same time, he acknowledges that "[n]ations of our day cannot have it that conditions within them are not equal"; thus, "it depends on them whether equality leads them to servitude or freedom, to enlightenment or barbarism, to prosperity or misery."[160]

Tocqueville's attentive reflections on the character of American democracy confirm the importance of remembering the founders' attitude toward religious freedom and the logic of jurisdiction that animated their dedication to freedom of conscience. In light of the preceding discussion of the founders' vision, and Tocqueville's subsequent reflections on tyranny, it is worth asking, *What is the will of the American majority today?*[161] What patterns and trends – socially, culturally, and legally – serve as a reflection of majoritarian thinking? What do these portend for a nation that, historically, has valued religious freedom? And finally, how do these developments affect the ability of the United States, as a nation, to help support and protect religious freedom in other parts of the world? Consider the core thesis of the landmark work *The Price of Freedom Denied*, alluded to in Chapter 1: *To the extent that governments and societies restrict religious freedoms, physical persecution, and conflict increase.*[162]

It is by no means an over-statement to assert that the American experiment in religious liberty is unique. In the words of two legal analysts, "some degree of American exceptionalism should [rightly] be preserved."[163] At the same time, ours is unquestionably an age of amnesia, of the material over the spiritual, of technology over history and philosophy, of personal experience over collective wisdom, and of entertainment over moral reflection. Adding to the challenges confronting us in the task of protecting religious freedom is an important dimension of the present social climate. I refer to a toxic mix of social egalitarianism and "tolerance" that is dominant and suggestive of irresolvable conflicts in the public sphere. This, in turn, raises serious questions about religious freedom. Once a foremost political virtue, tolerance in our day has transmuted into a vice. In the discussion that follows, we shall attempt to re-think the nature of "tolerance," properly understood. Given the contemporary *Zeitgeist*, however, this most assuredly will not be easy.

Notes

1 See the introduction to Daniel L. Dreisbach, Mark David Hall, and Jeffry H. Morrison, eds., *The Forgotten Founders on Religion and Public Life* (Notre Dame: University of Notre Dame Press, 2009).

2 Wilfred M. McClay, *A Student's Guide to History*, 3rd ed. (Wilmington: ISI Books, 2003), 73–4.

3 One need not resort to the sort of rabid resistance to the early American religious impulse that is found, for example, in Steven K. Green, *Inventing a Christian America: The Myth of the Religious Founding* (Oxford and New York: Oxford University Press, 2015). The problem with Green's scholarship is not lodged in the volume's title; rather, it is mirrored in the subtitle. Although the founders and framers did not envision a theocratic state, they *were* committed to ensuring that religious belief and religious freedom were public entities, and thus characteristic of the new republic. Hence, to resort to the language of "myth" and "revisionism" (see, esp., Chapter 5, pp. 199–241) in order to cast doubt on the religiously informed convictions and political intentions of many – if not most – of the

founders is to fail to follow the evidence wherever it leads, at best, or to deny the existence of the evidence, at worst. As suggested in his introduction and his endnotes (esp. on pp. 246–7), Green would appear to be reacting to literature by more fundamentalist authors rather than to serious scholarship being done in recent years within his own discipline. One wonders as well if Green has not engaged in a form of historical "revisionism" that has characterized the courts in the last seven decades. For more balanced and accurate assessments of the founders' beliefs and intentions, see, for example, Thomas Kidd, *God of Liberty: A Religious History of the American Revolution* (New York: Basic Books, 2010); Daniel L. Dreisbach and Mark David Hall, *The Sacred Rights of Conscience: Selected Readings on Religious Liberty and Church-State Relations in the American Founding* (Indianapolis: Liberty Fund, 2009); Daniel L. Dreisbach, Mark David Hall, and Jeffry H. Morrison, eds., *The Forgotten Founders on Religion and Public Life* (Notre Dame: University of Notre Dame Press, 2009); Daniel L. Dreisbach, Mark David Hall, and Jeffry H. Morrison, eds., *The Founders on God and Government* (Lanham: Rowman & Littlefield, 2004); and Thomas J. Curry, *The First Freedoms: Church and State in America to the Passage of the First Amendment* (Oxford and New York: Oxford University Press, 1986). Another helpful corrective, though for slightly different reasons, is Barry Alan Shain, *The Myth of American Individualism: The Protestant Origins of American Political Thought* (Princeton: Princeton University Press, 1994).

4 So Michael Novak, "Foreword: Religious Liberty," in Daniel L. Dreisbach, Mark David Hall, and Jeffrey H. Morrison, eds., *The Founders on God and Government* (Lanham: Rowman & Littlefield, 2004), ix.

5 Stephen D. Smith, *The Rise and Decline of America Religious Freedom* (Cambridge and London: Harvard University Press, 2014), 17–28.

6 Hence the longstanding tradition of "apostasy" and associated death sentences in Islam, depending on the school of interpretation and application of Islamic tradition.

7 I am less sanguine than Michael Novak, *The Universal Hunger for Liberty: Why the Clash of Civilizations Is Not Inevitable* (New York: Basic Books, 2004), 3–21 and 191–218, that Islam can nurture a "culture of liberty," as Novak calls it. This is not because there are not millions of Muslims who desire it. Rather, it is because Islam's theocratic – and frequently "totalitarian" – rule of society prevents meaningful interchange between Islam and the principles that help create a "culture of liberty." Evidence in the world today – and there are approximately 1.6 billion Muslims worldwide (www.pewresearch.org/fact-tank/2016/07/22/muslims-and-islam-key-findings-in-the-u-s-and-around-the-world/) – indicates that few, if any, Islamic nations around the globe truly tolerate, let alone exhibit, religious freedom. In fact, apart from North Korea and China, the worst offenders tend to be Islamic nations, as evidence adduced in Chapter 1 amply demonstrates. And this is fully aside from the religious terrorism, in varied forms, that it has exported over the last two decades.

8 Evidence from the New Testament is ubiquitous as to the non-coercive and reasoned character of true faith – for example, Jesus' use of parables in his teaching and persuading, Acts 5:27–33 (the apostles' declaration that obedience in matters of the heart is first due to the Creator, not men), Acts 17:16–34 (St. Paul's reasoning with both Jews and Greeks in the Athenian marketplace and in his Areopagus address), Acts 28 (St. Paul's trip to Rome to make his "appeal to Caesar"), 1 Cor. 9:19–23 (St. Paul's articulation of his "philosophy of ministry": i.e., being "all things to all men" through moral persuasion), Rom. 13:1–10 (St. Paul's teaching on the indispensable role of political authority and the "debt of love" that is owed all people), and 1 Pet. 2:13–17 (Peter's affirmation of the legitimacy of political rulers).

9 Novak, "Foreword," xi.

10 *Deficiencies of the Confederation*. George Washington to John Jay (August 1, 1786), accessible at http://press-pubs.uchicago.edu/founders/print_documents/v1ch5s11.html.

11 A notable exception is political historian Mark David Hall. See his essay "*Vindiciae, Contra Tyrannos*: The Influence of the Reformed Tradition in the American Founding," in Daniel L. Dreisbach and Mark David Hall, eds., *Faith and the Founders of the American Republic* (Oxford and New York: Oxford University Press, 2014), 34–52, esp. p. 52.

12 Significantly, in his *Memorial and Remonstrance against Religious Assessments*, Madison adduces arguments against an established church and *inter alia* stresses the element of private judgment. Nicholas P. Miller, *The Religious Roots of the First Amendment: Dissenting Protestants and the Separation of Church and State* (Oxford and New York: Oxford University Press, 2012), 154–5, writes, "It took both a Madison and a Witherspoon – a politically acute theologian and a theologically astute politician – to turn the right of private judgment into a truly national principle of church and state." Indeed, we are the better for it.

13 So, for example, James H. Hutson, *Forgotten Features of the Founding: The Recovery of Religious Themes in the Early American Republic* (Lanham: Lexington Books, 2003), 176–8, and Thomas Lindsay, "James Madison on Religion and Politics: Rhetoric and Reality," *American Political Science Review* 85 (December 1991): 1321–37. But it is necessary to maintain that "enlightenment rationalism" and deism did *not* make the founders "irreligious" or anti-Christian; rather, the sticking point seems to have been the establishment of a particular church. Concerning religious liberty, in the words of Frank Lambert, "the interests of the founding fathers converged with those of evangelicals" (*The Founding Fathers and the Place of Religion in America* [Princeton: Princeton University Press, 2003], 178).

14 Miller is one of those who properly discerns this line of thinking in Madison. See his "Theologian and Politician: John Witherspoon and James Madison Make a National Principle," Chapter 5 of *The Religious Roots of the First Amendment* (see n. 12). Garrett Ward Sheldon, "Religion and Politics in the Thought of James Madison," in Daniel L. Dreisbach, Mark David Hall, and Jeffry H. Morrison, eds., *The Founders on God and Government* (Lanham and Oxford: Rowman & Littlefield, 2004), 83–115, stands in basic agreement.

15 Scholars such as Allen Hertzke ("Introduction: A Madisonian Framework for Applying Constitutional Principles on Religion," in Allen Hertzke, ed., *Religious Freedom in America: Constitutional Roots and Contemporary Challenges* [Norman: University of Oklahoma Press, 2015], 6–10) are correct in pointing to evidence of this in the Virginia Declaration of Rights, drafted in 1776. Madison's role was crucial in framing the final version of the legislation, which underscored the free exercise of religion on the basis of transcendent obligations; it insists that "religion, or the duty which we owe to our Creator, and the manner of discharging it, can be directed only by reason and conviction, not by force or violence; and therefore all men are equally entitled to the free exercise of religion, according to the dictates of conscience; and that it is the mutual duty of all to practice Christian forbearance, love, and charity toward each other" (*Bill of Rights to the Virginia Declaration of Rights* no. 16, accessible at www.archives.gov/exhibits/charters/virginia_declaration_of_rights.html. A decade later Madison would repeat this argument in his important treatise "Memorial and Remonstrance against Religious Assessments" (1785). See, in general, and Merrill D. Peterson and Robert C. Vaughan, eds., *The Virginia Statute for Religious Freedom: Its Evolution and Consequences for American History* (Cambridge: Cambridge University Press, 1988).

16 *The Federalist* no. 51, accessible at www.constitution.org/fed/federa51.htm.

17 See, e.g., David L. Holmes, *The Faiths of the Founding Fathers* (New York: Oxford University Press, 2006); Hutson, *Forgotten Features of the Founding* (see n. 13); Frank Lambert, *The Founding Fathers and the Place of Religion in America* (Princeton: Princeton University Press, 2003); and Michael Novak, *On Two Wings: Humble Faith and Common Sense at the American Founding* (San Francisco: Encounter Books, 2002).

18 For both statistical and sociodemographic breakdowns of religious groups present at or around the time of the American founding, see Thomas S. Kidd, *The Great Awakening: The Roots of Evangelical Christianity in Colonial America* (New Haven and London: Yale University Press, 2007); Jon Butler, Grant Wacker and Randall Balmer, *Religion in American Life: A Short History* (New York: Oxford University Press, 2003), 1–162 (Part One: "Religion in Colonial America"); Edwin S. Gaustad and Leigh E. Schmidt, *The Religious History of America*, rev. ed. (New York: HarperCollins, 2002), 3–138; James H. Hutson, ed., *Religion and the New Republic* (Lanham: Rowman & Littlefield, 2000); and Sydney E. Ahlstrom, *A Religious History of the American People* (New Haven and London: Yale University Press, 1972), 1–384 (Parts One-Three).

19 Letter to Henry Lee (May 8, 1825), reproduced in Merrill D. Peterson, ed., *Thomas Jefferson: Writings* (New York: Library of America, 1984), 1500–1.

20 So Barry A. Kosmin and Seymour P. Lachman, *One Nation Under God: Religion in Contemporary American Society* (New York: Crown Publishers, 1993), 21–2.

21 For a fascinating description of Jewish beginnings in America from the mid-1600s until the late eighteenth century, see Jonathan D. Sarna, *American Judaism: A History* (New Haven: Yale University Press, 2004), 1–30. Even though, according to Sarna's estimate, Jews who fought in the American revolution numbered about 100 (32–3), George Washington, upon acceding to the presidency in 1789, found it necessary to acknowledge American Jews for their contributions in securing independence, as subsequent correspondence with several synagogues indicates (one of which being the famous 1790 letter to the "Hebrew congregation" in Newport, Rhode Island). And despite the fact that the major documents bearing on questions of religious liberty in American life do not mention them, and while "the revolution did not ultimately usher in the messianic age for American Jews," nevertheless "it did effect changes in law and in the relationship of religion to the state that transformed American Jewish life forever after" (ibid., 36). By the 1840s, Sarna observes, "The structure of the American Jewish community mirrored in organization the federalist pattern of the nation as a whole, balanced precariously between unity and diversity" (61). For correspondence between four of the founders – George Washington, Alexander Hamilton, John Adams, and Thomas Jefferson – and individual Jews, correspondence which throws light on the founders' engagement with Judaism, see David G. Dalin, "Jews, Judaism, and the American Founding," in Daniel L. Dreisbach and Mark David Hall, eds., *Faith and the Founders of the American Republic* (Oxford and New York: Oxford University Press, 2014), 66–76. Dalin summarizes the founders' attitudes toward the Jewish people perhaps most succinctly: it was one of ambivalence and admiration (76).

22 For representative recent scholarship which presses this argument persuasively, see Daniel L. Dreisbach and Mark David Hall, eds., *The Sacred Rights of Conscience: Selected Readings on Religious Liberty and Church State Relations* (Indianapolis: Liberty Fund, 2009); Mark David Hall, "The Sacred Rights of Conscience: America's Founders on Church and State," *Oregon Humanities* (Fall/Winter 2005): 40–6; and Daniel L. Dreisbach, Mark David Hall, and Jeffrey H. Morrison, eds., *The Founders on God and Government* (Lanham: Rowman & Littlefield, 2004).

23 Much of this imagery is conspicuously biblical in its derivation. What's more, this imagery was adduced on specific occasions by the more "rationalist" and

heterodox of the founders, as Daniel L. Dreisbach, "The Bible and the Political Culture of the American Founding," in Daniel L. Dreisbach and Mark David Hall, eds., *Faith and the Founders of the American Republic* (Oxford and New York: Oxford University Press, 2014), 152–9, points out. After John Adams, Thomas Jefferson, and Benjamin Franklin were appointed to a committee in July of 1776 to design a seal for "the United States of America," no less than the Franklin himself proposed the image of Moses as he parted the Red sea, with Jefferson recommending the "cloud by day and pillar by night" imagery from Israel's wilderness sojourn. This should strike us as rather remarkable for "sons of the Enlightenment," as Dreisbach is quick to observe. Which illustrates the conspicuous bias of historical scholarship: "Largely missing from the literature on the American founding is a serious discussion of the Bible's influence on the founders' political ideas and rhetoric . . . . The Bible's influence is not merely ignored in the scholarship; rather, some scholars contend that the leading founders, informed by rationalism, rejected biblical ideas" (144). An example of what Dreisbach is criticizing is Wilson Carey McWilliams, "The Bible in the American Political Tradition," in Myron J. Aronoff, ed., *Religion and Politics* (Political Anthropology Series 3; New Brunswick: Transaction Books, 1984), 11–45 (reproduced in Patrick J. Deneen and Susan J. McWilliams, eds., *Redeeming Democracy in America* [Lawrence: University Press of Kansas, 2011], 29–54). McWilliams argues that the Bible is "the second voice" in "the grand dialogue of American political culture" (29) and that "the founding generation rejected or de-emphasized the Bible and biblical rhetoric" (39).

24 This residue is still present in the early twentieth century in the presidency of Woodrow Wilson, the son of a Presbyterian minister, who framed America's "mission" to be "the liberation and salvation of the world" (as noted by Kosmin and Lachmann, 22). One might argue that this residue is still present in the speeches of most of late-twentieth-century U.S. presidents, for that matter.

25 To illustrate, historian Edwin S. Gaustad classifies the "famous five" in the following manner: "The Libertarians: Jefferson and Madison," "The Icons: Franklin and Washington," and "The *Philosophes*: Adams and Jefferson" in Chapters 3,4, and 5, respectively of his *Neither King nor Prelate: Religion and the New Nation 1776–1826* (Grand Rapids: Eerdmans, 1993).

26 Daniel L. Dreisbach, "Famous Founders and Forgotten Founders: What's the Difference, and Does the Difference Matter?" in Daniel L. Dreisbach, Mark David Hall, and Jeffry H. Morrison, eds., *The Forgotten Founders on Religion and Public Life* (Notre Dame: University of Notre Dame Press, 2009), 17–21.

27 Ibid., 10. In an endnote to his thoughtful essay, Dreisbach estimates that in 2009, the year *The Forgotten Fathers* was published, the collected papers projects of the "famous five" would be as follows when all done: Washington – ca. 90 volumes, the Adams family – 100 volumes, Jefferson – ca. 75 volumes, Madison – ca. 50 volumes, and Franklin – ca. 50 volumes (ibid., 24, n. 28). As I write (August of 2016), I have just visited the websites of those five projects and found the following projections: Washington papers (University of Virginia) – copies of 135,000 documents, Adams family papers (Massachusetts Historical Society) – ca. 27,000 documents, Jefferson papers (Princeton University) – ca. 70,000 documents, Madison papers (University of Virginia) – ca. 38,000 documents, and Franklin papers (Yale University) – ca. 30,000 documents.

28 Ibid., 18. Hall, "*Vindiciae, Contra Tyrannos*" (see n. 11), 53–4, has argued similarly. In point of fact, in comparing Jefferson's indirect role (given his absence from the country at the time) with that of Roger Sherman, a serious Reformed Christian and leader in the Congregational church who was intimately and extensively involved in drafting the First Amendment, Hall notes that "when U.S. Supreme Court justices have used history to help them interpret the First Amendment clauses they have made 112 distinct references to Jefferson but have

mentioned Sherman only three times" ("Jefferson Walls and Madisonian Lines: The Supreme Court's Use of History in Religion Clause Cases," *Oregon Law Review* 85 [2006]: 568–9).

29 Dreisbach, "Famous Founders," 18. See as well Daniel L. Dreisbach, *Thomas Jefferson and the Wall of Separation Between Church and State* (New York: New York University Press, 2002).

30 See n. 12.

31 In addition to taking those scholars to task who insist that the American founding was chiefly a product of the Enlightenment, Miller is also critical of those interpreters who view political ideas *per se*, rather than religion, as the chief cause of the pluralistic American experiment in religious liberty. He is especially critical of Anthony Gill, *The Political Origins of Religious Liberty* (Cambridge: Cambridge University Press, 2008), and of Lambert, *The Founding Fathers and the Place of Religion in America* (see in particular Miller's discussion of "Taking Religious Ideas Seriously" in the Introduction, pp. 9–12). William Lee Miller, *The First Liberty: America's Foundation in Religious Freedom* (Washington, DC: Georgetown University Press, 2003), 129–30, frames the matter helpfully: "America's tradition of religious liberty is not the work of Jefferson, Madison, and the Enlightenment alone, nor simply the result of expediency and necessity . . . The stream of liberty does not run straight from the Protestant Reformation, or from the main body of the Puritan movement in England, or from the largest group of Puritan settlers in America . . . It does, however, run crookedly, as it were, from those sources, a tributary that grows."

32 For a very thorough and carefully written description of this evolution, see Thomas J. Curry, *The First Freedoms: Church and State in America to the Passage of the First Amendment* (Oxford and New York: Oxford University Press, 1986).

33 Perhaps, as Michael Novak argues, it is necessary to distinguish between "secular" and "secularist" since the difference is great. "Secularism" is to be understood as a worldview, a metaphysical conclusion – what Novak calls a "willful atheism" or a "principled atheism" (*No One Sees God: The Dark Night of Atheists and Believers* [New York: Doubleday, 2008], 233–49).

34 Matthew J. Franck, "Two Tales of Freedom: Getting the Origins of Religious Liberty Right Matters," *Touchstone*(July/August 2016): 19–26.

35 Ibid., 19–21.

36 Ibid., 19.

37 Ibid.

38 Representative of recent scholarship that has assumed a significant deist element in the wider political thinking of the founders are Steven Waldman, *Founding Faith: How Our Founding Fathers Forged a Radical New Approach to Religious Liberty* (New York: Random House, 2009); Gary Kowalski, *Revolutionary Spirits: The Enlightened Faith of America's Founding Fathers* (New York: Blue Bridge, 2008); and Brooke Allen, *Moral Minority: Our Skeptical Founding Fathers* (Chicago: Ivan R. Dee, 2006).

39 Darrren Staloff has charted the lines of this division with considerable insight in "Deism and the Founders," in Daniel L. Dreisbach and Mark David Hall, eds., *Faith and the Founders of the American Republic* (Oxford and New York: Oxford University Press, 2014), 13–33.

40 Ibid.,15.

41 Ibid., 18.

42 Ibid., 20.

43 Ibid., 30.

44 Frank, "Two Tales of Freedom," 21.

45 Ibid. One might reasonably argue with Michael Novak (*On Two Wings* [see n. 16], 77–95) that Enlightenment thinking on equality and human rights is parasitic; that is, it borrowed these from Judeo-Christian metaphysics.

46 Barry Alan Shain, "Afterword – Revolutionary-Era Americans: Were They Enlightened or Protestant? Does It Matter?" in Daniel L. Dreisbach, Mark David Hall, and Jeffry H. Morrison, eds., *The Founders on God and Government* (Lanham and Oxford: Rowman & Littlefield, 2004), 291.
47 Ibid., 291–2.
48 Frank, "Two Tales of Freedom," 21–2.
49 So Thomas S. Kidd, "Epilogue," in Thomas S. Kidd, ed., *God of Liberty: A Religious History of the American Revolution* (New York: Basic Books, 2010), 255.
50 In speaking of basic "rights" and "liberties," the obvious needs re-stating: the libertarian strains of thinking so prevalent today which insist on personal autonomy and "choice" could not have even been *envisioned* by the founders.
51 Representative of this line of thinking are Wilson Carey McWilliams, "Protestant Prudence and Natural Rights," in Patrick J. Deneen and Susan J. McWilliams, eds., *Redeeming Democracy in America* (Lawrence: University Press of Kansas, 2011), 55–71; Steven K. Green, *The Second Disestablishment: Church and State in Nineteenth-Century America* (New York: Oxford University Press, 2010), 3–77; Michael P. Zuckert, *Launching Liberalism: On Lockean Political Philosophy* (Lawrence: University Press of Kansas, 2002); Michael P. Zuckert, *The Natural Rights Republic: Studies in the Foundation of the American Political Tradition* (Notre Dame: University of Notre Dame Press, 1997), 1–89; Leo Strauss, *Natural Right and History*, rev. ed. (Chicago: University of Chicago Press, 1999), 202–52; Peter C. Myers, *Our Only Star and Compass: Locke and the Struggle for Political Rationality* (Lanham: Rowman & Littlefield, 1998); and Thomas L. Pangle, *The Spirit of Modern Republicanism: The Moral Vision of the American Founders and the Philosophy of Locke* (Chicago and London: University of Chicago Press, 1988), 131–279.
52 Representative of this interpretative tendency is John Marshall, *John Locke, Toleration and Early Enlightenment Culture* (Cambridge: Cambridge University Press, 2006), and John Marshall, *John Locke: Resistance, Religion and Responsibility* (Cambridge: Cambridge University Press, 1994). An accompanying assumption by most interpreters is that "religious intolerance" finds its origin in Constantine. While the challenges to religious freedom of the fourth century fall outside of the scope of the present discussion, suffice it to say that most treatments of "Constantinianism" fail to appreciate the context – i.e., the sheer magnitude and ferocity – of (Diocletian) religious persecution that preceded Constantine's rule.
53 One scholar who sees both in Locke is Mark David Hall, who concludes, "Locke's political philosophy is best understood as a logical extension of Protestant resistance literature rather than as a radical departure from it" (*Roger Sherman and the Creation of the American Republic* [Oxford and New York: Oxford University Press, 2013], 21). See in particular Hall's discussion of "What About John Locke?" (20–7).
54 Ibid., 24.
55 So, e.g., Zuckert, *The Natural Rights Republic* (see n. 51), 172.
56 Significantly, many political leaders in the founding period were graduates of Harvard, Yale, or Princeton, which at that time were Reformed institutions in terms of theological outlook.
57 Hall, *Roger Sherman*, 26.
58 In this regard, a balanced and circumspect account of the interaction of Locke's theological assumptions and political thought can be found in Greg Forster, *John Locke's Politics of Moral Consensus* (Cambridge: Cambridge University Press, 2005). To his credit, Forster acknowledges the importance of natural law in Lockean thought.
59 Miller, *The Religious Roots of the First Amendment*, 85–8.

60 John Witte Jr., and Joel A. Nichols, *Religion and the American Constitutional Experiment*, 3rd ed. (Boulder: Westview Press, 2011), 21–40, argue that four groups – puritan, evangelical, enlightenment and civic republican – informed the early American experiment in terms of religious rights and liberties, even when each offered "different accents and interpretations" as to the specific role of religion (41).

61 This connection extends even to William Penn's influence in the royal family of the Stuarts, inasmuch as both Quakers and Catholics had interests at the time in religious dissent and freedom. Henry Richard Fox Bourne's biography reads as follows: "While his friends in Amsterdam were thus helping Locke to hide for his life . . ., his friends in London were working no less heartily in his interests. The most active of these . . . was William Penn, whom Locke had known as a promising youth at Oxford, and had probably, then and afterwards, helped in unrecorded ways" (*The Life of John Locke*, 2 vols., rep. [Darmstadt: Scientia Verlag Aalen, 1969], 23). Roger Woolhouse, *Locke: A Biography* (Cambridge and New York: Cambridge University Press, 2006), pours through a rich and remarkably extensive amount of letter correspondence from Locke. On Locke's connections to Penn, see correspondence penned between December 1686 and January 1689, pp. 251–2 and 258–60.

62 For helpful background to the work of Backus and his interaction with Locke, see William Gerald McLoughlin, ed., Isaac Backus on Church, State, and Calvinism (Cambridge: Harvard University Press, 1968), 223–6; Stanley Grenz, *Isaac Backus, Puritan and Baptist: His Place in History, His Thought and Their Implications for Modern Baptist Theology* (Macon: Mercer University Press, 1983), 86–7; and Miller, *The Religious Roots of the First Amendment*, 101–13.

63 So Miller, *The Religious Roots of the First Amendment*, 52.

64 Woolhouse, *A Bibliography*, 40.

65 Miller, *The Religious Roots of the First Amendment*, 49–90 ("The Philosopher and the Enthusiast: The Collaboration of John Locke and William Penn"), traces this connection and argues with thoroughness and persuasiveness that this in fact was the case.

66 John Locke, *Second Treatise of Government* (Chapter 2), accessible at www.constitution.org/jl/2ndtr02.htm.

67 Thomas Sowell, *A Conflict of Visions: Ideological Origins of Political Struggles* (New York: Basic Books, 2002).

68 Sowell is attentive to the fact that clashing political opinions and arguments result from people reasoning from fundamentally different premises. These premises, or assumptions, in turn inform different visions of how the world works, and how it should work. Visions are subjective, incomplete, and pre-theoretical in nature, and often implicit, so that their effects "do not depend upon their being articulated, or even on decision-makers' being aware of them" (8). Like maps, they are simultaneously indispensable and dangerous – dangerous "precisely to the extent that we confuse them with reality itself" (4). See his introductory chapter "The Role of Visions."

69 Ibid., 12.

70 Ibid.

71 Ibid., 13, citing *The Correspondence of Edmund Burke* (Chicago: University of Chicago Press, 1967), 6:48.

72 Ibid., 17, citing Edmund Burke, *Reflections on the Revolution in France* (London: J.M. Dent & Sons Ltd., 1967), 60.

73 Ibid., 23–4.

74 Sowell contrasts the two major revolutions of the eighteenth century – in France and in America – to illustrate the difference between the two differing visions (ibid., 24–8).

75 I am dependent on *The Federalist Papers* (New York: The Modern Library, 1961), 322.

76 *Federalist* no. 15, cited in ibid., 110.

77 Sowell, *A Conflict of Visions*, 32.

78 An example of this sort of violation in Western societies today would be the encouragement and/or training of religious radicals and terrorists in the mosque/"holy place" setting, even when Western societies are generally governed by the fear of being labelled "Islamophobia" and hence would be reticent to monitor such activity.

79 Franck, "Two Tales of Freedom," 23.

80 James W. Ceaser, *Designing a Polity: America's Constitution in Theory and Practice* (Lanham and Plymouth, UK: Rowman & Littlefield, 2011), 3.

81 Ibid., 4.

82 The image of a "high" and "impregnable" wall, of course, was memorably and perhaps most forcefully created in 1947 by Supreme Court Justice Hugo Black in the landmark *Everson v Board of Education* decision. Black declared: "In the words of Jefferson, the [First Amendment] clause against establishment of religion by law was intended to erect "a wall of separation between church and State." "That wall," he continued, "must remain high and impregnable. We could not approve the slightest breach."

83 Miller, *The First Liberty* (see n. 31), 257.

84 Daniel L. Dreisbach, *Thomas Jefferson and the Wall of Separation Between Church and State* (New York and London: New York University, 2002).

85 Dreisbach writes, "Simply state, insofar as the judiciary appropriated Jefferson's metaphor and then misconstrued that metaphor in its application, as critics allege, church-state jurisprudence may lack analytical merit and legitimacy"(ibid., 5–6).

86 Of note is the fact that Jefferson, whatever his personal theological convictions, consistently supported religion and as President attended church services in the Capital, which itself suggests that his view of "separation" was only "restrictive" and not absolute. It is significant as well that the famous Danbury letter, sent to the President by Baptists for whom religious liberty was paramount, celebrated Jefferson's election rather than expressing fear. See hereon James H. Hutson, *Religion and the Founding of the American Republic* (Washington, DC: Library of Congress, 1988), 84–94; Dreisbach, *Thomas Jefferson*, 25–54 (= Chapter 3: "Sowing Useful Truths and Principles: Thomas Jefferson and the Danbury Baptist Association"); and Thomas E. Buckley, "The Religious Rhetoric of Thomas Jefferson," in Daniel L. Dreisbach, Mark David Hall, and Jeffry H. Morrison, eds., *The Founders on God and Government* (Lanham and Oxford: Rowman & Littlefield, 2004), 53–82. Attempting to furnish perspective, Buckley writes, "In his religious references Jefferson was searching for common ground, for a language which his fellow citizens could understand and accept, whatever their political differences" (72).

87 Kurt T. Lash, "The Second Adoption of the Establishment Clause: The Rise of the Non-establishment Principle," *Arizona State Law Journal* 27 (1995): 1133.

88 Daniel L. Dreisbach, "Defining and Testing the Prohibition on Religious Establishments in the Early Republic," in T. Jeremy Gunn and John Witte Jr., eds., *No Establishment of Religion: America's Original Contribution to Religious Liberty* (Oxford and New York: Oxford University Press, 2012), 252–3.

89 On the scope and rationales for establishment throughout the colonies, see Michael W. McConnell, "Establishment at the Founding," in T. Jeremy Gunn and John Witte Jr., eds., *No Establishment of Religion: America's Original Contribution to Religious Liberty* (Oxford and New York: Oxford University Press, 2012), 45–69.

90 This is the chief argument of Vincent Phillip Munoz, *God and the Founders* (New York: Cambridge University Press, 2009).

91 In the opinion of Forrest Church, Madison by comparison "remained true to the difficult symmetry of *E pluribus unum*" (*So Help Me God: The Founding Fathers and the First Great Battle over Church and State* [Orlando: Harcourt, 2007], 420). For a most thoughtful account of the "interaction" between Madisonian and Jeffersonian views during the formative years of 1776 to 1786, see Miller, *The First Liberty*, 3–67.

92 In the words of the Continental Congress, "true religion and good morals are the only solid foundation of public liberty and happiness." See Worthington Chauncey Ford, ed., *Journals of the Continental Congress, 1774–1789*, 34 vols.,(New York: Johnson Reprint Corp., 1968), 12:1001.

93 Paul Leicester Ford and George Haven Putnam, eds., *Autobiography of Thomas Jefferson, 1743–1790* (New York: Putnam's Sons, 1914), 71.

94 So Michael I. Meyerson, *Endowed by Our Creator: The Birth of Religious Freedom in America* (New Haven and London: Yale University Press, 2012), 12.

95 Kidd, *God of Liberty*, 226.

96 By the designation "Reformed," I am referring in early America to those groups with a Calvinist lineage, including New England puritans, French Huguenots, Dutch and German Reformed, Scottish Covenanters, Presbyterians, and Congregationalists. One historian of American religion estimates that the "Reformed" theological heritage constituted three-quarters of the American population by 1776 – a population that numbered approximately three million. See Ahlstrom, *A Religious History of the American People* (see n. 18), 344, 350.

97 Hall, "*Vindiciae, Contra Tyrannos*," 54.

98 Ibid.

99 What was the European experience? In England, the Church of England was established by law; in France it was Roman Catholicism; in Germany and Scandinavia it was the Lutheran Church, and in Holland, it was the Reformed Church. Moreover, on the eve of the American revolution, nine of thirteen colonies had established churches.

100 Smith, *The Rise and Decline of American Religious Freedom* (see n. 5), 66.

101 Ibid., 70.

102 See "The Williamsburg Charter" (1988), accessible at http://web.mit.edu/bcf/www/BSJ97/wmsburg.html

103 The objection that the founders were inconsistent with regard to the equality of all human beings – e.g., given the presence of slavery – is here beside the point.

104 What were the principle elements of establishment? These included government control over doctrine, liturgy and structure; the appointment of bishops and clergy; mandatory attendance at worship services; public financial support (including taxation); prohibiting worship in other denominational contexts; the use of the state church for civil functions; and the limitation of political participation. See Michael W. McConnell, "Establishment and Disestablishment at the Founding, Part 1: Establishment of Religion," *William and Mary Law Review* 44 (2003): 2107–208.

105 Cf. Matt. 22:15–22, Mark 12:13–17, Acts 5:27–33, Rom. 13:17, and 1 Pet. 2:13–17. Indeed, one can justifiably argue, contra Philip Hamburger, *Separation of Church and State* (Cambridge: Harvard University Press, 2002), that the tradition of separation of church and state has far deeper roots – in fact, biblical roots. Consider that in ancient Israel the king could not serve as priest or enter the sanctuary to perform priestly duties.

106 Jacques Maritain considers the recognition and distinction of two powers in the Western cultural tradition as its "crowning achievement" (*The Things that Are Caesar's*, trans. James F. Scanlan [New York: C. Scribner's Sons, 1930], 1–43). And despite all of the controversy and fighting – often with disastrous effects – the understanding evolved and was clarified that that two independent spheres co-existed.

107 Of course, not all agreed with this consensus. In fact, at the time of the drafting of the First Amendment, in 1789, seven of the original 13 states still had some form of religious establishment, even though this would change.

108 This latter point was a particular point of emphasis in Madison's thinking.

109 Thus, Meyerson (*Endowed by Our Creator*, 236–41) seems justified in arguing that, as descriptions, both "Christian nation" and "secular nation" are illegitimate and miss the mark; the framers would have rejected both.

110 T. Jeremy Gunn, "The Separation of Church and State Versus Religion in the Public Square," in T. Jeremy Gunn and John Witte Jr., eds., *No Establishment of Religion: America's Original Contribution to Religious Liberty* (Oxford and New York: Oxford University Press, 2012), 28–9.

111 George Washington to James Madison (May 5, 1789), accessible also at http://founders.archives.gov/documents/Washington/05-02-02-0157.

112 "Mr. Cotton's Letter Lately Printed, Examined, and Answered" (February 5, 1644), reproduced in Perry Miller, *Roger Williams: His Contribution to the American Tradition* (Indianapolis: Bobbs-Merrill, 1953), 98. Williams, who was banished from Massachusetts and established Rhode Island, advocated a "soul liberty" by which he argued that attempts at coercive belief or disbelief only breed defiance. His own view was that as long as Jews, Catholics, even "Mohammedans" willingly accepted the responsibilities of citizenship, they were welcome. As he understood it, "freedom" was a freedom both *from* and *for* religion. See in particular Timothy L. Hall, *Separating Church and State: Roger Williams and Religious Liberty* (Urbana: University of Illinois, 1998); Edwin S. Gaustad, *Liberty of Conscience: Roger Williams in America* (Grand Rapids: Eerdmans, 1991); and Edmund S. Morgan, *Roger Williams: The Church and the State* (New York: W.W. Norton, 1967).

113 *Of the Laws of Ecclesiastical Polity* VIII.1.2. On the use of the "wall of separation" metaphor before Jefferson's time, instances of which Jefferson surely would have known, see Chapter 5 of Dreisbach, *Thomas Jefferson*, 71–82.

114 So, for example, Gunn, "Separation," 28, and Dreisbach, *Thomas Jefferson and the Wall of Separation Between Church and State*, 1–9, 71–82.

115 Dreisbach, *Thomas Jefferson and the Wall of Separation Between Church and State*,56. Dreisbach's rationale behind this "jurisdictional" or "structural" interpretation is set forth in Chapter 5 ("What the Wall Separates"). Smith, *The Rise and Decline of America Religious Freedom*, 48–75, concurs: "So the religion clauses were primarily jurisdictional in nature . . . The purpose of religion clauses . . . was to confirm in writing that jurisdiction over such matters would remain with the states, where virtually all Americans wanted it to remain" (57, 60–1). The context of the First Amendment is clearly *national* authority over religious life. The argument to the contrary by Ellis West, *The Religion Clauses of the First Amendment: Guarantees of States' Rights?* (Lanham and Plymouth, UK: Rowman & Littlefield, 2011), esp. 159–67, simply does not obtain. At the most basic level, it ignores the most obvious – namely, the First Amendment's language, which reads "*Congress* shall make no law respecting the establishment of religion . . ." West challenges Dreisbach and others in arguing that the First Amendment is not "jurisdictional" in its design but rather absolute; that is to say, it was intended to speak *both* to individual states *and* to the federal government. *Pace* West, it was not developments within individual states that the founders feared; rather, it was the likelihood of *federal encroachment*, on the one hand, and *federal establishment* of a church, on the other hand, that exercised them.

116 James Madison to the Reverend F.L. Schaeffer (December 3, 1821), in *Letters and Other Writings of James Madison*, 4 vols. (Philadelphia: J.B. Lippincott, 1865), 3:242–3, cited in Gunn, "Separation," 29.

117 Dreisbach, *Thomas Jefferson and the Wall of Separation Between Church and State.*

118 Hall, "Jefferson Walls and Madisonian Lines" (see n. 28), 568–9.

119 Meyerson, *Endowed by Our Creator*, 233–5.

120 In correspondence in December of 1790 with Noah Webster Jr., Jefferson defends "freedom of religion" in light of the continual attempts of civil authorities to suppress such. In this vein, he notes that there exist "certain fences" that "experience has proved peculiarly efficacious against wrong" and which the governing authorities "have ever shewn a disposition to weaken or remove" (Letter from Thomas Jefferson to Noah Webster Jr., December 4, 1790, *The Papers of Thomas Jefferson*, ed. Julian P. Boyd [Princeton: Princeton University Press, 1971], 18:132, cited by Dreisbach, *Thomas Jefferson*, 87–8).

121 In the end, it is difficult not to concur with Meyerson (*Endowed by Our Creator*, 233): "No simply metaphor can describe how the founding generation understood freedom of religion, and the 'Jeffersonian wall' has proved incapable of capturing the complexities of this inquiry." The problem, however, lies less with Jefferson's image than with modern interpretations – and interpolations – of Jefferson.

122 Letter from James Madison to the Rev. Jasper Adams, September 1833, reproduced in Daniel L. Dreisbach, ed., *Religion and Politics in the Early Republic: Jasper Adams and the Church-State Debate* (Lexington: University Press of Kentucky, 1996), 120–1, emphasis added.

123 Tellingly, Dreisbach writes, "A line, in contrast with a wall, is fluid and adaptable to changing relationships and can be overstepped" (*Thomas Jefferson*, 88).

124 Contra Justice Hugo Black, majority opinion, *Everton v. Board of Education* (1947).

125 If this is not the case, then Stephen Carter is correct: the "wall" becomes one-sided and represents "little more than an effort to subdue . . . religion," in its essence, becoming a veritable "prison wall" (Stephen L. Carter, *God's Name in Vain: The Wrongs and Rights of Religion in Politics* [New York: Basic Books, 2000], 78–80).

126 Chief Justice Warren Burger, majority opinion, *Lynch v. Donnelly* (1984).

127 James W. Skillen, "Conclusion: The Religion Puzzle," in Luis E. Lugo, ed., *Religion, Public Life, and the American Polity* (Knoxville: University of Tennessee Press, 1994), 249, illustrates the foolishness of rabidly separationist and absolutist sentiments of some in our own day when, at the practical level, he writes, "If government funds fire departments, those departments should protect all properties whether belonging to Christians or to atheists. If government chooses to fund schooling, those funds should extend proportionately to all school-age children whether they attend schools of one faith or another." As it applies to educational opportunity, Skillen has developed this line of reasoning with more sophistication in "Religion and Education Policy: Where Do We Go from Here?" *Journal of Law and Politics* (Spring 1990): 503–29.

128 Recall that for seventeenth-century settlers of American, "liberty of conscience" and "religious freedom" were what someone has called a "negative liberty," that is, the freedom to be left alone and go about their lives

129 John Courtney Murray, *We Hold These Truths: Catholics Reflections on the American Proposition* (New York: Sheed and Ward, 1960), 364.

130 I am drawing from Murray's typology of church-state relations as presented in ibid. (362–3). A different threefold typology is suggested by Brian F. LeBeau, *Religion in America to 1865* (Washington Square: New York University Press, 2000), 85, who distinguishes diverse understandings of church-state relations in early America according to the categories of "enlightened separatists," "political centrists," and "pietistic separationists." And Carl H. Esbeck, "A Typology of Church-State Relations in Current American Thought," in Luis

E. Lugo, ed., *Religion, Public Life, and the American Polity*, sets forth "the six common positions" to be found in Americans' thinking: "strict separationists," "freewill separationists," "institutional separationists," "structural pluralists," "non-preferentialists," and "restorationists."

131 So John Witte Jr., "One Public Religion, Many Private Religions: John Adams and the 1780 Massachusetts Constitution," in Daniel L. Dreisbach, Mark David Hall, and Jeffry H. Morrison, eds., *The Founders on God and Government* (Lanham and Oxford: Rowman & Littlefield, 2004), 47.

132 So Smith, *The Rise and Decline of American Religious Freedom*, 36.

133 Tellingly, Washington cautioned, "And let us with caution indulge the supposition, that morality can be maintained without religion. Whatever may be conceded to the influence of refined education on minds of peculiar structure, *reason and experience both forbid us to expect that national morality can prevail in exclusion of religious principle*" ("Farewell Address," in William B. Allen, ed., *George Washington: A Collection* [Indianapolis: Liberty, 1988], 521).

134 Early moderns would not have erected the dichotomy of public-versus-private morality as we moderns and ultra-moderns are inclined to do.

135 This term is owing to Jean Bethke Elshtain, "How Should We Talk?" *Case Western Reserve Law Review* 49, no. 4 (1999): 732.

136 This dual function has been eloquently stated by Gaustad, *Neither King nor Prelate* (see n. 25), 139.

137 Franck, "Two Tales of Freedom," 24.

138 Ibid.

139 James Madison, *Memorial and Remonstrance against Religious Assessments* no. 1.

140 Ibid.

141 Providing a thoughtful understanding of the notion of "providence" as it informed the beliefs of Witherspoon and his contemporaries is L. Gordon Tait, *The Piety of John Witherspoon* (Louisville: Geneva Press, 2001), 143–77 (= Chapter 5, "Providence"). On Witherspoon's political theology and the manner in which politics and religion coalesced in Witherspoon, see Jeffry H. Morrison, *John Witherspoon and the Founding of the American Republic* (Notre Dame: University of Notre Dame Press, 2007), and Jeffry H. Morrison, "John Witherspoon's Revolutionary Religion," in Daniel L. Dreisbach, Mark David Hall, and Jeffry H. Morrison, eds., *The Founders on God and Government* (Lanham and Oxford: Rowman & Littlefield, 2004), 117–46.

142 Most contemporary scholars concede that the founders believed religion needed special protection yet hold this "protection" to be unacceptable for today.

143 Joseph Cardinal Ratzinger (Benedict XVI), *Values in a Time of Upheaval*, trans. Brian McNeil (New York and San Francisco: Crossroad and Ignatius, 2006), 52.

144 So Miller, *The First Liberty*, 236.

145 Alexis de Tocqueville, introduction to *Democracy in America*, ed. and trans. Harvey C. Mansfield and Delba Winthrop (Chicago and London: University of Chicago Press, 2000), 3, 12. Tocqueville opens his account with the following: "Among the new objects that attracted my attention during my stay in the United States, none struck my eye more vividly than the equality of conditions," which he notes, "gives a certain direction to public spirit, a certain turn to the laws, new maxims to those who govern, and particular habits to the governed" (ibid., 3).

146 George W. Pierson, *Tocqueville in America* (Baltimore: Johns Hopkins University Press, 1996), 782–6. This volume originally appeared as *Tocqueville and Beaumont in America* and was published by Oxford University Press in 1938.

147 Ceaser, *Designing a Polity* (see n. 80) refers to a "two-founding thesis" (24) and attributes the term to Michael Zuchert, *The Natural Rights Republic* (Notre Dame: University of Notre Dame Press, 1996). As cultural historian Wilfred M. McClay notes, "The United State is distinctive in even having a founding, a clear moment in time in which the nation-state and its institutions were created, in full view of the world, out in the open air" (*A Student's Guide to History* [see n. 2], 49).

148 Tocqueville, *Democracy in America* I.2.9 (275).

149 Ibid. (280).

150 The egalitarian tendency, so important the American democratic impulse, was much in Tocqueville's view as he penned *Democracy in America*.

151 Tocqueville, *Democracy in America* I.2.7 (237).

152 Ibid. (243).

153 Ibid. (244).

154 Ibid. I.2.9 (282).

155 Ibid.

156 Tocqueville's observations force us to reject the rather remarkable conclusion offered by James H. Hutson, who writes, "If the American Revolution introduced into American life new ways of thinking about things and new ways of doing them," then "*its innovative impulse produced little novelty in the realm of religion and government*" (*Church and State in America: The First Two Centuries* [New York: Cambridge University Press, 2008], 188, emphasis added). Very much to the contrary.

157 Tocqueville, *Democracy in America* II.2.15 (519).

158 It would be mistaken to view Tocqueville's views on religion as purely instrumental, as some sort of artificial support or cultural baggage. It was his conviction that Christianity imparted moral values without which democracy cannot survive. In this way he shared many of the baseline assumptions of the founders themselves.

159 Ibid. II.4.7 (666).

160 Ibid. (676).

161 The new orthodoxy that is being advanced in our day, a sort of "secular egalitarianism" (so Smith, *The Rise and Decline of America Religious Freedom*, 156–8), is quite conspicuously hostile to religion, as evidenced by advocates of "gay rights" and same-sex marriage who are demanding legislation prohibiting "discrimination" on the basis of sexual orientation ("hate crimes"). While a very small minority of the citizenry actually affirms "gay rights," its force – socially and politically – is incomparable. I take this increasing *prohibition* from articulating a traditional and *natural* view of marriage in the public sphere and in public discourse – a view that has been normative for millennia – to be an indication that is nothing less than a genuine issue of religious freedom.

162 Brian J. Grim and Roger Finke, *The Price of Freedom Denied: Religious Persecution and Conflict in the Twenty-First Century* (Cambridge and New York: Cambridge University Press, 2011), 1–24, 222.

163 Witte and Nichols, *Religion and the American Constitutional Experiment* (see n. 60), 282.

4 Second thoughts on "pluralism," "neutrality," and "tolerance"

"Pluralism" and the public square

The public pursuit of truth

Surely few topics generate in our day as much heated discussion and controversy as the matter of Christianity's relationship to other cultures, religions, and value systems. No topic, that is, except one: Christianity's relationship to democratic culture.[1] What remains non-controversial amidst heated public debate on a variety of fronts is the recognition of the radically pluralist and tolerant character of the contemporary *Zeitgeist*. At the heart of the debates raging around us is lodged the need for many to question the very notion and nature of truth, a term that more often than not finds itself surrounded by quotation marks. But where did these grammatical indicators originate? And why?

This need to challenge the very notion and nature of truth is simultaneously moral, philosophical, theological, and sociological, raising questions of enormous importance not merely for those who embrace religious faith but for all citizens. For the committed Christian believer, it challenges at the most basic level an outlook that, from its origin, has claimed to know truth (however imperfectly), sought to embody this truth (however imperfectly), and been committed to proclaim this truth (however imperfectly) as revealed by the one true God through the Savior of the human race.

For those of us in the Western cultural context, questions of pluralism, diversity, and tolerance confront us at multiple levels. Not only must we face up to the tensions that issue out of the presence of religious pluralism and competing claims of religious authority in the twenty-first century, but we in democratic cultures have presumed the necessity of a morally "neutral" public sphere. This, of course, is the subject of endless debate, public discussion, and parsing of political and philosophical categories.[2] Certainly, in the latter half of the twentieth century and particularly since the end of the Cold War, many have taken as *a given* that the democratic process itself is the guarantor of our individual freedoms. In order to ensure and justify these freedoms, we assume that to press claims of "truth" in the public sphere is to adopt an attitude of undemocratic intolerance. Such claims, therefore, are best restricted to the private sphere, where they remain non-offensive. Consequently, in its appearance, the notion of "truth" would seem *not* to be a public good and means to preserve freedom but rather an impediment to freedom. Correlatively, democracy as most of our contemporaries understand it would seem to be indissolubly linked to relativism, which takes on the cast of being the authentic guarantor of democratic freedoms, since it is ever vigilant in its crusade to detect intolerance, rigidity, bigotry, and those attitudes that we deem highly offensive.

At this point, we shall need to pause and . . . breathe in. For the purposes of clarity, we must acknowledge certain questions that force themselves upon us. To wit, can justice, a universal predisposition that has been acknowledged by all international canons from 1948 onward (beginning with the UDHR) be defended? On what moral basis can such a defense be made? From the vantage point of secular fundamentalism, is it permissible to allow the religious viewpoint to enter the public realm and express its conviction, given the broadly held assumption that the public realm must remain "neutral?" The following discussion will assume a fundamental distinction between classical pluralism, which does not shy away from considering and offering truth-claims in the marketplace of diverse ideas, and relativism (or its cousin nihilism), which many mistake for "pluralism" today. In making this fundamental distinction, I am struck by the relevance of John Stuart Mill's observation:

> The peculiar evil of silencing the expression of an opinion . . . is that it is robbing the human race, posterity as well as the existing generation; those who dissent from the opinion, still more than those who hold it. If the opinion is right, they are deprived of the opportunity of exchanging error for truth: if wrong, they lose . . . what is almost as great a benefit, the clearer perception and livelier impression of truth, produced by its collision with error.[3]

Mill's reflections confront us with a difficult task, insofar as "tolerance," "pluralism," and "diversity," as someone has aptly noted, are among those "thought-killer" terms and concepts that tend to be accepted and imbibed uncritically – terms and concepts that desperately need a critical divorce from postmodern theorizing. And as such, they too have a discernible history, even when their usage today has extended virtually to the place of insanity.

Whether in antiquity or in the present day, whether in the Western or non-Western context, whether among the religiously minded or the rigidly secularist, whether in the sphere of democratic polity or within religious communities, to take up particular truth-claims and bring them into the public square remains nothing short of scandalous. Certainly, the adamantly agnostic and cynical question posed two millennia removed by Pilate, Rome's emissary, to Jesus – *What is truth?*[4] – loses none of its relevance.

However, the same may be said of Christ's response to the extent that it desacralized and relativized political power: *You would have no authority over me at all unless it had been given to you from above.*[5]

The bottom-line issue, then, is unavoidable: can claims to normative truth and ultimate reality – claims that offend ancient, modern, and ultra-modern sensibilities alike – still be made? And in the context of democratic pluralism, do not Christian claims about "truth" seem intolerant and wholly inappropriate to the world in which we live?

In all humility, those responding to these vexing questions will need initially to make a fundamental distinction. To question Christianity's claims to authority is to question not the reality of religious experience *per se*; after all, *all people* everywhere make such claims, which are inordinately subjective. Rather, it is to question the *possibility* of universal truth norms existing (*outside of* our personal existential experience) and whether – and to what degree – that truth is *knowable*. These, of course, are theological and philosophical matters of the first order and thus are as timely for us today as they were when Jesus responded to Pilate's *What is truth?* query in a radically political context.

Given the American context in which I am embedded and write, I am struck by the evolving arguments for religious tolerance that were antecedent to – and contiguous with – the American Revolution. In August of 1790, a Jewish congregation in Newport, Rhode Island, sent a message of praise and congratulations to President George Washington on the occasion of his visit to Newport. The message expressed gratitude for a government "which to bigotry gives no sanction, to persecution no assistance" but which affords everyone "liberty of conscience" and "immunities of citizenship."[6] This renowned exchange between the first President of the United States and a Jewish congregation is rather remarkable on several counts. These people are members of a religious community that had been oppressed and persecuted by much of the world, including Christendom, for centuries. Washington's response may indeed be taken as eloquent testimony to the central importance of religious toleration and freedom of religious expression upon which the nation was founded. Recall, as well, that the Bill of Rights, becoming part of the U.S. Constitution in 1791, a year after the aforementioned exchange between the Jewish congregation and Washington, prevents the government from establishing any state religion. Whether or to what extent Americans have always lived up to this standard is beside the point. What needs emphasis is that this nation has never known any state-imposed barrier to religious pluralism and religious expression.

(In the campaign for the ratification of the new U.S. Constitution, James Madison, in *Federalist#* 10, argues that "factions" within society will be both inevitable and tolerable. These pluralistic expressions have the cumulative effect, he believes, of balancing one another. At the same time, Madison assumes that all people will agree on rationally discerned standards of justice, on human equality and legitimate rights, and on social behavior that is "wicked" and hence deserving of censure.)

But the question still evades us: *how and where did the notion of religious tolerance and freedom originate?* What influences bore upon the founders and framers of our nations' charter documents? Much of their understanding of liberty, happiness, religious toleration, and freedom of expression was the product of their reflections on the European experience. The rationale for religious toleration is at once theological, moral, and philosophical, forged in part in the bitter controversies of religious strife during the preceding two and a half centuries.[7]

Locke and religious intolerance

Much recent scholarship has produced ample documentation of sixteenth- and seventeenth-century religious intolerance, both Catholic and Protestant, in relationship to longstanding patristic, late-medieval, and early modern justifications for intolerance. Historians of this era have sought to mirror elements of "high enlightenment" thought – for example, reason, civility, humanism, and tolerance – over against authoritarianism, incivility, barbarism, and intolerance. Students of the Enlightenment have tended to focus on atheistic and materialistic strands of Enlightenment thought while ignoring or downplaying Christian Enlightenment thinkers. At the same time, political historians have paid considerable attention to issues of political sovereignty, resistance, and natural rights while devoting relatively little attention to exploring the role of religious toleration in the constellation of late seventeenth-century thinking. The Netherlands provides a fascinating case study since, in contrast to England and France, it provided shelter for diverse religious and political refugees and was perhaps the most tolerant European society in the seventeenth century, advancing toleration for Catholics and unorthodox Protestants (for example, non-trinitarians and Socinians) alike, as well as for Jews and Muslims. Each of these groups was allowed to exist alongside the Calvinist "public church." Nevertheless, growing anti-Catholic sentiments are to be detected late in the century, and while religious toleration was practiced, it was legally restricted.

It is accurate to view religious intolerance during this period as part of a broader argument against political tyranny and oppression. John Locke, for example, watched with concern at the suppression of Protestants by Catholics in France and elsewhere. And with good reason he feared a growing absolutist tendency in England, which in the end provides part of the rationale for his Treatises on the subject of tolerance. Even the intolerance of Protestant dissenters by England's state church contributed substantially to his arguments. Irrespective of their provenance or geographical context, efforts toward religious toleration in the seventeenth century were not merely intended to combat abusive practice (though they included this). They were also meant to opposed deep-seated and longstanding justifications for religious intolerance, whether aimed across the Reformational aisle or by Protestants at fellow dissenting Protestants. The voices raised against religious intolerance may strike the modern reader as seemingly few, particularly against the backdrop of the general thinking of the masses. These voices – among them, Sebastian Franck, Sebastian Castellio, Dirck Cornhert, Roger Williams, John Milton, John Locke, Jean Le Clerc, and Pierre Bayle – are nonetheless significant, not only for their day but also for future generations.

Locke's arguments for religious toleration, it turns out, are indebted to a distinctly Christian view of the cosmos and to a broadly "integrated" understanding of an ordered, civil society. I suggested in the previous chapter that the general stereotype of "Enlightenment" thinking as rationalist, deist, empiricist, materialist, and skeptical is not wholly accurate. While it included those things, it was more. The product of a Puritan upbringing, Locke was a deeply devoted Christian who was committed to obedience to God as mankind's Creator. Authentic conviction, Locke maintains, cannot be forced upon people since belief does not arise merely out of the power of the will. Not confiscation of one's property or estate, not imprisonment, not torture, not any sort of external coercion can affect a person's inward judgment. Penalties, Locke writes, are "absolutely impertinent," since they are not "proper to convince the mind."[8] It is "only Light and evidence that can work a change in men's opinions; which Light can in no manner proceed from corporal sufferings, or any other outward penalties."[9]

At the psychological level, early tolerationists understood that when coercion is applied to belief, it risks creating either hypocrisy or atheism. Counterfeit profession or belief for the purposes avoiding punishment or unpleasant consequences, Locke knew, bred less honesty. Ultimately, forced belief, in addition to undermining the credibility of belief, develops an indifference to religious truth, the fruit of which is often impiety and wickedness. Locke describes this dynamic in the following manner:

> All the life and power of true religion consists in the inward and full persuasion of the mind . . . Whatever profession we make, to whatever outward worship we conform, if we are not fully satisfied in our own mind that the one is true, and the other well pleasing to God, such profession and such practice . . . are . . . great obstacles to our salvation . . . [and] we add unto the number of our other sins, those also of hypocrisy, and contempt of his Divine Majesty.[10]

What often is taken for granted, or simply ignored, is the fact that arguments for religious tolerance are *virtually non-existent* outside of societies that are indebted to Christian thinking about reality. Radical pluralists and multiculturalists, of course, will take umbrage at this suggestion, but it is nevertheless true, and one can state this fact in utter humility, without falling prey to "cultural imperialism." But why? What lies behind this socio-cultural and religious reality? Perez Zagorin, in his important volume *How the Idea of Religious Toleration Came to the West*, demonstrates a willingness – rare among historians of our era – to acknowledge this fact:

> The modern concepts of religious toleration and freedom are thus Western in origin and the offspring of European civilization. They are almost entirely due . . . to the work of Christian thinkers . . . of the sixteenth and seventeenth centuries . . . It is only in Western society . . . that there has appeared a massive body of writings by many different authors exploring the problem of religious intolerance from different angles and presenting an array of arguments in behalf of the principles of liberty of conscience, mutual tolerance, and religious coexistence and diversity.[11]

Even when this is not a major emphasis in his work, Zagorin is to be commended for doing what few scholars seem willing to do – i.e., acknowledging that arguments for religious toleration are difficult to find outside of societies that are indebted to a Christian heritage.[12] Moreover, one cannot simply ignore the "vast array of argument in behalf of the principles of liberty of conscience, mutual tolerance, and religious coexistence" that are unique to the Western cultural context.[13]

But what about the treatment of Jews and Muslims, that is, those "outside the camp?" While Zagorin restricts his study to intra-Christian manifestations of intolerance and their responses, John Marshall, in his massive (and cumbersomely titled) volume *John Locke, Toleration and Early Enlightenment Culture: Religious Intolerance and Arguments for Religious Toleration in Early Modern and "Early Enlightenment" Europe*,[14] devotes several chapters to an account of late seventeenth-century Christian attitudes toward the "heathen." Marshall traces patristic and late-medieval arguments that Jews, Muslims, and pagans should be tolerated, whereas "heretics" and "schismatics" should be punished. While he does recognize the existence of two strands of thinking in patristic and medieval texts – namely, tolerations and coercive opposition – he acknowledges that European Christians were far from consistent in applying religious toleration. That Locke argues for toleration as well as citizenship for both Jews and Muslims is an indication for Marshall that an "enlightened" Christianity distinguished itself both in conceptualization and in practice. According to the Lockean perspective, the cultural and ecclesiastical mindset that fosters coercive credalism and superstition, even barbarity on occasions, is to be set aside in favor of civility and humanity.[15]

Second thoughts about "tolerance": from unchaste "moral neutrality" to a chastened and principled pluralism

Truth and tolerance: probing the moral bottom line

Earlier, I attempted to distinguish between a principled understanding of pluralism, which does not shy away from considering and offering truth-claims, and relativism, which in our day not infrequently masquerades as "pluralism." This approach to pluralism, I maintain, tolerates and evaluates dissenting opinion, which in the end as Mill observed, affords a "clearer perception and livelier impression of truth" due to the interaction of truth and error. To reiterate, can *claims to normative truth and ultimate reality – claims that offend ancient, modern, and ultra-modern sensibilities alike – still be made?* And in an environment of democratic pluralism, are Christian claims about "truth" in fact "hate-filled," "bigoted," and "intolerant," as we often hear today? Again, the issue before us concerns the *possibility* of universal truth norms existing – whatever our personal experience might suggest – and whether, to some degree, some truth is knowable.

While religious tolerance as it developed in the seventeenth century is characterized by a willingness to recognize and permit dissenting views (views that perhaps even are mingled with error), another aspect of tolerance will require a greater willingness of citizens to be confrontational, a posture that contemporary Western societies are loath to "tolerate." A delicate question presents itself: in our concern to be forbearing toward and tolerant of others, is it possible, or even likely, that we lose the ability to defend and advance any sort of objective understanding of truth in religious dialogue, in ethics, and in political discourse? Is it possible – is it indeed necessary – to affirm personal, religious, and political commitments to truth in a manner that is not averse to true tolerance, given the symbiotic relationship between truth and tolerance?

Intolerance, it should be acknowledged, is a universal and manifestly human problem and not the provenance of Western or non-Western cultures. It is imperative that we be reminded of this fact, given the presence, even in the West, of multiple ideologies that are blatantly anti-Western and choose to overlook or ignore the humane achievements of the Western cultural heritage. Chiefly at the academic level but also in some popular circles in our day, objective notions about truth are held in high suspicion and derided. That the idea of truth as knowable and objectively verifiable is deeply doubted should strike us as not only erroneous – how, in fact, do we *know* that truth *cannot* be objectively known? – but also socially tragic in its consequences. Any society that doubts both the existence and the parameters of truth and moral reality cannot long endure. This is simply to say that tolerance properly understood needs truth in order to be a coherent, functional, and ordering concept in public life. To deny or call into question these foundations of social and political life is to prepare the way for totalitarianism. This reality is especially relevant in light of the extreme versions of secularism, with attendant nihilism, that presently typify Western thinking.[16] And in stating this, I reject any paternalistic claims, usually coming from the academy, that I am being "narrow," "imperialistic," or "intolerant." Please read further.

Tolerance old and new

Along with its siblings "diversity" and "compassion," "tolerance" has achieved remarkable status in our culture's hierarchy of values. In fact, the Commandment "Thou shalt not judge" seems to have superseded all revealed commandments – even rationally discovered ones.[17] But how is tolerance best understood and practiced as a social mandate? In the English language, tolerance in the sense of """bearing," "forbearing" or "indulging" (Latin: *tolerare*) dates from the mid-eighteenth century. Originally, "tolerance" denoted a policy of forbearance in the presence of something disliked or disapproved. It was foremost a political virtue, demonstrated by a government's readiness to permit a variety of religious beliefs. The notion that government should not enforce a specific religion comes to expression perhaps most forcefully in Locke's *Letter on Toleration* (1689) and *Two Treatises of Government* (1690). Removed from its political context, tolerance gradually came to be understood as a forbearance, an enduring of those behaviors or practices that we dislike.[18]

In its conception, tolerance took on the cast of a virtue because of its concern for the common good and its respect for people as persons. We endure particular customs, behaviors, or habits of people – sometimes even (relatively) bad ones – in the interest of preserving a greater unity. In the Lockean context, tolerance was advocated for religious non-conformists. Never was it construed, however, to imply, much less sanction, *morally questionable* behavior. Consider, however, the devolution of a public concept. What was a public virtue in its prior state becomes a vice if and when it (a) ceases to care for truth, (b) ignores the common good, and (c) disdains the values that uphold a community. The culture of "tolerance" in which we presently find ourselves is a culture in which people believe nothing and are remarkably indifferent to this precarious state of affairs. As a result of this transmutation, "tolerance" becomes indistinguishable from an intractably intolerant relativism. The challenge facing people of good will and people of faith is learning how to purify tolerance so that it remains a virtue without succumbing to the centripetal forces of relativism and the spirit of the age.

Any discussion of the notion of tolerance, of course, must first presuppose a context of pluralism. But we encounter problems, supremely illustrated by the sheer diversity of ways and contexts in which "pluralism" in our day is understood and defined. At minimum, in the interest of clarity, two uses of the term must be identified. Pluralism can, on the one hand, simply signify the phenomenological reality of differing cultures, ethnic groups, and traditions, as well as the social structures and mechanisms that order a society. These cultural phenomena are a social fact of life. It is out of this "structured"[19] form of pluralism that the American experience emerged; hence, the nation's motto *E pluribus unum* ("out of many one"). Herein different communities, different identities, and different ethnic traditions agree to co-exist; they do so because of a commitment to an over-arching common cause.

"Pluralism," however, can also operate under the assumption – tacit or explicit – that among competing ideological viewpoints, worldviews, or religious understandings of reality, none has (or is permitted to have) a privileged placed as a framework for interpreting reality. On this view, all religious positions possess an essential unity and all religious viewpoints stand on equal footing in terms of substance. Pluralism thus construed has a leveling effect. Hence, to argue for the authority and supremacy of Christianity is thought to manifest religious and cultural imperialism. This allegation, of course, places "pluralism" intrinsically at odds with Christian truth-claims, which are uncompromising in their nature. Undergirding these claims is that God the Creator has revealed himself universally through "general revelation" (for example, through the natural moral law) as well as uniquely and definitively through Jesus Christ.

For this reason alone, it is crucial to distinguish between pluralism as a social-cultural fact of life and pluralism as an ideology.[20] And precisely because people use the term "tolerance" indiscriminately and in both aforementioned contexts, preserving this distinction is critically important. In the context of the former, tolerance is a genuine manifestation of virtue. Social, cultural, and ethnic pluralism is to be welcomed and praised; it is the soil in which the gospel exists and is furthered, since it mirrors the splendor and rich diversity of creation. At stake in this form of pluralism are negotiable issues – issues such as language, cultural customs, ethnic habits, group preferences, and so forth. In the context of the latter form, however, discernment is necessary, since ideological pluralists demand that we "tolerate" alternative explanations of reality, while at the same time pressuring us to negotiate – and abdicate – claims to ultimate truth. In American culture, a shift in understanding "tolerance" has occurred – a shift that calls for vigilance. "Tolerance" has devolved into an indifference toward the possibility and parameters of truth, often belligerently and intolerably so; the result is a baneful permissiveness toward all manner of evil. Thereby a virtue has been transmuted into vice.

The tone of the ideological pluralist or "inclusivist," of course, sounds so epistemologically modest, so eminently reasonable. By contrast, exclusivists like Charles strike us as rather arrogant and bigoted, even oppressive. Yet precisely the opposite is in fact the case.[21] This is why martyrdom is an abiding Christian reality. Ideological pluralists, after all, do not offer up their lives in the name of being "radically inclusive."

Tolerance properly construed

Let us recall that tolerance, in our wider cultural tradition, emerged as a political and social virtue. And as such, it has private as well as public or communal dimensions. While we may disagree with another's opinion, vice, or lifestyle, we extend (in principle, at least) that person's "right" to a specific opinion or behavior which we may find objectionable. This duty, of course, to include all points of view inheres in what some call "classical pluralism." Christians and non-Christians of all varieties tolerate one another's differences because of what they all share in common – the laws of nature, inalienable rights, and a dignity that inheres in personhood. When, however, a person – in the name of "tolerance" – is making claims on the public square that issue out of an indifference or hostility toward truth, tolerance must then cease, for *we tolerate what we dislike until it begins making claims on the wider community in a way that undermines the common good*. Thus, we are compelled to draw a strict distinction between the freedoms of an individual, practiced in private, and the needs of the community, of which we all are contributing parts. This distinction is not necessarily owing to Christian insight, for Locke himself makes the basic observation – a important one for contemporary Americans – that a great deal of difference can be tolerated *provided that it does not endanger social cohesion*.

But in practical terms, what does this mean? As it concerns morally objectionable behavior, where exactly do we draw the line? How do we as a society determine what behavior is acceptable and what is unacceptable? A well-worn bit of conventional wisdom among religious folks is that we should "hate the sin while loving the sinner." While there is some truth to be granted herein, this nice-sounding piece of piety can easily descend into sloppy sentimentalism if it severs truth from love. To "speak the truth in love"[22] is to embody a moral honesty that refuses to compromise, in the name of "tolerance" or "diversity," the consequences of ultimate reality. At the same time, it is cognizant of the fact that fellow human beings are to be treated as bearers of the image of God. Love and truth are not mutually exclusive, despite the ethical propaganda that emanates from common culture (and, sadly, much religious teaching). Those who would call us to "love the sinner" frequently really are requiring of us that we sympathize non-judgmentally with him, by which they mean we should refrain from stigmatizing and expressing disapproval. The person, then, will feel better. But as one social critic has quipped, this attitude only "makes the world safe for moral dereliction."[23]

An anatomy of tolerance and neutrality

In our wrestling with where and how to draw the line between what is acceptable and unacceptable in the public sphere, let us step back for the moment and think through the process. We have assumed at the outset that, properly understood, tolerance is a patient endurance of a practice, opinion, or behavior of which one (or a majority of citizens) disapproves. To censure opinions or behaviors is to acknowledge that there are moral guidelines and moral limits that cause what is "good" and "true" to cohere and be intelligible. The evaluation of what is "tolerable" or "intolerable" is not measured by one's sincerity, one's personal experience, one's personal preference, or the insistence with which one holds particular convictions. If any of these themselves were moral barometers, then morality would reduce to personal whim and preference. You like chocolate, I happen to like strawberry, and the result is that we will simply have to agree to disagree. At the communal level, no one thereby is technically "right" or "wrong." At the policy level, however, if the "common good" is not informed by moral principle but rather by preference, in the end it becomes fluid and the "preferences" of the cultural and ruling elite are enshrined in power. Thus, the moral evaluation of "tolerable" and "intolerable" depends on the limits of what can be identified as good and true, and these limits are made known and confirmed, as we argued in Chapter 1, by the natural law. Positive and civil law owe their authority to natural law, without which they become fluid and arbitrary. For this reason, religious and non-religious people alike contend together in the public sphere, working for standards that just and equitable.

Furthermore, we shall need to distinguish between "intolerance" popularly construed and a genuine *critical discernment* that guards the common good, without which "civil society" cannot survive. In our day, this distinction is absolutely crucial, given the widespread tendency to denounce people of principle as "intolerant," "bigoted," and "hate-filled." If those decrying others as "intolerant" are philosophically indifferent to what is good, true, and real, society will need to *discern* this tendency and *name* it publicly for what it is. This responsibility is especially important in a cultural environment such as ours, given our fear of confrontation and our unwillingness to make moral judgments.

If "tolerance," "diversity," and "compassion" are not rooted in moral principle, they end up corrupting both the practitioner and the object. Elevating them to the status of cardinal virtues, while disengaging them from unbending moral realities, sends the signal to the unscrupulous that

> a good strategy for getting their way is to play on other people's pity, which is dreadfully destructive to character. It encourages malingering, self-pity, and claims of victimhood. It encourages not self-sufficiency, but dependence . . . not strength, but weakness; not honesty and integrity, but shameless and vicious exploitation of others; not cheerfulness in adversity, but whining; not acceptance of life's vicissitudes, but a readiness to find fault.[24]

Locke would concur, emphasizing in his *Letter on Tolerance* that if lawmakers did not establish laws against the prejudices and passions of men, society could not subsist. While autonomy was for him important, it was limited, and in no way did it entail license with regard to morality. Locke presupposed a rationally discerned morality shared by all – the natural law.

But where and how do responsible citizens – and religious believers in particular – "draw the line" between the tolerable and intolerable? Our answer must be this: we draw the line where private preferences that undermine the communal good and violate the natural moral law make claims in the public sphere. Are Christians called to tolerate an individual whose sexual behavior differs? Indeed. Are Christians called to tolerate the theoretical and practical promotion of that behavior in the form of social or public policy? By no means. Whereas sexuality is a private matter, educating on human sexuality (at least through *public* – i.e., tax-supported, institutions) ceases to be private; it is very much a public and communal concern.[25] Therefore, assuming an open marketplace of ideas in the classical pluralist sense, people of religious conviction – especially Christians – are not only free to contend but also *required* to do so, whatever the cost and inconvenience. They do so for the purposes of preserving social cohesion and the moral order.[26] This task, it goes without saying, will not be easy, particularly given the inclination of Western societies to tolerate the intolerable in our day.

A willingness to make the distinctions for which I argued earlier will doubtless lead to charges *ad nauseum* that as cultural "imperialists" and "bigots," we are "imposing" our morality on those around us and that the public sphere must remain "neutral." In the last several decades, of course, vigorous debate has transpired between professors of law, political scientists, and philosophers over interlocking questions of justice, "rights," and the public square. The strongest advocates of "tolerance" in our day insist on the idea that the public realm must remain morally "neutral." And because it is thought to be "neutral," the state and public affairs therefore must remain "neutral" in adjudicating various claims to "rights." But is there such a thing as moral "neutrality?"

If there are particular goods identified that need protecting, then society cannot be "neutral" with regard to those goods. It has a vested interest in maintaining and preserving them. Those "goods," of course, are established on the basis of what a society considers to be ultimate and authoritative.[27] Moral neutrality is neither self-evident not self-justifying; rather, it must be shown to be true or correct. When its proponents press their argument in the public sphere for a particular position – for example, on the nature of the family or marriage, same-sex unions, free speech, abortion rights, or capital punishment – they argue that competing notions are controversial, mistaken, and therefore to be rejected. Thus, "moral neutrality" is much like moral relativism insofar as its proponents attempt to demonstrate through arguments for or against competing positions the falsehood of its alleged existence.[28]

The point needing emphasis is this: there exists an inescapably *public morality*. Some moral force, represented by some subset of the population, will make policy decisions that affect the whole. Thus, no one is neutral with regard to the common weal. Furthermore, classically conceived pluralism and tolerance do not require that the community – or various communities – sacrifice their deeply held moral beliefs for the sake of individual preferences.

It is here that we must stress the symbiosis between tolerance and the common good – a point often ignored or neglected in present-day policy debates. Tolerance as an authentic virtue, as we have argued, is rooted in a firm commitment to what is true and good for society. Conversely, as a vice tolerance is indifferent to these realities. Therefore, tolerance is not – indeed, it cannot be – neutral toward what affects society. Even staunchly secular approaches to public and political life themselves are thoroughly religious in nature. That is to say, they arise out of deeply held or binding commitments (from the Latin verb *religare*, "to bind") to what people believe to be right and wrong, acceptable and unacceptable. Thus, any comprehensive orientation toward life has an inherently "religious" character, and every political and legal mode of reasoning begins and ends with fundamental assumptions, pre-commitments, and preconceptions about the origin, nature, and goal of life.[29]

Precisely what people are prepared to tolerate pivots on what is ultimate in their personal lives. And what society tolerates is predicated on its hierarchy of values. Social consensus is possible where there are overlapping realms of agreed-upon moral-social capital. Where there is no overlapping agreement, consensus is impossible, and anarchy is invited.[30] Therefore, it is necessary to expose the falsehood of the philosophical and sociological notion that a pluralistic society can be neutral on moral matters. This we might illustrate at the most basic level. If someone claims the "right to die," society is morally constrained to respond on the basis of the natural law: as an objective "good," human life has intrinsic value that must be protected by the state (if, that is, the state is legitimate). "Neutrality," which would permit right-to-die advocates the luxury of finding a constitutional "right to privacy," is not an option. Likewise, in response to homosexual activists who insist that gay marriage is a "civil right" to be on par with heterosexual marriages, we might argue that neither government nor the public can seek refuge in a purported "neutrality," since there exists a particular "nature" and function of human activity that is consensually demonstrable throughout human civilization. (In the penultimate chapter of this volume, I develop the tragic social ramifications of a "right-to-die" ethos, by which the intrinsic value of human life has *not* been protected by the state. My intention is to argue that human "freedom" is capable of annihilating itself.)

The fathers of the American experiment assumed that people will broadly agree on rationally discernible moral norms, a *consensus juris*, that will inform a society's understanding of rights, justice, good, and evil. This consensus, it should be noted, guards against a tyranny of both the minority and the majority, since "tyranny" *per se* is a fundamental violation of human (or natural) rights that are inalienable. There is, then, no moral "neutrality" as envisioned by this nation's founders and framers; in the interest of all of society, particular "goods" will need to be defended.[31]

In the end, the public nature of the marketplace (of both ideas and goods) as well as of social institutions, coupled with the very public nature of debating what constitutes the common good, compels people of good will – and especially people of religious faith – to work for the common good using and all means. This they must do, so long as democratic pluralism resists the centripetal slide into a soft form of totalitarian statism. And in response to the potential objection that a balance of power – i.e., judicial, executive, and legislative – excludes the possibility of political tyranny of various degrees in the United States, or, like democracies, I would simply pose a question. What if all three branches of "democratic" government, mirroring the values of elitist culture, are (more or less) committed to a bleaching of the religious viewpoint and an eradication of Christian participation in the moral, legal, as well as political process? For those of us who tend to shy away from confrontation and simply wish for greater "toleration" in an unqualified way, we do well to remember that a society

> cannot function well, cannot survive, and cannot protect the innocent . . . from harm and evil, without a large measure of intolerance. Yes, intolerance – of theft, burglary, cruelty, classroom hooliganism, disrespect for parental authority, and violent crime of all sorts; of substance abuse, infidelity, illegitimacy, perversion, pornography, rape, and child molestation; of fraud, envy, covetousness, and knavery; of sloth, mediocrity, incompetence, maleducation, improvidence, irresponsibility and fecklessness. A society tolerant of those things would soon find itself in serious trouble, even facing dissolution, and many people in that society would be in peril of their lives.[32]

Alas, tolerance properly construed *cannot avoid* the unpleasant task of making moral judgments. In fact, all people in truth *do* make moral judgments; that is, all people do draw the moral line between "acceptable" and "unacceptable." The difference is *where* we all choose to draw that line. In the end, then, *someone's* morality *will* be imposed in the public sphere; there is, quite honestly, no such thing as "moral neutrality." The ostensible neutrality of the modern secular state, in the words of constitutional scholar Stephen D. Smith, "turns out to be, upon closer examination, a sort of political optical illusion."[33]

Everyone has claims on the public square – most notably Christian believers, whose cultural mandate rests on a firm commitment to the redemption of all things.[34] While it is surely not a given that everyone's claim will be "tolerated," tolerance properly understood mirrors a strong and principled commitment to promote moral truth and work for the common good.[35] It is perhaps high time to return a good word that has been hijacked and reinstate its proper meaning,

Truth and tolerance: again, the moral bottom line

In his important volume *Truth and Tolerance: Christian Belief and World Religions*, former Pope Benedict XVI neither shies away from the exclusive nature of Christian claims nor is inattentive to the need of Christians to enter into dialogue, courageously yet humbly, with those who imbibe the radically pluralist spirit of the age. For Benedict, religion can have two trajectories: one the one hand it can be preparatory, and on the other hand, it can be repressive to the extent that it prevents acknowledgment or affirmation of greater truth. Scripturally, Christian faith understands the existence of both of these trajectories and engages both in a humble, tolerant, and truth-seeking fashion. Christian believers will seek to exploit common ground with our contemporaries, attentive to themes, values, and truths that are partially grasped by the rational non-Christian. At the same time, they will be critically discerning in this engagement, at times resistant or in opposition to the error that might accompany the pluralist *Zeitgeist*.

Benedict aims to address the perspective on religious belief that is dominant today, which is markedly skeptical and typically secularist in character. This perspective views Christianity's exclusivist claims over against other worldviews as a sign of arrogance and religious imperialism. No one, it is thought, can declare any religious viewpoint to be false or less "true"; "truth," after all, is multiple, subjective, and multiperspectival. To confess a perspective of truth that is objective, knowable, and unified is to commit the cardinal sin of "judgmentalism" – to be rigid, bigoted, and culturally imperialistic.

For Benedict, the real test of competing "truth"-claims amidst cultural and religious diversity is graphically demonstrated in one's ability to withstand suffering in a hostile cultural environment and, if need be (from the Christian vantage point), suffer martyrdom. In the aftermath of the former pope's appointment – then as Cardinal Ratzinger – in 1992 as a member of the Academy of Moral Sciences and Politics of the Institut de France and successor to the Russian scientist and (former Soviet) dissident Andrey Sakharov, Ratzinger paid homage to Sakharov in ways that are significant. Sakharov, he recognized, "accepted the price of suffering and of persecution" in order to uphold human dignity, ethical integrity, and freedom, even when it meant giving up his scientific work. From 1968 onward, Sakharov had been excluded from work on projects that included state secrets while he was advocating universal human rights. Though loving his country deeply, Sakharov was forced to accuse a regime that oppressed his people and reduced them to servitude. For Ratzinger, Sakharov's commitment to human dignity, freedom, and human rights is an enduring lesson. The Russian dissident resisted those forces – at once philosophical and political – that destroyed what it meant to be truly human.

In Western culture, these forces have expressed themselves in a stubborn nihilism, even when it is a nihilism with a happy face. Freedom, alas, can annihilate itself, and that annihilation may be the fruit of absolutizing the majority viewpoint. In his address, Ratzinger confronts his audience with candor: neither National Socialism nor Communism nor secular naturalism of the West regards any particular action *per se* as universally evil or immoral; all of these cultural idolatries, he laments, are characterized by an emptying of the soul.[36]

In his pontificate, Benedict continued to advance what was a major theme in the writings of John Paul II by arguing that freedom, properly construed, must be tethered to truth if it is legitimate.[37] In his 1995 encyclical *Evangelium Vitae*, John Paul observed a profound confusion between good and evil resulting in the corruption of conscience that is taking place in our "culture of death" – a culture that, in the view of some, is becoming re-paganized.[38] His commentary, it should be remembered, came after the extraordinary events in Eastern Europe of 1989 and 1990 and was *directed at those living in Western democracies*:

> Today, when many countries have seen the fall of ideologies which bound politics to a totalitarian conception of the world – Marxism being the foremost of these – there is no less grave a danger that the fundamental rights of the human person will be denied and that the religious yearnings which a rise in the heart of every human being will be absorbed once again into politics. This is *the risk of an alliance between democracy and ethical relativism*, which would remove any sure moral reference point from the political and social life, and on a deeper level make the acknowledgement of truth impossible.[39]

Does John Paul resort to over-statement by warning of "an alliance of democracy and ethical relativism" and by the potential for this to "make the acknowledgment of truth impossible?" This theme, it should be remembered, was a common feature in his writings and mirrored the conviction that *if there is not ultimate truth to guide and direct the activity of a society, then ideas and priorities are easily manipulated for the purposes of raw, corrosive political power*. John Paul seems to have in mind lessons of recent history when he reiterates that a "democracy without values readily turns into open or thinly veiled totalitarianism."[40] John Paul's burden calls to mind the words of the social philosopher Michael Novak, who had a knack for understanding the times in which we live:

> During the next hundred years, the question for those who love liberty is whether we can survive the most insidious and duplicitous attacks from within, from those who undermine the virtues of our people, doing in advance the work of the Father of Lies. "There is no such thing as truth," they teach even the little ones. "Truth is bondage. Believe what seems right to you. There are as many truths as there are individuals. Follow your feelings. Do as you please. Get in touch with yourself. Do what feels comfortable." Those who speak in this way prepare the jails of the twenty-first century. They do the work of tyrants.[41]

Significantly, the "crisis of truth" was a recurring theme in the encyclicals of John Paul and in none more so than *Veritatis Splendor* ("The Splendor of Truth"). Throughout *VS*, John Paul analyzes different facets of morality, at the heart of which are lodged the natural law and the Ten Commandments. Divine revelation, he argues, comes initially through the natural law – i.e., "the law written on the heart" of every human being – illuminating the human heart at the most basic level with regard to moral first things. There is a common thread that unites John Paul with Augustine, Aquinas, Calvin, and even the American founders, whose language of "self-evident truths" mirrors the shared conviction of a "nature" that is ordered by "nature's God." All ascribe to a view of reality, expressed through the natural law, which requires that humans, regardless of cultural context, pursue the good and just for the sake of the common weal of society. To pursue the good is, in the words of Jesus, to "love your neighbor" and to "treat others as you would have them treat you." This moral intuition, it should be emphasized, was not limited to Jesus's teaching or to Christian faith; Plato also uses this formulation, which serves to illustrate that it is universal in its scope and applicability, an expression of "general revelation," of natural moral law.

Because the human person is "by nature a social animal,"[42] the human social order depends on a commitment to preserve the good and resist what is evil, transcending differences in religion and culture. To fail to do so is to pervert justice and breed moral anarchy.[43] Society's laws, then, out of necessity must deliberately seek to affirm and reinforce the natural law; the common good depends on it. Members of society are to advance and uphold human positive laws that embody the ethical contours of the moral law. The Decalogue, properly viewed, provides the ethical contours of the natural law.[44] Those moral norms contained therein protect and sanctify critical social elements such as family and parental authority, human life, material property, and respect for others. As moral obligations, they are self-evident and unchanging with time and culture. While the natural law does not guide us and instruct us in the construction and application of *all* laws in *every* given situation, laws must mirror and accord with the moral basis of the natural law if they possess any moral authority.[45]

It becomes apparent that in the historic Christian moral tradition, the problem of cultural and religious diversity, of pluralism and tolerance, is in truth no "problem" at all. In fact, pluralism has been the environment in which Christian faith – indeed, Israel's faith before it – always found itself. Indeed, this was the true scandal of Israel's faith from the start – namely, that she was "rigidly" monotheistic in a radically polytheistic and pluralistic world. For this reason, not only Aristotle and classical philosophers, who grasped partial truth about the universe but also Christian moral thinkers from Augustine to Aquinas to C.S. Lewis to John Paul II have argued for the application of natural-law thinking in the realm of public discourse, irrespective of provenance. All were cognizant of the need to argue for moral "first principles" on the basis of human nature. To do so is to reckon with the reality of pluralism and begin at the place of common ground between believer and non-believer.[46]

It is significant that both John Paul II and Benedict XVI have argued that human freedom requires moral content. Human freedoms and rights depend on moral realities that transcend the body politic and the democratic process. These moral realities are not subject to assorted demands for "pluralism," "tolerance," or "diversity," however commendable or acceptable these may be. Authentic freedom is grounded in objective notions of law and the good. If and where these notions are fluid, then human rights and freedoms vary; indeed, they may even be eliminated. But such is the danger not merely of the totalitarian state; it is the potential for any "democratic" society, since values derive their validity and inviolability precisely from the fact that they are true and universally normative.[47] Otherwise, we cannot address moral atrocity at any level in any sphere of human activity.

Whether or not the reader is willing to grant the "re-paganized" character of Western culture, as some social critics have maintained, important challenges confront us. How does the religious believer engage not only a surrounding pluralistic culture but also a plurality of cultures? And on what moral basis? Interculturality – and with it, religious and philosophical pluralism – is the undeniable context in which discussions of basic human issues occurs today, whether political, legal, social, or moral in nature. The Christian believer will need to engage secular materialists within our own Western context as well as diverse people-groups and religions of the world, between which there exist great differences and tensions. But secular rationalism,[48] which has been thought by many in Western societies to be universal and govern the world, in fact is quite limited as an explanatory outlook, not merely from the religious perspective but seen logically. At the philosophical level, it is unable to offer a satisfactory and definitive explanation of ultimate reality and of moral first principles. Viewed practically, it would seem to breed social and political consequences that render it deficient in terms of responsible social policy. It is surely not insignificant that even leading proponents of secularism's dogmas have suggested this deficiency at the social policy level.

Secularism and the post-secular shift

Reason and religion

During the last decade-and-a-half, the idea of the "post-secular" has acquired growing currency in contemporary academic discourse.[49] Longstanding and relatively unexamined assumptions about reigning "modes of secularism" have been revisited across a variety of academic disciplines. Whatever our own assessment of this supposed development might be, it raises questions of enormous importance concerning the place of religion in society, as suggested by an attendant skepticism vis-à-vis scientific naturalism.[50] These questions, at the very least, challenge our understanding of public life. Accompanying these questions is the realization that secularism, whatever it is, is not "neutral." In what follows, I take note of a fascinating – and in many ways, significant – exchange between two leading intellectual figures that illustrates the need for rethinking not only what "secularism" entails but also the role that religion plays in any society.

At the invitation of the Catholic Academy of Bavaria, in January of 2004 two intellectual "antipodes" agreed to dialogue on the political and moral foundations of secular Western society. The meeting of Jürgen Habermas, one of the most influential contemporary philosophers and secular theorists alive, and Joseph Cardinal Ratzinger, the then Prefect of the Roman Congregation for the Doctrine of the Faith (to become Pope Benedict XVI one year later) was remarkable for several reasons. Not least was the high profile of these interlocutors – one a preeminent secular theorist and the other arguably the most visible Christian leader in the world. Consider as well the parallels between the two. Both were born in the 1920s – Habermas in 1929, Ratzinger in 1927. Both took their doctorate in the twelve-month span between 1953 and 1954. Both settled into their eventual influential positions in the early 1980s – Ratzinger as Prefect of Congregation for the Doctrine of the Faith in 1981 and Habermas assuming his final professorial position in 1983 in Frankfurt. Both, however, appear to be the ultimate embodiment of secular and religious conviction.[51]

The dialogue between Habermas and Ratzinger, it needs pointing out, coincided with the aftermath of significant geopolitical developments. Hence, we must back up. Three weeks after the terrorist attacks on September 11 of 2001, Habermas had given his acceptance speech of the "Peace Prize" at the German Booksellers convention. His remarks created no little controversy. Acknowledging his own inclination to be "tone deaf" with regard to religion, Habermas surprised many by insisting that secular society must acquire a new appreciation for the role of religion. This he declared even when such poses a "cognitive challenge" to philosophy. Habermas challenged his audience to take seriously the realm of religious belief, which he characterized as significantly more than simply a vestige of the past. Part of the controversy generated by Habermas's remarks issued from the fact that up until the early 2000s, Habermas had depicted religious belief as antithetical to the modern liberal state. Since then, that has changed. In his more recent writings, he has argued for the need of recognizing religion's value in democratic liberalism.[52]

The two interlocutors had agreed to address the topic of *pre-political foundations of a democratic state*. For Habermas, the topic mirrors the basis of a "postmetaphysical," secular mode of thinking, whereas for Ratzinger the subject permits reflections on distinctly metaphysical realities – moral realities – which give life and meaning to all. Few can miss the antithesis. At the same time, what is noteworthy is the common ground shared by these two individuals at the social and political level. And given this common ground, it is appropriate to rehearse the fruits of this dialogue.

Habermas asks at the outset whether a free (= democratic) state presupposes as its basis what it cannot in fact guarantee. Is it still possible to offer secular – which is to say, "postmetaphysical," non-religious – justification for the state? And what precisely is it that unites the citizenry? Moreover, what happens if society degenerates, "goes off the rails," and collapses? Habermas's own response is surprising. He suggests that society must understand "secularization" as a "double learning process that compels both the traditions of the Enlightenment and the religious doctrine to reflect on their own respective limits."[53] This he maintains, even when he rejects the overt assumptions that religion and natural law theory bring. To his credit, Habermas is able to ask *why* human rights are rooted in democracy from the very beginning. His response is that a democratic state is constituted, at its core, by the rule of law, although he is quick to renounce the antecedent moral realities of the natural law.[54] Legality, not morality, govern Habermas's way of thinking.

But in spite of his rejection of inherently *moral*, and thus pre-political, foundations of the democratic state, Habermas acknowledges that not only a common language and nationalism contribute to a society's collective identity but also its common religious heritage; these, he concedes, *are* "pre-political." But when these societal bonds break, it would seem that we are left with "market" forces that increasingly regulate peoples' lives, leaving the citizenry with a "depoliticized" sense of belonging. Reacting to this social-cultural tendency of "modernism" is postmodern theory in its variant forms. Habermas takes this reaction one step further by positing that "when reason reflects on its deepest foundations, it discovers that it owes its origins to something else."[55] At bottom, then, "philosophy has good reasons to be willing to learn from religious traditions."[56]

Where does this leave us? Habermas concludes, albeit in a somewhat surprising fashion to some, "It is in the interest of the constitutional state to deal carefully with all the cultural sources that nourish its citizens' consciousness of norms and their solidarity." This awareness, he notes, which has become conservative, "is reflected in the phrase: 'postsecular society.'"[57] But this "post-secular" concession mirrors not only the fact that religion is important to many people but also reflects "a normative insight that has consequences for the political dealings of unbelieving citizens with believing citizens."[58] For the citizen who is "unmusical" in religious matters, Habermas concludes that this dual respect – i.e., the awareness that the "secular" and the "sacred" cannot be partitioned or separated – "demands" that he or she acknowledge the *rational* character of public disagreement (to a limit, of course) between religious and non-religious viewpoints.[59] In the public and political arena, a naturalistic worldview does not trump competing religious worldviews. In practical terms, this means for Habermas that "neutrality" of the state should mean that every citizen has the same ethical freedom – a freedom that is "incompatible" with the political universalization of a secularist worldview. In fact, "a liberal political culture can expect that the secularized citizens play their part in the endeavors to translate relevant contributions from the religious language into a language that is accessible to the public as a whole."[60]

Given the enormous potential for doing good and doing evil in our day, Joseph Cardinal Ratzinger finds it necessary to accentuate what Habermas in theory initially denies – namely, that science, technology, and politics *per se* cannot address the question of doing good and *why* we must do the good. This, rather, is the reserve of moral philosophy and religion, which must shed light on basic questions of human personhood and the reason and purpose for our existence. The task of politics, Ratzinger insists, is to structure the use of power in a moral and meaningful way. Law must be rooted in its antecedent, the moral law. Freedom without law is nothing less than anarchy, which, in turn ends up destroying freedom. Moreover, there will always arise suspicion of the law and rebellion against the law when and where "law itself appears to be no longer the expression of a justice that is at the service of all, but rather the product of arbitrariness and legislative arrogance on the part of those who have the power for it."[61]

This, for Ratzinger, forces upon us an antecedent question: what is the genesis of law? The answer cannot be public sentiment, social trends or a "majority decision," since "majorities" themselves "can be blind or unjust, as history teaches us very plainly."[62] Rather, there must be "self-subsistent" values, pre-political beliefs, universal moral principles that are rationally discerned and inviolable – values that inform basic "human rights," upon which no one can infringe.[63] Ratzinger anticipates the secularist's question: what about the global problem of religiously inspired terrorism? Doesn't this phenomenon require that religion "be placed under the guardianship of reason," with the boundaries of religion carefully marked off?[64] But the problem of religiously inspired terrorism is not the only global threat. Another concerns the implications of "reason" unbounded. Because through technology humankind is now capable of "producing" other human beings artificially, Ratzinger worries that man becomes a product, no longer a *gift* of nature and nature's Creator God. And surely, the temptation, then, to produce the "right" person is well within reach, the very logical next step in human "progress."

Whether the danger is religion that terrorizes or reason which is ethically unrestrained, Ratzinger is led to conclude that there is a law that is *discovered*, not created. It is a law that transcends legal systems and cultures, a law binding on men *qua* men in their mutual relationships that tells them what are their moral obligations.[65] This law – the natural law – "transcends the confessional borders of faith by establishing reason as the instrument whereby law can be posited in common."[66] And because it seeks a rational basis for a moral consensus in a pluralistic cultural context, the natural law remains central to dialogue and debate between religious and secular interlocutors and communities. Without the natural law, there are no "human rights," Ratzinger insists. Without human moral obligations, human rights in truth cannot exist. Whence, then, come human obligations?

This question, of course, is not some intra-Christian or narrowly Western matter. The basic questions that concern human existence – *Who am I? What is my purpose? What is ultimate?* – are universal and not culturally bound. In fact, it is reasonable to argue that of the "two great cultures" of the Western world – namely, the culture of Christian faith and the culture of secular rationalism – the latter is *not* universal. It might well be argued that "European secularization is an *exceptional* development and *one that needs to be corrected.*"[67] Evidence thereof for Ratzinger is that it comes up against its limitations when it attempts to demonstrate itself, and it is incapable of being reproduced in the whole of mankind.

What, then, might we conclude from dialogue between secular and religious viewpoints? Some agreement exists between Ratzinger and Habermas insofar as Habermas mirrors a shift toward a "post-secularism." At the very least, a "post-secular" bearing would appear more tolerant of – and open to – the religious viewpoint, and for this, we can be grateful. In addition, we may acknowledge in humility, as Ratzinger does, that there are pathologies in religion just as there are pathologies of reason. That is, religion can be divorced from reason with results that are unspeakably tragic, just as there is a dangerous hubris of reason that refuses to acknowledge any sort of accountability to a higher authority. Both pathologies stand in need of purging. As Ratzinger reminds us, faith and reason are symbiotic in the historic Christian tradition; in the words of John Paul, they are like two wings of a bird in flight in their pursuit of the truth.[68]

The secular west: retrospect and prospects

In his book *Values in a Time of Upheaval*, Benedict XVI reflects on Europe's past, present, and future. His reflections serve as an occasion for North Americans to do the same, given the secularization process that has been afoot. Despite the fact that America was birthed in reaction to certain tendencies of European culture, and despite the many potentially divisive cultural identities that comprise "Europe," one factor remains clear, even when it is a source of embarrassment. The "founding fathers" of Europe regarded the Christian heritage as the core of their historical identity: "That which is common to all Christians, transcending denominational borders, seemed to them to supply a force strong enough to harmonize political conduct in the world."[69] Moreover, "this did not appear incompatible with the great moral impulses of the Enlightenment, which had displayed the rational side of Christianity . . ."[70]

Even when these basic assumptions about Christian faith were acknowledged in the aftermath of the Second World War, during which time the great universal declarations of human rights based on natural law thinking were formulated, various ideological trends radically broke with this tradition. Foremost among these was a Marxist understanding of human nature and society, coupled with a Hegelian view of history. Rationality thereby was subordinated to functionality, whether political, socioeconomic, or technological in its manifestation. Even in a post-Marxist era, the departure from the ethical tradition that shaped Europe remains, as debates over the European Union's constitution in the early 2000s well demonstrated. What should give us pause, as it does for Benedict, is the fact that secular rationalism, divorced from the ethical moorings of its religious heritage, becomes destructive to human personhood. *We ignore this heritage at our peril.* So Benedict: "The attempt to think and to live *without any contact with these great [ethical] traditions* [governing Europe's past] would be an arrogance that ultimately leaves man helpless and empty."[71]

An underlying assumption of the argument developed thus far in this volume is that to remove or restrict religion from politics and the public sphere (whether in the European or North American context), though advocated by many, illustrates a basic misunderstanding of the nature of pluralism. It is in fact in keeping with principled pluralism and the natural law that religious beliefs and religious arguments be integrated into the fabric of a democratic society. An ordered or "principled" pluralism mirrors the natural law to the extent that a society is ordered to the common good. We may insist that *every* individual citizen and *every* group within society is informed by a particular world- and life-view, and a sense of what is ultimate, even when such is implicit or unacknowledged. In this sense, "secularism" may be understood as a "worldview," informed by basic assumptions about what is ultimate.[72] Correlatively, religious belief is a reasonable world- and life-view as well, and hence must be part of the public sphere, *if* a society is truly democratic. No society, without being totalitarian, can exclude from the public sphere and from public debate over the momentous issues of the day any worldview that represents a large part of the population.[73] Unless, that is, this "majority" view is *per se* evil and destructive.[74]

To attempt to make a case for "principled" pluralism, which is the burden the present chapter, is not to argue chiefly for a particular legal or constitutional position. It is, rather, to make a foremost *moral* argument – one that will have momentous social and policy implications. Is it morally acceptable for religious conviction to have a role in the public sphere? The *legality* of any policy issue must be preceded by considerations of the *morality* of the matter. What is not needed in our day is that cultural "conservatives" – and religious "conservatives" in particular – move toward a social secession, sequestering themselves from secular culture and norms, however tempting that may be. When religion isolates itself from secular society, both sides lose, with religion losing more.[75]

Here we must humbly acknowledge that religious believers at times have been misguided in terms of their response to the challenges of relativism and secularism in the American context. Two tendencies are worth noting. One is to project the view that religious belief is purely a matter of "faith, that is, something that should not be judged by the standards of *reason*." Another is to sit by passively while secularists are mounting a very public campaign to have religion privatized or marginalized. Both inclinations need to be resisted. Stanley Carlson-Thies, senior director of the Institutional Religious Freedom Alliance, writes that for religious freedom to flourish three elements – or, "commitments to a particular conception of the good" – need to be expressed publicly by religious organizations and communities: (1) a faith-shaped identity that can be observed in its people and its mission, (2) faith-shaped standards for those who are employed or associated, and (3) a faith-influenced set of services that are tangible and ethically formed expressions of that community's worldview.[76]

What is needed in the broadly Western context is an approach to public moral persuasion that at times will *leaven* secular culture and at times *counter* an aggressively secular transformation of the culture. In arguing such I am making the assumption that we are not *too late*, culturally speaking, in our attempts at affecting the moral fabric of society. Any attempts to leaven or counter the cultural climate, of course, will not be popular; they will inevitably encounter the wrath of "majority" opinion. But the fear of what others think of us must not be our motivation, in the end. At their root, our attempts to influence the moral tenor of public discourse will proceed from a commitment to be faithful to what is true and real and good. Such a commitment, which more often than not will entail a very real cost, lies at the heart of a "principled" pluralism. After all, to resist majoritarian opinion requires moral *principle*.

In his inaugural address as the Regius Chair of Moral and Pastoral Theology at the University of Oxford, Nigel Biggar argues that in our day religious believers should affirm a "humane, polyglot liberalism," even when this responsibility requires critical levels of moral discernment. As suggested by the intriguing title "Saving the Secular," Biggar's address challenges the stifling bias of secularism which refuses to permit religious categories in public discourse. Why, Biggar asks, should religious and theological references "uniquely suffer ban from public conversation?" But the flip side of this bias also needs exposing: "Why should Aristotelians, Hobbesians, Marxists, Nietzscheans, and Social Darwinists be allowed to say what they mean in their own terms, but not orthodox Jews or Christians or Muslims?"[77] The bottom line for Biggar is that *it is indeed possible* for religious contributions to public discussion to be reasonable, and to be accessible. This, of course, assumes that religious believers are making serious attempts at accessibility; nevertheless, the possibility must not be denied. What is important, Biggar insists,

> is that we want to reach a common understanding of the truth, that we are prepared to explain how and why we see things as we do, that we are open to honest negotiation, and that we are inclined to exercise charity in our construction and reconstruction of each other's point of view. In sum, what matters is not the *language* of public discourse, but the *manner* of its conduct – and the motives and intentions that drive it.[78]

This strikes me as eminently good advice. While I might quibble ever so slightly with Biggar's suggestion that "what matters is not the language of public discourse" – for, indeed, it *does* matter, as anyone who has ever lived in a foreign culture can testify – the wider point is well taken. The manner in which our communication is conducted, as verified by our motives and our intentions, matters enormously. As the Germans say, *Schluss, Punkt, Fertig, Aus*.

***

Clashes over religious freedom between competing value systems not infrequently claim lives around the world. In democracies and relatively free nations, however, bloodshed is supposed to be averted. But because less blood is being spilled in so-called free societies does not mean that the dignity of the human person, in materialistic, immoral, or demeaning ways, is not being degraded. As one Canadian social commentator remarks, where religious communities are coerced to hollow out their beliefs and where young adults are seeing their futures eviscerated because of the culture's values, it is perhaps time to ask, *is our system of politics and law serving us well?*[79] And at what point to do policy disputes, representing the intersection of politics and law, in fact become issues of religious freedom?

In the chapter that follows, we must take one step back and probe the very reason *why* religious freedom – if there is such a thing – is the "first freedom."

Notes

1 Strangely, Western culture cannot (as of 2016) bring itself to acknowledge both the debt to its Christian heritage and the discordance between democratic values and aspects of other world religions.
2 The literature in this realm, it goes without saying, is virtually boundless. A useful starting-point is Jonathan Chaplin, "Rejecting Neutrality, Respecting Diversity: From 'Liberal Pluralism' to Christian Pluralism," *Christian Scholars Review* 35, no. 2 (Winter 2006): 143–75. Chaplin attempts to map the bewildering "plurality of pluralisms" that are thought to exist within Western liberal polity while examining responses thereto.
3 John Stuart Mill, *On Liberty*, ed. Alburey Castell (New York: Appleton-Century-Crofts, 1947), 16.
4 John 18:38.
5 John 19:11.
6 Both the letter to Washington and his response are to be found at www.tourosynagogue.org/history-learning/gw-letter.
7 To say "in part" is accurate, since the founders' other fear, political tyranny, is ever present, instructing us throughout all of human history.
8 John Locke, *An Essay on Toleration*, reproduced in Mark A. Goldie, ed., *Locke: Political Essays* (Cambridge Texts in the History of Political Thought; Cambridge: Cambridge University Press, 1997), 137.
9 Ibid.
10 Ibid.
11 Perez Zagorin, *How the Idea of Religious Toleration Came to the West* (Princeton: Princeton University Press, 2003), xii–xiii.
12 This remains the case even when most historians of the era, Zagorin included, view Luther, Calvin et al., as "the great persecuting Protestant reformers" (ibid., xiv) until toleration reformers such as Locke and Bayle appear on the scene.
13 Again, whether and to what extent Western societies adequately mirror these theological and philosophical commitments in the present day is beside the point.
14 John Marshall, *John Locke, Toleration and Early Enlightenment Culture: Religious Intolerance and Arguments for Religious Toleration in Early Modern and "Early Enlightenment" Europe* (Cambridge Studies in Early Modern British History; Cambridge: Cambridge University Press, 2006).
15 Tolerance, however, was not to be extended to atheists. Locke's own position, set forth in *A Letter on Toleration*, was that neither promises nor oaths nor covenants were sufficient to morally obligate those who do not believe in God; hence, at its base atheism raises questions of honesty and trustworthiness. This view, however, was not shared by all, even when it was normative. Pierre Bayle (1647–1706), a French Huguenot and contemporary of Locke who lived in exile in the Netherlands and witnessed the flood of Protestant refugees escaping persecution in France, wrote that morality was independent of (though not unrelated to) religion. The upshot of this is that atheists could in fact be more virtuous than Christians, who, truth be told, were also capable of committing crimes. See Bayle's *Pensées diverses sur la comète*, reproduced in volume 3 of *Oeuvres diverses*, ed. Elizabeth Labrousse, 5 vols. (Hildesheim: Georg Olms, 1965–1970).
16 Useful works that attempt to address this contradiction are Brad Stetson and Joseph G. Conti, *The Truth about Tolerance: Pluralism, Diversity and the*

Culture Wars (Downers Grove: InterVarsity Press, 2005), Benedict XVI, *Truth and Tolerance: Christian Belief and World Religions*, trans. H. Taylor (San Francisco: Ignatius, 2004); J. Budziszewski, *The Revenge of Conscience: Politics and the Fall of Man* (Dallas: Spence, 1999); and J. Budziszewski, *True Tolerance: Liberalism and the Necessity of Judgment* (New Brunswick: Transaction, 1992).

17 So, correctly in my view, Adam Wolfson, "What Remains of Toleration?" *The Public Interest* (Winter 1999): 37–51, esp. 40.

18 In a volume with the fascinating title *The Long Truce: How Toleration Made the World Safe for Power and Profit* (Dallas: Spence, 2001), A.J. Conyers has traced the modern history of the notion of tolerance in an attempt to answer the question of whether tolerance can be considered a virtue in the strictest sense. Conyer's answer is that, narrowly speaking, it is not a virtue; rather, it is to be viewed as a "strategy" or policy that directs virtues such as patience, humility, moderation, and prudence to a desired end. In the end, the "goodness" of tolerance is dependent upon the nature of the goods that it serves.

19 "Structured pluralism" is what James W. Skillen, in *Recharging the American Experiment: Principled Pluralism for Genuine Civic Community* (Grand Rapids: Baker, 1994), 83–95, uses to describe "the diversity of organizational competencies and social responsibilities" in society. Skillen's work through the years as the former director of the Center for Public Justice has been aimed at reinvigorating a principled pluralism.

20 Very helpful attempts to make this distinction are found in Lesslie Newbigin, *The Gospel in a Pluralist Society* (Grand Rapids: Eerdmans, 1989); Alister E. McGrath, *A Passion for Truth* (Downers Grove: InterVarsity Press, 1996), especially, Chapter 5; and Alister E. McGrath, "The Challenge of Pluralism for the Contemporary Christian Church," *Journal of the Evangelical Theological Society* 35, no. 3 (1992): 361–73.

21 Peter J. Leithart has very succinctly pressed this point in "Pluralism's Pride," *Touchstone* (September 2005): 15–17.

22 Cf. Eph. 4:15.

23 John Attarian, "In Dispraise of Tolerance, Sensitivity and Compassion," *The Social Critic* (Spring 1998): 16.

24 Ibid., 18.

25 A brief but useful overview of both the limitations of tolerance within the communal context and the contours of Christian responsibility is to be found in Kent Weber, "How Far Is Tolerance a Virtue?" *Regeneration Quarterly* (Winter 1996): 29–31.

26 Adopting the appropriate language with which to contend, it needs emphasizing, is of vital importance.

27 This has been argued succinctly and forcefully by J. Budziszewski, "The Illusion of Moral Neutrality," *First Things* (August/September 1993): 32–7. Cf. as well Budziszewski's *True Tolerance* (see n. 16), which develops this thinking more fully.

28 For example, what we have in competition today are contrasting visions of marriage, not a "moral" and a "morally neutral" vision of marriage. Hence, sound marriage laws are not those that aspire to "moral neutrality"; rather, they are those that accord with moral reality and human nature. To "tolerate" through public policy the normalizing of those practices that are in defiance of moral truth and unnatural, and to transmute it into an issue of "discrimination" and "human rights" as activists have done, is to undermine human *dignity*, deny that humans have a fundamental *nature*, and destroy the *very basis* of "civil society." Hereon see Robert P. George, " 'Same-Sex Marriage' and 'Moral Neutrality,' " in *The Clash of Orthodoxies: Law, Religion, and Morality in Crisis* (Wilmington: ISI Books, 2001), 75–89.

29 Hence the inherent fallacy in John Rawls' understanding of and approach to "comprehensive doctrines" as developed in *A Theory of Justice* (Cambridge:

Belknap Press, 1971) and *Political Liberalism* (New York: Columbia University Press, 1993). On the wider role of assumptions and philosophical pre-commitments, see Roy Clouser, *The Myth of Religious Neutrality: An Essay on the Hidden Role of Religious Belief in Theories* (Notre Dame: University of Notre Dame Press, 1991).

30 One might consequently argue that the metaphor of "culture wars" is no mere metaphor; at stake is the clash of two competing, all-encompassing visions of humanity and society.

31 While the question of whether deliberation over "moral goods" in the public sphere should be handled judicially, in the courts, rather than democratically, in the political sphere, is a fair one, it is beyond the scope of the present volume. Genuine disagreement within the context of democratic pluralism is possible – indeed, likely. For representative views on both sides, see Amy Gutman and Dennis Thompson, *Democracy and Disagreement: Why Moral Conflict Cannot Be Avoided in Politics, and What Should Be Done about It* (Cambridge: Harvard University Press, 1996), and Robert P. George, "Law, Democracy and Moral Disagreement," in Robert P. George, ed., *In Defense of Natural Law* (Oxford: Clarendon, 1999), 315–34.

32 Attarian, "Dispraise," 22.

33 Stephen D. Smith, *The Rise and Decline of American Religious Freedom* (Cambridge and London: Harvard University Press, 2014), 130.

34 See, for example, Col. 1:17–20, 1 Tim. 2:1–7, and Heb. 1:2.

35 Christian conviction and cultural witness – and I write from a confessionally Christian viewpoint – will necessarily be anchored in two fundamental orientations. First, we must insist that the religious perspective, even highly confessional forms of religious belief, be allowed in the public arena, thereby refusing to succumb to the temptation – and mandate of secularists – to privatize faith. Second, we must be cognizant of the limits of political and legal action within pluralistic society and not view activism as salvific.

36 For an English translation of Ratzinger's address to the Institut de France, "Wahrheit, Werte, Macht: Prüfsteine der pluralistischen Gesellschaft" (translation: "Truth, Values, Power: Touchstones of a Pluralistic Society"), first published in 1995, see *Values in a Time of Upheaval*, trans. Brian McNeil (New York and San Francisco: Crossroad and Ignatius, 2006), 45–52. In this volume, Ratzinger's essay appears under the title "Freedom, Law, and the Good: Moral Principles in Democratic Societies."

37 This linkage is pronounced and amplified in John Paul's 1993 encyclical *Veritatis Splendor* but is implicit elsewhere.

38 While the literature here is extensive, representative of this view – in its considerable diversity – are Morris Berman, *The Twilight of American Culture* (New York: W.W. Norton, 2000); Benjamin D. Wiker, "The Repaganization of the West," *New Oxford Review* (May 1996): 19–22; J. Daryl Charles, "Engaging the (Neo)Pagan Mind," *Trinity Journal* n.s. 16 (1995): 47–62; Michael Novak, "Awakening from Nihilism: The Templeton Prize Address," *First Things* 45 (August–September 1994): 18–22; Herbert Schlossberg, *Idols for Destruction: The Conflict of Christian Faith and American Culture*, rev. ed. (Wheaton: Crossway, 1990); and Alasdair MacIntyre, *After Virtue: A Study in Moral Theory* (Notre Dame: University of Notre Dame Press, 1981).

39 *Veritatis Splendor* no. 101, emphasis present. The encyclical is accessible at http://w2.vatican.va/content/john-paul-ii/en/encyclicals/documents/hf_jp-ii_enc_06081993_veritatis-splendor.html.

40 Ibid.

41 Novak, "Awakening from Nihilism" (see n. 38).

42 So Thomas Aquinas, *Summa Theologiae* [hereafter *S.T.*] I-II Q. 96, a. 4.

43 Ibid. I-II Q. 95, a. 2.

44 Aquinas understands the Ten Commandments in this way: "Now the precepts of the Decalogue contain the very intention of the lawgiver, who is God. For the precepts of the first table, which directs us to God, contain the very order to the common and final good, which is God; while the precepts of the second table contain the order of justice to be observed among men, namely, that nothing undue be done to anyone, and that each one be given his due . . . Consequently, the precepts of the Decalogue admit of no dispensation whatever" (*S.T.* I-II Q. 100, a. 8).

45 Hence the reality of just and unjust laws.

46 This is none other than the task of "apologetics."

47 Hereon see Joseph Cardinal Ratzinger, "What Is Truth? The Significance of Religious and Ethical Values in a Pluralistic Society," in Brian McNeil, trans., *Values in a Time of Upheaval*(New York and San Francisco: Crossroad and Ignatius, 2006), 53–72.

48 For the sake of clarity, I am making a fundamental distinction between *rationalism*, which severs itself from any sort of faith commitments in order to assert absolute autonomy, and *rationality*, which is part of the image of God within us based on created human nature and by which we seek, search, explore, and probe fuller understanding of reality. Historically, the Christian intellectual tradition understands no division between faith and reason; rather, the two operate harmoniously in humans' pursuit of truth. The Christian church of any era must wrestle with the implications of a "faith that seeks understanding" (*fides quaerens intellectum*). For this reason, the Christian faith should be known for a spirited defense of the unity of faith and reason. None has offered in our time a more penetrating analysis of the dangers of divorcing reason and faith than John Paul II in his final encyclical, *Fides et Ratio* (1998). For critiques of *Fides* from a sympathetic Protestant perspective, see "Faith and Reason: A Forum" (responses by Nicholas Wolterstorff and Alvin Plantinga), *Books & Culture* (July–August 1999): 28–30 and 32–5, and J. Daryl Charles, "Passionately Seeking the Truth: Unpunctual Protestant Reflections on *Fides et Ratio*," *Pro Ecclesia* 11, no. 2 (Spring 2002): 133–45.

49 Representative of the growing amount of literature are Philip Gorski, David Kyuman Kim, John Torpey, and Jonathan VanAntwerpen, eds., *The Post-Secular in Question: Religion in Contemporary Society* (New York: New York University Press, 2012); Craig J. Calhoun, Mark Juergensmeyer, and Jonathan VanAntwerpen, eds., *Rethinking Secularism* (Oxford and New York: Oxford University Press, 2011); Mark Juergensmeyer, "Beyond Words and War: The Global Future of Religion," *Journal of the American Academy of Religion* 78, no. 4 (2010): 882–95; Philip S. Gorski and Ates Altinordu, "After Secularization?" *Annual Review of Sociology* 34 (2008): 55–85; Jürgen Habermas, "Religion in the Public Sphere," *European Journal of Philosophy* 14 (2006): 1–25; Pippa Norris and Ronald Inglehart, *Sacred and Secular: Religion and Politics Worldwide* (Cambridge and New York: Cambridge University Press, 2004); and Peter L. Berger, "The Desecularization of the World: A Global Overview," in Peter L. Berger, ed., *The Desecularization of the World: Resurgent Religion and World Politics* (Washington, DC, and Grand Rapids: Ethics & Public Policy Center and Eerdmans, 1999), 1–18.

50 It is, of course, debatable whether in fact a "shift" truly is occurring, similar to the claims of "postmodernism" that "modernism" is passé.

51 See the Foreword to Jürgen Habermas and Jospeh Ratzinger (Pope Benedict XVI), *The Dialectics of Secularization: On Reason and Religion*, ed. Florian Schuller, trans. Brian McNeil (San Francisco: Ignatius, 2006), 13–15.

52 See, for example, Jürgen Habermas, *Dialektik der Säkularisierung: Uber Vernunft und Religion* (Freiburg am Breisgau and Basel: Herder Verlag, 2005) and Jürgen Habermas, *Zwischen Naturalismus und Religion: Philosophische Aufsätze* (Frankfurt am Main: Suhrkamp Verlag, 2005).

53 I am here dependent on the translation provided by Schuller, *The Dialectics of Secularization* (see n. 51). 23.
54 Ibid., 27.
55 Ibid., 40.
56 Ibid., 42.
57 Ibid., 46.
58 Ibid.
59 Ibid., 50.
60 Ibid., 51–2.
61 Ibid., 58.
62 Ibid., 60.
63 Ibid., 61.
64 Ibid., 64.
65 Ibid., 68.
66 Ibid., 69.
67 Ibid., 75, emphasis added.
68 It is with these words that John Paul introduces his important 1998 encyclical *Fides et Ratio*.
69 Ratzinger, *Values in a Time of Upheaval*, 152.
70 Ibid.
71 Ibid., 159.
72 "Secularism" – and here for our own purposes I will use the term interchangeably with "materialism" or "naturalism" – can be properly evaluated as a "worldview" based on its dominant presuppositions. Two warrant our consideration: (a) it understands all of reality as material or physical in nature rather than a complex composite of the material and non-material; (b) it holds the cosmos, with all living and non-living entities, to be a random occurrence. These baseline assumptions about ultimate reality, it needs emphasizing, have enormous social and political ramifications, including how science and technology are used, how law develops and is practiced, how education is furthered, how communications and media are advanced, and how government should operate.
73 This is essentially the argument that is advanced by Brendan Sweetman in *Why Politics Needs Religion: The Place of Religious Arguments in the Public Square* (Downers Grove: IVP Academic, 2006), and stated explicitly on pp. 13–14.
74 Examples of this might be Nazism, genocidal tendencies among people-groups, or scientific-technological attempts to eliminate parts of the population.
75 Thus argues Jonathan Rauch, "The Great Secession," *The Atlantic* (July/August 2014), accessible at www.theatlantic.com/magazine/archive/2014/07/the-great-secession/372288/. While there is truth in Rauch's argument, as a self-professing homosexual atheist Rauch wants parts of the Christian moral code to be changed, in order to be accepted. But this prescription, based on the broader assumption that Christian morality is toxic, "hate-filled," bigoted" and "intolerant," is itself unacceptable. It only subverts, rather than encourages, honest moral dialogue on contentious ethical issues.
76 Stanley Carlson-Thies, "Religious Freedom: The Cornerstone of Strong Social Architecture (Part One)," *Comment* (May 31, 2013), accessible at www.cardus.ca/comment/article/3974/religious-freedom-the-cornerstone-of-strong-social-architecture-part-one/.This essay is an adaptation of the 2013 Kuyper Lecture by Carlson-Thies, sponsored by the Center for Public Justice.
77 Nigel Biggar, "Saving the Secular: The Public Vocation of Moral Theology," *Journal of Religious Ethics* 37, no. 1 (2009): 166.
78 Ibid., 168, emphasis present.
79 So Ray Pennings, "The Secular Democracy and Its Victims," *The Cardus Daily* (June 19, 2014), accessible at www.convivium.ca/articles/the-secular-democracy-and-its-victims.

5 Natural law, human dignity, and human moral obligation

Whence and why "human dignity?"

Personhood and dignity

It has become increasingly evident in recent years that most – if not all – of our pressing ethical issues hinge in some ways on the question of personhood and the dignity of the human person. Almost prophetically, the Second Vatican Council, in words that retain all (if not *more*) of their relevance today, condemned with utmost clarity various crimes and attacks against human life that cry out for a response by people of good will:

> Whatever is opposed to life itself such as any type of murder, genocide, abortion, whatever violates the integrity of the human person such as mutilation, torments inflicted on body or mind, attempts to coerce the will itself; whatever insults human dignity such as subhuman living conditions, arbitrary imprisonment, deportation, slavery, prostitution, euthanasia or willful self-destruction; the selling of women and children, as well as disgraceful working conditions, where people are treated as mere instruments of gain rather than as free and responsible persons: All these things and others like them are infamies indeed. They poison human society, and they do more harm to those who, given the fact practice them than to those who suffer from injury. Moreover, they are a supreme dishonor to the Creator.[1]

Not helping matters in our own day, given the presence of the aforementioned scourges in the twenty-first century, is the role certain prominent "ethicists" play in our own cultural tradition. Though perhaps more visible than many, Peter Singer, the Ira W. DeCamp Professor of Bioethics at Princeton University's Center for Human Values and laureate professor at the Centre for Applied Philosophy and Public Ethics, University of Melbourne, is nevertheless representative of metaphysical materialists when he famously argues categorically that membership of the human species is not "morally relevant."[2] It follows, not only for Singer but also for many in Western culture, that "some nonhuman animals whose lives, by any standard, are more valuable than the lives of some humans."[3] In consequence, "[a] chimpanzee, a dog, or pig, for instance, will have a higher degree of self-awareness and a greater capacity for meaningful relations with others than a severely retarded infant or someone in a state of advanced senility."[4] How Singer knows this to be true we cannot know; nor can he. And whether Singer is genuinely convinced that membership of the human species is not "morally relevant" is debatable.[5] But by what moral standard or code can Singer – or *any* theorist, for that matter – make such a declaration? And what are the implications of such a view?

If, however, human personhood *is* a morally relevant question, as I argue, then our task is to identify the *nature* of what a person is. Of course, to identify and amplify human nature is to identify and underscore an abiding consensus about personhood. The fact that some ethicists, theorists, and social activists in our day call into question the very notion of personhood is not to grant them any particular authoritative status on the matter. Indeed, one of the strikingly salient features of contemporary Western culture – and our "post-everything" climate – is the sheer hubris with which it denies what generations, even millennia, of human civilization have affirmed to be true. Intractably severed from the past, cut off from inter-generational wisdom, and unaccountable to any moral authority whatsoever, we declare ourselves in the third millennium to be "autonomous." For this reason, then, it is necessary to view contemporary pronouncements about human nature and human personhood by metaphysical materialists for precisely *what they are*: in and of themselves they possess no more authority than rival pronouncements (for example, those of religious believers or the Christian Church). And if these pronouncements are found to be *outside* of the human and cultural consensus that has endured, we are justified in rejecting them in the interest of both intellectual honesty and the common good. In prior generations this conclusion would have been non-controversial and beyond debate.

An authentic understanding of personhood lays hold of the *nature* of what is characteristically and uniquely "human." When philosophers and scientists are accustomed to speak of the human being as a "rational animal," they invite qualification. At a rudimentary level, rationality is understood to convey sentience, self-conscious awareness, self-responsibility, and the ability to reflect. Hereby human beings distinguish themselves from other "animals" – in their aspirations, in their creativity, in their moral imagination, and in their pursuit of what is good. When we reason and when we judge (and when we realize that we will *be judged*), we demonstrate that human life transcends physical matter. This "consensual" understanding of human nature did not arrive yesterday. It is affirmed by both ancients and moderns, and as a consensus, it transcends individual cultures and social grouping. Moreover, what "science" discovers tomorrow will not alter this understanding.[6]

Illustrative of this abiding "consensus" is Aristotle's well-known example of the oak. Resident within the acorn is all the potential that distinguishes the genus oak. This potential furnishes a sufficient explanation of both the diversity and the sameness within the genus, and it offers an adequate description of the nature of the oak, at whatever stage of the oak's development along the way. Note that this description of "nature" has nothing to do with how the genus oak functions, or how it may be used, or the strength and characteristics of its wood, or how large it may eventually grow, or how it might weather the elements throughout the growth process. Nor does this understanding vary among Asians, Africans, Europeans, or North and South Americans. Rather, it corresponds narrowly yet precisely enough to what the oak is *in its essence*.

We are permitted then, summarily, to make certain conclusions regarding the existence and interrelation of the oak and acorn:

- Without the oak tree the acorn would not exist.
- The acorn is thus dependent on the oak tree for its existence.
- Conversely, the oak tree is dependent on the acorn for its continued existence.
- The acorn may or may not grow sufficiently, but this possibility does not bear on its essential nature.
- The oak tree may or may not grow to the size of other oak trees, but this possibility does not bear on its essential nature.

Our awareness of the essential nature of the genus oak does not vary, nor is it subject to debate. It corresponds to reality as humans experience it universally and perennially. Using another analogy, we might attempt to make the same point about "nature" through computers and computer processing. While a central processing unit, random-access memory, various drives, computer chips, and electromagnetic circuitry all constitute elements within each computer system and describe the functions of what a computer *does*, without the software the computer is not operational. The computer software may be said, albeit crudely, to have "intrinsic value."[7]

Thomas Aquinas offers a definition of personhood that simultaneously accords with the consensus of classical philosophy and is distinctly Christian. "Person" signifies *the individual substance of a rational nature*. "Personhood" thus denotes what is distinct about the human being; it implies a fundamental *dignity*. In Thomistic thought, personhood may even be applied to the Godhead to the extent that it is relational, even when the persons within the Godhead are not three isolated individuals.[8] For Aquinas, dignity is what distinguishes human beings through the act of creation, which bestows on them a status that is unique within all of the cosmos. Human beings, hence, possess an *intrinsic* dignity by virtue of their being human. Were this not the case, then their value would rise and fall according to the development or deterioration of their functions. Such valuation, based on functionality, is extremely subjective and relative to the interests of the valuer. We may call this valuation *extrinsic* dignity, which is external and imputed, measured by performance, status, utility, and usefulness.

Human sanctity and human rights are meaningless apart from the notion of inherent dignity and what we are by nature. Animals possess no "rights" in the proper sense of the term.[9] The great apes do not wrestle with "dignity," nor do they agonize over issues of justice, purpose, and meaning of their existence. Not for nothing has philosopher Bernard Lonergan observed that when non-human animals run out of biological opportunities and activities – for example, seeking food and shelter, mating and reproducing, playing and avoiding pain and predators – they fall asleep. When humans, however, run out of biological opportunities and activities, they ask questions.[10] Significantly, the nature of this questioning always and again returns to *what it means to be human*. Who am I? Where am I headed? Is there a knowable truth? Why do I suffer? What are the consequences of my actions? To what or whom am I morally accountable? Do I have an intrinsic worth? The nature of human dignity is such that, all too often, it is taken for granted. Only when it is threatened do we find ourselves contemplating it with any measure of seriousness. We see what becomes of "human dignity" when it disappears in the context of tyrannical regimes.[11]

But precisely *why* do humans ask questions in the first place? Considering this very question, educator and author Robert Spitzer frames the matter pointedly: "It is not simply the ability to ask questions" in the generic sense. It is rather the ability

> to ask questions about what is ultimate, unconditional, perfect, infinite, absolute and eternal with respect to love, goodness, truth, beauty and being. This is what humans seem to do uniquely by comparison with other members of the animal kingdom. It is reasonable to believe that these powers are unique to beings of human origin.[12]

It is proper, therefore, to speak of a certain "objectivity" to human nature insofar as we operate within a general consensus of what human beings, broadly speaking, collectively know, believe, and affirm. Even when in our "post-everything" cultural climate it is fashionable to *question or deny* this consensus, our "knowing" is based on evidence and convictions that are not dependent on subjective, private, or inaccessible data. It is a common fund accessible to all – to philosophers, scientists, social scientists, and theologians; to teachers, theorists, clinicians, and laypersons; to Kansans, Cambodians, Canadians, and Kazakhstanis. And it is a consensus around which there has been and remains fundamental agreement, even when that consensus has been dissipating of late. Our understanding of personhood and dignity, however, does not only concern beginning-of-life issues or end-of-life issues; it speaks as well to the matter of basic human rights and freedoms in a global context in which genocide, slavery, mass murder, and totalitarian political persecution are ever present.

Sadly, however, it is a sign of our time that virtually anyone who witnesses today to the sacrosanct nature of human life in any stage, whether at its margins or in its very constitution, can expect to be demonized by the high priests of secular culture. One thinks, for example, of the now-famous 2003 essay by philosopher Ruth Macklin, "Dignity Is a Useless Concept," and the 2008 essay by cognitive scientist and popular science-writer Stephen Pinker, "The Stupidity of Dignity."[13] The problem, Pinker opines, is that the notion of human "dignity" is "squishy" and "subjective," "hardly up to the heavyweight moral demands assigned to it." As it turns out, Pinker's ire is directed toward political and cultural conservatives, and he does no "heavyweight" lifting himself. After all, for the secular materialist matter is ultimate; there exists no higher moral authority. But such is the nature of ethics in a world turned on its head. In reality, however, it is the mindset of secular fundamentalism, not a Judeo-Christian approach to ethics, which is "hardly up to the heavyweight moral demands" that press upon it. One wonders what response the Macklins and Pinkers of the world will offer in the face of genocide, mass terror, and egregious human rights violations that manifest themselves around the globe; after all, human "dignity," as they insist, is meaningless.

In the end, based on common sense and the natural law, we must reject the secularists' rejection of human dignity as a concept; their rejection of human value, alas, is nothing short of undignified and inhumane. Without it, "civil society" as we know it dissipates and society collapses. Without it, the common good does not exist. Without it, society collapses. And without it, we cannot justify helping the oppressed.

The human being as the imago Dei

Because at its periphery – for example, in contentious bioethical debates of the day – and in its very constitution – as seen through gross poverty, slavery, genocide, and human rights atrocities worldwide – human personhood is being denied in ever-increasing ways, the dignity of the human person must be re-affirmed. Ruth Macklin and Steven Pinker only serve to illustrate, however crudely and unintentionally, this reality.

In Judaism and in the historic Christian tradition, the significance of the doctrine of the *imago Dei* is that every human creature points toward a Creator. The image is a reflection of its origin: "And God said, Let us make man in our image, after our likeness" (Gen. 1:26; cf. 5:1–3 and 9:5–7). It follows, then, that our full imaging of the Creator expresses itself through our fundamental nature and not merely our functionality, social utility, or qualitative development. That is, we live as knowing, loving, reasoning, serving beings, always mirroring the image or likeness of the Creator in our humanness, whether in our birthing, in our dying, or in between. Furthermore, because the image of God is an endowment, personhood is neither developmental nor incremental, nor is it the product of performance or achievement.[14] The true image of God in us is never removed from the human creature. The human person is a body-soul composite, with the soulish dimension continuing to exist beyond and transcending physical death.[15] Stated otherwise, in the words of moral theologian William May, God cannot incarnate himself in a pig or cow or ape because those creatures are incapable of reflecting the divine image.[16] God has, however, incarnated himself in a human, mysteriously choosing as the eternal uncreated Logos to become one of us.[17]

An important implication of human beings' mirroring of the divine image can be granted even by the non-theist: human moral action will transcend mere impulse and desire. It will conform to what is true, what is good, what is virtuous, and *what is in harmony with our intrinsic nature*. If humans have an intrinsic nature, issuing out of the *imago Dei*, then to honor this nature is to flourish, since human beings can distinguish between ultimate and less-than-ultimate, even destructive, ends. Human actions are morally good when human beings use their moral freedom in ways that correspond, rather than go counter to, their created nature. Therefore, *deep within the interior life human beings discover a law – the natural moral law – that they themselves did not create yet which they feel obliged to obey*. We sense this law in the context of social relations, whether it concerns speeding or strangulation, thievery or thuggery, exaggeration or perjury. The Ten Commandments merely describe the *general contours* of this law that for the sake of human flourishing may not be transgressed.

Affirming objective moral truth, as witnessed to by the natural moral law, yields the common moral judgment to protect and dignify human life, and particularly vulnerable human life. This moral-philosophical commitment results in a moral line that connects beginning-of-life issues with euthanasia,[18] slavery, genocide, and mass human rights violations amidst totalitarian rule. To eliminate innocent human life at the margins, on the one hand, and to fail to protect human lives who are oppressed and persecuted, on the other, are both *always* wrong. They are wrong not only because the Christian Church or the Christian moral tradition or religion in general teaches such but also because the moral law, "written on the heart" of every human being, witnesses to their wrongness.

A useful clarification of the concept of human dignity emerges when we contrast the Christian conception of the *imago Dei* with competing models of human nature. Consider, for example, metaphysical naturalism, or what often is called scientific materialism. Because metaphysical materialism denies the soulish dimension of human existence, it has the consequence of undermining human dignity. To speak of "human dignity" – which is defined by "our essential and inviolable humanity"[19] – yet deny the non-material uniqueness of the human species is to be caught in a contradiction. At the very least, it is to be parasitic by importing a belief in "dignity" that cannot be legitimately grounded by pure materialism itself. And it is to deny that there is a transcendent "good" that should order human behavior – a "good" that transcends "genes and memes," stimulus and response, appetites and instincts. For the materialist, the mind is simply processing these stimuli, and complex human behavior, involving emotions and choices, reduces to selfish desire and "survival." Is "dignity" simply a degree of biological complexity that an animal possesses, the accidental intersection of chance variation and natural selection? Or is it the evidence of our design, the imprint of the Creator? If the former, then there is no grounding of human response in a higher moral law, since human actions and responses can only be ascribed to the directionless (but determinative) forces of evolution and natural selection. By contrast, human dignity issuing out of the *imago Dei* mirrors a special status, a superior rank, in the created order among living creatures and confers special worth both to human life and to human procreation.[20]

But if we reject transcendent moral standards, if we deny accountability to a higher moral law (the natural law), where then do moral principles – if in fact they exist – originate? It is implausible to understand them, if they do exist, as arising out of an accidental universe, wherein no purpose and "design" are permitted to exist or be acknowledged. The materialist's world and life views make morality, moral purpose, and moral principle an impossibility. "Survival of the fittest" cannot lead to a distinction between "good" and "evil." It does not permit the existence of a "Good Samaritan." In fact, it expressly encourages the oppressing of the weak by the strong; thereby basic human "rights" vanish.

There is, then, an irreducible "religious" character to the notion of human dignity.[21] Modern secular ethics, by contrast, falls short of our human capacities since it ignores the human soul and as a result asks too little.[22] It asks us not to be morally accountable to a higher moral authority; rather, at bottom, it only asks that we obey our various instincts (*regardless* of how these have been learned or evolved), that we only be "true" to our own personal promptings. But this will not suffice if we wish to dissuade people from murdering others, abusing others, exploiting others, or depriving others. For if I wish to compel or restrain the behavior of others, it follows that, in addition to a certain noble view of human personhood, there must be *some authority* that transcends my own preferences and instincts.

Dignitatis humanae: a natural law argument for human dignity and religious freedom

With the universal declarations on human rights and human dignity that proceeded in the aftermath of the Second World War, one might reasonably argue that a sense and awareness of human dignity has been impressed upon the last three generations as never before in human history. As evidence thereof, one can speak of a "third wave" of democratization that has spread around the globe in the last two generations.[23]And what does this "wave" indicate? At the very least, it suggests that freedom – construed chiefly in social-political terms – accords with the human spirit and applies, first and foremost, to the powers of government as they respect, or refuse to encroach upon, the sanctity and dignity of human life. As previous chapters in this volume have attempted to clarify, the wider context of the historic Christian, indeed Judeo-Christian, tradition gives evidence (sometimes at great cost) that truth does not – indeed cannot – impose itself upon human beings. For this reason, religious freedom, which is rooted in a commitment to the sacredness of conscience, demands an immunity from coercion in society. It honors the individual's duty toward the Creator and his moral laws – or toward individual conscience, in the case of an atheist – as these apply (within reason) to human society.

One statement – or should we say, restatement – of this position followed in the years of Europe's in the aftermath of WWII. The papal encyclical *Dignitatis Humanae*, published in 1965 as part of the Second Vatican Council, re-formulated the age-old conviction that religious freedom is a human right in the most basic and applied sense. This freedom means that

> all men are to be immune from coercion on then party of individuals or of social groups and of any human power, in such wise that no one is to be forced to act in a manner contrary to his own beliefs, whether privately or publicly, and that "within due limits."[24]

This understanding of human dignity, the Council reinforces, is known to all "through the revealed word of God and by reason itself." Hence, "religious freedom is to be recognized in the constitutional law whereby society is governed" and thus is to be understood as a "civil right."[25] The right to religious freedom, the encyclical insists, does not inhere in "the subjective disposition of the person, but in his nature," regardless of whether or not people live up to their moral obligations to revealed truth.[26]

Further light is shed on these most basic of obligations. The highest norm of human life, according to the encyclical, is "the divine law – eternal, objective and universal – whereby God orders, directs and governs the entire universe and all the ways of the human community by a plan conceived in wisdom and love."[27] Human beings have been created in such a way as to "participate" in this law, as a result of divine providence, by means of the natural law. But because truth is discovered in accord with human beings' social nature, its inquiry and questioning proceed in a manner that is free, by means of personal assent, and through the mediation of personal conscience.[28] It follows, then, that humans are not to be forced to act in a manner contrary to personal conscience, nor are they to be restrained from acting in according with conscience. Thus, in matters of religious conviction, every manner of coercion should be excluded. Moreover, this social nature requires that humans should give *external and public* expression to these internal convictions, whether as individuals, as families, or as communities.[29] This collective reality underscores the importance of the common good, for which purpose government exists in the first place,[30] and it "makes no small contribution" to the creation of "an environment in which men without hindrance" are invited to respond to the deepest convictions of their hearts; no aspect of life can be excluded.[31]

This freedom to resist compulsion and be guided by the light of moral judgment, according to the encyclical, finds its ultimate expression in Jesus Christ, who both acknowledged the realm of the magistrate ("Render to Caesar the things that are Caesar's . . .") and gave clear warning that the higher obligations to God are to be kept inviolate (see Matt. 22:15–22). Although Christ bore witness to the truth,[32] he refused to impose the truth on those who rejected it. "Not by force of blows does His rule assert its claims."[33] Truth, if it is true, must ultimately have a persuasive power that compels.

The encyclical observes that the early Christian Church followed the same path as her master. Christ's disciples sought to *persuade* others, "not, however, by coercion or devices unworthy of the Gospel."[34] St. Paul, the apostle to the Gentiles, affirms the understanding of our "dual citizenship" set forth by Christ himself. On the one hand, we recognize all legitimate civil authority: "Let every soul be subject to the governing authorities. For there is no authority except from God, and the authorities that exist are appointed by God."[35] On the other hand, we do not recognize *illegitimate* authority.[36] The early believers "did not hesitate to speak out against governing powers which set themselves in opposition to the holy will of God: 'It is necessary to obey God rather than men' (Acts 5:29)."[37] Moreover, the same apostle reminds his readers that "each one of us is to render to God an account of himself,"[38] reflecting quite clearly the conviction that every person is bound to his or her conscience. For St. Paul, governing authorities exercise *derivative* power, and thus themselves will undergo a *moral accounting*.

According to the encyclical, it is therefore a matter of faithfulness to its own tradition that the Church recognizes and supports the principle of religious freedom. Religious freedom is a "sacred freedom," a freedom that has been endowed by the Creator.[39] This principle may be expressed as such:

> Where the principle of religious freedom is not only proclaimed in words or simply incorporated in law but also given sincere and practical application, there the Church succeeds in achieving a stable situation of right as well as of fact and *the independence which is necessary for the fulfillment of her divine mission*.[40]

This freedom is "sacred" in nature, and yet it is an endowment to all human beings, not merely those of religious faith. Because of this requisite "independence," both religious believers and the non-religious possess a "civil right" *not to be hindered* in leading their lives in accordance with their consciences.[41] Therefore, a harmony exists between the freedom of the Church and the religious freedom that is to be recognized as the right of all people and all communities. In consequence of this fundamental right, the encyclical denounces, with great sorrow, the fact that

> forms of government still exist under which, even though freedom of religious worship receives constitutional recognition, the powers of government are engaged in the effort to deter citizens from the profession of religion and to make life very difficult and dangerous for religious communities.[42]

Assuming the "independence" of religious believers to live their lives unimpeded, in accordance with the dictates of conscience, precisely what are they "free" to promote through belief and lifestyle, word and deed? To pose this question is to inquire into the nature of both rights and duties, which *together* constitute the essence of human moral obligation.

Human dignity, human obligations, and universal predispositions

Rights versus duties in a post-secular moment

The hallmark of our era, it scarcely needs mentioning, is its accent on "rights." However, "rights" have moral meaning when – and *only* when – they issue out of a particular understanding of human nature. They have meaning, as we have suggested, *if* we assume that dignity accords with a certain uniqueness about the human species. But we cannot conceptualize human "rights" properly unless we are willing to attach with this commitment an equal commitment to duties.

Social commentator David Gelernter has argued that the ethics of rights originated in Roman jurisprudence, while the ethics of duty originated in the Judeo-Christian moral tradition. While this reduction may not satisfy all readers, at its heart it is broadly accurate and broadly supported. In formal terms, a "right" confers an advantageous position," as it were; rights-based thinking focuses on what is *due* to you. Duty-based thinking, by comparison, concerns itself with what is *required* of you.[43] Properly construed, rights and duties are reciprocal in nature. If I have a fundamental right to something, others have the duty to guard and protect that right. But another distinction is necessary, especially in the present cultural climate. Rights-based thinking has transformed itself since the founders and framers wrote of "inalienable rights." Today we've grown accustomed to understanding "rights," first and foremost, in terms of personal freedoms and individual preferences.[44] This understanding, I think, would have the founders rolling in their graves.

In looking at the reciprocal nature of rights versus duties, Gelernter concludes, "The ethics of duty is intrinsically superior to the ethics of rights . . ., regardless of your views on religion."[45]In fact, he argues, it is well possible that the rise of rights-discourse, and not Darwinism or modern science, is responsible for the eclipse of religion, and hence, of an ethics of duty.[46] In any case, it is abundantly clear that people tend to welcome rights while eschewing duties. And if duties are required, most people demand to know, *On what authority?* This is the real question, in the end. On what authority? It is difficult to disagree with Gelernter, for whom the most plausible answer comes down to *transcendent authority*. While it is a fact that contemporary life is secularized, it is also a fact that most people – even in secularized societies – are religious in their conviction. If this is true, we do well to take the sort of argument made by Gelernter seriously and not allow ethics to be developed – and promulgated – in a *secular ghetto*. Religion cannot be discounted simply because the secular materialist wishes to banish it. That we are presently "post-secular," according to numerous cultural commentators, would suggest the truth of this reality. As noted in the previous chapter, the very fact that two high-profile representatives of both secularism and religion, Jürgen Habermas and Benedict XVI, have engaged in serious dialogue about the deficiencies of a secularist world-view to address fundamental questions of human existence is powerful evidence of this conviction.[47] What's more, even atheists themselves will benefit from this mutual understanding.[48]

One of the discoveries of the Habermas-Benedict exchange was that the two individuals appear to share common ground in construing certain pre-political moral foundations of a free state. Part of this agreement is the conviction that human beings are entitled to basic human rights on the basis of a fundamental dignity – a dignity that applies to all, irrespective of functionality or utility. Global pronouncements on such as we find in Article One of the UDHR in 1948 ("All human beings are born free and equal in dignity and rights."[49]) and Article One of the *Charter of Fundamental Rights of the European Union* in 2000 ("Human dignity is inviolable. It must be respected and protected."[50]) attest to this commitment. Moreover, these pronouncements are owing to natural law thinking, even when unbeknownst to their various signatories. This understanding of human nature and human rights presupposes that all human beings are endowed with a twofold sense of duty: (1) to do justice and (2) to express "neighbor-love," i.e., a duty toward and concern for the other as we would wish for ourselves. This, of course, finds expression in the so-called Golden Rule ethic. In the discussion that follows, I wish to argue that this twofold moral-philosophical commitment – justice and neighbor-love – underpins a basic commitment to guard and protect fellow human beings in a global context. This moral obligation to "protect" others begins with the sacred rights of conscience, what we call religious freedom.

The "Good Samaritan": a model for human dignity and moral obligation

The upshot of our argument thus far is that personhood and dignity, rooted in awareness that because human beings mirror the *imago Dei* they are accorded special moral status, require of us that we extend "neighbor-love" to those in great need. Here we need not look far in the Christian moral tradition, for the parable of the "Good Samaritan" (Luke 10:25–37) has much to teach us.

It is important to contextualize Jesus's use of the parable. The parable is introduced in response to a question by one of his listeners, a lawyer. The question concerned the requirements of what was "written in the Law." When asked in Socratic fashion by Jesus what the lawyer thought, the lawyer responds correctly by observing the Great Commandment: love God and love your neighbor (Luke 10:27–28). For this, he is commended. What needs fleshing out, however, is the meaning of the question that he poses to Jesus: "Precisely who is my neighbor?" After all, there are many "neighbors" out there, and some of them strike us as downright despicable.

With this, Jesus introduces to his listeners the "Good Samaritan." As is well known, this illustration for a first-century Judean audience will have a bite to it, since Jews and Samaritans generally detested one another. This history of animosity between the two people, of course, was longstanding, and that for ethnic, religious, and political reasons. So, to tell a first-century Jew that a Samaritan is his "neighbor," and then to epitomize this neighbor as "good" and exemplary (adding insult to injury) is to cross contemporary national, ethnic, and religious boundaries in a manner that was sure to offend. And to make matters worse, a priest and a Levite are depicted in the parable as initially coming upon the scene of the crime and yet being indifferent to the sufferer's plight. Recall the crime: a man from Jerusalem was attacked, stripped of his clothes, robbed, beaten, and left for dead. And recall the immediate response: the two representatives of Israel's religious establishment both "pass by on the other side" with studied indifference.[51]

In rather stark contrast, it is the Samaritan who shows himself to be the real "neighbor" to the victim in question. Taking pity on the victim, he ministers to his wounds, puts the victim on his donkey, takes him to an inn, and cares for him. The next day the Samaritan leaves money with the innkeeper to look after the victim's needs – until, that is, the Samaritan returns. If the parable teaches anything, it teaches that we may not "pass by on the other side" indifferently when we encounter those who are suffering. And this suffering, as it turns out, might be inconvenient or contrary to conventional views on nationality, ethnicity, or politics. The Samaritan is "good" because he has compassion and is sensitive to the sufferings of others, and because he gives expression to human solidarity through concrete deeds. He demonstrates the moral law – the "law written on the heart" – in bold contrast to two religious custodians of the written law. The irony could not be richer. The "Good Samaritan" serves as an enduring model of human dignity and moral obligation. In this model, we find a meeting-place, a uniting, of justice and neighbor-love, a moral-philosophical reality the substance of which underpins natural law moral reasoning.

In a fascinating way, ethicist Paul Ramsey takes the Good Samaritan model and extrapolates the wider implications of the parable in furnishing what he calls a "preferential ethics of protection."[52] He asks the reader to consider what might have been Jesus's response, had the Samaritan come upon the criminals in the very act. Would Jesus have required nonresistance, as pacifists maintain? For that matter, would Jesus have apprehended – or help apprehend – the criminals? Would he have sought criminal justice for the offenders? Would he have approved of a local police force on patrol in the highway region where the crime took place? For Ramsey, the response of charity, or neighbor-love, which is rooted in a covenantal loyalty to both God and one's neighbor,[53] is clear and in no way incompatible with Christ's commands, common sense, or Christian social ethics. In the case of an innocent third party being accosted, attacked, or subjected to oppressive abuse, we use morally guided force when and where appropriate to intervene, disarm, and incapacitate the offender, and to protect basic human rights that are being threatened or violated. We do this because of human dignity, to which justice and neighbor-love are tethered. This "ethics of protection," of course, extends to a wide range of activity and human endeavor. It might express itself through political engagement, diplomatic relations, private ventures, socially sensitive entrepreneurship, community service, and humanitarian social work. In more extreme cases, it also might be more "overt" in character, even taking the form of humanitarian intervention and the application of interventionary force where oppression and abuse are widespread and life threatening.

What follows, then, is a discussion of how justice and neighbor-love, consistent with natural law ethics and a commitment to human dignity, combine to underpin a right and a duty to defend the suffering and oppressed. I locate this "right and duty" in the collective wisdom of the "just war" tradition. Significantly, this tradition of qualifying the use of force, though not solely confined to the Christian moral tradition, nevertheless, over the last two millennia has been developed and refined chiefly by Christian moral thinkers through the ages. The specific context for the ensuing discussion is humanitarian intervention.

The obligations of justice and neighbor-love in humanitarian intervention: a test-case

Discerning our moral obligation: to intervene or not to intervene?

In the aftermath of the Rwandan tragedy, just war historian James Turner Johnson rightly observed that, with the end of the Cold War, policy-makers were ill prepared to deal with geopolitical crises that have arisen since, not to mention the fact that it exposed an utter lack of moral discourse regarding international affairs.[54] And indeed this was the case. Making matters worse, those who might have viewed Cold War tensions as the fruit of defects in the international order, and thus envisioned a post-Cold War increase in the United Nations' prestige, surely have had their hopes dashed. The truth of one Burmese human rights activist is patent: "There are no countries in the world which have gained liberation through the help of the United Nations."[55] And this is fully aside from the fact that, based on its politics and its constituency, the U.N. is just as capable of sanctioning injustice as justice. However, that is a story for another day.

The question that I wish to raise is this: how might those in relatively free nations – particularly those who serve in political, humanitarian, or military capacities – propose to deal with the scale of humanitarian need in our day that is massive and frequently the result of unstable regimes?[56] And for the purposes of this particular test-case, what moral and political resources might inform our response to what has been called "complex humanitarian emergencies"[57] – situations that fall short of formal war *per se* but which require a measure of military force for the purposes of humanitarian concern?[58]

The following discussion attempts to address this question by marshaling much neglected – and not infrequently misunderstood – resources of the just war tradition, resources that are permanent and applicable to the humanitarian dilemma. Herewith I am assuming, as I have argued in a previous chapter, that moral "neutrality" in life is impossible and thus untenable. Most mainstream debates about foreign policy and humanitarian intervention proceed from questionable – and surely contestable – assumptions about state sovereignty, human rights, and cultural relativism that, alas, are anything but "neutral." But I will assume that the "just war" idea,[59] when its moral framework is properly understood, is the *only* legitimate means of attempting to think responsibly about the dilemma of humanitarian intervention.[60]

Writing on the ethics of intervention two generations ago, Paul Ramsey set forth the argument that military intervention for the sake of justice and charity remains *both* a right *and* a duty.[61] In Ramsey's view, the failure of relatively free nations to intervene in humanitarian emergencies would be "tragically to fail to undertake responsibilities that . . . are not likely to be accomplished by other political actors."[62] Responding to the common objection that intervention can be unjust and illicit, Ramsey acknowledged both possibilities – unjust as well as just causes. However, the mere *possibility* of unjust causes, Ramsey insisted, does not release us – whether we are political actors, the "extended hands" of the military, humanitarian workers, members of nongovernmental organizations (NGOs), or private citizens – from our moral responsibility. Not intervening can also be unjust. Therefore, the precise form of one's obligation toward one's "neighbor" based on charity requires discernment.[63]

The viewpoint that I am assuming is that humanitarian intervention is justified in *some*, not all, cases. The reason for this is that the purpose of government is to protect and secure basic human rights of all persons by virtue of human personhood, worth, and dignity. Those regimes that violate these basic rights in the end forfeit their own right to be protected by international law. State sovereignty is not an intrinsic value, as is human personhood. Sovereignty must serve human ends.[64] In respecting those basic human rights, we are hence obligated to assist and rescue others at reasonable cost to ourselves, and, where possible, assist in the social-political reconstruction of those victims' lives. This is none other than the "Golden Rule" ethic: we do unto others as we wish that they would do unto us.[65]

A proper understanding of human nature and human dignity must undergird any conception of "human rights." This understanding is necessarily rooted in moral realism[66] – a moral realism that lies at the heart of just war thinking. By virtue of their common humanity, human beings have moral duties. These duties are intuited through reason and understood to be universal and immutable. Moreover, they are not limited to family, ethnicity, or politics but extend to our "neighbor," which is to say, *whoever stands in need*. Such duties, then, can be described as "pre-political," anchored in an awareness of a higher law, the natural law, from which any form of civil or positive law must derive.[67] The moral is supra-legal; it is antecedent to any and all legal questions. Only in this way are we able to posit any sort of grounding for "universal human rights." If that were not so, then "Nuremburg was nothing but victors' vengeance dressed up in a fiction of 'justice,'" in the words of one cultural commentator.[68]

Just war thinking allows us to conceptualize the assistance of a "neighbor" in need, through its morally justified and morally guided application of limited force. This is because of its fundamental moral-philosophical commitment to desire the highest, the best, for fellow human beings. The just war concept, it needs to be emphasized, is not just about war; it is a way of thinking about broader political life. For this reason, it has been described as an "ethic of responsibility."[69] In its essence, this just war "ethic of responsibility" concretizes human duties in the direction of those who stand in dire need, seeking to restore a justly ordered peace, which is to say, an environment in which human beings can flourish. Hence, the ethic is *not* some "dirty hands" conception of armed force that utilizes some "lesser evil" to achieve some good or remove some greater evil. It is rather a necessary, though limited, means by which to bring about a *good* result, based on a *good* intention, just as criminal justice and law enforcement are designed to achieve a *good* result – an ordered peace in which people can reasonably flourish – in domestic life.[70] The just war ethic, then, is rooted in civic virtue.[71]

The conjoining of justice and charity in just war moral reasoning

Even when "humanitarian intervention" finds little support in modern international law, an older tradition, anchored in just war thinking, justifies force not only to correct wrongs but also to protect the innocent. It is this tradition that best explains – and "re-locates"[72] – humanitarian intervention, and at the heart of this "tradition" is the conjoining of justice and charity.

To divorce justice and charity is to do irreparable damage to the character of both virtues as well as to alter the very moral foundation upon which just-war thinking rests. Both justice and charity are non-fluid in character. As quintessential *human* virtues, they are deemed universally binding, and hence, are "owed" all people. As already noted, evidence of this universality is the transcultural "Golden Rule" ethic surfacing in the teaching of both Plato and Jesus. And as I attempt to argue more fully in the next chapter, this ethic, wherein justice and charity embrace, gives tangible embodiment to the natural law.

Charity, as Augustine conceives of it, must motivate all that we do, including the application of coercive force. Not merely the external act but our internal motivation determines the morality of our deeds.[73] As a social force, this "rightly ordered love"[74] is foremost concerned with what is good – good for the perpetrator of criminal acts, good for victims of criminal acts, good for society which is watching, and good for future/potential offenders.

To read Thomas Aquinas's treatment of both charity and justice in the *Summa Theologica* is instructive. Therein he examines the nature of charity, its moral dimensions, and its consequences. Charity, according to Aquinas, must be developed *through habit* and thus is "a principle of action."[75] Moreover, what is noteworthy is the fact that *war* is contextualized in the middle of Aquinas's discussion of charity (Q. 40 of II-II). For Aquinas, charity and justice meet and guide us in applying coercive force. Because "justice directs a man in his relations with others,"[76] justice and love meld in Thomistic thought.

Two innovative, early modern thinkers in the just war tradition who saw the symbiosis of justice and charity applying in distinctly "humanitarian" situations of their day were Francisco de Vitoria and Francisco Suárez. Their context – Spanish "New World" discovery – is important, for it placed them at odds with conventional thinking of the day. Vitoria's task in particular was to challenge Spanish imperial pretensions and the unjust treatment of Native Americans. "The barbarians are all our neighbors," he wrote, "and therefore anyone, especially princes, may defend them from . . . tyranny and oppression."[77] Spanish intervention could *not* mean *conquest*, based on the natural law and the natives' innocence, even when their customs might seem strange. Recall Vitoria's context: he advances natural law and just-war reasoning on behalf of *those outside his cultural world*, that is, those who technically were not his "neighbors."

Like Vitoria before him, Suárez taught at a leading university of his day. Trained both as a lawyer and a theologian, he addressed the subject of war as did Augustine and Aquinas – as a duty of charity. This element, coupled with the belief that moral principles based on the natural law must guide the use of coercive force in war, formed the main argument of his treatise *On the Three Theological Virtues, Faith, Hope, and Charity*.[78] Following Aquinas, Suárez argued that not merely natural justice[79] but also the norm of charity constitutes the proper motivation for war and coercive force.

Two twentieth-century thinkers, to whom greater detail is devoted in the following chapter, share this commitment to prevent love and justice from being disengaged, though in differing ways. Reinhold Niebuhr, as clouds were forming on the European horizon in the 1930s, grew impatient with standard Protestant ethics of his day. In the end, Niebuhr rejected the divorce of love and justice (even when his theological reasoning must be viewed as deficient).[80] The divorce of love and justice, he believed, is tragic: we end up abetting *injustice*.[81]

The noted Princeton ethicist and just war theorist Paul Ramsey, whom I cite in several contexts throughout this volume, cautioned that someone who is "impelled by love" simply "cannot remain aloof . . . toward the neighbor."[82] Love, Ramsey insisted, originates in justice.[83] Neighbor-love is the primary feature of Ramsey's construal of love because it is cognizant of the dignity and worth of others. And out of this conviction, as indicated earlier, Ramsey speaks of a "preferential ethics of protection"[84] that has the innocent neighbor or third party in view.[85] "[N]o authority on earth," he writes, can withdraw from charity or justice their inclination to "rescue from dereliction and oppression all whom it is possible to rescue."[86] To his great credit, Ramsey's theological orientation always had responsible policy in view – something that, sadly, cannot be said about many theological thinkers today.

"Interventionist" thinkers, then, from Augustine to Ramsey and beyond illustrate why, particularly in *our* day, charity or "neighbor-love" will need to be redefined once more.

The costs and character of non-intervention: a caveat

Assuming that all moral conditions for intervention have been met, charity and human dignity bring us to the conclusion that we have not only a right but also a responsibility to intervene where atrocity is afoot. And *who* should do the rescuing? Our answer must be those states that are (a) best placed and (b) able to assist. While agreement on specifics of those options may elude us, *that* human beings are morally obligated to intervene and come to the aid of victims of gross injustice, where possible, should be beyond controversy.[87]

A word of caution here is in order. Current unpopularity among the American public and American policy-makers regarding humanitarian intervention *may or may not* represent moral principle. While no nation on earth *can or should* "police the world," and while no outcomes are guaranteed, a general attitude of moral detachment *may* in fact serve as a smokescreen for our inability to make moral judgments and engage social-political evil head-on. Full disclosure: I happen to believe, perhaps somewhat offensively to my readers, that the United States, because of its influence and power in the world, has corresponding responsibilities. That does not mean that the United States should involve itself in every – or even most – geopolitical conflicts around the globe. It does mean, however, that the United States, for better or worse, has responsibilities around the world that few nations have. This, let me be quite clear, is *not* imperialism. Rather, it is a conviction, anchored in a moral realism, that *to whom much has been given, much will be required*. I prefer to think about these responsibilities in terms of national and global *stewardship*. Stewardship, it needs emphasizing, entails not only rights but also *duties* – duties that are motivated, or *should* be motivated, by a dual commitment to justice and neighbor-love.

But *what about humanitarian interventions where we have no national interests?* This is a legitimate question. While acknowledging our responsibilities at home, these do not preclude responsibilities abroad. They simply remind us that there are finite limits on the responsibilities that we owe others. And these responsibilities abroad, of course, will vary according to the situation.[88]

Finally, let it be said that "national interest" as it concerns security issues is not merely "selfish"; it is inevitably tied to the security of *other* nations. Granted, it is *not* unreasonable to ask, *Why* should *we* be bearing the burden of military intervention in remote parts of the world? Nor is it unreasonable to ask, *Why* should *our soldiers* in particular be bearing that burden? These are eminently fair questions. But national interest, in the end, need not vitiate the motivation to assist other nations where the need is dire. And should we be accused of hypocrisy or a double standard regarding intervention, as is inevitable, it is "better to be inconsistently responsible than consistently irresponsible."[89]

Justice, neighbor-love, and human dignity

In an important address in 1997 at the U.S. Holocaust Museum, South African Justice Richard Goldstone, who had previously been chief prosecutor of the International Criminal Tribunals for the former Yugoslavia and Rwanda, had this to say,

> The one thing that I have learned in my travels to the former Yugoslavia and in Rwanda and in my own country is that where there have been egregious human rights violations that have been unaccounted for, where there has been no justice, where the victims have not received any acknowledgement, where they have been forgotten, where there's been a national amnesia, the effect is a cancer in the society. It is the reason that explains, in my respectful opinion, spirals of violence in the former Yugoslavia for centuries and in Rwanda for decades.[90]

In this speech, Goldstone recommends doing four things for the sake of those who have suffered: (1) exposing the truth of specific guilt and avoiding general guilt; (2) recording the truth of moral atrocity for the historical record in order to counter attempts by the guilty to avoid guilt; (3) publicly acknowledging the loss of the victims, who, as terrified people, need justice; and (4) applying the deterrent of criminal justice, since human nature tends to be deterred from criminal behavior by the fear of punishment. Goldstone's remarks, fresh on the heels of unprecedented genocidal violence, serve to remind us that Paul Ramsey was right. No authority on earth can withdraw from "social charity" and "social justice" their intrinsic and justifiable tendency to rescue from dereliction and oppression all whom it is possible to rescue.[91] That justification can never be withdrawn; it can only be limited, supplanted, or suspended temporarily.

It has been said that people will not cherish their own freedom if they are unwilling to intervene on behalf of others in need. Ancient proverbial wisdom beckons people of principle, irrespective of their location in life, to act on behalf of the traumatized. Such a call bears repeating, especially in a post-consensus cultural climate and at a moment when nations suffer from "humanitarian fatigue":

> If you faint in the day of adversity,
> How small is your strength.
> Rescue those who are being led away toward death,
> Hold back those stumbling toward the slaughter.
> If you say, "But we knew nothing about this,"
> Does not He who weighs the heart consider it?
> Does not He who guards your life not know it?
> And will He not repay each person
> According to what that person has done?[92]

To "rescue those being led away to death" and to "hold back those stumbling toward slaughter" – *this* is the work of justice and neighbor-love.

Notes

1 *Gaudium et Spes* no. 27.
2 This is an underlying theme in *Animal Liberation: A New Ethics for Our Treatment of Animals* (New York: Random House, 1975) and in Chapter 3 of *Practical Ethics* (Cambridge and New York: Cambridge University Press, 1980). Re-titled *Animal Liberation: The Definitive Classic of the Animal Movement*, the former volume appeared in 2015 in its fortieth anniversary edition.
3 Singer, *Animal Liberation*, 19.
4 Ibid.
5 What goes relatively unpublished by Singer is the fact that he is inconsistent with his published views. In recent years, his own mother has suffered from conditions that would require her to be euthanized, based on what he himself has argued so stridently. To the best of my knowledge, however, Singer has not called for his mother's elimination.
6 This is not to argue that science, properly construed, cannot elucidate various aspects of physical nature. It is only to argue that human creativity, self-consciousness, moral imagination and self-responsibility are *metaphysical*, not purely physical, questions.
7 Robert J. Spitzer, Robin A. Berhhoft and Camille E. De Blasi, *Healing the Culture: A Commonsense Philosophy of Happiness, Freedom, and the Life Issues* (San Francisco: Ignatius, 2000), 43–4, develop this way of thinking in a helpful manner.
8 Thomas Aquinas, *Summa Theologiae* I-II Q. 29, art. 1, 3, and 4.
9 This is not to argue that they are not to be cared for and cherished as part of the created order by human beings who are stewards of that order. It is only to point out, contra "animal-rights" activists, that "animal rights" has the unintended (or perhaps intended) consequence of demeaning human personhood and undermining the very notion of human dignity.
10 Bernard Lonergan, *Insight: A Study of Human Understanding*, eds. Frederick E. Crowe and Robert M. Doran (Toronto: University of Toronto Press, 1992), 34.
11 Few have expressed this reality with clarity as has Edmund D. Pellegrino, in his essay "The Lived Experience of Human Dignity," in Leslie A. Meltzer, ed., *Human Dignity and Bioethics: Essays Commissioned by the President's Council on Bioethics* (Washington, DC: President's Council on Bioethics, 2006), 503–39.

12 Spitzer et al., *Healing the Culture*, 47.

13 Ruth Macklin, "Dignity Is a Useless Concept," *British Medical Journal* 327 (December 18, 2003): 1419–20, and Steven Pinker, "The Stupidity of Dignity," *The New Republic* (May 28, 2008), accessible at https://newrepublic.com/article/64674/the-stupidity-dignity. Macklin's argument, it needs to be pointed out, was made in the context of bioethics. She attempted to criticize the President's Council on Bioethics during the George W. Bush administration for its rather strong emphasis on human dignity, which, she insisted, was a "hopelessly vague" concept. But contra Macklin, human dignity is a moral entity and outweighs any need for an individual's "autonomy," a concept which is central to her understanding of bioethical concerns.

14 The implications of human personhood and dignity for contemporary bioethical debates are developed thoughtfully by Patrick Lee in "Personhood, Dignity, Suicide, and Euthanasia," *National Catholic Bioethics Quarterly* (Autumn 2001): 329–43, and Pellegrino, "The Lived Experience of Human Dignity" (see n. 11), 503–39.

15 I am rejecting a dualism that permeates Western thought and separates the person from his or her body. If either the body or the soulish part of human nature does not in fact constitute part of personhood, then human existence becomes subhuman, and hence destructive of life.

16 William E. May, "The Sanctity of Human Life," in William Bentley Ball, ed., *In Search of a National Morality: A Manifesto for Evangelicals and Catholics* (Grand Rapids and San Francisco: Baker and Ignatius, 1992), 105.

17 See John 1:1–5.

18 In both Judaism and Christianity, it is immoral and unlawful either to take your own life or to instruct anyone else to take it.

19 So Adam Schulman, "Bioethics and the Question of Human Dignity," in Leslie A. Meltzer, ed., *Human Dignity and Bioethics: Essays Commissioned by the President's Council on Bioethics*(Washington: DC: President's Council on Bioethics, 2008), 3–18.

20 Quite clearly, this has enormous implications for bioethics. Human dignity based on the special moral status of the human species suggests that science, while it can tell us much about the material and physical realm, cannot answer the deepest questions about the soulish dimension of the human person – questions that concern the why and wherefore of human existence. For this reason, as they respect this mystery human beings set moral limits in terms of utopian visions that through genetic engineering, cloning and certain methods of biotechnology threaten the *natural order* of things as they are designed. Technology, it needs emphasizing, can exalt or imperil human dignity. On the various challenges that bioethics presents to the concept of human dignity, see the essays collected in *Human Dignity and Bioethics: Essays Commissioned by the President's Council on Bioethics* (Washington, DC: President's Council on Bioethics, 2008).

21 David Gelernter, "The Irreducibly Religious Character of Human Dignity," in Leslie A. Meltzer, ed., *Human Dignity and Bioethics: Essays Commissioned by the President's Council on Bioethics* (Washington, DC: President's Council on Bioethics, 2008), 387–405.

22 Ibid., 389.

23 See Samuel P. Huntington, *The Third Wave: Democratization in the Late Twentieth Century* (Norman: University of Oklahoma Press, 1991).

24 *Dignitatis Humanae* [hereafter *D.H.*] no. 2. I am using the version of this encyclical accessible at www.vatican.va/archive/hist_councils/ii_vatican_council/documents/vat-ii_decl_19651207_dignitatis-humanae_en.html.

25 Ibid.

26 Ibid.

27 Ibid., no. 3.

28 Ibid.
29 Ibid., nos. 4–5.
30 Ibid., nos. 6–7.
31 Ibid., no. 10.
32 John 18:37.
33 *D.H.* no. 11.
34 Ibid. Here we might consider as well 1 Cor. 2:3–5 and 1 Thess. 2:3–5.
35 Rom. 13:1.
36 The conundrum for many lies in the seeming contradiction here between "legitimate" and "illegitimate' authority. A necessary starting-point is to recognize that moral reality is *pre-political*. This means that political authority is not *absolutely* autonomous and that human beings, when coerced to do wrong, are morally obligated to resist that authority, regardless of the personal costs.
37 *D.H.* no. 11. Cf. here as well Acts 4:4:19–20.
38 Rom. 14:12.
39 *D.H.* no. 13.
40 Ibid., emphasis added.
41 Ibid.
42 Ibid., no. 15.
43 Gelernter, "The Irreducibly Religious Character of Human Dignity" (see n. 21), 397–8.
44 Hereon see Mary Ann Glendon, *Rights Talk: The Impoverishment of Political Discourse* (New York: Free Press, 1991).
45 Gelernter, "The Irreducibly Religious Character of Human Dignity," 404.
46 Ibid.
47 For Habermas and Benedict, "human dignity" is a "translational" concept in that it furnishes us with "human rights" (J rgen Habermas and Joseph Cardinal Ratzinger [Pope Benedict XVI],*The Dialectics of Secularization: On Reason and Religion*, ed. Florian Schuller, trans. Brian McNeil [San Francisco: Ignatius, 2006], 71).
48 So Gelernter, "The Irreducibly Religious Character of Human Dignity," 404–5.
49 United Nations, "Universal Declaration of Human Rights," accessible at www.ohchr.org/EN/UDHR/Documents/UDHR_Translations/eng.pdf.
50 "Charter of Fundamental Rights of the European Union," accessible at http://eur-lex.europa.eu/legal-content/EN/TXT/?uri=CELEX:12012P/TXT. The Charter became "legally binding" on the EU in 2009.
51 Luke 10:3–32.
52 Ramsey develops the notion of a "preferential ethics of protection" in several of his writings but perhaps most thoroughly in *Basic Christian Ethics* (New York: Scribner's, 1950), 166–71. See as well "Christian Vocation and Resistance," in William Werpehowski and Stephen D. Crocco, eds., *The Essential Paul Ramsey: A Collection* (New Haven and London: Yale University Press, 1994), 41–59, originally published in *Basic Christian Ethics*.
53 On the twofold command to love God and neighbor, see Matt. 22:36–40, Mark 12:31, and Luke 10:25–28.
54 James Turner Johnson, "Humanitarian Intervention, Christian Ethical Reasoning, and the Just War Idea," in Luis E. Lugo, ed., *Sovereignty at the Crossroads? Morality and International Politics in the Post-Cold War Era* (Lanham: Rowman & Littlefield, 1996), 127.
55 Ludu Sein Win, veteran Burmese (and Rangoon-based) journalist, cited in *Irrawaddy*, April 2008, p. 5 (the *Irrawaddy* online website has since been removed).
56 This instability might be characteristic of new states, failed states, or those states on the verge of collapse.
57 We may define humanitarian intervention as "the proportionate international use or threat of military force, undertaken in principle by a liberal government

or alliance, aiming at ending tyranny or anarchy, welcomed by the victims, and consistent with the doctrine of double effect" (Fernando R. Tesón, "The Liberal Case for Humanitarian Intervention," in J.L. Holzgrefe and Robert O. Keohane, eds., *Humanitarian Intervention: Ethical, Legal, and Political Dilemmas* [Cambridge: Cambridge University Press, 2003], 94). Characteristic of "complex humanitarian emergencies" are several factors: they are crises that are (1) multi-dimensional (involving a wide array of disasters such as war, widespread violence and human rights violations, famine and disease, widespread suffering, social-political disorder, mass displacements of people-groups, etc., resulting in massive death rates), (2) man-made (and thus not "natural disasters"), and (3) essentially political and politicizing. See Jeni Klugman, *Social and Economic Policies to Prevent Complex Humanitarian Emergencies: Lessons from Experience* (Helsinki: United Nations University, World Institute for Development of Economics Research, 1999), 1–2.

58 Indeed, the sheer number and intensity of geopolitical horrors since the Cold War – from Bosnia and Kosovo, Rwanda, Sudan, Sierra Leone, and Liberia to East Timor, Iraq, Syria and the Central African Republic – force us to reconsider the *necessity* of military force in "humanitarian intervention." The tragic lesson of genocide in Rwanda and ethnic cleansing in the Balkans is that large-scale violations of human rights may be *impossible* to prevent or punish *without* military intervention. And where the problems are internal – that is, where they are rooted in particular social structures, a particular political culture, a collapsed infrastructure, or a mindset that gives rise to ethnic hatred, resentment, and violence – the conundrum of humanitarian intervention requires us to ponder the costs of nation-building. My own position is that states in faraway places do indeed have an obligation to intervene, where they have the wherewithal and when the costs are not unreasonable. Politically, I assume that stable states in particular have this obligation, given that they have a stake in global security. From a moral standpoint, I understand stewardship to be based on the principle that to whom much is given, much will be required.

59 Since no war is perfectly "just," it is more accurate to speak of "justified war," by which both *whether or not* to enter armed conflict and *how* to proceed in that conflict are subjected to severe moral qualification.

60 Elsewhere I have argued similarly in "The Ethics of Humanitarian Intervention," in Jonathan Chaplin and Robert Joustra, eds., *God and Global Order: The Power of Religion in American Foreign Policy* (Waco: Baylor University Press, 2010), 145–69.

61 More recently, Michael Walzer has also made a similar argument in Chapter 5 ("The Politics of Rescue") of *Arguing about War* (New Haven and London: Yale University Press, 2004), 67–81. This essay originally appeared in the journal *Dissent* (Winter 1995): 35–41.

62 Paul Ramsey, *The Just War: Force and Political Responsibility* (New York: Scribner, 1968), 23.

63 In his writings on social ethics, war and force, Ramsey shares the Augustinian conviction that charity must motivate all that we do, inclusive of restraining social-political evil. On charity as a governing motive of going to war or intervention, see as well Hugo Grotius, *The Rights War and Peace* 2.1.9; 2.17.9; 2.25.3, 9; 3.1.4; 3.2.6; and 3.13.4. Multiple times in this work, Grotius refers to the "rules of charity" as they relate to – and support – formal justice.

64 So Tesón, "The Liberal Case for Humanitarian Intervention," 93–129.

65 Both Plato and Jesus taught a version of the "Golden Rule," thereby illustrating the fact, based on human dignity, that it is universal in scope.

66 In his important book *A Conflict of Visions: Ideological Origins of Political Struggles* (New York: Basic Books, 2002), Thomas Sowell contrasts two competing visions of human nature in our world today – what he calls the "constrained"

and "unconstrained" visions. The difference between the two understandings cannot be over-stated. Sowell's great service is to point out the ethical, social, and political consequences of the latter while arguing for a more modest and, ultimately, realistic or "constrained" understanding of human nature.

67 Hugo Grotius observes that the natural law "remains still in Force where there are no Courts of Justice" (*The Rights of War and Peace* II.20.8, art. 5). I am here using the version edited by Richard Tuck (Indianapolis: Liberty Fund, 2005).

68 Nigel Biggar, *In Defence of War* (Oxford and New York: Oxford University Press, 2013), 214. Although the political development of "human rights" is more recent, our cultural tradition's understanding of human respect – and hence basic "rights" – has deep roots, anchored in the Judeo-Christian emphasis of human dignity and intrinsic worth and issuing from the conviction of human beings being fashioned in the "image of God." This "natural-law" understanding of human nature, wherein human beings are understood to be morally "free" agents (and hence morally responsible), has been coupled with the Judeo-Christian belief in a transcendent moral order, has contributed to a social-cultural environment in which the very notion of human "rights" and human flourishing has been bred. Since 1948, major international declarations have borrowed and assumed these essential truths, even when such declarations have been clothed in secular language. The problem with cultural relativism, for those who would deny or question the notion of a fundamental human "nature" and inherent human "rights," is that if cultural relativism and moral pluralism are true, then nations could never pass judgments – indeed, *any* judgments – on "crimes against humanity." If, however, there is such a thing as "universal human rights," then preventing genocide, mass murder, ethnic cleansing, and the like must be a part of our foreign policy. And although historically such abuses have been due to dictatorial regimes, the reality is that in our day these atrocities more often than not occur in failed or collapsing states. This burden, in 2001, led the International Commission on Intervention and State Sovereignty (ICISS) to argue for a "re-conceiving" of the notion of sovereignty in its report "The Responsibility to Protect," which was endorsed with strong support again at the 2005 United Nations World Summit. Whether "R2P" has been effectual is, of course, another matter.

69 Jean Bethke Elshtain, "Just War and an Ethics of Responsibility," in Eric Patterson, ed., *Ethics beyond War's End* (Washington, DC: Georgetown University Press, 2012), 123. This, of course, places just war thinking at odds with pacifism, which rejects the essence and significance of political activity *qua* politics. Because it ignores questions of power, pacifism can offer little in terms of authentic peace building in a fallen world, despite its claims.

70 Grotius insists that the laws governing the ethics of war and peace are anchored in the same principles of justice that hold together all domains of civil society (*The Rights of War and Peace*, prol. no. 24; cf. also 2.1.9–11). In the same vein, Augustine writes that it is good – and charitable – to resist, prevent, or subdue a wrongdoer; we do him a service by expressing a "benevolent harshness" (*Epistle* 138 ["To Marcellinus"]).

71 Jean Bethke Elshtain, "Epilogue: Continuing Implications of the Just War Tradition," in Jean Bethke Elshtain, ed., *Just War Theory: Readings in Social and Political Theory* (New York: New York University Press, 1992), 323–33.

72 Terry Nardin, "The Moral Basis of Humanitarian Intervention," *Ethics & International Affairs* 16, no. 1 (2002): 57–8.

73 *The City of God* 14.9.

74 All that was created is "good," for Augustine; however, when our loves are not rightly ordered, the ultimate good is violated (*City of God* 15.22).

75 *S.T.* II-II Q. 23–46, 58; cf. also *Commentary on the Nicomachean Ethics*, Lectures IV–VI.

76 Because "justice directs a man in his relations with others" (ibid. II-II Q. 58, a. 9, r. 3), justice and love meld in Thomistic thought.
77 Francisco de Vitoria, "On the American Indians," reproduced in Anthony Pagden and Jeremy Lawrance, eds., *Vitoria: Political Writings* (Cambridge Texts in the History of Political Thought; Cambridge: Cambridge University Press, 1992), 288.
78 This was published posthumously in 1621.
79 Cf. in this regard Aristotle, *Politics* 1333b–1334a. Suárez rejects the Aristotelian assumption of a natural moral "elite" within society who through their superior knowledge intuit justice over injustice and right over wrong.
80 In Chapter 6, I analyze this deficiency as it surfaces in Niebuhr's writings. An insightful corrective to Niebuhr's deficient theological orientation is offered by Paul Ramsey in "Love and Law," in Charles W. Kegley and Robert W. Bretall, eds., *Reinhold Niebuhr: His Religious, Social and Political Thought* (New York: Palgrave Macmillan, 1961), 79–123; see as well David D. Corey and J. Daryl Charles, *The Just War Tradition: An Introduction* (Wilmington: ISI Books, 2012), 207–26.
81 Ibid., 136.
82 *Basic Christian Ethics* (New York: Scribner's, 1950), 345–6.
83 Ibid., 367.
84 Ibid., 166–71.
85 In this vein, Ramsey takes Jesus' teaching on "turning the other cheek" in the Sermon on the Mount and notes that Jesus does not say, *If someone strikes your neighbor on the right cheek, turn to his aggressor the other as well* (170–1).
86 Ramsey, *The Just War* (see n. 61), 35–6.
87 Among those "first-order" priorities that inform the ultimate justification for intervening are the following: (1) embodied justice as it affects the people who stand in need, (2) creating order out of chaos in social-political terms, and (3) seeking the common good of those in need, and (4) seeking the international common good as it is affected by the crisis (thus Ramsey, *The Just War*, 28–33).
88 These realities are argued with great clarity in James Turner Johnson, "Moral Responsibility After Conflict," in Eric Patterson, ed., *Ethics Beyond War's End* (Washington, DC: Georgetown University Press, 2012), 17–33.
89 Biggar, *In Defence of War*, 233.
90 The transcript of this address appeared in the *Washington Post*(February 2, 1997), C4.
91 Ramsey, *The Just War*, 35–6: "No authority on earth can withdraw from "social charity" and "social justice" their intrinsic and justifiable tendencies to rescue from dereliction and oppression all whom it is possible to rescue . . . This justification can never be withdrawn; it can only be limited, supplanted, or put in abeyance."
92 Proverbs 24:10–12.

6 The natural-law underpinnings of religious freedom – a closer look

Justice and neighbor-love in symbiosis

Justice and neighbor-love in association: conflict or concord?

At its third annual ethics symposium, convened in 2012 at the Command and General Staff College at Fort Leavenworth, Kansas, the U.S. Army brought together ethicists, historians, political philosophers, and chaplains, from both military and civilian life, to reflect corporately on the ethics of coercive force in the contemporary geopolitical setting. One of the speakers addressed those assembled (predominately Majors and Lt. Colonels) on the moral-philosophical underpinnings of what consensually has been understood as the mainstream of the just-war tradition, a rich tradition of (frequently, though not exclusively, Christian) moral reflection stretching from Ambrose and Augustine to Aquinas to Vitoria, Suárez and Grotius to modern-day theorists such as Paul Ramsey, William V. O'Brien, Michael Walzer, James Turner Johnson, and Jean Bethke Elshtain. The title of his address was instructive: "Justice, Neighbor-Love, and the Permanent in Just-War Thinking."

The essence of his remarks was that the symbiosis of justice and charity undergirds and informs the tradition and doctrine of "just war," properly understood. To divorce these two virtues, therefore, would be to do irreparable damage to the character of both justice and charity as well as to alter the very moral foundation upon which just-war thinking rests. Both justice and charity, he reminded his audience, are non-fluid in character; as quintessential *human* virtues, they are deemed universally binding, and hence, are "owed" all people.[1]

These two ethical imperatives – doing justice and loving one's neighbor – are indeed lodged at the heart of our own cultural tradition in numerable ways (and ways surely taken for granted). Although the imperative to do justice derives from two strands of that cultural heritage – "Athens" and "Jerusalem," as one social commentator has encapsulated them[2] – the second, loving your neighbor as yourself, is unique to "Jerusalem." We may readily grant, of course, that the ancient Greeks highly esteemed various forms of "love," notably, *eros* and *philia*; however, it is the Judeo-Christian tradition alone that describes the outlines of – and rationale behind – *agape*.[3]

The present chapter concerns itself with the manner in which our own culture, and Western culture in general, approaches ethical issues and engages in moral reasoning. Specifically, its concern is to address the perceived opposition between – when not the outright divorce of – justice and charity.[4] This perceived tension is widely on display both in scholarly literature, whether among professional ethicists or philosophers or behavioral theorists, and at the popular level. And yet it is a tension that is rarely – if ever – addressed at the presuppositional level. This antagonism, moreover, typifies secular as well as religious thinking; both tend to assume either a tension or some measure of conflict between the two virtues. Justice, it is thought, at its base is cold, rational, harsh and exacting, while charity is considered to be personal, compassionate, forgiving, and hence, "humane." By way of illustration, the notion of retribution or punishment, which is foundational to any meaningful construal of justice, has long been the scourge of the social sciences. For generations, social scientists and behavioral theorists, including not a few criminologists, have viewed punishment in general as detrimental to human beings. Alas, it was only a matter of time before religious ethicists and theologians began imbibing this prejudice and promoting it, in both academic and popular discourse.

An important task, then, as we contemplate not only an "ethics of religious freedom" but also more generally, *any* responsible expression of social ethics is (a) to appropriate a proper understanding of the nature of both justice and neighbor-love and then (b) to understand properly the interrelationship of the two virtues. Because of the widespread misunderstandings that surround how the two virtues interact, this chapter will concern itself chiefly with the latter concern.

An anatomy of conflict: the influence of seminal thinkers

One representative sample of the sort of thinking that is dominant in religious circles today – a sample issuing from a mainline Protestant context – is the following: "I believe that Christians should engage politics with a love that risks not being reciprocated, an unconditional love for all, a love that makes no distinction between friend and enemy."[5] This statement, of course, utilizes language that is thought to mirror the teaching of the New Testament and Jesus himself. Moreover, it proceeds from the baseline assumption – an assumption that unites many sincere religious believers of diverse backgrounds – that love (at least, "Christian love") is both the goal of human existence and the means to that goal and that justice is secondary in priority.

Another contemporary exemplar serves as a useful illustration, given its succinctness and clarity. In the introduction to a book with the title *Moral Wisdom*, the author writes,

> I believe we need to start with the primacy of love and specifically the love of God . . . If we start with love instead of freedom or truth, what

> happens? Why start discussions of morality and ethics with love? Let me give you three reasons: from the scriptures, theology, and the tradition rooted in human experience.[6]

The author's position, that love is the *starting point* for morality – and not truth, for example[7] – should give us pause. Yet, this assertion places him squarely in the "mainstream" of contemporary thinking about ethics. Generally assumed is that love and justice stand in tension or opposition, resulting in a "primacy" or "priority" of love.

The upshot of this understanding of love is that to treat fellow human beings merely as moral law or justice *requires* is not the same – nor is it as noble – as to love others in the manner that Jesus ostensibly requires of us. In the words of one commentator, "[t]o act out of love is perforce not to treat the recipient as one does because justice requires it," and "to treat someone as one does because justice requires it is perforce not to be acting out of love."[8] This mindset is likely to take the form of writers arguing that the "priority of love" will potentially conflict with the rigid demands of justice – the flipside of which is to argue that fulfilling the requirements of justice, narrowly construed, will be unloving.

And although, as one social commentator has pointed out, "nobody has ever proposed that seeking justice should constitute the whole of one's ethical orientation," the same cannot be said of love. Quite the contrary: "Many have held that love should be the totality of one's orientation toward one's fellow human beings."[9] This preference for what we may call "agapism" helps account for a perceived conflict between the two virtues of justice and love and thus invites scrutiny. With its supporting assumptions, this mode of thinking will need a measure of critique. Where precisely does this understanding of the "priority of love" and of love's ethical demands originate? And what does it yield in terms of the common social good and responsible social policy? It should be emphasized from the outset that to examine the nature and reasons for the "conflict," whether at the theoretical or the practical level, is no mere exercise in philosophical gnat straining. Rather, a divorce of these virtues – and, conversely, their reconciliation and symbiosis – has enormous ramifications for not only a robust social ethic but also the maintenance of "civil society" as we presently know it. But the "priority" of love did not emerge yesterday. In fact, it has considerable support from important thinkers of the past.

Kierkegaard and Nygren

In his important and defining *Works of Love*, Søren Kierkegaard argues for love's transcendence by observing the anatomy of *agape*. Divine love, Kierkegaard insists, is our supreme duty, a fulfillment of the law, and our ongoing debt to others. Moreover, this love seeks not its own, it builds others up, it hides a multitude of sins, it believes and hopes all things, and it abides forever.[10] The nature of love, furthermore, is said to be indescribable and unfathomable, a mystery consonant with the divine nature. And it is uncalculating – a feature that will bear significantly on Kierkegaard's understanding of the ethical life.

A fascinating, though tantalizingly brief, discussion in *Works* is devoted to prudence or wisdom. Kierkegaard contrasts what he understands to be the work of prudence with that of charity. Prudence reckons or calculates, making us aware of our limits and cautioning us. But human wisdom has never been capable of reckoning all the chances that lie before us. Faith has taken all chances into account. If one must love, then the matter is eternally decided.[11] Kierkegaard worries that the large-heartedness that issues from love will be restricted by other virtues.

A critically important question for Kierkegaard is the following: "What is it that is never changed even though everything [else] is changed?" His response: "It is love" – i.e., "that which never becomes something else."[12] Love is eternal, "the only thing that will not be abolished."[13] The directive "You shall love," for Kierkegaard, is "the royal law."[14] Love makes no distinction between friend and enemy, and hence, is "blind" and "unconditioned."[15] The ethical implications of this "blind" and "unconditional" love – toward friend and enemy – can be seen in Kierkegaard's understanding of love's relationship to law. He writes, "The relation of love to the law is like the relation of understanding to faith. The understanding reckons and reckons, calculates and calculates, but it never attains the certainty which faith has. So it is with the law: it defines and defines but never reaches the sum, which is love."[16]

In the conclusion of *Works*, Kierkegaard writes tellingly, "The matter is very simple. Christianity has abandoned the Jewish like-for-like: 'An eye for any eye, a tooth for a tooth,' " and "it has established the Christian, the eternal's like-for-like in its place." Christianity, Kierkegaard concludes, "Turns attention completely away from the external" and "turns it inward."[17] This conclusion is thought to find confirmation in Jesus's teaching in the "Sermon on the Mount," wherein it is assumed by Kierkegaard – mistakenly – that Jesus is negating and abolishing the *lex talionis* as a measurement of justice and just retribution.[18] For Kierkegaard, the concept of restitution no longer exists with the advent of Christianity. In this "leap of faith," love becomes the *source and sum* of ethics, a transcendent norm that lies *beyond* the natural law and any moral parameters.[19]

Perhaps the most sophisticated – and forceful – apology for love's primacy is found in the seminal work of Anders Nygren (d. 1978), for whom the Christian idea of love involves "a revolution in ethical outlook without parallel in the history of ethics."[20] As the title of his work suggests, the main competitor to *agape* is the Platonic concept of *eros*. The challenge is therefore twofold: to distinguish the two forms of love and to purify *agape* of any cultural baggage. Nygren insists that *agape* is not merely *a* fundamental motif of Christianity; it is *the* fundamental motif.[21]

For Nygren, the character of love is understood to be "unmotivated," "indifferent to value," "uncalculating," "unlimited," "unconditional" and "blind" to the demands of justice.[22] This "blindness," it is thought, results in forgiveness, which is gratuitous and foregoing of any corrective rights. God's love, after all, is pure grace and does not recognize merit or value. Therefore, the moral vision of the New Testament is not merely a "fulfillment" of the Old; it is a *repudiation* of law and justice as revealed in the Old – that is, "agapic love does not supplement justice but supersedes it."[23]

Theologically, Nygren grounds his argument almost exclusively in the fact that God has expressed his love by means of forgiveness, a form of love that should serve as a model for how we love our "neighbor." The character of forgiveness is such that it is entirely gratuitous. Hence, it follows for Nygren that "fellowship with God is not governed by law but by love. God's attitude to men is not characterized by *justitia distributive*, but by agape, not by retributive righteousness, but by freely giving and forgiving love."[24] This leads Nygren to conclude,

> It is only when all thought of the worthiness of the object is abandoned that we can understand what Agape is. God's love allows *no limits to be set for it by the character of conduct of man.* The distinction between the worthy and the unworthy, the righteous and the sinner, sets no bounds to His love.[25]

God's love then, Nygren can declare, "Makes a mockery of all attempts at rational motivation."[26]

The conclusion of the matter for Nygren, in terms of ethics, is that to treat my neighbor appropriately because justice requires it is *less* – and hence inferior – than to treat my neighbor agapically. This is true because

> [a]gape shatters completely the legal conception of the relationship between God and man. That is the reason for the conflict of Jesus with the Pharisees and Paul's campaign against "the Law." Agape is the opposite of "Nomos," and therefore a denial of the foundation on which the entire Jewish scale of values rested.[27]

In this vein, Nygren is insistent that divine love as revealed in the Old Testament is qualitatively different from – and *inferior* to – that which is revealed in the New; the former is thought to be conditioned by law, covenantal demands and fear whereas the latter is unbounded, gratuitous, and unconditional.[28] Nygren would appear to be conflating certain distortions associated with rabbinic Judaism of the first century with the actual teaching of the Old Testament itself. (As evidence of this, Jesus says, "You have heard that it was said, 'Love your neighbor and hate your enemy,' but I say to you, love your enemies . . ." [Matt. 5:43]. In fact, the Old Testament does not teach enemy-hate; rather, this was an interpretive distortion that had entered by Jesus's day.) It is precisely because of these contemporary distortions and because of debates in the synagogues as to whether Jesus is setting aside the law that Matthew finds it necessary to include confrontations with Israel's teachers that neither Mark nor Luke include in their accounts. This would explain the context that informs Jesus teaching found in Matt. 5:17–48 ("You have heard it said but I tell you . . .") and Matt. 23:1–39 ("Woe to you scribes and Pharisees . . ."). And Nygren's inability to observe this distinction grants us insight into why justice, for him, stands in conflict with love.

At bottom, "[w]here spontaneous love and generosity are found, the order of justice is *obsolete and invalidated*."[29] "Motivated justice," Nygren insists, must give place to "unmotivated love."[30] Strictly viewed, justice and love will stand in conflict.[31] God's love, Nygren declares, "Has no place within a legal scheme, and to those who think of fellowship with God in terms of law and justice it is bound to seem nothing less than blasphemy."[32] Perhaps the reader will get the impression, as I did, that Nygren is inclined toward a "Marcionite" tendency in his opposition between Old Testament and New Testament ethics, between law or justice and agape. Indeed, in his chapter titled "The Agape Type in Marcion," we learn why. Therein Nygren paints the second-century heretic in quite glowing terms for his elevation of the *agape* motif and concomitant demoting of the *nomos* motif. For this reason, Nygren can conclude with this rather remarkable statement: "It was disastrous for the later history of the Christian idea of love that Marcion thus became the great arch-heretic."[33]

For "apapists" like Kierkegaard and Nygren, love is "blind" to justice and "unconditioned." But, alas, this *cannot* be neighbor-love, properly construed; such a position, ethically speaking, is quite simply untenable. If anything, "agapism" would seem to encourage *injustice* and make society unsafe for all.

Timothy P. Jackson

Numerous contemporary writers might be cited as examples of the primacy of love, a primacy that is more or less explicit in its demotion of justice when and where it is thought that the two virtues stand in opposition. One writer, given the thoroughness and creativity with which he has argued for this primacy, deserves particular attention. In his important work *The Priority of Love: Christian Charity and Social Justice*,[34] the self-professing "strong agapist"[35] Timothy Jackson writes,

> The contemporary fate of charity was sealed not so much by direct attacks on agapic love itself as by ill-considered defenses of three related virtues: prudence, freedom, and justice. (These defenses have been offered both by Christians and by those who see themselves as secular heirs to the Christian moral tradition.) Prudence, defined as healthy attention to one's peace and future prosperity; freedom, defined as absence of arbitrary or coercive external restraint; and justice, defined as keeping contracts civilly and distributing basic goods based on merit, all have their place. Indeed, it is the chief glory of liberal democracy

> to have deployed the language of "rights and duties" in an effort to safeguard these three essentials. But neither prudence, nor freedom, nor justice alone can do the work of agapic love, and in the absence of such love, all three of these other goods wither. When exponents of other virtues suggest (explicitly or implicitly) that they can *supplant* charity in some quarter of life, they cut morality's root in all quarters . . . Yet when either exponents or opponents of *agape* argue that it is "*directly in conflict*" with rights and duties, or with social justice generally, they pluck morality's modern flower.[36]

While this citation is too lengthy to exegete fully, it invites our consideration and well illustrates our central thesis. Notice for the author of the aforementioned discussion that "neither prudence, nor freedom, nor justice alone can do the work of agapic love, and in the absence of such love, all three of these other goods wither." While we may grant a partial truth in this statement – for example, we may agree that charity cannot be absent from human endeavor[37] – the author would seem to assume a tension, if not opposition, between justice, wisdom or truth (based on his definition of these virtues[38]) and love, as if they can be added to or subtracted from one another as supplements. Consider his assertion that neither wisdom, nor freedom nor truth "can do the work" of love. Such thinking would appear to drive a wedge, wittingly or unwittingly, between virtues that inhere in – and constitute – one another.[39] Is justice not in fact the *form* in which love manifests itself? Is not love the *way* of wisdom? And is not wisdom a *sensitivity* to what is just and charitable in human relations?

Further clarification as to love's "priority" is offered by Jackson:

> Being the "root of all virtue," a *meta value*, makes charity too important, too fundamental, to count as a (mere) duty of justice. Charity is the wellspring of rights and duties, justice, and the like, but it is not itself a right or a duty in the modern sense. *Agape* is *beyond all economies of exchange, all questions of desert or contract*, at least when human beings are the subjects and objects of love.[40]

Love, for Jackson, is "antecedent to *all* human goods" and "the root of *all* virtue."[41] Correlatively, justice, for Jackson, is clearly secondary to love; love, he insists, is "prior to" justice.[42] Unlike justice, "agapic love" is "constant and unconditional," and it "does not premise this [equal] regard on the even-handed appraisal of rational agents and their agency."[43]

How might one respond to these assertions? First, let us recognize that Jackson's understanding of "justice" is based on the assumption that authentic, "charitable" justice is *not* reciprocal, which it in fact *is*, as Thomas Aquinas is at pains to argue. Aquinas adheres to and yet builds upon, with Christian insight, the classical understanding of rendering to each what is *due*, without which understanding "criminal justice" and "civil society" would be impossible.[44] Society, though not the individual, *must* reciprocate, which is to say, it must restore a balance that was injured, and this for the common good.[45] Reciprocal or retributive justice should not be viewed as "regrettable violence" for the sake of a justice that is divorced from charity; rather, it is *part and parcel* of justice.[46]But at the wider level, it is necessary to respond to Jackson's assertion by questioning whether love indeed *is* "beyond all economies of exchange," "beyond all questions of desert or contract," and in fact a "meta value" that trumps truth, justice and other (cardinal) virtues. At the most basic level, what *indeed* happens to "criminal justice" and the maintenance of "civil society?" By placing "love," as Jackson does, *beyond* all economies and institutions of justice, or, in the language of Nygren, making love "blind" to the demands of justice, are we not in fact *making society unsafe for all*?[47] Is this vision not somewhat *utopian* in nature, given the fact that wider humanity – the "natural man" of St. Paul – does not love with an agapeistic love? Because Jackson claims to be representing the Christian tradition, let it be said that the New Testament nowhere insinuates, much less teaches, that love is "beyond all economies of exchange" and "all questions of desert," including reciprocal justice. Justice is neither "demoted" nor dispensed with simply because of the "love-imperative" found in the Christian scriptures. As empirical evidence thereof, we can rest assured that 70 years ago European Jews, as they were being liberated from Nazi concentration camps by Allied forces, were grateful not merely for the "love-imperative" but for a commitment to reciprocal justice that inheres in a proper understanding of "neighbor-love."

In his recently published *Political Agape: Christian Love and Liberal Democracy*, a volume that completes his trilogy on Christian love,[48] Jackson has extended his argument by contending the love is the "first political virtue."[49] Love, he writes, "Is the foundational norm that ought to structure political principles and policies, from the death penalty to war to marriage to adoption."[50] And as a "political virtue," justice is clearly secondary to love, which is *the* "primary social value."[51] Part of the rationale for Jackson's book is the centrality that justice has had in Western political thinking ancient and modern – from Plato to John Rawls. But because "[f]or millennia, we have habitually misunderstood or at least misstated our relations to one another," love and not social justice should be the glue that binds citizens together.[52]

Whether love, as opposed to justice, should order society, however, is a questionable thesis. Significantly, secular liberal democracy fully aside, it is a thesis that somehow has escaped leading Christian moral and political thinkers through the ages, and Jackson seems indifferent to the fact that this priority of love in the *political* realm lies outside the mainstream of historic Christian thought (which is *not* to say that love is not important in Christian moral theology). Jackson correctly understands the "cross of Christ" as an ultimate expression of love – and self-sacrifice – which he believes should inform liberal society as a result of "prophetic Christian voice."[53] But to argue that love is the "first political virtue" and the basis for public policy in a pluralism wherein religious and non-religious agree to co-exist is quite another matter. In summing up his position, he insists that a "prophetic liberalism" (his term) should "supplant an *erotic democracy* [his term] that emphasizes justice and human dignity with an *agapic democracy* that accents love and human sanctity."[54] But this will mean, according to Jackson, *inter alia* that we go "beyond America's founding documents"[55] and understand that "liberty and justice for all" – whatever these words entail – "must be governed by faith in the God who is agapic love."[56]

Surely such a vision of politics begs many questions and invites scrutiny at a level that is well beyond the scope of my book. Several things, however, need to be said. One is to ask, "What if most people *don't wish* to 'be governed by faith in the God who is agapic love,'" as Jackson writes? Here we must reiterate the importance of principled pluralism, as discussed in a previous chapter. A pluralism that is "principled" does not require religious faith as a common denominator. It does, however, require that there exist a broader consensus about moral reality; hence, the importance of the natural law and a justly ordered peace that helps order the structure of society.

We must also ask, as was noted earlier, why leading Christian political and moral thinkers through the ages did not theorize in terms of love's *priority* (which does *not* mean that love was unimportant to them). Rather, in the main they tended to affirm a version of natural law ethics that assumed the symbiosis of justice and neighbor-love, without necessarily giving one or the other "priority." In this regard, we may also disagree – and here I stand in vigorous disagreement – with one of Jackson's assumptions about the American founding. *Pace* Jackson, we need *not* "go beyond the founders" (whatever that means), as if the founders and framers somehow over time embodied, or attempted to embody, a "Christian nationalism," or that they were misguided, based on the European experience, in their desires for constructing – however tentatively – the American experiment. Quite the contrary, *even when we may be honest about the founders' flaws and about the nation's grievous sins*. As I have attempted to argue in Chapter 3, what is desperately needed is that we rediscover, in *some* measure, the founders' vision, at the heart of which was lodged natural-law thinking, the sacred rights of conscience, a resultant understanding of religious freedom and an environment of (relatively) principled pluralism. It is supreme irony that several chapters of *Political Agape* are devoted to the examples of Abraham Lincoln and Martin Luther King Jr. as models of a "charitable" and "prophetic" witness. What goes largely unsaid – and what apparently goes relatively unnoticed by the author – is that both Lincoln and King were informed by natural law thinking; this simply cannot be missed in their writings and speeches.[57] Natural law ethics, as we have attempted to argue up to this point, assumes the wedding, rather than a tension or the separation, of justice and neighbor-love – a wedding that informs responsible social policy in both domestic and international affairs.[58]

But I have digressed a bit. Let us return to the baseline assumption that informs Jackson's thinking. It is the precedence and "priority" – which is to say, the "stand-alone-ness" – of love as a virtue in conceptualizing the ethical life. In *The Moral Vision of the New Testament: A Contemporary Introduction to New Testament Ethics*, Richard Hays writes,

> Some readers will be surprised to find that I have not proposed love as a unifying theme for New Testament ethics. It is widely supposed that love is the basic message of the New Testament. Indeed, the letters of Paul, the Gospel of John, and the Johannine epistles explicitly highlight love as a (or the) distinctive element of the Christian life: it is the "more excellent way" (1 Cor. 12:31–13:13). The fulfillment of the Law (Rom. 13:8), the new commandment of Jesus (John 13:34–35), and the revelation of the character of God that is to be reflected in relationships within the community of believers (1 John 4:7–8). Certainly, in these writings love is fundamental to the moral life.[59]

At the same time, Hays responds, in no uncertain terms, to the common objection that love *should* have primacy in the ethical life: his omission of love from a list of *unifying images* in biblical literature is *not* an oversight. "For several reasons," he assures the reader, "love cannot serve as a focal image for the synthetic task of New Testament ethics."[60] Chief among these is that "[f]or a number of the major New Testament writers, love is not a central thematic emphasis."[61] Hays identifies Mark, Luke, and Acts, as well as the writer of Hebrews and Revelation as offering little or no attention to this theme. These works, Hays insists, "resist any attempt to synthesize their moral vision by employing love as a focal image."[62] To these, I would argue, we might also add the Pauline prison epistles, the pastorals, and the Petrine epistles, as well as Jude. If anything, I think, Hays may be understating the matter in attempting to evaluate the "priority" of love. Hays is not alone in taking issue with the priority-of-love interpretation of the New Testament. Philosopher Nicholas Wolterstorff devotes a chapter of his important work *Justice: Rights and Wrongs* to the "de-justicizing" of the New Testament.[63] Wolterstorff observes, "Justice, along with its negative, injustice, is one of the main themes in the New Testament. Wolterstorff is countering what he views as "a powerful strand of thought" among interpreters of the New Testament who contend that the New Testament is primarily about love.[64]

Perhaps my reader, at this point, has little interest in the biblical text or in New Testament ethics. I respect that lack of interest and do not presuppose it on the part of the reader. My purpose here is simply to demonstrate that even theological voices themselves object to the argument that love should have "priority." But before shifting our focus to a "concordant" view of the moral life, we must consider yet one more version of love's "priority" that continues to show enormous appeal and invites serious scrutiny.

Ideological pacifism

Given its basic pre-commitment to peace as "non-violence" (or peace as the absence of conflict), ideological pacifism, perhaps the most influential subset of "priority-of-love" thinking, places love and justice in frequent and fundamental tension or opposition. While pacifism can be either secular or religious in its orientation, not infrequently it derives its inspiration from religious sources. For religious pacifists, this outlook expresses itself in a reading of the Christian scriptures that extols peace as *the* virtue of the Kingdom of God. In our day, it finds its most forceful expression in the writings of people like John Howard Yoder, Stanley Hauerwas, and other Anabaptist types. Because of particular ideological pre-commitments to "peace" and "non-violence," certain tendencies that inform faith and ethics flow from this outlook. Among these are the following:

- extolling of love and "peace" as the highest virtues;
- understanding the so-called Sermon on the Mount not only in terms of personal discipleship but also statecraft as well;
- understanding "turning the other cheek" as the equivalent of "enemy-love";
- assumption of moral purity in the early, pre-Constantinian church, followed by the decline and apostasy of the Church from Constantine onward (so-called Constantinianism);
- assumption, correlatively, that the Church since the fourth century, with the exception of the "radical Reformation" of the sixteenth century, has been in apostasy;
- failure to distinguish between a just peace (*pax iusta*) and an unjust peace (*pax iniqua*) as well as a corresponding failure to distinguish between "force" – which is morally neutral, able to be used for either good or ill, and supportive of law and justice when morally guided – and "violence";
- failure, in reading the Christian scriptures, to distinguish between Romans 12 (a *pro*scribing of justice) and Romans 13 (a *pre*scribing of justice)
- rejection of the natural law, which expresses the moral law as constitutive of the creation orders; and
- false dichotomizing of Old Testament and New Testament ethics in one's reading of the Christian scriptures.

Lest the reader conclude that I am unfairly caricaturing religious pacifism, permit me to say that I grew up in the Anabaptist tradition and thus understand – and appreciate – it from "the inside." The strengths of the pacifist perspective are multiple and certainly compelling. Whether secular or religious in character, it is sensitive to the violent tendencies that permeate both human experience in general and American culture in particular. In addition, it recognizes diverse – and in many ways – creative avenues for political and social action. In the words of Jean Bethke Elshtain, pacifism puts "violence on trial" in that it views social life from the standpoint of the potential victim and not the victor.[65] Furthermore, it is keenly sensitive to the distortions of faith that come with an uncritical view of the state that fades into nationalism – a continual problem throughout history and not one that is uniquely American.[66]

Though perhaps surprising to some, mainstream Christian thinking through the ages takes exception to pacifist pre-commitments at several critically important levels. These criticisms are theological, historical, moral-philosophical, and hermeneutical in nature.[67] One objection to religious pacifism is its failure to make the fundamental moral distinction that exists – supported in the Old and New Testament – between shedding *innocent* blood and shedding *any* blood. This distinction can be seen in the Sixth Commandment, in the post-flood covenant with Noah (Genesis 9), and in the rationale for the cities of refuge (Numbers 35, Deuteronomy 19, and Joshua 20). Not all killing is murder. To fail to acknowledge this important distinction not only undermines the common good but also can even be said to prepare the ground for totalitarianism.[68]

The mainstream of historic Christian thinking differs with religious pacifism on another critically important front. Politics and guarding the common good (which encompasses a host of civil service vocations) are not a "necessary [or "intrinsic"] evil"; rather, they are part of our stewardship in tending all of creation (unless, of course, Scripture explicitly condemns certain vocations as intrinsically immoral). Notice that for John the Baptist, in a context of soul-searching and repentance (Luke 3:14), the "sin" of the soldiers is not *being soldiers*, any more than Zacchaeus's "sin" (Luke 19:1–10) was collecting taxes. Rather, in both cases it was the temptation to be unjust.[69] Notice, as well, that two officers of the Roman Legions are paradigms of faith. One is praised by Jesus for his utterly remarkable willingness to believe (Matt. 8:5–13), and another is used to open the eyes of the apostle Peter to the divine purpose (Acts 10 and 11). Significantly, a centurion is the first baptized Gentile (Acts 11:44–48). In the New Testament, soldiers or those in authority are never called away from their vocation.[70] The inability of many, then, to read beyond a truncated understanding of the "Sermon on the Mount" – an understanding that is anchored in pacifistic pre-commitments – would seem to be part of the reason that Aquinas begins his discussion of war in the *Summa* by asking, "Is it always sinful to wage war?"[71]

Mainstream Christian thinking about stewardship in the world, including political realities, is perhaps best captured by the "two cities" imagery that forms the bedrock of Augustinian thought. Our dual citizenship and our attendant responsibilities call us to live "between the times," as it were, with allegiances to both the "city of man" and the "city of God." While Christians acknowledge an ultimate allegiance to the latter, they take seriously *both* citizenships. In refusing to engage in policy and politics, pacifism creates the morally awkward (and inconsistent) dilemma of keeping its hands clean while non-believers dirty their hands in the business of maintaining justice and preserving the social order, from which even pacifists themselves benefit.[72]

Yet another qualification, in some ways suggested earlier, needs emphasis which pacifism is inclined to overlook. "Peace" can be unjust and therefore illicit in character. Insofar as thugs, terrorists, pirates, and criminals – in any age and context – maintain an obit of "peace" around themselves in order to flourish in their activity, peace must be *justly* ordered.[73] In the words of Aquinas, "peace is not a virtue, but the fruit of virtue."[74] Peace and justice are both human goods, but neither is an absolute good. The Christian position, it needs emphasizing, is *not* "peace at any price."[75] Mainstream Christianity's disagreement with pacifism does not simply concern the *means* of establishing peace; rather, it concerns the *nature* of that interim, geopolitical worldly peace. Because of its pre-commitment to "non-violence" and consequent refusal to resist evil directly through action, ideological pacifism would seem to bestow upon evil and tyranny an advantage. Michael Walzer worries that pacifism concedes the overrunning of a country or people-group (let alone a community) needing defending, something that no government (whether federal, state or local) has ever done willingly.[76] Walzer is simply stating the obvious, and it is difficult to disagree with him. For this reason, C.S. Lewis observed, "If war is ever lawful, then peace is sometimes sinful."[77]

Given the praise that is universally showered on Gandhi, it needs to be said that the moral distinction between a just and an unjust peace highlights the logical conclusion and – in the end – moral obtuseness of Gandhi's "non-violence." Doubtless, few people recall the advice given by Gandhi to European Jews who were being delivered to extermination camps by the Nazis. What was this advice? It was to *commit suicide in order to get the world's attention* and speak to the conscience of nations.[78] Notice the contradiction here: whereas violence toward others was viewed by Gandhi as immoral, violence directed toward *the self* was to be countenanced. One is justified in arguing that Gandhi's "pacifism" was only possible in relatively free nations like India, a British colony, and not in totalitarian societies like the Soviet Union or Nazi Germany.[79]

Martin Luther is said to have quipped that if we insist in the present life that the lion lay down with the lamb, *the lamb will need constant replacement*. And indeed it will. The "prophetic" images of lion and lamb, adder and infant, leopard and goat, compelling as they are in a universal sense, are intended to be eschatological; it is utopian and fantastic to expect – and interpret – these as lying together, playing with each other, and co-existing harmoniously in the present life. Human obligations short of the eschaton concern guarding and justly ordering – however imperfectly – a *temporal* peace, not the *perfect* peace of the city of God. This will include, even when it does not limit itself to, protecting religious freedom, that most basic of all human freedoms.

An anatomy of concord: necessary correctives to split thinking

Theological reflections on the unity of the virtues

Elsewhere, I have attempted to show, in expressly theological terms, that it has been a confession of Christian theology through the ages that the nature and character of the Trinitarian God subsist in a unity.[80] Again, permit me to say that my argument does not depend solely on the theological component. My non-theistic readers will still find common ground. Nevertheless, it well illustrates my thesis. Theologians speak of the divine nature in terms of communicable and incommunicable attributes.[81] Among the latter, which are the present focus of our discussion, are eternality, infinity, omnipotence, omniscience, transcendence, immutability, invisibility, sovereignty, and self-sufficiency. A related feature, which tends to suffer from short shrift, is the attribute of divine indivisibility. This doctrine counters the notion – whether implicit or explicit – that the divine nature is constituted by separate parts. A God whose being is understood or assumed to be composite, thus, is assumed ultimately to be more creaturely than otherly or transcendent in nature.[82] Divine attributes are not to be understood as additions, elements, trappings, or supplements – i.e., qualities that are "added" or in need of being "balanced." They do not exist in a certain "combination." At bottom, the Judeo-Christian God is not a deity of parts or divisions,[83] nor does he "develop" or "emanate." Rather, his actions are an expression of his perfection, unity, and timelessness. We might even argue that God does not *have* attributes; he *is* his attributes. And for our purposes here, I am assuming that his love *is* his justice, that his judgments *are* his mercy, and vice versa, even when they manifest themselves in differing (and seemingly irreconcilable) ways.[84]

The ethical implications of the doctrine of divine indivisibility become readily apparent. Because the divine nature is not composite or a sum of many parts but rather a unity, divine action is to be understood not as a setting aside or "negating" or "demoting" of various attributes but rather as a different expression or form of the same attributes. To be sure, from the human standpoint, the qualities of divine mercy and compassion would appear the opposites of divine judgment and wrath. And yet, historic Christian confession calls us to reject this "opposition" or tension and affirm that these are but different manifestations of the same attributes. The divine nature, after all, does not change.

The ethical upshot of this doctrinal position requires reiterating. Divine justice and love may not be severed or viewed as standing in tension (or opposition). And because Christians are "called" to imitate the divine nature, they are prohibited from divorcing justice and charity as these "cardinal virtues" impact persons and people-groups. It is in this way – namely, via creation and divine image-bearing – that the human moral impulse is to be understood. Christian theology posits that humans are created in the image of God; hence, we are to bear his likeness by mirroring the *imago Dei* through our lives and our actions.

A fundamental part of this image-bearing is to manifest and work for justice in the context of human relations. Motivation for this work is summarized by the so-called Golden Rule ethic that surfaces in the teaching of both Plato and Jesus: we do to others as we would want others to do to us. This entails advancing standards of moral good and resisting or countering evil. For Thomas Aquinas, precisely this – doing good and avoiding evil – constitutes the heart of the natural moral law, the "first principles of practical reason."[85] In his brief but richly discerning essay "The Humanitarian Theory of Punishment," alluded to in the previous chapter, C.S. Lewis argues that it is precisely *because of* the image of God in others, not *in spite of* it, that we hold fellow human beings accountable for their actions. To hold them accountable, Lewis insists, is to dignify the *imago Dei* in them, and to fail to hold them accountable is to disavow the *imago Dei*.[86]

Lest one assume that Christian theology loosens the demands of justice by means of a presumed "priority" of love, two important qualifications are in order. First, the definition of "love" needs severe qualification. "Love" needs stripping of the cultural baggage to which we have grown accustomed. When we speak, in biblical and theological terms, of "loving one's neighbor," we understand charity to mean *the desire for another's best or highest*. It is in this light that we are to understand "enemy-love" as taught by Jesus. We wish for fellow human beings what is *best* for them – even for criminals and evildoers. To restrain or inhibit evildoers is indeed best for them, best for society at large, and best for future offenders.

Secondly, the teaching of the New Testament is univocal in its emphasis: *love fulfills the law*. Which is another way of saying that charity and justice are one and cannot be divorced. Which is another way of saying there is no "priority" of love. This is the explicit teaching of Jesus, Paul, and James.[87] Consider the context and implications, for example, of Jesus's teaching. As recorded in Matt. 5:17–48, his teaching is designed to counter contemporary religious thinking that might loosen the demands of the moral law. Moreover, it should be viewed as going hand-in-hand with his two-fold "great command" to love God and love neighbor (Matt. 22:35–40 = Mark 12:28–34 = Luke 10:25–28). To argue that love "fulfills" the law (Matt. 5:17 = Rom. 13: 8, 10 = James 2:8) is to insist that love is the *meaning* of the law,[88] which is to say that law provides the content and structure of love. Justice, therefore, becomes the instrument of love.[89] Stated differently, the "great command" is internal and external; that is, it is both personal and social. Both realms are united, with the second issuing out of the first insofar as the first confers value and dignity on the second.[90]

The context of the epistle of James indicates that the author is responding to tensions within an emergent Christian community in which the role of law is being hotly debated. Hence, he finds it necessary, utilizing techniques from wisdom literature, to admonish and exhort on the basis of the conviction that Christian faith, if it is authentic, will be *verified by good works*. For James, neighbor-love will do justly and thereby be a "fulfillment" of the law. And in the apostolic teaching recorded in Romans 13, Paul is arguing that justice as meted out by the governing authorities is divinely sanctioned for the express purpose of preserving justice and social order in a fallen world. In the apostle's rationale, retributive justice and individual conscience are necessarily linked because of the "debt" of charity, which "fulfills the [moral] law." Notice the Pauline response to "agapism": retributive justice and charity are not mutually exclusive (Rom. 13:1–10).

While readers of this volume may or may not have theological interests, my purpose here is simply to demonstrate the considerable inconsistency that exists even in much standard religious thinking. Moreover, both secular and religious alike are inclined to pit love against justice. In fact, I would contend that after having taught nearly three decades in a "Christian liberal arts" environment at the collegiate level and having done public policy research in criminal justice in Washington, DC, religious believers are perhaps *more* prone to this false dichotomy. This unfortunate state of affairs suggests several things for our consideration: religious believers (at least those in the Christian tradition) (a) are taught that love has *priority* over all virtues, including justice; (b) tend to be ethically deficient, given this lacking theoretical (= theological) foundation; and (c) consequently lack the tools to apply their faith properly in terms of responsible public policy. What's more, these deficiencies would seem to be found equally among theological "liberals" and "conservatives," with both groups being inclined to "spiritualize" the ethical demands of justice by means of the "priority of love."

A superficial view of ethics is prone either to view justice and love as separate aspects of human relations or to assume that the two virtues have different ethical criteria.[91] Hence, one might then conclude that love transcends all rational ethical criteria or that it constitutes mere "self-sacrifice," while justice is concerned to accommodate to – or be negotiated by – human expectations and human needs. Correlatively, one might as well conclude that "strict justice" is less than "humane" while "love" has the best interests of the person in view.

The Christian scriptures, it needs emphasizing, never present justice as a lesser good or lesser virtue. Rather, from a theological, ethical as well as logical standpoint, one might argue that love and justice are woven together in the divine character and thus are to be manifest in a robust ethic of "neighbor-love"; hence the significance of the "great command," as we have noted. This ethic will be sensitive *inter alia* to the needs of the weak, the poor, the defenseless, and those whose basic human rights are being violated. Neighbor-love is inseparable from justice, so that it is accurate to insist, in Augustinian terms, that justice is the "service" of love.[92] In fact, for Augustine, perfect charity *is* perfect justice.[93] This comports with Jesus's teaching – namely, that loving God and loving the neighbor are a unified entity. Justice is not simply "added on" to love; it is, rather, the embodiment of love, the very order or structure which love requires, without which love collapses into sentimentalism.[94] And because justice arbitrates, as it were, between competing claims and interests in society, we would expect to find clashing theories about justice in the public sphere.[95] What illuminates the character of justice when viewed through the lens of the Hebrew and Christian scriptures is an explanation of its origin – the divine nature – and its rationale: we act justly because God acts justly. But one need not be religious to see the truth of this line of reasoning: in non-religious terms, we treat others *as we ourselves wish to be treated* (justly), and we do not treat others *as we ourselves would not wish to be treated* (unjustly).

The influence of seminal thinkers

Because the Christian social ethic rests on a bedrock of moral and theological foundations, chief of which is the character of God himself, we would expect to find a mainstream of thinking about charity and justice among the Church's fathers of any era. And indeed we do, both ancient and modern.

1 *Augustine and Aquinas*

Augustine is important *inter alia* because he reminds us of our two citizenships – one in the "city of God," one in the "city of man." When push comes to shove, as it were, and our allegiances are tested, Augustine is very clear in *De Civitate Dei* that our ultimate allegiance is to the divine city. However, that does not release us from our responsibilities to the city of man, and in *that* city, there is a critical need for ordering society because of the effects of sin.

For Augustine, whose views would survive in whole or in part well through the Reformation of the sixteenth century and to a remarkable extent even to the present day, wars occur because of the fallen nature of human beings. Most wars, he believed, are rooted in concrete sins such the implacable lust for power (*libido dominandi*) and vengeance.[96] Augustine's foundational emphasis on the fallenness of the human condition has led some commentators to label him a "realist."[97] It was Augustine's belief that there was no perfect justice on earth. All regimes are flawed, all politics mirrors the effects of sin, and human conflict is simply inevitable. In a famous passage of the *City of God*, Augustine likens human political associations to bands of robbers:

> Justice removed, then, what are kingdoms but great bands of robbers? What are bands of robbers themselves but little kingdoms? The band itself is made up of men; it is governed by the authority of a ruler; it is bound together by a pact of association; and the loot is divided according to an agreed law. If, by the constant addition of desperate men, this scourge grows to such a size that it acquires territory, establishes a seat of government, occupies cities and subjugates peoples, it assumes the name kingdom more openly. For this name is now manifestly conferred upon it not by the removal of greed, but by the addition of impunity.[98]

On the surface, it would appear that Augustine is thoroughly pessimistic about the possibility of any connection between justice and politics. Yet it would be inaccurate to conclude that he viewed justice and politics as divorced. While Augustine was among the first great political writers to break from the ancient view that politics might somehow make human nature good or bring about a state of *eudaimonia* (happiness, blessedness), he was nevertheless convinced that politics was indispensable for creating a modicum of peace on earth.

Hence he speaks of the *tranquillitas ordinis*, the justly ordered peace, a space in which the chaotic violence of fallen men might be mitigated to a degree (i.e., justice) so that individuals might flourish.[99] Because of evil and the obligation of *Christian love* to defend and protect the innocent third party, to not apply what he calls "benevolent harshness" (*benigna asperitas*)[100] to stop the evildoer is itself to be an accomplice in doing evil. In Augustine's "benevolent harshness," love and justice necessarily merge.

The concept of "benevolent harshness" may sound paradoxical, yet it is both facilitated and illuminated by certain philosophical and theological distinctions. "In correcting a son however severely," writes Augustine, "paternal love is surely never lost sight of." This love is internal, a matter of one's purpose and intent, while the acts or acts of discipline are external and may appear harsh. Even when applied to international relations, and even to war, justice may be done with benevolence if the welfare of the victims as well as the conquered becomes the principal concern.[101]

Charity, as Augustine conceives of it, must motivate all that we do, including the application of coercive force. Not the external act but our internal motivation determines the morality of our deeds.[102] As a social force, this "rightly ordered love"[103] is foremost concerned with what is good – good for the perpetrator of criminal acts, good for the society which is watching, and good for future/potential offenders. This understanding, of course, inheres in what we denote as justice. Justice, for Augustine, is "the love of God . . . diffused through all the others [i.e., the other virtues]."[104]

It was noted earlier that the influence of Augustine's thinking was far-reaching, and in the work of Thomas Aquinas, we witness to what extent that was true. To read Aquinas's treatment of both charity and justice in *Summa Theologica* is instructive. Questions 23–46 of the *secunda secundae partis* (i.e., the second part of the second part) are devoted to the nature of charity, its priorities, its moral dimensions, and its consequences. In Aquinas's understanding, charity is the *form* of all the virtues, whether theological or moral.[105] Why is it the "form" of all virtues? Because charity is included in the very definition of virtue; that is, *every virtue depends* on it. Given the fact that the relationship of charity to all other virtues is central to Aquinas's vision, we must probe a bit deeper.

In considering a potential objection that justice, charity, beneficence (i.e., doing good), and mercy are distinct entities, he writes, "Just as friendship or charity sees in the benefit bestowed . . . the general aspect of good, so does justice see therein the aspect of debt, while pity considers the relieving of distress or defect."[106] For Aquinas, the act of doing good unites the virtues. In fact, Aquinas states, "All the virtues that are directed to another person may by reason of this common aspect be annexed to justice."[107]

To the interrogatory, "Is a command to love really necessary?" Aquinas answers, yes, any moral obligation requires a command, given sin and the human propensity for hatred. In fact, the command to love is implicit in all ten commands of the Decalogue. The virtues, of which *caritas* is one, are developed habitually and, therefore, must be both commanded and practiced. As a virtue, then, love for Aquinas is "a principle of action."[108] At the same time, the requirements of charity as we consider the ethical life are not unlimited: we cannot assist everyone. Which is to say that charity, in Aquinas's understanding, is not "unconditional"; rather, it is conditioned and constrained in the human experience. Therefore, we do not – indeed, we cannot – mandate "equal charity for all" since our ability to display charity is governed by human need.[109]

What is noteworthy in Aquinas's discussion is the fact that the problem of *war* is contextualized in the middle of his treatment of *caritas* (Q. 40) – a fact that not infrequently is ignored in modern commentary. Not only the effect of human virtues in general but also the specific virtue of love itself helps frame human moral obligation in the application of coercive force. Here we see the mark of Augustine's thinking on Aquinas's reflections, as is the case in much of Aquinas's wider analysis. The guiding principle of loving one's neighbor is linked to numerous virtues in Thomistic thought, including justice, joy, peace, and mercy. Each virtue, however, is opposed by a corresponding vice in a narrower sense, and war, according to the structure of Thomistic thinking in the *Summa*, is best understood as a vice opposed to peace. And because war is so clearly a vice in extreme form, it is quite natural to wonder whether it is *always* wrong. Precisely for this reason, Aquinas begins his commentary with the words *utrum aliquod bellum sit licitum* (whether some kind of war is ever lawful). After all, war would seem contrary to the precept expressed in Matthew 5:39, "Do not resist the one who is evil." Therefore, one might reasonably conclude, war is evil. Period. Which is why the discussion of war in Question 40 begins with the question of whether war is always a sin.

While a fuller treatment of his response to the question "Can war ever be just?" is beyond the scope of the present discussion, Aquinas proceeds to argue, "In order for war to be just, three things are necessary." Recall, again, the context of the question of war: it is lodged in the middle of Aquinas's discussion of *caritas*. Consider the second and third of the three justifications for war noted by Aquinas (the first being legitimate authority). Regarding the second, just cause, he writes that punishing a wrong can be a virtue – the virtue of justice in action. But this particular expression of virtue, he is well aware, runs a high risk of being transmuted into a vice. That is to say, it risks violating the requirements of charity. Therefore, it falls to Aquinas to show how coercive force can be just as well as true to the demands of charity.[110]

And precisely this rationale is found in his third requirement. In order for a war not to be unjust, the intention of the belligerents must be to act with the advancement of the good in mind or the avoidance of evil. This, of course, echoes Aquinas's first precept of natural law: do good and avoid evil. It may happen, for example, that a war is waged for a just cause and with the authority of a legitimate sovereign and yet in the end be unjust. Why? So crucial is *right intention* that if the belligerents' motivations and designs are not right, then every act will be unjust. Right intention, then, will guide the process so as not to oppose a justly ordered peace. Charity – the good of both the belligerents and those whom they are subduing – is the only means of reconciling justice and peace, according to Aquinas.

Although Aquinas's debt to Augustine is evident throughout his discussion in Question 40, he accomplishes something that neither Augustine himself nor those who subsequently drew from Augustinian thought achieved. Aquinas places the problem of war within a coherent framework of human virtues (and specifically charity) in order to illuminate its proper and improper manifestations more clearly. Charity and justice meet and guide us in applying coercive force. And one of the three classic criteria for a war to be considered "just" is right intention. Right intention is measured by the presence of both charity – which desires the best for the neighbor – and justice (Q. 58) – which is protective of the basic rights of the innocent neighbor. Because "justice directs a man in his relations with others,"[111] justice and love meld in Thomistic thought.

2 *Niebuhr and Ramsey*

Two Christian thinkers closer to our time share this commitment to prevent love and justice from being disengaged, though in differing ways. I consider first the example of Reinhold Niebuhr. Niebuhr appeared in 1948 on the cover of *Time* Magazine's twenty-fifth anniversary issue, and when he died in 1971, he was hailed by the same magazine as "the greatest Protestant theologian in America since Jonathan Edwards."[112] At the height of Cold War tensions in the early 1960s, Niebuhr was applauded by University of Chicago political theorist Hans Morgenthau, a leading figure in twentieth-century political realism, as "perhaps the greatest living political philosopher in America."[113] Niebuhr, interestingly enough, was a Marxist and a pacifist in his early years. But as storm clouds were forming on the European horizon in the 1930s, he grew impatient with standard Protestant ethics of his day and abandoned his pacifism for what he called an "Augustinian realism."[114] By 1949, he had abandoned his earlier Marxist views for a distinct brand of democratic liberalism grounded in a biblical understanding of human nature. The influence of his mature ideas cannot be overstated, and that influence, as is well known, helped to shape the thinking of political realists such as George Keenan, Hans Morganthau and Arthur Schlesinger Jr. Even today, he is routinely cited as influential by leading statesmen or commentators on public affairs, and he is the subject of continuing analysis as a theological and political thinker.[115] Niebuhrian realism, then, is deserving of our attention. Much of its significance has to do with how Niebuhr, in his own iconoclastic, nuanced and, and in some respects, deficient way, refused to allow justice and charity to be divorced.[116]

Among other things, Niebuhr is perhaps best known for his now famous words "the impossible possibility" to describe Jesus's love ethic.[117] In *An Interpretation of Christian Ethics*, Niebuhr writes, "The faith which regards the love commandment as a simple possibility rather than an impossible possibility is rooted in a faulty analysis of human nature."[118] What Niebuhr called "Christian idealism" creates an illusion; what is needed, rather, is a "Christian realism." Niebuhr believed that "the final law in which all other law is fulfilled is the law of love"; however, he insists, this finality is eschatological in nature; it cannot be realized as a law among the nations in the present life. Tellingly, he writes, "The gospel is something more than the law of love. The gospel deals with the fact that men *violate* the law of love."[119] Though acknowledging the reality of self-sacrifice as part of love, he does not hold the view, with the Christian "sentimentalist," that self-sacrificial love can make for responsible public policy *on this side of the eschaton*. "That degree of love is an impossibility for nations."[120] At the same time, Niebuhr insists that "in the ideal of equality," which is "always the regulative principle of justice," there is resident "an echo of the law of love."[121] Niebuhr worries that that *both secular and religious understandings of the relationship of justice and love tend to exclude justice from love.* In the end, Niebuhr rejects the divorce of love and justice, even when his theological reasoning must be viewed as deficient.[122] Because he contrasts love and justice without placing them in opposition, Niebuhr cannot technically be called an "agapeist."[123] Summarizing his own position in *Christian Realism and Political Problems*, he writes, "Broadly speaking, the end of law is justice. But we have seen that justice is related to love. Thus there is a dialectical relation between love and law even as there is between love beyond law and love as law."[124] Law and justice, therefore, can be viewed as "an approximation of the law of love on the one hand and an instrument of love on the other hand."[125]

A helpful way to probe Niebuhr's "realist" stance in foreign affairs is to observe how it emerges from his rejection of pacifism in the now classic essay "Why the Christian Church is Not Pacifist,"[126] written in the early years of WWII. The essay argues that most (though not all) forms of pacifism are "heretical" (his word). That is, when judged by either the gospel's account of human nature or by the facts of human experience throughout history, modern forms of pacifism fail to correspond with reality. And both of these criteria – the human condition and human history – are for Niebuhr related, anchored in a Christian anthropology that acknowledges both the "law of love" and the presence of sinful fallenness.[127] The problem with pacifism, insists Niebuhr, is that it appears one-sided in its emphasis; it stresses one of these two poles – the law of love – and then mistakenly attempts to apply this "law" to public policy, in the naïve belief (or hope) that human conflict will wither away.

Christian idealism, Niebuhr laments, is tempted toward two errors: it is tempted either to withdraw from participating in the world of political and economic affairs or to have an exaggerated view of his influence in the culture. It is tempted, in other words, toward "defeatism" or toward sentimentality.[128] In its essence, it is incapable of deriving any significant politico-moral principles from "the law of love." It thereby destroys a dynamic relationship between the ideal of love and the principles of justice. The result of this divorce, he believes, is tragic: we end up abetting *injustice*.

The folly of such a view is demonstrated not only by the Christian gospel but also by historical experience. And on this point, Niebuhr is characteristically brilliant, finding it necessary to lampoon Protestant naïveté on the eve of the Second World War:

> If we believe that the only reason men do not love each other perfectly is because the law of love has not been preached persuasively enough, we believe something to which experience does not conform. If we believe that if Britain had only been fortunate enough to have produced 30 percent instead of 2 percent of conscientious objectors to military service, Hitler's heart would have been softened and he would not have dared attack Poland, we hold a faith which no historic reality justifies.[129]

Whatever Christianity entails, Niebuhr insists that it does not require one to believe that self-sacrifice always, or even usually, yields politically desirable – and responsible – results. In fact, history suggests precisely the opposite, and it is a foolish idealism that seeks to deny such.[130] Love may triumph over evil at the end of time, but in history, where human beings remain sinful and fallen, loves does not solve the political problem. The fundamental and permanent political problem, according to Niebuhr, concerns the aggregate effects of sin and the human condition: selfishness, greed, lust for power, and self-assertion that goes beyond the limits of fairness and justice. What is needed to offset this problem is not love (not simply, at least) but resistance – that is, a balance of power and love that produces justice. Here we see the human need for government, insofar as coercion – not *oppression*, but coercion by government – is necessary because of the human condition. Were it not for the governing authorities, social life would degenerate quickly into anarchy; at the same time, were it not for checks upon governmental power, life would degenerate quickly into tyranny.[131] Realistically speaking, the closest approximation of civil society that mediates between the two extremes of anarchy and tyranny in a fallen world is a "justice" in which "life is prevented from destroying life."[132]

Before we leave Niebuhr, several remarks are needed regarding his theological orientation. As it applies to public policy and especially international affairs, it is Niebuhr's conviction that Christians, no less than anyone else, should recognize the need for robust participation in society and the reality of coercive force, even when and where this includes participation in war or humanitarian intervention. Resistance to tyranny, Niebuhr is wholly convinced, is not optional for relatively free societies, and he is to be commended for countering many fellow Protestants in his day who denied any Christian basis for this conviction. Here we gain insight into the reasons why Niebuhr was so critical of pacifism. In fairness, however, it must be said that Niebuhr's theological rationale leaves much to be desired, even when he intuited that justice must not be severed from love.[133] His understanding of love is anchored in a perception of the "ethic of Jesus," which, he believes, is characterized by "absolute" moral imperatives – for example, "resist not evil," "love your enemies," "be not anxious for your life," and "be perfect even as your Father in heaven." While these commands are to be lauded, Niebuhr believes that they spell disaster for socio-political life: "No appeal to social consequences could fully justify these demands of Jesus" in the geo-political sphere.[134] Not only are these demands unjustifiable in terms of their social-political consequences, they are also impossible to fulfill. Thus, on the one hand, this perceived "ethic of Jesus" is a standard by which we will ultimately be judged, but, on the other hand, it is a standard we can never meet. It creates, in Niebuhr's famous phrase, an "impossible possibility" for the present.[135] This split in Niebuhr's thinking leads him to give modern pacifists a choice: either break from the ethic of Jesus and become politically "responsible" (as the "Christian realist" does when necessity calls) or else attempt to live by the ethic of Jesus, to the extent that this is humanly possible, yet become politically "irrelevant." There is a place for Christian pacifism, he concedes, but it is not a *political* place. Its home is in the monastery or the withdrawn Christian community, and its value lies in its testimony to those who take the problems of politics seriously.[136]

One generation closer to us, the noted Princeton ethicist Paul Ramsey believed that the ethical principles of Christian faith were relevant to the world's political economic and social problems. Ramsey demonstrated keen insight into the ethical dilemmas of our time as well as a remarkable fluency in relating those insights in the wider public arena. He was without equal in his ability to enter cross-disciplinary conversation and debate with not only theologians and ethicists but also social scientists, politicians and policy analysts of his day, and to do so in a manner that was knowledgeable and timely. Not surprisingly, Ramsey was influenced by the writings of Niebuhr at an early age. And tipping his hat to Niebuhr in the mid-1960s, Ramsey could write, "There is a need for more, not less, Christian realism in our premises [about international affairs]."[137] That influence would be felt in strategic ways, for few other individuals in the twentieth century have done more to link Christian ethics in a responsible manner to public policy.

A primary feature of Ramsey's writings is to apply Augustinian thinking to contemporary ethical challenges. Ramsey insists that one who is "impelled by love" simply "cannot remain aloof . . . toward the neighbor."[138] Although Ramsey views love as central to any viable social ethic, he qualifies the character of love in ways that are probing, creative, and ethically necessary. For this reason, he regularly speaks in his writings of "the ethics of *obedient* love."[139] Love, Ramsey insists, originates in righteousness and justice.[140] And justice, he observes, is "what Christian love does when confronted by two or more neighbors."[141] Which is why, he concludes, Jesus's teaching emphasizes a rule – i.e., a kingdom – and *not simply love*.[142]

Neighbor-love is the primary expression of Ramsey's "obedient" love because it is cognizant of the *imago Dei* in others. For this reason, Ramsey speaks of "a Christian ethic of resistance"[143] and a "preferential ethics of protection"[144] that has the innocent neighbor or third party in view. Hence, "Love can only do more, it can never do less, than justice requires."[145] Thus, "no authority on earth," he insists, can withdraw from charity or justice their inclination to "rescue from dereliction and oppression all whom it is possible to rescue."[146] In the end, Ramsey opposed what he called "pure agapism," which mistakenly assumes that no basic ethical principles other than "the law of love" are valid. There *are* general rules of practice, as he argues in his important work *Deeds and Rules in Christian Ethics*,[147] even when Ramsey was not a natural-law theorist.[148] To his great credit, Ramsey's theological orientation always had responsible policy in view.

Part of our difficulty, as Ramsey sees it, is that we have frequently distorted the meaning of Jesus's teaching. He notes, as an example, the oft-cited admonition to "turn the other cheek" (Matt. 5:39). Jesus directive is this: "If someone strikes *you* . . ." The matter, Ramsey observes, is *personal* – between you and someone else. Jesus does not say, nor does he advocate, "If someone strikes *your neighbor* on the right cheek, turn to him *your neighbor's* other cheek . . ." That is, while people are free to forego self-defense, they are *not* free to ignore the plight of the innocent third party.[149]

Although in his career Ramsey addressed a wide range of ethical issues, his work in the sphere of the ethics of war and peace has had a notably enduring effect on just-war thinkers to the present day. Commentary taken from his important volume *The Just War* well illustrates his understanding of how justice and love, while differentiated in their qualities, nevertheless are unified and may not be disengaged either in theory or in practice:

> The Western theory of the just war originated, not primarily from the considerations of abstract or "natural" justice, but from the interior of the ethics of Christian love, or what John XXIII termed "social charity." It is a work of charity for the Good Samaritan to give help to the man who fell among thieves. But one step more, it may have been a work of charity for the inn keeper to hold himself ready to receive beaten and wounded men . . . By yet another step, it might well be a work of charity to resist, by force of arms, any external aggression against the social order that maintains the police patrol along the road to Jericho. This means that, where the enforcement of an ordered community is not effectively present, it may be a work of justice and a work of social charity to resort to other and available and effective means of resisting injustice: What do you think Jesus would have made the Samaritan do if he had come upon the scene while the robbers were still at their fell work?[150]

Summarizing his orientation, Ramsey writes, "This is what I mean by saying that the justice of sometimes resorting to armed conflict originated in the interior of the ethics of Christian love."[151] For Ramsey, it is the work of love and justice together to deliver people from tyranny and oppression.[152] As with Niebuhr, Ramsey realized that justice is not simply "added" on to (or subtracted from) love; rather, it is the order which love requires.[153]

3. *Benedict XVI*

In his important 2009 encyclical *Caritas in Veritate*, Benedict XVI writes, "Charity in truth, to which Jesus Christ bore witness by his earthly life and especially by his death and resurrection, is *the principal driving force behind the authentic development of every person and of all humanity*."[154] Charity in truth. Permit me, in the discussion of Benedict which follows, to substitute the word "truth" for "justice." Up to this point, I have argued for the unity, the symbiosis, the in severability of love and justice. I have done so not only for theological but also for ethical as well as socio-cultural reasons, all of which are interrelated. What may be argued of love and justice regarding their character and constitution may also be extended to the relationship between love and truth. One cannot exist with the other. Each needs the other.

In this final encyclical of the pontificate of Benedict XVI, we find the extension of a theme that was recurring not only in his work but also in that of his predecessor, John Paul II.[155] Charity in truth. "*Only in the truth does charity* shine forth, *only in the truth* can charity be authentically lived. Truth is the light that gives meaning and value to charity."[156] "Agapism," as we have seen (or at least "strong agapism"), is inclined to assert itself on the basis of the theological declaration "God is love"; therefore, it is thought, a robust social ethic must have love as its "priority." Benedict does not deny love's importance, but he does argue that "love," at least as it is understood today, needs strong qualification. Charity in truth. Benedict encourages his readers, for eminently ethical reasons, not only to look at God as love but also to look at Christ, who expresses, with precision, the very image of the Father (John 1:14, 18; Col. 1:15): "In Christ, charity in truth becomes the Face of his Person, a vocation for us to love our brothers and sisters in the truth of his plan. Indeed, he himself is the Truth (cf. Jn 14:6)." Charity in truth.

Benedict continues,

> To defend the truth, to articulate it with humility and conviction, and to bear witness to it in life are therefore exacting and indispensable *forms of charity*. Charity, in fact, 'rejoices in the truth' (1 Cor 13:6). All people feel the interior impulse to love authentically: love and truth never abandon them completely, because these are the vocation planted by God in the heart and mind of every human person.[157]

Charity in truth.

Lest one conclude that Benedict denies the centrality of love, he reiterates what he had written in his first Encyclical Letter, *Deus Caritas Est* ("God is love"): "Everything has its origin in God's love, everything is shaped by it, everything is directed towards it. Love is God's greatest gift to humanity; it is his promise and our hope."[158] Charity, therefore, must be at the heart of the Church's social doctrine. Every responsibility and every commitment, Benedict avers, must ensure that the Church's social ethic is derived from charity – a charity which, he notes, is "the synthesis of the entire Law," based on Jesus's teaching (cf. Mt 22:36–40).[159] This linkage – charity representing the synthesis of justice as represented by the Law – confers "real substance to the personal relationship with God and with neighbor."[160] Moreover, it is a guiding principle "not only of micro-relationships" such as family, friendships and small groups "but also of macro-relationships" such as social and economic ties.[161] Therefore, "[f]or the Church, instructed by the Gospel, charity is everything."[162]

But there is a problem. Benedict is aware of ways in which "charity has been and continues to be misconstrued and emptied of meaning, with the consequent risk of being misinterpreted, detached from ethical living and, in any event, undervalued." But this emptying also occurs "in the social, juridical, cultural, political and economic fields" – that is, contexts which are "most exposed to this danger" and where moral responsibility is urgently needed.[163] Hence the need to link charity with truth not only in the sequence given by St. Paul, *veritas in caritate* (Eph 4:15), but also in the inverse and complementary sequence of *caritas in veritate*. Truth in charity. Charity in truth.

Not only does truth need to be "sought, found and expressed within the 'economy' of charity" but also "charity in its turn needs to be understood, confirmed and practised in the light of truth."[164] The reason for this mutual and reciprocal relationship is significant and should give pause to anyone who takes the moral life seriously. Of this mutuality and reciprocity Benedict writes,

> In this way, not only do we do a service to charity enlightened by truth, but we also help give credibility to truth, demonstrating its persuasive and authenticating power in the practical setting of social living. This is a matter of no small account today, in a social and cultural context which relativizes truth, often paying little heed to it and showing increasing reluctance to acknowledge its existence.[165]

Relativizing the truth. In a cultural context that downplays truth at best and despises it at worst, Benedict worries that "love" – perhaps properly understood in generations past – now is devoid of meaning. He elaborates:

> Without truth, charity degenerates into sentimentality. Love becomes an empty shell, to be filled in an arbitrary way. In a culture without truth, this is the fatal risk facing love. It falls prey to contingent subjective emotions and opinions, the word "love" is abused and distorted, to the point where it comes to mean the opposite. Truth frees charity from the constraints of an emotionalism that deprives it of relational and social content, and of a fideism that deprives it of human and universal breathing-space. In the truth, charity reflects the personal yet public dimension of faith in the God of the Bible, who is both Agápe and Lógos: Charity and Truth, Love and Word.[166]

The implications of the organic linkage between charity and truth become apparent. Because of this linkage, charity can be "understood," "shared," and "communicated," even cross-culturally, transcending the normal cultural barriers that limit communication and communion.[167] Truth, thus seen, has the capacity to open minds and unite people in their experience. In the present social and cultural climate wherein the tendency is to relativize truth, Benedict wishes to admonish us that "practising charity in truth helps people to understand that adhering to the values of Christianity is not merely useful but essential for building a good society and for true integral human development."[168]

And what would a Christianity consisting of charity without truth breed, if tolerated? In Benedict's assessment, it would be "more or less interchangeable with a pool of good sentiments, helpful for social cohesion, but of little relevance."[169] But more specifically, "there would no longer be any real place for God in the world. Without truth, charity is confined to a narrow field devoid of relations. It is excluded from the plans and processes of promoting human development of universal range, in dialogue between knowledge and praxis."[170]

For this reason, Benedict reminds his readers, the Church's social teaching is *caritas in veritate in re sociali*; it is "the proclamation of the truth of Christ's love in society,"[171] and "the principle around which the Church's social doctrine turns."[172] Therefore, while social ethics is a service of charity, "its locus is truth," which will have a "preserving" and "liberating" power in the face of "ever-changing events of history."[173] At the same time, truth vindicates faith and reason, "both in the distinction and also in the convergence of those two cognitive fields."[174] Furthermore, without truth, "without trust and love for what is true, there is *no social conscience and responsibility*."[175] Thereby "social action" ends up serving private or misguided interests, gutting the very source and goal of moral action.

The "guts" of the social ethic Benedict wishes to preserve, contra the assumptions of agapists, consist of two integral components: justice and the common good. As Benedict's encyclical suggests, these will need some unpacking. First, concerning the cardinal virtue of justice: "*Ubi societas, ibi ius*: every society draws up its own system of justice."[176] While Benedict acknowledges, with agapists and non-agapists alike, that charity can go beyond justice, it is also true that charity "never lacks justice," since justice

> prompts us to give the other what is "his," what is due to him by reason of his being or his acting. I cannot "give" what is mine to the other, without first giving him what pertains to him in justice. If we love others with charity, then first of all we are just towards them.[177]

Charity in justice.

But there is more. Not only is justice "not extraneous to charity," and not only is it "not an alternative or parallel path to charity," but justice, rather, is "inseparable from charity . . . and intrinsic to it"; it is "the primary way of charity" and "an integral part of the love."[178] There are two ways of viewing the relationship of love and justice. Viewed from one angle, "charity demands justice" based on "recognition and respect for the legitimate rights of individuals and peoples," to the extent that charity "strives to build the earthly city according to law and justice."[179] Viewed from another angle, charity "transcends" justice and "completes it in the logic of giving and forgiving," based on communion and relationship. Charity will give "theological and salvific value" to a commitment for justice, *without suspending or demoting the necessity of justice.*[180] Charity in justice.

The second component of a credible social ethic and reason why charity does not – indeed cannot – stand-alone is the common social good. To desire the common good and strive toward it, insists Benedict, is "a requirement of justice and charity."[181] The rationale is not difficult to apprehend:

> To take a stand for the common good is on the one hand to be solicitous for, and on the other hand to avail oneself of, that complex of institutions that give structure to the life of society, juridically, civilly, politically and culturally, making it the pólis, or "city."[182]

This after all, constitutes the realm of justice. And yet, "[t]he more we strive to secure a common good corresponding to the real needs of our neighbours, the more effectively we love them."[183] The "institutional path" of charity will require that it is wed to other cardinal virtues. Charity in justice and truth.

Love anchored in truth – *caritas in veritate* – is said by Benedict to be "a great challenge for the Church in a world that is becoming progressively and pervasively globalized."[184] The great risk of our time, as he sees it, is that the sum total of global developments "is not matched by ethical interaction of consciences and minds that would give rise to truly human development."[185] For without truth, in addition to love collapsing into subjectivism and sentimentalism,

> it is easy to fall into an empiricist and sceptical view of life, incapable of rising to the level of praxis because of a lack of interest in grasping the values – sometimes even the meanings – with which to judge and direct it.[186]

To be faithful to human nature, for Benedict, is to be faithful to the truth, which *alone* is "the guarantee of freedom (cf. Jn 8:32) and of the possibility of integral human development." Charity in truth.

Both love and justice have as a major component in their constitution the moral primacy – i.e., the moral "priority" – of responding to *human need.* Charity works through justice; the one is not an alternative to the other.

The recent work of Nicholas Wolterstorff

Rethinking the character of love and justice

In his 2011 work *Justice in Love*, Nicholas Wolterstorff, the Noah Porter Emeritus Professor of Philosophical Theology at Yale University, notes the "persistence and prominence" of the question *How do justice and love relate to each other?*, which emerged as he was writing his previous book, *Justice: Rights and Wrongs*.[187] That volume, however, "became too long for any additional chapters," and it became clear to Wolterstorff, after no more than preliminary reflection, that "a serious treatment of the topic would require not a chapter (as originally thought) but a book."[188] The chief burden of *Justice in Love*, then, is the perceived tension between justice and love and the possibility of an "unjust love" and an "unloving justice." To his credit, the author realizes that this is no mere academic question, for *inter alia* it is lodged "at the center of the controversies swirling around truth and reconciliation commissions of the past thirty years."[189]

Moreover, Wolterstorff is struck by the lack of nuanced treatments of charity, at least in the literature, when compared, for example, with the discussions of justice and its variations. The resultant migration for many toward "agapism" mirrors a perceived conflict between the two virtues that invites serious investigation. And it illuminates the structure of *Justice in Love*, which seeks to probe the character and contours of love in both theological and moral-philosophical terms as it stands in relationship to justice. *Justice in Love* is organized according to four principal parts. Part 1 ("Benevolence-Agapism") examines several classical texts of modern-day *agapism* and argues for a "compatibilist" perspective in understanding the imperatives of love and justice. Part 2 ("Care-Agapism") expands the examination of both classical and non-classical agapism and finds the author defending a non-classical variety that pays particular attention to how the justice-imperative relates to the love-imperative. In Parts 3 ("Just and Unjust Love") and 4 ("The Justice of God's Love"), the reader is confronted with particular examples cited by Wolterstorff of perceived conflict between the two virtues, based on his promotion of the "care-agapism" model. Therein the author identifies specific contexts in which a malformed version of either justice or love, as he understands it, might be on display. The volume ends with the author's reflections on theological justification in light of God's justice and God's generosity toward humankind.

Following an examination of influential "agapists" – Søren Kierkegaard, Anders Nygren, and Reinhold Niebuhr (the latter of whom Wolterstorff, perhaps strangely to some readers, categorizes as a "non-classical agapist"[190]) – Wolterstorff attempts to rethink conventional definitions of justice and love as well as to reconsider their application in light of human well-being and what is deemed "good." At one point, he writes summarily, "Treating the neighbor justly is an example of loving the neighbor."[191] While this statement is true as far as it goes, in its simplicity it does not offer a definition of justice in which the roots of this cardinal virtue are illuminated. A classical definition of justice – a consistent will to render to each person his or her due – is a likely starting-point which contains, at least implicitly, the notions of "right" and desert." But Wolterstorff intuits that rights are meaningless apart from some sense of moral *obligation*, that is to say, some intuition of universal, normative social bonds between fellow human beings.[192] And it is the absence of moral obligation in contemporary society, with its exaltation of personal autonomy, that distorts our thinking about justice.[193]

Authentic love, for Wolterstorff, will embody justice for the simple fact that people are fashioned in the image of God and thus possess an intrinsic dignity. What's more, a Christian understanding of love will put self-love in proper perspective – a perspective that eschews both self-indulgence and self-deprecation. In addition to the "Golden Rule," Wolterstorff cites the so-called Sermon on the Mount as evidence of love's application. Here he has in mind specifically what he believes to be a repudiation of the Old Testament's "reciprocity code," of which the *lex talionis* (Matt. 5:38–39) is a part.[194] In this context, Wolterstorff distinguishes between punishment and retribution, operating on the assumption that the notion of retribution is "the idea of redressing harm done to some victim by the imposition of an equivalent harm on the victimizer." Jesus's command to forgive the wrongdoer, Wolterstorff believes, was part of Jesus's rejection of retribution: "To forgive someone for the wrong he did me is to bestow on him the good of not holding it against him."[195] This presupposition, with its ethical implications, will need re-visiting.

Part 3 of the volume offers the reader a variety of contexts in which the symbiosis of justice and love might be tested. As suggested earlier, Wolterstorff is attentive to the place of forgiveness in the Christian social ethic and devotes important space and discussion to the relationship between repentance, forgiveness, and reconciliation. Not all readers will be satisfied with his baseline conviction: "Full and complete forgiveness . . . requires foregoing reprobative punishment . . . [and] such foregoing does not, as such violate or undermine justice."[196] Nevertheless, the searching questions that Wolterstorff poses are an important starting-point for meaningful discussion on the viability of Christian conviction in the public sphere.

After deliberating on whether generosity and paternalism can express themselves in either just or unjust forms, Wolterstorff concludes the volume with theological reflections from the epistle to the Romans on God's generosity and justice, revisiting the theme of the alleged tension between love and justice. The conclusion to the matter is this: God is just and justified in offering justification to Jews and Gentiles alike.[197] Although this justification is pure gift, it is nevertheless "just," by virtue of the fact that it is reckoned (i.e., imputed) to us.

Justice in Love is an important volume, not least because the author correctly senses a disconnect in the thinking of many. One is challenged to find similar volumes in our day that wrestle with the widely perceived tension between justice and love, and for addressing this need Wolterstorff is to be commended. What's more, the volume is significant because of the exemplary manner in which the author seeks to persuade, mixing a blend of theological insight with moral-philosophical arguments in matters of (potentially) enormous social consequence. The volume's lucid exposition of historic arguments, bringing to bear important insights from the past for present consideration, is laudable and assuredly pertinent to our time. Correlatively, its argument for a proper grounding of human rights is one of its great strengths; Wolterstorff is incisive and forthright when pressing his argument that neither the ancient philosophical account of human rights – eudaimonistic or utilitarian in nature – nor the modern secularist account is capable of adequately grounding these rights in the way that a theistic (and specifically Judeo-Christian) account does.[198] And it may be that the author has done a further service, whether intended or not, by exposing a peculiarly – when not universally – Protestant tendency of constructing false dichotomies. Whether these oppositions consist of faith versus works, law versus grace, grace versus nature, general versus special revelation, Old Covenant versus New Covenant ethical norms, personal piety versus social witness, or love versus justice, there is something inherent in Protestant thinking that is inclined toward the creation of false dichotomies. This defect, which has not always been part of the Protestant legacy, is most unfortunate, and it afflicts professionals and non-professionals, clergy and laity, mainline and evangelical types alike.

Caveats and qualifications

Most readers will resonate with Wolterstorff's burden as I did, whether or not they are satisfied with his conclusions. Indeed, in contemporary thinking it is not uncommon to find love and justice standing in tension, if not conflict, and love given priority over justice. The perceived opposition between the two virtues, as we have suggested, expresses itself in a variety of ways. One common feature is to misconstrue charity as harsh legalism or unjust paternalism under the assumption that love and "grace" loosen what justice and law rigidly demand. This misunderstanding very often derives from a particular reading of the so-called Sermon on the Mount, by which it is thought that charity somehow cancels out the public need for retribution and restitution. Here I depart from Woltertorff on two fronts: first, in his contention that Jesus rejects a "reciprocity code" as taught in the Old Testament, and second, in what I view to be his unnecessary distinction between punishment and retribution.

As to the former, it needs emphasizing that Jesus is rejecting *private* attempts to carry out "justice" – "vigilante justice," if you will – but he is *not* rejecting the *lex talionis* as a principle of justice implemented in the proper context – namely, by the authorities – any more than he is abrogating the sanction against murder, adultery or integrity in one's speech (cf. Matt. 5:17ff). With respect to retaliation, Jesus intends to challenges his listeners to consider their attitudes in the face of *personal* insults. The fact that insult (i.e., personal injury), rather than assault (i.e., public injury), is at issue here is further suggested by the mention of the cheek being slapped (Matt. 5:39), in addition to the three other related illustrations – giving "the short off your back," going "the second mile," and giving or lending to whoever asks.[199] The meaning of Jesus's teaching here cannot be that when a third party is being injured, I am required to stand by and allow injustice to proceed. Were this the case, even if non-resistance were intended as "compassion," in the end, it would result in cruelty toward society. There is nothing in the teaching of Jesus prohibits normal police work or soldiering, which may entail coercive force for the purposes of restraining evil and maintaining justice. Charity may or may not express itself in resisting evil, based on the public-versus-private distinction. To interpret Matthew 5:38–42 as an absolute prohibition of coercive force is to misunderstand the teaching of the Christian scriptures broadly and the "Sermon on the Mount" more narrowly. What's more the *lex talionis* expresses several universally valid legal principles that inhere in justice: it seeks to levy *proportionality* in society's response to criminal acts, and it establishes both *upper and lower limits* to that response.[200] Both aspects – proportionality and limitation – inhere in the abiding character of justice, a "cardinal" virtue. Never did the *lex talionis*, as delineated in the Old Testament, convey upon the *individual* the right to retaliate. Penalties and punishments were administered judicially, not privately. Jewish sources, moreover, indicate that monetary penalties were being assessed for injuries that were incurred in the first century.[201] By Jesus's day, legal compensation had become *illegal*, negating the very spirit of the law.

As to my latter disagreement with Wolterstorff (and here I realize that the former and the latter concerns are related), "retribution" properly construed needs to be distinguished from revenge or retaliation, not "punishment" *per se*. Retribution also is to be distinguished from *retributivism*.[202] The spirit behind revenge, on the one hand, and retribution, on the other, is captured quite tellingly by St. Paul in Romans 12 and 13. In Romans 12 the apostle makes it abundantly clear that justice is not personal but public; that is, it is lodged with the governing authorities, which divine providence has ordained to preserve the moral-social order. To equate – and thereby confuse – revenge or retaliation, which is subjective and often personal in character, with moral retribution, which is objective, public, and part of the common good, is to distort the character of justice at the most fundamental level.[203] To argue that retributive justice for wrongdoing (which includes restitution) is not a requisite part of human affairs, whether it affects the religious believer or non-believer, is to dismiss both common sense and human experience in history (fully aside from the mainstream teaching of the Christian moral tradition). And it is to miss (or deny) the therapeutic or restorative purpose that is lodged at the core of the image of God.[204] C.S. Lewis expresses this reality exquisitely in his essay "The Humanitarian Theory of Punishment," in which he argues that contrary to contemporary behaviorist theory, we punish precisely *because* human beings are moral agents, made in the image of God.[205] We dignify human beings as moral agents by holding them accountable for their actions. Not to hold them accountable would be to "undignify" them, to treat them as *less* than fully "human." In the words of Michael Sandel, "As the therapeutic ethic represents the flight from moral responsibility, the retributive ethic represents the yearning to recover it."[206] Here it may be the case that Wolterstorff has promoted the very dichotomy – love over justice – that his book sets out to correct.

A corollary of rejecting retribution is to view love as a necessary renunciation of coercive force, such as in my own father's Anabaptist heritage, noted earlier. Ideological pacifists, due to past or potential abuse of coercive force ("violence"), reject in principle the possibility that force can ever serve just purposes. To maintain the important distinction between "violence" and "force." Here it is necessary, with John Courtney Murray, to maintain the critically important distinction between "violence" and "force":

> Force is the measure of power necessary and sufficient to uphold the valid purposes both of law and politics. What exceeds this measure is violence, which destroys the order both of law and of politics . . . As an instrument, force is morally neutral in itself.[207]

A related assumption, for religious pacifists, is that authentic justice is reserved for the next life and divine providence, insofar as only the Almighty can right the wrongs of the present life. Both of these views – that force *per se* is immoral and that retributive justice is reserved for the next life – seriously undermine any legitimate attempts at criminal justice.

One further view of love requires our consideration. It derives from the inaccurate, though widespread, assumption that justice prevents us from truly forgiving others. Because of Wolterstorff's concern to address forgiveness as it relates to the retaliatory impulse and Jesus's teaching on retaliation in the "Sermon on the Mount" (Matt. 5:38–42), a number of remarks are in order. And while this particular accent does not bear directly on the question of religious freedom, it does bear on it indirectly to the extent that it concerns our response to victims of outrageous evil. It is widely believed, by religious and non-religious people alike, that insisting on the demands of justice cheapens or inhibits our attempts at forgiveness, or that an offender cannot be genuinely "forgiven" and simultaneously be forced to pay his debt to society. Several elements usually remain unexamined, or at least clouded, in typical discussions of "forgiveness." Among these are (1) the centrality of the role of repentance and contrition in the entire forgiveness process; (2) the moral (and theological) fact that people in truth *do* pay for their sins in the present life, even when "forgiveness" allows them to be restored to those people whom they have offended (and, from a theological standpoint, enter communion with a holy God); and (3) whether political actors and nations can or should be "forgiven" for perpetrating social-political evil and gross injustice.

At the most fundamental level, it needs to be stated that although persons can "forgive" others for wrongdoing, *governing authorities cannot*. And if they would, society would collapse in chaos. In addition, it is necessary to distinguish between two models of "forgiveness," which have already been insinuated earlier. Traditionally, at least in our own cultural tradition, "forgiveness" has been understood as a *social exchange or transaction* between two parties – offender and victim – following an offense and subsequent confrontation. Forgiveness is bestowed upon the offender by the victim in response to the offender's contrition and repentance. Another approach is to understand "forgiveness" as *psychological and therapeutic release* by the victimized, *regardless* of whether or not the offender (a) is confronted by the victim and (b) has shown contrition for his wrongdoing. The latter understanding, which does not correspond to "forgiveness" in the technical and transactional sense, would nevertheless seem to be the dominant view in our day of the concept of "forgiveness."[208] Authentic forgiveness – as distinct from psychological release based on a therapeutic model – is predicated on repentance and contrition of the offender.

But further qualifications are necessary at this point. In his treatment of forgiveness, Wolterstorff writes, "To forgive is not to treat the *act* as not having been done but to enact the resolution *not to hold the act* against *the wrongdoer*."[209] Wolterstorff's belief that we should not hold the act – however heinous and evil – against the *wrongdoer* as a person, interestingly, finds no support in either the Hebrew or the Christian scriptures (a fact that would take many sincere Christian believers by surprise). In this vein, one is reminded of the old adages "To forgive is to forget" and "Let bygones be bygones." But what does the judge say to the family members of victims of genocide? What should the courts say to family members of a murder victim? And what should a counselor, therapist, or pastor say to the woman who has been raped? Especially, when in each of these cases the perpetrators remain implacable and non-contrite? Does "Christian spirituality" – the kind that both Wolterstorff and I at least affirm "on paper" – teach such a concept of "forgiveness" – a concept that continually and agonizingly disrupts the most sincere efforts of the victim to forgive? Are human beings *required* to forgive in such desperate situations?

Our answer must be no. But not merely because such an understanding of forgiveness falls short of justice and love properly construed. As it is, neither the Old Testament nor the New Testament teaches such a concept. A careful examination of relevant New Testament texts reveals that the common assumption to "forgive and forget" and to "let bygones be bygones" – ostensibly out of "Christian love" – is a distortion of the transaction of forgiveness which, properly understood, entails two requisite steps: (1) confrontation and accountability and (2) contrition and repentance.[210]

This pattern is confirmed by the classic New Testament text of Matthew 18:15–17, which concerns confronting someone who "sins against" you. Notice that Jesus prescribes the initial step of confrontation. And if the offender remains intractable, notice the pattern which follows: members of the community are to be witnesses to the confrontation. Notice, too, that forgiveness is not prescribed when and where the community has confronted the offender and he or she remains obstinate; quite the opposite, in fact, is prescribed by Jesus (15:17). And not only does Jesus teach this method, he also practices it, as New Testament scholar Troy Martin observes,

> Jesus does not simply forgive the offences of his generation. Instead, he summons his generation to repent . . . He confronts the Pharisees and scribes with their hypocrisy . . ., the Sadducees with their error . . ., the citizens of Nazareth with their shame . . ., and his disciples with their lack of faith . . . Jesus predicts stern judgment upon the unrepentant . . . Jesus confronts his generation and holds it accountable for its deeds.[211]

But I can hear my reader's objection. Following immediately on the heels of this "confrontation text" in Matthew 18 is Peter's follow-up question: *how often must I forgive?* On the surface, Jesus's response would seem to support the well-worn adage that, without any qualification, I should forget the wrong done to me and forgive the wrongdoer: "I say to you, [do this] not seven times but seventy times seven" (Matt. 18:22). But compare this particular occasion as it is recorded in Matthew with a parallel and abbreviated account in Luke 17:1–4. Again Troy Martin said,

> Luke's version of Jesus' response explicitly requires repentance before forgiveness is extended. Is Luke's explicit requirement of repentance also implicit in Matthew's version of the response? The Parable of the Unforgiving Servant that immediately follows in Matthew's Gospel [18:23–35] stipulates an affirmative answer to this question.[212]

I take Martin's exegetical conclusion to be correct. In support of that interpretation, notice what occurs at the end of the parable: the master recalls the "forgiven" debtor and *reinstates the entire original debt* (Matt. 18:34). Throughout the Hebrew and Christian scriptures, the declaration of divine forgiveness is always – *always* – preceded by a call for contrition and repentance. If, as Martin points out, repentance is a *prerequisite* for divine forgiveness to be extended, and if divine forgiveness is a *paradigm* for a Christian understanding of forgiveness, "then repentance is also a necessary prerequisite" in the forgiveness process.[213]

Wolterstorff's conclusion, then, regarding forgiveness is inadequate. It fails to distinguish between the private and public requirements before justice. Moreover, and just as important, it trivializes the degree to which the victim's survivors – for example, in the kinds of tragedies I identified earlier– suffer. Surely Wolterstorff does not expect that the family members of a murder victim can and should "forgive" the murderer of their kin who remains intractable. To forego "reprobative punishment," as Wolterstorff calls it, in the case of, say, premeditated murder would be to prevent the family members from ever burying their pain, achieving a modicum of emotional closure, and resuming their lives. And if we dismiss retribution for the most heinous of crimes, on what basis, *on what possible grounds*, can we uphold just rewards for lesser offenses?[214] For *any* crimes?

Thus, despite Wolterstorff's thorough attempts to qualify forgiveness in a manner that is intended to express both justice and love, his understanding of the concept remains deficient.[215] At this point, recall the observation in Chapter 5 made by Richard Goldstone, former prosecutor of the International Criminal Tribunals for the former Yugoslavia and Rwanda, in a speech at the U.S. Holocaust Museum:

> Where there have been egregious human rights violations that have been unaccounted for, where there has been no justice, where the victims have not received any acknowledgment, where they've been forgotten, where there's been a national amnesia, the effect is a cancer in society.[216]

Notice that Goldstone is not calling for mercy or "forgiveness" as many might construe it today. Authentic justice in a broken and fallen world, rather, is retributive as well as reparative and reconstructive. Highly instructive in this regard are comments made in 1976 by John Paul II – still Archbishop Karol Wojtyla of Kracow at the time – on the relationship between temporal punishment and cleansing/purification from sin. In this remarkable homily, Wojtyla offered penetrating reflections on the "anatomy" of punishment. Guilt incurred by moral breaches (i.e., "sin"), the future pontiff noted, constitutes a debt in the present life that must be paid. Punitive dealings, he maintained, provide the necessary atonement and restore the balance of justice and moral order that has been disturbed. This "law of purification," as Wojtyla described it, "reveals both the temporal and the eternal perspectives" of human moral accountability. The "purification" process occurs "by way of suffering."[217] A necessary qualification is required: "Although punishment in itself causes suffering, humiliation, depravation and freedom – things which grievously wound a person – it nevertheless a good purpose."[218]

Doubtless, at this point, some of my readers are protesting – quite understandably, I might add – that so-called punishment is the *effect and result* of misguided attempts at administering "justice." This is admittedly a fair objection. In response to this objection, Wojtyla offers the following qualification in his discussion of punishment as a means of "purification":

> We have all heard about terrible indictment – sometimes followed later by rehabilitation–and sentences inflicted upon people disgracefully liquidated in the name, so it is said, of law and order. Nonetheless, theses abuses cannot change the basic truth about punishment. Unjust application of judicial systems on the part of men only underlines the need for ultimate justice.[219]

This point cannot be overstated. Despite unjust applications of judicial systems, despite the flaws of the criminal justice system (and they are many), we do not simply abandon the justice system. Rather, we should re-double our efforts to work for a truer justice, as victims of genocidal treatment and egregious human rights violations remind us. Thus, Wolterstorff's conclusion to the matter – "Full and complete forgiveness . . . requires foregoing reprobative punishment"[220] – must be rejected in its failure to distinguish adequately between *personal* reaction to wrongdoing and the *public* requirements of justice rightly understood, part of which is to restore what has been ruptured.[221]

In addition to the aforementioned qualifications, Wolterstorff's volume begs certain questions by virtue of its inattention to – indeed, the wholesale absence of – several critically important elements that would strengthen his thesis. One concerns a thinker whose work and writings were not compromised by the love-justice opposition; here I refer to Princeton ethicist Paul Ramsey, to whom I have given considerable attention in the present volume. It is strange that Ramsey is cited only once by Wolterstorff – and briefly so – in his entire volume, and this one lone allusion gives the impression, mistakenly in my opinion, that Ramsey is part of the problem created by "modern day agapists."[222] In spite of some of my misgivings about part of Ramsey's theological orientation,[223] I would argue that Ramsey serves as an *antidote* to the "agapeist" fallacy. To his great credit, Ramsey very much stood in contrast to "agapeist" ethicists, theologians, and thinkers of his day, challenging their inclination to sever the demands of justice from charity; indeed, in his writings we find that neither love nor justice is sacrificed to the other. In Ramsey's work, which not infrequently strikes the reader as complex and perhaps even contradictory at times (much like that of Niebuhr), justice and love remain wedded, which is why his work in the spheres of medical ethics, bioethics, war and peace, humanitarian intervention, and Christian social witness remains significant.

Two further and related deficiencies require comment. I refer here, firstly, to the lack of any discussion of the natural law (especially as developed in the Christian moral tradition, since Wolterstorff represents himself in this very tradition), and secondly, to the absence of significant interaction with Catholic sources. This twofold omission seems odd, given both the richness of resources at our disposal and the unfortunate (and particularly Protestant) tendency toward the creation of false dichotomies – a defect that afflicts ethicists, theologians, activists, and laypersons. Although Protestants in their more recent history have been distrustful of natural law thinking, for reasons that I have enumerated elsewhere,[224] the important contribution – and the great necessity – of natural law ethics is demonstrated not only in the fact that it has resided in the mainstream of Christian moral thinking through the ages but also in the fact that it has presumed the harmony of justice and charity. This double omission in *Justice in Love* raises significant questions,[225] not least of which is what Protestants in general might gain in their understanding by interacting ecumenically with other – foremost, Catholic – ethical viewpoints. At the very least, Catholic perspectives have not been beholden to the sorts of false dichotomies – and compromised thinking – that have plagued Protestants in recent history.[226] What's more, Catholic social ethics has much to teach us about fruitful dialogue with the surrounding culture.

A final caveat is in order. Beyond the limitations noted earlier, in *Justice in Love* Wolterstorff does not appeal to any conception of the "common good," which is notable in a volume that concerns itself with social ethics, more broadly, and the interaction of justice and love, more narrowly. Here sources past and present beckon us. For both Aquinas and Augustine, all virtues, whether they are political or theological in denomination, derive from a common source. And because in their essence justice and love belong together insofar as *they principally concern our relations to others*,[227] they furnish *the very basis* for the common good. Although it is not the focus of much examination in our day, the common good in Aquinas's writings is central to his social thought. Because (a) the human being is a social creature, (b) people are inclined toward self-interest, and (c) the primary moral impulse of human beings – i.e., the first precept of the natural law – is doing good and avoiding evil,[228] it follows for Aquinas that all human action and human community are directed to the good.[229] The natural law thus has as its telos, its goal, to seek "the supreme human good" or the common social good, and for Aquinas, the common good is superior to the good of the individual.[230] Moreover, general justice provides us with the broader precepts that establish this common good,[231] at the same time that the common good is assumed in much of Aquinas's discussion of charity, even when it is not explicit.

Closer to our time, the *Catechism of the Catholic Church*, in calling its readers to engage the cultural environment in thoughtful and judicious ways, anchors our obligation to promote the common good in *the dignity of the human person*.[232] Defining this social good as "the sum total of social conditions which allow people, either as groups or as individuals, to reach their fulfillment more fully and more easily,"[233] the *Catechism* identifies three constitutive elements thereof:

> First, the common good presupposes respect for the person as such. In the name of the common good, public authorities are bound to respect *the fundamental and inalienable rights* of the human person . . . In particular, the common good resides in the conditions for the exercise of the natural freedoms indispensable for the development of the human vocation, such as "the right to act according to a sound norm of conscience and to safeguard . . . privacy, and rightful freedom also in matters of religion."
>
> Second, the common good requires *the social well-being and development* of the group itself. Development is the epitome of all social duties. Certainly, it is the proper function of authority to arbitrate, in the name of the common good, between various particular interests; but it should make accessible to each what is needed to lead a truly human life: food, clothing, health, work, education and culture, suitable information, the right to establish a family, and so on.

> Finally, the common good requires peace, that is, *the stability and security of a just order*. It presupposes that authority should ensure by morally acceptable means the security of society and its members. It is the basis of the right to legitimate personal and collective defence.[234]

Dignity, social well-being, justly ordered peace. This, then, constitutes the "common good" which is required of any relatively free society, and particularly one in which the relationship between "justice" and "love" is being seriously contemplated.

In the end, our assessment of Wolterstorff must remain mixed. *Justice in Love* responds, appropriately and in many respects creatively, to a perceived deficiency in wider thinking about the relationship between two "cardinal" virtues, justice, and love. It does so with a trenchant examination of "agapist" thinking of previous generations that has left its indelible mark, even to the present. At the same time, the volume would seem to lean on a somewhat unsteady and insecure ethical foundation in terms of how Wolterstorff understands love and justice to be interwoven.[235] In fact, the volume's title itself is mildly suggesting that Wolterstorff, in the end, still believes in a "priority" of love.

***

The discussion of "agapism" and pacifism earlier in this chapter suggested the inadequacy of "spiritualizing" the ethical demands of justice by means of the "priority of love" as it concerns law and public policy. In the following chapter, we will attempt to make application by considering a test-case for religious freedom. If justice and love are not viewed as constitutive of each other, if they are perceived as potentially standing in conflict and hence permitted to be separated, what are the ramifications of this divorce in the realm of social policy and civil society? The argument for their unity, in the context of inevitable social and ethical dilemmas, cannot escape controversy. Nor will it be very popular. But these are controversies that are unavoidable in our day, notwithstanding the "post-everything" and hypertolerant *Zeitgeist* regnant in Western societies which *refuses* to allow moral arguments in the public sphere.

In the chapter that follows, I attempt to argue that massive cultural shifts need "preparation." Although history is replete with such examples, I shall confine my argument in Chapter 7 to more recent history, chiefly because my own marriage brought me years ago into direct contact with that piece of history in a way that was sobering and sensitizing. *Inter alia*, it sensitized me to the enormous responsibility that we have to defend human dignity – a dignity that is *intrinsic* and not extrinsic, the fruit of *inherent* worth and not the product of power, performance, or achievement. The wedding of justice and charity will cause us, when and where we have the wherewithal, to assist the "neighbor" who stands in need. Today, as was the case 70 years ago, those standing in gross need are often found at the fringes of life. In order to illustrate the need to protect the "sacred rights of conscience" and the most basic of liberties, we shall consider the plight of those who were deemed "unworthy" of being allowed to live. This determination, which quickly became policy in 1933, did not occur overnight. It needed preparation.

Notes

1 J. Daryl Charles, "The Ethics of Humanitarian Intervention and the Just War Tradition: Rethinking the Implications of Neighbor-Love in the 21st Century," The Ethics of Humanitarian Military Operations and Intervention, April 18–21, 2016, U.S. Army Command and General Staff College, Fort Leavenworth, KS.
2 Nicholas Wolterstorff, *Justice in Love* (Grand Rapids and Cambridge, UK: Eerdmans, 2011), vii.
3 See, in this regard, Lev. 19:13, 15 and 18; Matt. 22:39; Mark 12:31; Luke 10:27; and Rom. 13:9.
4 Throughout this chapter, I am using "charity," "love," and "neighbor-love" interchangeably, even when differentiation in some contexts is warranted.
5 Ellen Ott Marshall, *Christians in the Public Square: Faith that Transforms Politics* (Nashville: Abingdon, 2008), 3. This citation comes from a section in the first chapter titled "Unconditional Love as a Starting Point." In this chapter, the author – an ideological pacifist who is arguing for "non-violent" expression – is countering what she believes to be forms of "hatred" in the U.S. politics that need confrontation with love.
6 James F. Keenan, *Moral Wisdom* (Lanham and Oxford: Rowman & Littlefield, 2004), 14.
7 As a helpful antidote to this false dichotomy, see the important 1993 papal encyclical of John Paul II, *Veritatis Splendor*, accessible at http://w2.vatican.va/content/john-paul-ii/en/encyclicals/documents/hf_jp-ii_enc_06081993_veritatis-splendor.html.
8 Wolterstorff, *Justice in Love*, vii.
9 Ibid., 1.
10 Søren Kierkegaard, *Works of Love*, ed. and trans. Howard V. and Edna H. Hong (New York: Harper & Row, 1962), Part 2.
11 Ibid., Part 9.
12 Søren Kierkegaard, *Eighteen Upbuilding Discourses*, trans. Howard V. and Edna H. Hong (Princeton: Princeton University Press, 1990), 56.
13 Ibid., 71.
14 Ibid.; cf. James 2:8.
15 Kierkegaard, *Works of Love*, 69, 79.
16 Ibid., 111.
17 Ibid., 405.
18 Consider the context of Matt. 5:21–48, which is devoted to six "test-cases" (often called "antitheses") for the moral law – murder, adultery, divorce, loathing, retaliation, and enemy-love. The purpose of this teaching is not to *repudiate* the moral law; recall Jesus' introductory declaration (5:17): "Do not suppose that I have come to abolish the law or the prophets; I have not come to abolish them but to fulfill them." Rather, it is to affirm them be showing that they begin in the heart. The rabbinic formula "You have heard it said but I tell you . . ." used repetitively in this block of teaching indicates that Jesus is correcting conventional rabbinic teaching, *not* setting aside Mosaic law. Jesus is not rejecting the *lex talionis* as a principle of justice, a principle that establishes upper and lower limits; rather, he is taking issue with the manner in which the *lex* had been used – and abused – in rabbinic interpretation and Jewish practice. Here we must reject the standard approach to these verses which misses the exegetical mark. So, for example, Timothy P. Jackson, in *Love Disconsoled: Meditations*

on Christian Charity (Cambridge and New York: Cambridge University Press, 1999), 5, writes, "These words [Matt. 5:38–48] are not fundamentally at odds with the Hebrew Bible as totality, but they do override the *lex talionis* and call for an extremely stringent life of charity." Contra the author, nothing of the sort is being done by Jesus. Jesus is *not* negating the *lex talionis*, just as he is not negating (= "overriding") other aspects of the moral law – e.g., against murder, dishonest speech, adultery, etc. – as recorded in Matt. 5:21–48. He is, however, clarifying the nature of the moral law, getting at the heart of people's actions by exposing human intention. Jackson, who has been a chief spokesperson for the "priority-of-love" viewpoint and thus is critiqued later in this chapter, is representative of conventional commentary. Standard commentary errs at two levels. First, it misconstrues the nature and contours of the *lex talionis*; second, it fails to read Matt. 5:38–42 in context, ignoring the framing of the six test-cases (of which 5:38–42 is one) that appears in 5:17–20. Far from repudiating the universal principle of proportionate compensation, Jesus is speaking to the dynamic of interpersonal relationships. He is forbidding application of the *lex talionis* to *private matters*, which doubtless would include personal vendettas. That is, his intent is to curtail the spirit of revenge. Never did the *lex talionis* as a principle of justice and as expressed in the Old Testament convey upon the *individual* the right to retaliation. In addition, see n. 199. Elsewhere I have examined the background and meaning of Matt. 38–42 in greater detail; see J. Daryl Charles, "Do Not Suppose That I Have Come": The Ethic of the Sermon on the Mount Reconsidered," *Southwestern Journal of Theology* 46, no. 3 (2004): 47–70.

19 Daryl J. Wenneman, "The Role of Love in the Thought of Kant and Kierkegaarad," accessible at www.bu.edu/wcp/Papers/Reli/ReliWenn.htm, develops this insight with particular clarity. Although making sense of Kierkegaard can be maddening, given the complexity (and at times seeming contradictory nature) of his thought, useful interpretations of his work include M. Jaime Ferreira, *Love's Grateful Striving* (Oxford: Oxford University Press, 2001), and C. Stephen Evans, *Kierkegaard's Ethic of Love: Divine Commands and Moral Obligations* (Oxford: Oxford University Press, 2004).

20 Anders Nygren, *Agape and Eros*, trans. Philip S. Watson (London: SPCK, 1953), 28. Nygren, writes Stephen J. Pope, "Love in Contemporary Christian Ethics," *Journal of Religious Ethics* 23, no. 1 (1995): 167, "set the terms of the debate for subsequent theological ethics," and indeed this would seem to be the case.

21 Nygren, *Agape and Eros*, 61–7, 81–91, 105–45, and 146–59. The primary biblical components of Nygren's thesis are Jesus' reiteration of the "two greatest commandments" (Matt. 22:37–40; Mark 12:29–31), the parable of the Prodigal Son (Luke 15: 11–32), and the centrality of "God is love" in Johannine literature.

22 Ibid., 75–80, 91.

23 Wolterstorff, *Justice in Love*, 46.

24 Nygren, *Agape and Eros*, 70.

25 Ibid., 78, emphasis added.

26 Ibid., 99.

27 Ibid., 200–1.

28 Ibid., 70–1.

29 Ibid., 90, emphasis added.

30 Ibid., 74.

31 Nygren anchors this conclusion, that love demotes and negates strict justice, in his interpretation of the Parable of the Laborers (Matt. 20:1–16) and the Parable of the Unmerciful Steward (Matt. 18:23–35), although Nygren misidentifies the latter in Matthew's Gospel (ibid., 86–91, esp. 91).

32 Ibid., 71.

33 Ibid., 333.

34 Timothy P. Jackson, *The Priority of Love: Christian Charity and Social Justice* (Princeton and Oxford: Princeton University Press, 2003).

35 Ibid., 10.

36 Ibid., 6.

37 Jackson's general burden, laid out in the introductory chapter ("The Fate of Charity"), is the "eclipse of charity" both in public discourse and within the Christian community (2); "agapic love," he notes, "is what we are made for" (5).

38 Depending on how one defines "wisdom," "justice" and "freedom," one might grant Jackson's concern at face value. However, adopting Jackson's own position that virtue derives from the Creator, we may argue that wisdom, justice, and freedom – properly construed – have their source in the character of God.

39 Here we must maintain with Aquinas and others in the Christian moral tradition that the virtues are *united* and cannot be divorced from one another. This unity, of course, allows for both their perfection *and* their corruption. See Thomas Aquinas, *De Caritate* a. 13 and *Summa Thelogica* [hereafter *S.T.*] II-II Q. 24, a. 12.

40 Jackson, *The Priority of Love*, 13, emphasis added.

41 Ibid., 11, 13.

42 Ibid., 39.

43 Ibid., 69. "Reciprocal justice," he worries, without love is *itself* – that is, *per se* – "volatile and destructive" (ibid., 18–19).

44 Jackson writes, "Love only resorts to punishment when . . . the retributive steps will likely benefit all concerned" (ibid., 154). But this is an impossible explanation because *it is impossible* to know when punishment *will* "work" and when it *will not*. Often we will *never* know, and there exist some criminals who are – and remain – incorrigible. It is highly doubtful that the apostle Paul had such a qualification in mind when he penned his admonitions to Roman believers on the divinely "ordained" role of the governing authorities. Consider alone the Pauline statement framed in 13:4! Nowhere in the argument of Romans 13 do we read of the authorities "forgiving" and "cancelling the debt" of wrongdoers on the basis of charity. Hence, in this sense, love never "transcends" justice, as religious ethicists are often inclined to argue.

45 Forgiveness, hence, is "beyond" or "outside of" justice; that is, it renders the logic of just desert and punishment, which are foundational to justice, irrelevant. For this reason, the role of the state is not to "forgive" criminal behavior, which damages the common good. Hereon see Jiwei Ci, *The Two Faces of Justice* (Cambridge and London: Harvard University Press, 2006), 190.

46 For a helpful corrective to much contemporary thinking about punishment and forgiveness as they relate to justice, see Ci (ibid.), especially, Chapter 10 ("Individual Forgiveness, Social Resentment").

47 Consider the applications of such thinking. By placing "love" beyond justice Jackson can hence write the following concerning the abortion issue: "To insist, legally and medically, that women carry fetuses to term, against their will, is to intrude on a matter that is best left to individual conscience and to guarantee that women remain second-class citizens, tied coercively to childbearing and childrearing" (*The Priority of Love*, 177). Notice the fruit of "love" as Jackson understands it: not concern for the sanctity of life, from its conception, and not what the Christian Church, from the beginning, has *always* taught and affirmed, but rather, the individual's "choice" as to whether she wishes to carry the child to term or end its life. Let us speak the truth charitably here: this sort of thinking is neither charitable, nor just, nor Christian; it simply mirrors the values of surrounding culture. But it well illustrates the morbid confusion described by Benedict XVI's in his 2009 encyclical *Caritas in Veritate*: "Without truth, charity degenerates into sentimentality. Love becomes an empty shell, to be filled in an arbitrary way. In a culture without truth, this is the fatal risk facing love. It falls

prey to contingent subjective emotions and opinions, [and] the word 'love' is abused and distorted, to the point where it comes to mean the opposite" (no. 3).

48 The first volume, published by Cambridge University Press in 1999, was titled *Love Disconsoled*.

49 Timothy P. Jackson, *Political Agape: Christian Love and Liberal Democracy* (Grand Rapids and Cambridge: Eerdmans, 2015), 2.

50 Ibid.

51 Ibid. This prioritization is forcefully made in the book's introduction (1–9) and throughout the volume (see, for example, 47–55 and 337–41). Even when Jackson writes that love is not "at odds with justice" (2), it is "prior" and "antecedent" to justice (11; cf. also *The Priority of Love*, 39).

52 Ibid., 2. This line of thinking is developed in Chapter 1 of the book. In theory, Jackson believes that love should rise above justice without subverting it and that love has "major policy implications" (ibid., 47). At the same time, virtually the whole of the volume is devoted to demonstrating, in Jackson's understanding, that justice is secondary to love.

53 Ibid., 48–9.

54 Ibid., 48.

55 Ibid., 59–61.

56 Ibid., 83.

57 Jackson does acknowledge that natural law thinking was a part of Lincoln's repertoire (ibid., 60), yet he writes of Lincoln's "evolving political faith" that the "charity for all" which is commanded in Hebrew-Christian Scripture "inspires, governs, and *finally transcends* both of America's founding documents and both positive and natural law" (ibid.). My hunch is that most natural law theorists who are of the Christian faith would find this statement rather remarkable. At the very least, it creates a false dichotomy, once more, between justice and love.

58 Elsewhere in *Political Agape*, Jackson writes, "In spite of its historical commitments to forms of 'natural law,' Christianity ought to be wary of too readily identifying the 'natural' with the normative" (378). This is a hint that seems to confirm why Jackson, in another chapter of the book, argues that Christian love will lead us to welcome same-sex marriage. See Chapter 11, which has the incongruous title "Keeping Marriage Sacred: The Christian Case for Gay and Lesbian Wedlock" (317–52). Notice the moral logic at work here: what is "natural" is not "normative," or at least it shouldn't be "normative." And what the Christian Church, the entire Christian moral tradition, common sense, and yes, *nature* teach about human sexuality is to be discarded by a "prophetic" embodiment of "love" as Jackson understands it. For those whose thinking is so predisposed, truth and moral reality can be "unloving."

59 Richard B. Hays, *The Moral Vision of the New Testament: Community, Cross New Creation. A Contemporary Introduction to New Testament Ethics* (San Francisco: HarperCollins, 1996), 200.

60 Ibid.

61 Ibid.

62 Ibid., 202. Jackson has responded to Hays' assertion that "the concept of love is insufficient as a ground of coherence for the New Testament's moral vision" in *The Priority of Love*, 15–16 and 20–7. Jackson responds by arguing that Hays' three organizing images for New Testament ethics – "community, cross, and new creation" – might be said to "triangulate on charity as God's essence" (26). In closing his argument for love's "priority," Jackson writes, "When properly understood, love's priority cannot be pressed into service of a reductionism that would make moral propositions deductively certain and moral persons sublimely self-sufficient, but it can be a crucial aid in countering an errant 'pluralism' that would make moral claims utterly relativistic and moral persons psychologically fragmented" (27). In response, I would simply say that the agapist reductionism

itself contributes precisely to the problem identified by Jackson. It devalues justice, truth and other "cardinal" virtues that necessarily shape (and express) love, so that, as Benedict XVI has presciently argued, in the end love is reduced by an "errant pluralism" to the point where "[i]t falls prey to contingent subjective emotions and opinions, [and] the word 'love' is abused and distorted, to the point where it comes to mean the opposite" (*Caritas in Veritate* no. 3).

63 Nicholas Wolterstorff, *Justice: Rights and Wrongs* (Princeton: Princeton University Press, 2008).

64 Ibid., 96. Here Wolterstorff has Stanley Hauerwas (*After Christendom* [Nashville: Abingdon, 1991]) and Anders Nygren (*Agape and Eros* [see n. 20]) chiefly in his sites.

65 Jean Bethke Elshtain, *Women and War*, rev. ed. (Chicago and London: University of Chicago Press, 1995), 123, 132.

66 At least for a previous generation of "conscientious objectors" like my own father (a Mennonite who performed alternative service in a Veteran's Hospital during WWII), it has shown a willingness to sacrifice and count the cost of one's own convictions. Of course, conscription was the reality of the Second World War, unlike today with soldiering in our culture a voluntary matter, which renders pacifism as "policy" in a wholly different light. Today there is essentially *no cost* in maintaining pacifist convictions.

67 For all the high praise that was showered upon Richard Hays' *The Moral Vision of the New Testament: A Contemporary Introduction to New Testament Ethics* (New York: HarperCollins, 1996) following its publication (and the praise was *effusive* from all corners), Hay's pacifist reading of the New Testament (Chapter 14: "Violence in Defense of Justice?") is exceedingly disappointing at multiple levels – theologically, historically, moral-philosophically and hermeneutically. More recently, Nigel Biggar, *In Defence of War* (Oxford and New York: Oxford University Press, 2013), especially, Chapters 1 and 2, has subjected Hays's pacifist reading of the scriptures to withering – and much needed – scrutiny.

68 This fundamental moral distinction has been succinctly emphasized by philosopher E.M.B. Anscombe in her essay "War and Murder," in Malham M. Wakin, ed., *War, Morality, and the Military Profession* (Boulder: Westview, 1979), 285–98.

69 Luke 3:14: "In the same way the soldiers asked him, "What shall we do?" So he said to them, "Don't intimidate anyone or accuse falsely, and be content with your wages.' "

70 In his writings, Anabaptist theologian John Howard Yoder mistakenly asserts that Revelation 13, not Romans 13, is the true – and only legitimate – portrait of governing authorities. Yoder's position goes one step further than his Anabaptist forebears. Article 6 of the Schleitheim Confession of 1527, the earliest formal declaration of Anabaptist beliefs, confesses: "The sword is ordained of God outside the perfection of Christ. It punishes and puts to death the wicked, and guards and protects the good. In the Law the sword was ordained for the punishment of the wicked and for their death, and the same (sword) is (now) ordained to be used by the worldly magistrates." What Schleitheim rejects is that Christians themselves can wield the sword or serve as magistrates.

71 *S.T.* II-II Q. 40.

72 While debating two Anabaptist pacifists alongside Boston College philosopher Peter Kreeft several years ago at the renowned Fanueil Hall in Boston, I simply asked the two whether they would prefer that drivers of Brinks trucks, which transport *their* life savings from ABC Bank to XYZ Savings and Loan, should be unarmed (or, at most, carry only water pistols and plastic bullets). Their Anabaptist forebears of the sixteenth century at least acknowledged the role of the magistrate: the "sword" is ordained by God for the punishment of evil and the preservation of the social order (Schleitheim Confession no. 6), an order from which pacifists benefit enormously.

73 Augustine distinguishes between a *pax iusta* and a *pax iniqua*, a just and an unjust peace.
74 *S.T.* II-II Q. 29.
75 Therefore, Jesus' words "Blessed are the peacemakers" need severe qualification.
76 Michael Walzer, *Just and Unjust Wars: A Moral Argument With Historical Illustrations*, 4th ed. (New York: Basic Books, 2006), 329–35.
77 C.S. Lewis, "The Conditions for a Just War," in Walter Hooper, ed., *God in the Dock: Essays on Theology and Ethics* (Grand Rapids: Eerdmans, 1970), 326.
78 See in this regard George Orwell, "Reflections on Gandhi," *Partisan Review* 16, no. 1 (1949): 85–92, accessible online as well at www.online-literature.com/orwell/898/.
79 Reacting to Gandhi's insistence on distinguishing between non-violent resistance and non-resistance, Reinhold Niebuhr quipped: "All this is a pardonable confusion in the soul of a man who is trying to harmonise the insights of a saint with the necessities of statecraft, a very difficult achievement. But it is nevertheless a confusion" (*Moral Man and Immoral Society* [New York: Scribner's, 1960], 243).
80 J. Daryl Charles, "The Moral Underpinnings of Just Retribution: Justice and Charity in Symbiosis," *Providence: A Journal of Christianity and American Foreign Policy* 3 (Spring 2016): 5–16.
81 "Incommunicable" attributes distinguish themselves from "communicable" attributes that are understood to be "shared" with human creation.
82 Hence, the response by Athanasius and the Council of Nicea to Arian distortions.
83 Hereon see more recently James E. Dolezal, *God Without Parts: Divine Simplicity and the Metaphysics of God's Absoluteness* (Eugene: Pickwick Publications, 2011).
84 For example, a proper understanding of the doctrine of atonement, and penal substitution in particular, will refuse to pit an angry, wrathful Father against a loving, merciful Son.
85 *S.T.* I-II Q. 94.
86 C.S. Lewis, "The Humanitarian Theory of Punishment," in Walter Hooper, ed., *God in the Dock: Essay on Theology and Ethics* (Grand Rapids: Eerdmans, 1970), 287–300. This essay was originally published in the *Australian Quarterly Review* 3, no. 3 (1949): 5–12.
87 Matt. 5:14–48, 22:37–40, Rom. 13:6–10, and James 2:8–11.
88 So Stephen Charles Mott, *Biblical Ethics and Social Change*, 2nd ed. (Oxford and New York: Oxford University Press, 2011), 41.
89 Ibid., 45, 53.
90 Oliver O'Donovan, *Resurrection and Moral Order: An Outline for Evangelical Ethics* (Leicester and Grand Rapids: InterVarsity Press and Eerdmans, 1986), 226–9.
91 So, correctly, Daniel Day Williams, *The Spirit and the Forms of Love* (New York: Harper & Row, 1968), 243.
92 Augustine, *On the Morals of the Catholic Church* no. 15.
93 Augustine, *On Nature and Grace* 70.84.
94 Williams, *The Spirit and the Forms of Love*, 245, 250.
95 A cursory review of the literature in political science and in the social sciences reveals the existence of rival theories and assumptions about the very nature of "justice." Some accept the concepts of desert and retribution, while others deny them. Some studies affirm the effectiveness of deterrence, while others deny or call into question its efficacy. Some appeal to "inalienable rights" that accord with natural law and human dignity, while others appeal to social contract or utility. And at a rudimentary level, there is a fair amount of disagreement as to what constitutes basic "goods." For a theoretical appraisal of this diverse landscape, see Alasdair MacIntyre, *Whose Justice? Which Rationality?* (Notre Dame: University of Notre Dame Press, 1988), especially Chapters 1 and 20.
96 Augustine, *City of God* 4.6 and 14.28.

97 For example, see Reinhold Niebuhr's famous essay "Augustine's Political Realism," in Reinhold Niebuhr, ed., *Christian Realism and Political Problems* (New York: Scribner's, 1953), 119–47.

98 Augustine, *City of God* 4.4. Whether in fact this accurately represents Augustine's view is difficult to say, given its strong rhetorical character. Moreover, kingdoms as bands of robbers appears earlier in Cyprian (*Epistle* I.6 = *Anti-Nicene Fathers* 5.277). By Augustine's day it may have become a standard jab at the Roman tendency to equate empire with justice.

99 Ibid. 19.17.

100 Augustine, *Epistle* 138 ("To Marcellinus").

101 Ibid.

102 *The City of God* 14.9.

103 All that was created is "good," for Augustine; however, when our loves are not rightly ordered, the ultimate good is violated (*City of God* 15.22).

104 Augustine, *City of God* 61.4.

105 *S.T.* I-II Q. 62, a. 2–4 and II-II Q. 23, a. 8; cf. also *De Caritate* 3.

106 Ibid. II-II Q. 31, a. 1–3.

107 Ibid. II-II Q. 80, a. 1.

108 Ibid. QQ. 23–46, 58; cf. also *Commentary on Nicomachean Ethics*, Lectures IV–VI.

109 Ibid. Q. 31, a. 2 and 3.

110 In fact, Aquinas argues that where the public good is at stake and wrongdoers fail to mend their ways, they are to be slain. This, he reasons, is done not out of hatred but out of charity (*S.T.* II-II Q. 25).

111 Ibid. Q. 58, a. 9, r. 3.

112 "Death of a Christian Realist," *Time*(June 14, 1971).

113 Hans J. Morgenthau, "The Influence of Reinhold Niebuhr in American Political Life and Thought," in Harold R. Langdon, ed., *Reinhold Niebuhr: A Prophetic Voice in Our Time* (Greenwich, CT: Seabury, 1962), 109.

114 See Niebuhr, "Augustine's Political Realism" (see n. 97), 119–46.

115 See, for example, Elizabeth Sifton, ed., *Reinhold Niebuhr: Major Works on Religion and Politics* (New York: Library of America, 2015); Daniel Rice, *Reinhold Niebuhr and His Circle of Influence* (Cambridge: Cambridge University Press, 2013); Charles LeMert, *Why Niebuhr Matters*(New Haven and London: Yale University Press, 2011); John Patrick Diggins, *Why Niebuhr Now?*(Chicago and London: University of Chicago Press, 2011); Richard Harries and Stephen Platten, eds., *Reinhold Niebuhr and Contemporary Politics: God & Power* (Oxford: Oxford University Press, 2010); Arthur Schlesinger Jr., "Forgetting Reinhold Niebuhr," *The New York Times*(September 18, 2005), accessible at www.nytimes.com/2005/09/18/books/review/18schlesinger.html; and David Brooks, "A Man on a Gray Horse," *The Atlantic* (September 2002), accessible at www.theatlantic.com/magazine/archive/2002/09/a-man-on-a-grey-horse/302558/.

116 Niebuhr's thinking is simultaneously eclectic, nuanced and at times difficult to follow. Moreover, he is admired by both theological "liberals" and "conservatives" and tends to defy neat categorization by his eschewing of reductionism.

117 Reinhold Niebuhr, *Christianity and Power Politics* (New York: Scribner's, 1940), 3.

118 Reinhold Niebuhr, *An Interpretation of Christian Ethics* (Cleveland and New York: Meridian, 1956 [repr.]), 134.

119 *Christianity and Power Politics*, 18 (emphasis added).

120 Niebuhr, *An Interpretation of Christian Ethics*, 129.

121 Ibid., 108.

122 An example of this deficiency may suffice; in *The Nature and Destiny of Man*, vol. 1 (New York: Scribner's, 1943), 295, he writes, "Love is thus the end term of any system of morals. It is the moral requirement in which all schemes of

justice are fulfilled and negated. They are fulfilled because the obligation of life to life is more fully met in love than is possible in any scheme of equity and justice. They are negated because love makes an end of the nicely calculated less and more of structures of justice."

123 Contra Wolterstorff, *Justice in Love*, 62–72, and correctly, Gene Outka, *Agape: An Ethical Analysis* (New Haven: Yale University Press, 1972), 79.

124 Niebuhr, *Christian Realism and Political Problems* (see n. 97), 171.

125 Ibid., 171–2.

126 Originally published in 1939 as a pamphlet, "Why the Church Is Not Pacifist" was subsequently included in *Christianity and Power Politics*.

127 Ibid., 2.

128 Niebuhr, *Moral Man and Immoral Society* (see n. 79), 75–6.

129 Niebuhr, *Christianity and Power Politics*, 6.

130 See Reinhold Niebuhr, "The Ethic of Jesus and the Social Problem," in D.B. Robertson, ed., *Love and Justice: Selections from the Shorter Writings of Reinhold Niebuhr* (Louisville: Westminster John Knox Press, 1992), 34–5.

131 Niebuhr, "Why the Church Is Not Pacifist," 14.

132 Ibid., 27.

133 On this theological deficiency in Niebuhr, see David D. Corey and J. Daryl Charles, *The Just War Tradition: An Introduction* (Wilmington: ISI Books, 2012), 207–26 (= Chapter 11: "Why Have Our Churches Lost the Tradition? Two Temptations: Christian Realism, Christian Pacifism").

134 Niebuhr, *An Interpretation of Christian Ethics*, 46.

135 Ibid., 56–8.

136 Niebuhr, "Why the Church Is Not Pacifist," 31.

137 Ramsey, *The Just War: Force and Political Responsibility* (repr.; Lanham: Rowman & Littlefield, 2002), 488. This and related comments on "Christian Realism" were published originally in 1966 in the journal *America*.

138 Paul Ramsey, *Basic Christian Ethics* (New York: Scribner's, 1950), 345–6.

139 Ibid., xvii (emphasis added).

140 Ibid., 367.

141 Ibid., 243 and 347.

142 Ibid., 24–35.

143 Ibid., 171–84.

144 Ibid., 166–71.

145 Ibid., 347–8, herewith citing Emil Brunner, *Justice and the Social Order* (New York and London: Harper & Bros., 1945), 129.

146 Ramsey, *The Just War* (see n. 137), 35–6.

147 Paul Ramsey, *Deeds and Rules in Christian Ethics* (New York: Scribner's, 1967).

148 Here I take issue with Ramsey, who in Chapter 2 of *Basic Christian Ethics*, in the section titled "What the Christian Does without a Code," writes the following: "What should be done or not done in a particular instance, what is good or bad, right or wrong, what is better or worse than something else, what are degrees of value – these things in Christian ethics are not known in advance or derived from some preconceived code. They derive backward by Christian love from what it apprehends to be the needs of others" (78–9). Here Ramsey is attempting to apply Pauline teaching from Galatians and 1 Corinthians to argue for a "Christian" view of liberty notably in contrast to Pharisaical and Judaism's *legalistic* tendencies. But Ramsey overreaches. Paul himself declares, in no uncertain terms, that "love fulfills the law" (Rom. 13:8–10). Not only the natural lawyer but also the historic Christian moral tradition in general rejects Ramsey's line of reasoning here insofar as it wrongly assumes that no moral code, no moral principles and/or no moral standards exist in the universe apart from "love." *Pace* Ramsey, good and bad, right and wrong, varying "degrees of

value" are *indeed* known "in advance" – not in great detail but in their essence (thus Rom. 2:14–15). Hence, we cannot say that they "derive backward" by or from love, even when we concur that they agree with and *embody* authentic love. Nevertheless, whatever our quibbles with Ramsey's theological rationale, like Niebuhr, Ramsey in the end refuses to lift or abrogate the demands of justice; for Ramsey, justice properly construed *is* social charity.

149 This line of reasoning is found in his *Basic Christian Ethics*, in *War and the Christian Conscience* (Durham: Duke University Press, 1961), and in *The Just War*.

150 William Werpehowski, and Stephen D. Crocco, eds., *The Essential Paul Ramsey: A Collection* (New Haven and London: Yale University Press, 1994), 62. This is reproduced from *The Just War*.

151 Ibid., 62–3.

152 Here Ramsey is not only responding to Barthian ethics, which rejects the natural law but also to more likeminded thinking such as that of Emil Brunner, who countered Barth on the matter of "natural theology" (correctly, in my view) and yet argued that justice is "a totally different thing" from love, insofar as justice is "rational" and "compensational," whereas love is not (incorrectly, in my view). See Emil Brunner, *Justice and the Social Order* (New York and London: Harper & Bros., 1945), 127–8.

153 On both the similarities and differences between Niebuhr and Ramsey, both avowed Augustinians, see William R. Stevenson Jr., *Christian Love and Just War: Moral Paradox and Political Life in St. Augustine and His Interpreters* (Mercer: Mercer University Press, 1987), 115–48.

154 Benedict XVI, *Caritas in Veritate* no. 1, emphasis added. The encyclical is accessible at http://w2.vatican.va/content/benedict-xvi/en/encyclicals/documents/hf_ben-xvi_enc_20090629_caritas-in-veritate.html.

155 See *Veritatis Splendor* (1993), accessible at http://w2.vatican.va/content/john-paul-ii/en/encyclicals/documents/hf_jp-ii_enc_06081993_veritatis-splendor.html.

156 Ibid., no. 3, emphasis added.

157 Ibid., no. 1, emphasis added.

158 Ibid., no. 2.

159 Ibid.

160 Ibid.

161 Ibid.

162 Ibid.

163 Ibid.

164 Ibid.

165 Ibid.

166 Ibid., no. 3.

167 Ibid., no. 4.

168 Ibid.

169 Ibid.

170 Ibid.

171 Ibid., no. 5.

172 Ibid., no. 6.

173 Ibid.

174 Ibid.

175 Ibid., nos. 5–6, emphasis added.

176 Ibid., no. 6.

177 Ibid.

178 Ibid.

179 Ibid.

180 Ibid.

181 Ibid., no. 7.
182 Ibid.
183 Ibid.
184 Ibid., no. 9.
185 Ibid.
186 Ibid.
187 See n. 63.
188 Woltertorff, *Justice in Love*, vii.
189 Ibid., viii.
190 Here I take issue with this categorizing of Niebuhr. While Niebuhr evades a neat and tidy classification, and while his theological rationale leaves much to be desired (as noted earlier), I grant that his thinking is perhaps more nuanced than Wolterstorff maintains. In the end, Niebuhr's ethic caused him, to his credit, *not* to divorce justice from love but rather to affirm justice when and where it was needed – for example, as storms clouds were gathering on the European horizon in the 1930s. In time, Niebuhr became impatient with and highly critical of fellow Protestants who tended to be "love-orientated." On Niebuhr's deficient theological thinking, see n. 122 and n. 133.
191 Wolterstorff, *Justice in Love*, 85.
192 Ibid., 91. Wolterstorff argues in his previous volume, *Justice: Rights and Wrongs*, that rights are not grounded in *duties* but rather in respect of human worth (264–310). I would contend that the proper grounding of rights does not require the "either . . . or . . ." opposition that Wolterstorff creates; honoring *both* are requisite of human beings, if for no other reason, duties (= moral obligations) issue out of human dignity.
193 Most of *Justice: Rights and Wrongs* is devoted to an account of human "rights" based on Wolterstorff's distinction between "primary" justice and "rectifying" or "corrective" justice.
194 Wolterstorff, *Justice in Love*, 123–6.
195 Ibid., 129.
196 Ibid., 206.
197 Ibid., 256.
198 Here, in addition to the work of Immanuel Kant, Wolterstorff interacts with Jonathan Glover (*Humanity: A Moral History of the Twentieth Century* [New Haven: Yale University Press, 2001]) and Ronald Dworkin (*Freedom's Law: The Moral Reading of the American Constitution* [Cambridge: Harvard University Press, 1999]; Ronald Dworkin, *Life's Dominion: An Argument About Abortion, Euthanasia, and Individual Freedom* [New York: A.A. Knopf, 1993]; and Ronald Dworkin, *Taking Rights Seriously* [Cambridge: Harvard University Press, 1987]).
199 Like the first of the four illustrations ("turning the other cheek"), the second, legally contesting someone taking an article of clothing (cf. Luke 6:29, although see Exod. 22:26–27 and Deut. 24:13), does not constitute robbery *per se*, and thus is not a matter of public justice; it is private and therefore to be settled accordingly. As with the slap, this scenario is most likely mirroring a question of honor and shame. The point is that by giving away not only the "tunic" but also the "cloak" as well, one can diffuse particular contentious situations. The third illustration resembles the second. Being compelled to go "the second mile" might refer to aristocratic imposition of power or the common practice of soldiers in an "occupied" territory conscribing civilians to carry their baggage, against which there was no law (cf. Matt. 27:32). Generosity, even for those who are undeserving, can diffuse potentially hostile situations. The fourth illustration, giving and lending to those who ask, merely reinforces what the prior three had illustrated. If we pause to reflect for a moment on the consequences of our interpretive strategy, we discover the folly of absolutizing "giving to anyone

who asks" to mean that we would need to honor *every* request or demand for money, including that of every irresponsible child and every irresponsible beggar or thug on the street.

200 In truth, for punishment to be deemed "proportionate," both upper and lower limits are implied. Punishment is "just" to the extent that it "fits the crime."

201 Numerous commentators cite a Talmudic source, *m. Baba Qamma*, with its exhaustive instructions regarding penalties for particular actions. One of these is slapping with the back of the hand. On the rabbinic background to Jesus' teaching in Matthew 5:38–42, see Hermann Strack and Paul Billerbeck, *Kommentar zum Neuen Testament aus Talmud und Midrash* (München: Beck, 1922), 1.342.

202 "Retributivism" would assert that justice, not the offender as a person, is an end in itself. Thus, in extreme cases, it would even demand the unjust sacrifice of innocent individuals for collective, supposedly "just," ends.

203 On the important moral distinction between revenge and retribution, see J. Daryl Charles and Timothy J. Demy, *War, Peace, and Christianity: Questions and Answers from a Just-War Perspective* (Wheaton: Crossway, 2010), 259–63; J. Daryl Charles, "Capital Crime and Punishment: Reflections on Violating Human Sanctity," *Touchstone* 15, no. 2 (September 2002): 19–26; and J. Daryl Charles, "The Moral Underpinnings of Just Retribution," *Providence: A Journal of Christianity and American Foreign Policy* 3 (Spring 2016): 5–16. See as well David A. Crocker, "Retribution and Reconciliation," *Philosophy and Public Policy* 20, no. 1 (2000): 1–6, who helpfully illustrates this moral distinction in the context of foreign policy.

204 Wolterstorff's position is laid out extensively in Chapter 17.

205 Lewis, "The Humanitarian Theory of Punishment," 287–94 (see n. 86).

206 Michael J. Sandel, "Should Victims Have a Say in Sentencing?" in Michael J. Sandel, ed., *Public Philosophy: Essays on Morality in Politics* (Cambridge and London: Harvard University Press, 2005), 108.

207 John Courtney Murray, *We Hold These Truths: Catholic Reflections on the American Proposition* (New York: Sheed and Ward, 1960), 288.

208 For a penetrating look at both models, see Troy Martin and Avis Clendenen, *Forgiveness: Finding Freedom through Reconciliation* (New York: Crossroad Publishing Co., 2002). The co-authors combine insights from both the social sciences and theology, making this volume exceedingly helpful. They argue for the necessity of distinguishing between the "social-exchange" model and the "psychological" model. While acknowledging the importance of therapeutic "release" in the victim toward the offender, they argue that this *in and of itself* is *not* "forgiveness" in the proper sense. Rather, authentic forgiveness requires, in situations where it is possible, a person-to-person confrontation and exchange that involves repentance and contrition (by the offender) and subsequent forgiveness (by the offended), leading to some measure of reconciliation.

209 Wolterstorff, *Justice in Love*, 170.

210 Hereon see Troy Martin, "The Christian's Obligation Not to Forgive," *The Expository Times* 108, no. 12 (September 1997): 360–2, and Clendenen and Martin, *Forgiveness* (see n. 208).

211 Martin, "The Christian's Obligation Not to Forgive," 360.

212 Ibid., 361.

213 Ibid. In the end, Martin is sensitive to the commonly raised (and important) question that many would raise in objection: *what about those tragic instances when wrongdoers remain implacable and unrepentant?* And *what if death – or impossible circumstances – prevent confrontation and accountability from occurring?* In those sorts of situations, Martin argues that the victim then should "transfer the responsibility of forgiveness to God," a process which he distinguishes from the "forgive and forget" mentality (ibid., 362; cf. also Clendenen and Martin, *Forgiveness*, 92–101).

214 Few have argued this point more succinctly, and persuasively, than Robert James Bidinotto, "Crime and Moral Retribution," in Robert James Bidinotto, ed., *Criminal Justice? The Legal System Versus Individual Responsibility* (Irvington-on-the-Hudson: Foundation for Economic Education, Inc., 1994), 181–200. In this vein, if capital punishment does not serve to deter the potential murderer, the abolitionist will therefore need to acknowledge the grim reality that *neither will any other form of punishment*. Thus, we are faced with a rather sobering possibility: *any* punishment is arbitrary. Although the topic is beyond the scope of the present discussion, elsewhere I have written extensively on the ethics of capital punishment. See, for example, "Capital Crime and Punishment," *Religion & Politics* (January 19, 2016), accessible at http://religionandpolitics.org/?s=capital+punishment, and "Outrageous Atrocity or Moral Imperative? The Ethics of Capital Punishment." *Studies in Christian Ethics* (Fall 1993): 1–14.

215 Interestingly, Wolterstorff does not address Jesus' admonition, found in the context of confronting an offender, *not to forgive* the person who remains unrepentant (Matt. 18:17). Nor in briefly mentioning the parable of the unmerciful servant (Matt. 18:21–35) does he consider an important implication of Jesus' teaching, given the fact that the unmerciful servant's original debt was *reinstated* due to his lack of thoroughgoing repentance (Matt. 18:32–34; cf. also 1 Cor. 5:1–15). Wolterstorff *does* comment on Peter's reaction, recorded earlier in Matthew 18, to Jesus' exhortation to forgive "seventy times seven," that is, boundlessly (*Justice in Love*, 162–3). Finally, neither does Wolterstorff consider the fact that, from a theological perspective, in the final analysis God does not forgive all people – only those who, having realized their need, have repented and embraced his mercy and forgiveness. This is the clear teaching of the Christian scriptures and the historic Christian tradition.

216 Richard Goldstone, "Healing Wounded People," *The Washington Post* (February 2, 1997), C4.

217 Karol Wojtyla, *Sign of Contradiction* (New York: Seabury Press, 1979), 166–9.

218 Ibid., 166.

219 Ibid.

220 Wolterstorff, *Justice in Love*, 206. This position is neither Christian, nor charitable, nor just. It is, rather, an exceedingly "cruel mercy."

221 Moral retribution, after all, is the core strategy of the criminal justice. In the end, one does not need recourse to religion to intuit the fundamental character of justice. As I have argued, this is part of the function of the natural law.

222 Wolterstorff, *Justice in Love*, 24.

223 See n. 148.

224 J. Daryl Charles, *Retrieving the Natural Law: A Return to Moral First Things* (Critical Issues in Bioethics; Grand Rapids and Cambridge, UK: Eerdmans, 2008), especially, Chapter 4, and J. Daryl Charles, "Burying the Wrong Corpse: Protestants and the Natural Law," in Jesse Covington, Bryan McGraw and Micah Watson, eds., *Natural Law and Evangelical Political Thought* (Lanham: Lexington Books, 2012), 1–19.

225 This omission in *Justice in Love* is not accidental. In Wolterstorff's previous volume, *Justice: Rights and Wrongs*, a scant five pages are devoted to the natural law, and these five pages have less to do with natural law thinking than with Woltertorff's argument that Thomas Aquinas, from whom most accounts of the natural law derive, in the end "gives no account of justice" that allows him adequately to ground inherent rights (42).

226 Perhaps no better example of this can be found than John Paul II's exceedingly important 1993 encyclical *Veritatis Splendor* ("Splendor of Truth"). *Veritatis Splendor* is foremost concerned with the ethical life, and John Paul is burdened by the relative weakness of moral teaching – and moral formation – to be found

in the Christian community, given its mandate to participate in and inform the wider culture.

227 Augustine, Augustine, *City of God* 19.23 and *Epistle* 155.13, 15 ("To Macedonius"); Thomas Aquinas, *S.T.* I-II Q. 62; II-II Q. 23; and II-II Q. 80 and 81.

228 Aquinas, *S.T.* 1-II Q. 94.

229 Ibid.

230 Ibid. II-II QQ. 39 and 58. In fact, the person who seeks the common good (the good of many) in reality seeks his own good, if for no other reason, argues Aquinas, that the individual good is impossible without the common good (ibid. Q. 47, a. 10).

231 Ibid.

232 *Catechism of the Catholic Church* (Washington, DC: United States Catholic Conference, 1994), nos. 1907 and 1913.

233 Here the *Catechism* is citing the Vatican II document *Gaudium et Spes* no. 26.

234 *Catechism of the Catholic Church*, nos. 1907–1909.

235 Here I concur broadly with Joseph Clair, "Wolterstorff on Love and Justice: An Augustinian Response," *Journal of Religious Ethics* 41, no. 1 (March 2013): 138–67.

7 Human personhood, moral truth, and what is at stake

A test-case

A recurring theme in the encyclicals of John Paul II (d. 2005) was the necessity of freedom being harnessed to truth. Apart from this linkage, he forcefully argued, freedom annihilates itself. Speaking from the vantage point of one who had intimate acquaintance with political tyranny, during his lifetime John Paul addressed those of us who live in relatively "free" societies by reminding us that the wedding of democratic pluralism and moral relativism constitutes a thinly veiled totalitarianism.[1] And indeed, the historical record would seem to vindicate the former pontiff: the century immediately behind us constitutes a sobering reminder that freedom in fact is capable of annihilating itself.

Although the exact numbers vary and, by any measurement, are difficult to grasp, we do well to ponder the sobering dimensions of the eclipse of good and evil in the century just removed. Consider, for just a moment, the mind-boggling statistics – again, approximate – which illustrate the disappearance of the distinction between evil and good in notable twentieth-century regimes. French historian Stéphane Courtois, in his introduction to *The Black Book of Communism*, places the number of human deaths due to political and ideological oppression in the vicinity of 100 million.[2] Compare this with military historian Robert Conquest's estimates, in *Reflections on a Ravaged Century*, which are in the neighborhood of 170 million.[3] Truly, the stench of death is omnipresent. After we have considered the incalculable dimensions of evil and have done the math, surely all of these human lives matter – a fact for which pacifists and separatists, who reject natural law thinking and the just use of force, lack any legitimate answer.

But ideological pacifism and religious isolation are not my primary concern, even when they contribute to the undermining of religious freedom. The movement toward self-extermination occurs when human freedom and moral agency are no longer tethered to a universal moral law, that is, when freedom is "beyond good and evil," as we have intimated earlier in this volume.[4] The result, prepared over several decades, is a moral vacuum that only power – *brute power* – can fill.

Scarcely more than a half-century removed, Europeans and North Americans seem to have forgotten a most disturbing fact of recent history. Moral atrocity, couched in broadly acceptable justification at *both* academic and popular levels, is the end result of the encroachment on ethics of "biological" and material explanations of human life that imbeds itself in the public – and in time, political – realm. This "function-oriented" strain of thinking, perhaps relatively subdued for several generations, would appear to have emerged once more in our own day in full force. But, as always, it is couched in "scientific" garb.

As evidence of contemporary culture's preference for a "social-utility-over-human-dignity" model of personhood, based on the trumping of morality by utilitarian considerations and biology, I propose that we consider attitudes toward personhood as they surface in debates and legal developments surrounding euthanasia. The fact that in our day assisted suicide – whether it goes by the name of "mercy killing," "death with dignity," or "physician-assisted suicide" – is gaining traction in the United States, with significant encouragement from European models,[5] is by no means a new development. Already 25 years ago, John Harris, at the time the Sir David Alliance Professor of Bioethics and Director of the Institute of Medicine Law and Bioethics at the University of Manchester, wrote in the pages of the *Kennedy Institute of Ethics Journal*:

> Normally we use the term "person" as a synonym for 'human beings,' people like us. However, we are also familiar with the idea that there are nonhuman persons, and humans who are not, or may not be [,] persons or full persons . . . Human nonpersons or humans who are not fully fledged [sic] persons may include zygotes and embryos, or individuals who are 'brain-dead,' anencephalic infants, or individuals in a persistent vegetative state.

Note the source of this rather remarkable declaration. It comes from someone considered an authority on bioethical issues. Which is to say, he is not speaking as an "outsider"; rather, he is representative of many influential secular bioethicists who have been calling for a radical revisioning of our understanding of human personhood. Consider, as well, a similar statement by another respected secular bioethicist of the day: "Although nonhuman animals are not plausible candidates for moral personhood, humans too fail to qualify as moral persons if they lack one or more of the conditions of moral personhood."[6] And consider, too, the fact that both of these pronouncements appear in the journal published by the Kennedy Institute of Ethics, which is a part of Georgetown University, a supposedly Catholic institution. Strangely, the Institute's website, with supreme modesty, reads, "The Kennedy Institute of Ethics at Georgetown University helped to invent the field of bioethics, beginning a tradition of creative leadership in practical ethics that continues into the twenty-first century."[7] If the visitor to the Kennedy Institute of Ethics website is like me, he or she is genuinely perplexed by such a claim. One would hope that the serious study of "ethics" might cause us to operate within an *existing* (and time-tested) tradition of moral reflection – what in past generations was viewed as *wisdom*– rather than "inventing" new approaches to perennial ethical questions through self-imagined human "creativity."[8]

Full disclosure: perhaps because I married into a German family and spent the early years of marriage living in (former West) Germany, where the first of our children was born, and studying at a German university, I am particularly sensitive to the character of moral atrocity that lies in the not-too-distant past. Perhaps, too, it is because my German father-in-law who died in 1984 – an exceedingly good man whom I loved dearly and who raised six children – spent the five years of the Second World War working for *der Deutscher Bundesbahn* (the German railroad) in *Poland* as a railroad-car switcher. (Side note: while the Spanish or the French or the Portuguese, for example, might claim to be a fairly "loving" people, the recent historical record prevents the Germans from making such a claim. Whether this judgment is "fair" or not is beside the point. And let the reader please know that I make this comment as an observation, not as a criticism.) In contemplating the depth and width of ethical dilemmas, I am less concerned to "invent" a new ethical approach to pressing issues of the day by means of "creative" activity than I am to wrestle with perennial ethical dilemmas by drawing on the resources of *time-tested* wisdom – a wisdom that is lodged in the natural law tradition.

In this chapter, I wish to examine the evolution of the notion of *lebensunwertes Leben* ("life not worth living") in German academic thought that occurred in the roughly forty-year period between 1890 and 1933, when Nationalism Socialism officially took power. Hereby I hope to illustrate, in support of my argument for the linkage between religious freedom, natural law, and human dignity, that "totalitarian" tendencies – whether they originate with the minority or the majority of the population – require *preparation.* (In case the reader is struggling with "whiplash" at this point, as a result of my "linkage," I simply ask that he/she be patient. My wider burden is to show that without universally applicable moral principles, intuited through the natural law, human beings have *no means by which to prevent or retard socio-political evil.*)

I am, of course, well aware that some of my readers will view this rhetorical strategy as an "over-reaction" to present cultural developments, or an unfair application to the present of past moral atrocity. I can well imagine that some of my readers will deny the validity of my drawing a connection between European versions of tyranny of the twentieth century with present trajectories in Western culture that mirror a disdain for moral law. In response, I wish only to say that ideological "preparation" for radical shifts in cultural thinking is particularly significant as we undergo *shifts in our social understanding of the notion of human personhood.* Even my potential critics cannot deny that shifts in this vein in fact are proceeding at a breathtaking pace.

Legal scholar Michael J. Perry has noted, "The internationalization of human rights" that began to occur in 1945.[9] Two particular events among others were critical to this development. One was the signing of the Charter of the United Nations in October of 1945 with its provisions for "fundamental freedoms" and "human rights." The second was the adoption, in December of 1948, by the U.N. General Assembly of the UDHR, which marked a "dramatic break" with the past.[10] Up until the Second World War, it was generally assumed that international law would not intrude into a nation's sovereignty for the purposes of preventing that nation from egregious "human rights" violations. Thus, W. Michael Reisman stated,

> In 1942, for example, a member of the British House of Commons characterized Adolph Hitler's treatment of Jews of Allied nationality as a matter of international concerns but characterized the treatment of Jews of Axis nationality as no one else's business; it was a domestic matter.[11]

From 1945 onward, Reisman observes, that conception changed for the most part, with governments from this point forward having to give some form of accountability in terms of how it treated its citizens.

But let us pause to consider the declaration by the British House of Commons member – a declaration made as late as 1942, well after institutional "reforms" had been codified by German National Socialists – along with its far-reaching implications: violations of "human rights" are a "domestic matter" and "no one else's business." At the very least, we are justified in asking the most basic of questions. How did even *Allied* thinking come to accept this unacceptable form of logic?[12] But, more fundamentally, how did German society come to accept the very practices and policies that tolerated egregious human rights violations and inverted "life" and "death?"

The social and cultural preparation of a way of thinking

Biological arguments

One of the tragic legacies of social Darwinism is that it assisted in giving justification to the elimination of *lebensunwertes Leben*, life that is "not worth living," or, in the language of Darwinists themselves, life that is simply unfit.[13] While it is commonly assumed that the moral atrocities associated with the Holocaust were the exclusive domain of Adolf Hitler and those loyal to him (people such as Joseph Goebbels, Hermann Goering, Heinrich Himmler and Albert Speer), this was only the final act.[14] Indeed, it would appear, as authors with such diverse backgrounds as Alexander Mitscherlich,[15] Robert Jay Lifton,[16] Robert Proctor,[17] Michael Burleigh[18] and Wesley Smith[19] have documented, the path to scientific, medical, and social-political evil was prepared *long before Nazism was even a cloud on the German horizon.*

In addition to the ascendancy of biological determinism,[20] an important step in legitimizing the killing of the weak, the infirm, the terminally ill and the incompetent was the shift in ethos among medical doctors and psychiatrists several decades prior to WWII. Historian Robert Proctor has argued persuasively that the Nazi experiment was rooted in *pre-1933 thinking* about the essence of personhood, racial hygienics and survival economics, and that the "caring professions" were instrumental both in pioneering research and in carrying out this program.[21] Based on the evidence available, I am inclined to agree with Proctor's argument. Proctor is adamant that academics, scientists, and medical practitioners were *pioneers and not merely pawns* in this process. By 1933, however, when political power was consolidated by National Socialists, resistance within the medical community was too late. As evidence, Proctor notes that most of the fifteen-odd journals devoted to racial hygienics were established long before the rise of National Socialism as a political party.[22] This social-cultural development raises important questions and should give us pause.

Few accounts of this period are more thoroughly researched than Michael Burleigh's *Death and Deliverance: "Euthanasia" in Germany ca. 1900–1945*. Particularly riveting is Burleigh's discussion of psychiatric reform and medical utilitarianism during the Weimar period.[23] Based on a German source that agrees with Burleigh, during the years of WWI, an estimated 140,000 people died in German psychiatric asylums.[24] This would suggest that about 30 percent of the entire pre-war population died as a result of hunger, disease, or neglect.[25] Following the war, evidence indicates that a shift in the moral climate was in progress. In the spring of 1920, the chairman of the German Psychiatric Association, Karl Bonhoeffer, testified before association members at the GPA annual meeting that "we have witnessed change in the concept of humanity"; moreover,

> In emphasizing the right of the healthy to stay alive, which is an inevitable result of periods of necessity, there is also a danger of going too far: a danger that the self-sacrificing subordination of the strong to the needs of the helpless and ill, which lies at the heart of any true concern for the sick, will give ground to the demand of the healthy to live.[26]

According to Burleigh, Bonhoeffer went on in the 1930s to offer courses that trained those who in time would be authorized with implementing sterilization policies introduced by the National Socialists.[27] (Karl's well-known son, Dietrich, would study theology at Union Theological Seminary in New York City and, to his credit, return to Germany to identify with the so-called confessing church – a decision that in the spring of 1945 would result in his execution literally weeks before liberation by Allied forces.)

Already in the 1890s, the traditional view of medicine that physicians are not to harm and only to cure was being questioned in some corners by a "right-to-die" ethos. Voluntary euthanasia was being supported by a concept of *negative human worth* – i.e., by the combined notion that suffering negates human value and the incurably ill and mentally defective place an enormous burden, whether economically or socially or emotionally, on families and their surrounding communities. It is at this time that the expression *lebensunwertes Leben*, "life not worth living,"[28] seems to have emerged and became the subject of heated debate by the time that WWI ended.[29]

Several late nineteenth-century German proponents of involuntary euthanasia deserve recognition. In 1899, influential biologist and Darwinian social theorist Ernst Haeckel published *The Riddle of the Universe*, which achieved an enormous amount of success, becoming one of the most widely read science books of the era. According to historian Daniel Gasman, *Riddle* sold more than 100,000 copies in its first year, went through ten editions by 1919, had sold over 500,000 copies by 1933, and in time was translated into 25 different languages.[30] Gasman describes Haeckel as "Germany's major prophet of political biology."[31] One of several influential voices contending for the utility of euthanasia, Haeckel combined the notion of euthanasia as an act of mercy with economic concerns, resulting in the social argument that considerable cost – both human and economic – might be saved.

Further justification for euthanasia in the pre-WWI era was provided by people such as social theorist Adolf Jost and Nobel-Prize-winning chemist Wilhelm Ostwald. According to Ostwald, "in all circumstances suffering represents a restriction upon, and diminution of, the individual and capacity to perform in society of the person suffering."[32] In his 1895 book *Das Recht auf den Tod* ("The Right to Death"), Jost set forth the argument – an argument almost 40 years in advance of Nazi prescriptions – that the "right" to kill existed in the context of the higher rights possessed by the state, since all individuals belong to the social organism of the state. What's more, this was couched in terms of "compassion" and "relief" from one's suffering. Finally, and not least importantly, the "right" to kill compassionately was predicated on biology, in accordance with the spirit of the age: the state must ensure that the social organism remains fit and healthy.[33]

Legal and medical arguments

Well before the outbreak of WWI, multiple influential voices appear in the literature agitating for a legalization of assisted death. One such proposal, published in 1913, contains the following provisions:

- Whoever is incurably ill has the right to assisted death.
- The right to assisted death will be established by the patient's petition to relevant juridical authorities.[34]
- On the basis of this petition, the court will instigate an examination of the patient by a court-appointed physician and two qualified specialists.[35]
- The record of the examination must demonstrate that the illness is more likely to follow a terminal course rather than leading to recovery with the patient's permanent ability to work.[36]
- Whoever painlessly kills the patient as a result of the latter's express and unambiguous request is not to be punished, provided that the patient

has been accorded the right to die under clause 5 of the law, or if post-humous examination reveals that he was incurably ill.[37]

- Whoever kills the patient without his express and unambiguous request will be punished with hard labor.
- These qualifications apply equally to the elderly and the handicapped.[38]

In many respects, the most significant contribution to the debate over euthanasia was the publication in 1920 of *Die Freigabe der Vernichtung lebensunwerten Lebens: Ihr Mass und Ihre Form*,[39] by esteemed law professor Karl Binding and psychiatrist Alfred Hoche.[40] The title of this volume is normally translated from the German as "The Permission to Destroy Life Unworthy of Life." This translation, however, does not capture the nuance and the euphemism that inhere in the German original. A better rendering would be "Release for the Extermination of Life Unworthy of Being Lived." The German verb *freigeben*, from which the noun *Freigabe* is derived, can mean "permit," but more often it carries the sense of "release" or "set free." Hence, "*Freigabe*" in this context is a partner-term standing alongside another German euphemism, *Gnadentod* ("mercy death"). In my research, I came across only one historical source that rendered *Freigabe*as "Release": Robert Proctor's *Racial Hygience*.[41] Hence the title of Binding and Hoche's volume is likely intended to convey a therapeutic nuance and not merely a descriptive or prescriptive function. From the standpoint of euthanasia advocacy, people are "released" or "set free" by the act of "mercy killing."

By 1920, the subject of euthanasia was no longer merely a matter of academic debate. Binding and Hoche argued with considerable precision that the medical profession had the professional responsibility not only of promoting health but also, where necessary, facilitating death (*Sterbehilfe*). The Binding-Hoche book is significant for several reasons. One is the fundamental assumption undergirding its argument: people are autonomous or sovereign in terms of the right to decide how to live or dispose of their lives. Another is the way in which the authors seek to mainstream the distinction between *lebenwertes Leben* ("life worth living") and *lebensunwertes Leben*("life not worth living").[42] Binding attempts to extrapolate from what he believes to be a "weakness" in the German criminal code by suggesting that certain life, for example, someone who is "deathly ill or fatally wounded,"[43] consequently "no longer merits full legal protection."[44] Binding laments the fact that the distinguishing between "worthwhile" and "unworthwhile" life "has made no progress" in the actual practice of German criminal law, although in the academic literature it has "gained a lively reception."[45]

What's more, Binding and Hoche stressed that ending "life unworthy of living" had a *therapeutic* goal. But in what instances was the facilitation of death necessary? The authors carefully reason that certain categories of persons were living "unworthy" lives but also that assisting in their death is ethically, medically, and economically justifiable. These categories include the retarded, the deformed, the mentally ill,[46] and the severely disabled.[47]

Freigabe consists of two essays, the first being a "legal explanation" by Binding, whose reflections followed 40 years of teaching law at the university level, and the second a "medical explanation" by Hoche. What follows is a summary of their two-pronged argument – an argument that is remarkably similar to the one being advocated by present-day proponents of assisted death.[48]

Binding, one of Germany's leading constitutional scholars, restates a question that has "much occupied" his thinking for many years, "but which most people timidly avoid because it is seen as delicate and hard to answer."[49] Hs question is this:

> Should permissible taking of life be restricted, except in emergency situations, to an individual's act of suicide as it is in current law, or should it be legally extended to the killing of fellow human beings, and under what conditions?[50]

Binding is a passionate and deeply committed secularist. Foreclosing any debate, he asserts unequivocally:

> Religious reasons have no probative force in law for two reasons. First, in this instance, they rest on a wholly unworthy concept of God. Second, law is thoroughly secular and is focused on the regulation of our external common life. Additionally, the New Testament says nothing about the problem of suicide.[51]

Binding's prejudice against religion allows him to re-cast traditional Christian morality as the true villain, thereby paving the way for a universal "right to die":

> After an extended, deeply unchristian, interruption in the recognition of this right [the right to end one's life] (an interruption demanded by the church and supported by the obscene idea that the God of love could wish that human beings not die until they undergo endless physical and spiritual suffering) . . ., it has now been fully reestablished (except in a few backward countries) as an inalienable possession for all time . . . For the law, nothing else remains except to regard the living person as the sovereign of his own existence and manner of life.[52]

Based on these two guiding presuppositions – i.e., that religious belief is dangerous and individual persons possess sovereignty – Binding reasons that the right of persons to kill themselves is to be protected legally.[53] Moreover, this "right" is "transferrable" to "all so-called accomplices who act with the suicide's express consent."[54] In fact, Binding asserts, "this act must be considered not legally forbidden even when the law does not explicitly recognize it."[55] The practical rationale for euthanasia is that it "replaces a death which is painful . . . with a less painful death."[56] To reassure his audience, Binding adds, "This is not 'an act of killing in the legal sense' but is rather the modification of an irrevocably present cause of a death which can no longer be evaded. *In truth it is a purely healing act.*"[57] Such "healing intervention" must extend even to "unconscious patients," since "the permission of the suffering patient is not required."[58] Further qualification of this "healing act" will be needed.

The compassion argument

Anticipating objection among his readers, Binding assures them that "in truth it [assisted suicide] arises from nothing but the deepest sympathy."[59] "The act of euthanasia," he intones, "must be a consequence of free sympathy."[60] Thus, given the combination of his illustrious career teaching law and his thinking about "the hopelessly ill" that is motivated by the "deepest sympathy," Binding seems well positioned to pose questions that "raise an uneasy feeling in anyone who is accustomed to assessing the value of individual life."[61] One such question is this: "Are there human lives which have so completely lost the attribute of legal status . . . that their continuation has permanently lost all value, both for the bearer of that life and for society?"[62] Binding's own response has the ring of authority as well as common sense:

> It is impossible to doubt that there are living people to whom death would be a release, and whose death would simultaneously free society and the state from carrying a burden which serves no conceivable purpose, except that of providing an example of the greatest un selfishness.[63]

Binding's reflections compel him to tread – and agitate – where German society heretofore has not legally trod:

> Is it our duty actively to advocate for this life's continuance . . . or to permit its destruction under specific conditions? One could also state the question legislatively, like this: Does the energetic preservation of such life deserve preference . . .? Or does permitting its termination, which frees everyone involved, seem the lesser evil?[64]

Because his logic is airtight, Binding is resolute:

> I cannot find the least reason – legally, socially, ethically, or religiously – not to permit those requested to do so to kill such hopeless cases who urgently demand death; indeed I consider this permission to be simply *a duty of legal mercy* (a mercy which also asserts itself in many other forms).[65]

Binding then proceeds to discuss "the necessary means" of carrying out this "duty of legal mercy." "With good reason," he observes, "permission always presupposes a clinical diagnosis." This diagnosis, moreover, "requires competent objective verification, which cannot be placed in the agent's own hands,"[66] even when instigation of the request may originate with *relatives or the person's doctor*. Two steps are recommended by Binding:

1 "The initiative must take the form of an application for permission from a qualified applicant."
2 "This application goes to a government board, whose primary task is limited to investigating whether the presuppositions for permission are met."[67]

According to the Binding prescription, each case subsequently was to be evaluated by a three-person panel consisting of a physician, a psychiatrist, and a lawyer, who "alone have the right to vote."[68] This "Permission Board" was authorized to decree that

> after thorough investigation on the basis of current scientific opinion, the patient seems beyond help; that there is no reason to doubt the sincerity of his consent; that accordingly no impediment stands in the way of killing the patient; and that the petitioner is entrusted with bringing about the patient's release from his evil situation in the most expedient way . . .[69]

Only then was death, based on this protocol, to be "expertly" administered by a physician, in whom the right to grant death was a "natural extension of the responsibilities of the attending physician."[70] Moreover, the "final release must be completely painless, and only qualified persons are justified in applying the means."[71]

And what about the possibility of error? Binding is confident that "scientific" consensus operates beyond the realm of error. At the same time, he realizes that because of the morally promiscuous era of which he is a part, objections to "mercy killing" are to be expected. Proof of "alleged error by the Permission Board would be very difficult to come by," he assures the potential "Board" member; nonetheless, "the possibility of error by the Permission Board is undeniable."[72] Indeed,

> Error is possible in all human actions, and no one would draw the foolish conclusion that, considering this possible defect, we must forego all useful and wholesome activities. Even the physician in private practice can make errors which have serious consequences, but no one would bar him from practice because he is capable of erring. *What is good and reasonable must be done despite the risk of error.*[73]

Ultimately, even the possibility of fatal mistakes should not stand in the way of carrying out the "good and reasonable" prescription of Prof. Binding, which is the elimination of "life unworthy of living." Binding's self-proclaimed "deepest sympathy" for "valueless lives" comes to full expression at the conclusion of his essay: "But humanity loses so many members through error that one more or one less really scarcely matters."[74]

The complicity of medical ethics: from healing to harming

In the second essay of *Freigabe*, Alfred Hoche examines the medical relationship of physicians to their patients and physicians' relationship to killing. Hoche opens the essay by observing that "a code of medical ethics is nowhere explicitly established":

> There is no medical moral law set out in paragraphs, no Moral Service Regulations. The young physician enters practice without any legal definition of his rights and duties – especially regarding the most important points. Not even the Hippocratic Oath . . ., with its generalities, is operative today.[75]

In practice, what physicians *may* do, or *ought* to do, emanates from peer opinion. Indeed, writes Hoche, in some instances, physicians "are compelled to destroy life" – for example, in "killing a living child during delivery for the purpose of saving the mother, terminating pregnancy for the same reason."[76] This is done "in the interest of serving a higher good."[77] Furthermore, "in all surgical procedures, one tacitly counts on a certain percentage of fatal outcomes," and these "can never be wholly avoided. Our moral sensibility is completely reconciled to this."[78]

One recurring "inner dilemma" that "not infrequently touches the physician" is whether or not, through "passive acquiescence," to yield to "the temptation to let nature run its course" in matters of dying. Hoche is convinced that in certain cases such "passive acquiescence" to natural death is to be resisted. For example, "when the patient is incurably mentally ill, then death is at all events preferable."[79] Hoche emphasizes how "immensely complicated it has already become for doctors to balance, in daily life, the rigid basic principles of medical ethics and the demands of a higher conception of life's value," and when these two stand in conflict, the physician must recognize that "he has no absolute relation to this [latter] obligation in all circumstances."[80] Rather, "this relation is merely relative, alterable under new conditions, and always open to question"; medical ethics, as Hoche understands it, "cannot be viewed as an eternally fixed pattern."[81] So, for example,

> If killing incurables or eliminating those who are mentally dead should come to be regulated (and generally acknowledged) as not only unpunishable but also as desirable for the general welfare, then, from that very moment, no opposing grounds for excluding this could be found in medical ethics.[82]

Hoche is not unmindful of practical concerns as he ponders the ethical duties of the medical profession. Extreme cases of "hopeless illness" that require the continuation of life, in his view, render "nonsensical" the need for life-saving measures. In posing the question, *Is there human life which has utterly forfeited its claim to worth . . . that its continuation has forever lost all value both for the bearer of that life and society?*, Hoche answers, "With certainty: Yes." One example of this is what he calls "mental death," i.e., the condition of people who are deemed "complete idiots," those "whose existence weighs most heavily on the community."[83]

When all else fails: economics as trump card

Hoche instinctively moves to the economic dimensions of caring for those who are said to "burden the community." He calculates, based on the number of "complete idiots" cared for in German institutions in his day, the amount of money and resources that would be saved. His calculations are as follows. Were Prof. Binding's recommendations acted upon, "it is easy to estimate what incredible capital is withdrawn from the nation's wealth for food, clothing, and heating – for an unproductive purpose."[84] This great loss due to "such dead weight" of "valueless lives" calls for "the liberation of every available power for productive ends."[85] Here, as with his co-author Binding, the sheer inhumanity of Hoche strikes the reader as remarkable. He writes, "Naturally no doctor would conclude with certainty that a two- or three-year-old was suffering permanent mental death. But even in childhood, the moment comes when this prediction can be made without doubt."[86]

Hoche is by no means naïve in realizing that overturning conventional thinking, especially at the popular level, takes time and conditioning. Legislative as well as religious roadblocks serve as an additional impediment to the advancement of scientific thinking. Hoche waxes realistic:

> The enormous difficulty of trying to address these problems legislatively will continue for a long time. Likewise, the ideas of gaining relief from our national burden by permitting the destruction of wholly worthless mentally dead persons will (from the start and for a long time) encounter lively, strident, and passionately stated opposition. This opposition will draw its strength from many different sources: resistance to the new and unfamiliar, religious ideas, sentimental feelings, and so on.[87]

Up to now, Hoche laments, when "the individuals subjective right to exist" has clashed with "objective expediency and necessity," the former has typically won. This "difficult" problem has been a result of "the essential participation of Christian ideas." However, Hoche asserts, "alien perspectives" should not prevent us from realizing and acting on the conviction that "valueless lives" and "dead weight existences" are a drain to society as a "civil organism."[88]

Putting euthanasia in perspective: the preparation of an idea

In 1933, with the ascension of the National Socialists to power in Germany, two developments that had reached their critical mass were promptly codified into law. One was the long-discussed sterilization program, which had been debated but had not achieved majority support. The second was authorized euthanasia. The proposal, issued by the German Ministry of Justice, was reported on the front page of *The New York Times* on October 8, 1933. Summarizing the ministry's proposal, it stated: "'It shall be made possible for physicians to end the tortures of incurable patients, upon requests, in the interests of true humanity.'" Moreover, the ministry ensured, 'no life still valuable to the state will be wantonly destroyed.'"[89]

Dr. Andrew C. Ivy, asked in 1946 by the board of trustees of the American Medical Association to serve as a consultant at the Nuremberg trial of Nazi physicians who had been indicted for "crimes against humanity," reflected on his difficult experience with the following observation:

> It was inconceivable that a group of men trained in medicine and in official positions of power in German governmental circles could ignore the ethical principles of medicine and the unwritten law that a doctor should be nearer humanity than other men . . . [W]e had assumed that the sacred aspects of medicine and its ethics would certainly remain inviolate.[90]

Although, according to Ivy, "fewer than two hundred German physicians participated directly in the medical war crimes," it became clear to Ivy that these atrocities were only "the end result" of the "complete encroachment on the ethics and freedom of medicine" by those in positions of influence.[91] But where did this process begin? Indeed, the encroachment of crass utilitarianism on the spheres of ethics and medical science, not to mention psychiatry and law, had begun to surface 40 years before National Socialism ascended to power in 1933. Its propagators displayed an artful and calculated mix of intellectual justification and popular agitation. Where the influence of the Church and morally principled intellectuals was during these preparatory years is a matter of question.

Perhaps dormant for several brief decades, this utilitarian strain of thinking appears to have emerged once more in full force, at least in the Western context. Where it dominates current bioethical debates, we find it most conspicuously on display in contemporary discussions of *what constitutes personhood*. But utilitarian thinking about ethics is ubiquitous. It is the air we breathe, surfacing among professional ethicists, health-care practitioners, social theorists, "new biologists," and various consultants who weigh the value of personhood against the economics of health care and the cumulative "burden" on individuals, families, and society. Utilitarian ethics informs beginning-of-life issues, life-enhancement issues, and end-of life issues. Lacking any antecedent moral commitment to the sanctity and dignity of human life, utilitarian theorists and practitioners adopt a "quality-of-life" ethic. The inevitable question that follows is this: Does human life reduce to a "choice," or is it an endowment? Rightly, as social theorist Leon Kass warned, "There is the very real danger that what constitutes a 'meaningful life' among the intellectual elite will be imposed on the people as the only standard by which the value of human life is measured."[92]

Let us return to pre-war Germany. Consider the following dilemma, "Problem 97," found in a German mathematics textbook published in 1935:

> A mental patient costs about 4 RMS[[93]] a day to keep, a cripple 5.50 RMS, a criminal 3.50 RMS. In many cases a civil servant only has about 4 RMS, a salaried employee scarcely 3.50 RMS, an unskilled worker barely 2 RMS for his family. (a) Illustrate these figures with the aid of pictures. According to conservative estimates, there are about 300,000 mental patients, epileptics, etc. in asylums in Germany. (b) What do they cost together per annum at a rate of 4 RMS per person? . . . How many marriage loans at 1,000 RMS each could be awarded per annum with this money, disregarding later repayment?[94]

The solution to "Problem 97" is given as follows. "Assuming an average daily outlay of 3.50 RMS," the results are (1) a "daily savings" of 245.955 RMS, (2) an "annual saving" of 88,543.98 RMS, and over the long term, 885,438.800 RMS will have been, or has already been, saved by 1 September 1951 by reason of the *disinfection of 70,273 persons* which has been carried out to date."[95] This "solution," it should be pointed out, was part of a digest found in 1945 at Schloss Hartheim, one of several killing centers where organized euthanasia was being performed on adults during the wartime.

Historian Robert Proctor has argued that the primary argument for forcible euthanasia in the 1930s was economic; assisted death was justified as a kind of "preemptive triage" to free up bed space.[96] This may have been the manner in which the euthanatic impulse eventually expressed itself, but the notion of *lebensunwertes Leben* does not *begin* with a financial question; it begins with the *human* question. *What does it mean to be a human being?* Persons who were considered a "burden" on German society included handicapped infants, the mentally ill, the terminally ill, the comatose, and the criminal element. They were initially perceived as a "burden" because of a deficient – a *thoroughly inhumane* – view of personhood. By 1941, euthanasia had become part of normal hospital routine,[97] at which point this disposal or "disinfection" of human lives, nevertheless, was to be done "humanely and economically." Lest we think that "that was then but this is now," or that German thinking on the matter was isolated in 1942, Proctor has noted that until reports of wholesale Nazi exterminations began to appear in American newspapers in 1942, the merits of forced euthanasia were being vigorously debated in various American scholarly journals, including the *Journal of the American Psychiatric Association*, which had called for the killing of retarded children ("nature's mistakes").[98]

Writing already in 1989 shortly before his death, Cardinal John O'Connor of New York City, an ardent pro-life advocate, predicted that euthanasia would "dwarf the abortion phenomenon in magnitude, in numbers, in horror."[99] When one considers the sheer number of abortions performed each year in North America, let alone in the last 25 years since O'Connor's pronouncement (and forget the entire Western world, for the moment), this statement borders on fantasy. In his lifetime, it needs to be said, Cardinal O'Connor was not someone given to exaggeration. And while there is nothing inevitable about human predictions, surely O'Connor's words, spoken a quarter-century removed, should haunt us. What is it that can hinder this "prophecy" from coming to pass?

Following a public referendum in the state of Washington that turned back the permission to assist death, but before Oregon's approval of the same in 1997, the Ramsey Colloquium of the Institute on Religion and Public Life, named after ethicist Paul Ramsey (1913–1988), produced an eloquent statement of the Jewish and Christian understanding of euthanasia. "Always to Care, Never to Kill" first appeared in the November 27, 1991, edition of the *Wall Street Journal* and subsequently was published in the February 1992 issue of the journal *First Things*.[100] The statement is notable for its understanding of personhood, at the center of which stands the concept of human dignity.

"Always to Care" begins by declaring that to deal with the problem of suffering by means of eliminating those who suffer is an evasion of moral duty and a great wrong. It rehearses the fact that deeply embedded within the moral and medical traditions of our own culture is the distinction between *allowing to die*, on the one hand, and *killing*, on the other. Never is it permitted to take any action that is aimed at the death of ourselves or others; it is always prohibited.

> Medical treatments can be refused or withheld if they are either useless or excessively burdensome. No one should be subjected to useless treatment; no one need accept any and all lifesaving treatments, no matter how burdensome. In making such decisions, the judgment is about the worth of treatments, *not* about the worth of lives. When we ask whether a treatment is useless, the question is: "Will this treatment be useful for this patient, will it benefit the life he or she has?" When we ask whether a treatment is burdensome, the question is: "Is this treatment excessively burdensome to the life of this patient?" The question is *not* whether this life is useless or burdensome. Our decisions, whether for or against a specific treatment, are to be always in the service of life. We can and should allow the dying to die; we must never intend the death of the living. We may reject a treatment; we must never reject a life.[101]

The statement points to a four-fold source of wisdom that helps safeguard the worth of the human life. That wisdom is religious, moral, political, and institutional – a wisdom that prevents us from transgressing boundaries that teach us always to care, never to kill.

> Guided by this wisdom, we will not presume to eliminate a fellow human being, nor need we fear being abandoned in our suffering. The

> compact of rights, duties, and mutual trust that makes human community possible depends upon our continuing adherence to the precept, *Always to care, never to kill.*[102]

It is one thing to believe – and argue – that human beings have a "right" to die without intolerable suffering or without the use of extraordinary measures. In fact, Catholic social ethics has traditionally made the important distinction between "ordinary" and "extraordinary" measures when addressing end-of-life matters. It is, however, quite another thing to pressure certain individuals (or groups) and eventually *require* that they die – as "lives not worthy of living." In our own day, as was the case in pre-WWII Germany, there exists the widespread perception that when family members and doctors assist patients with suicide they are acting out of charity, perhaps even justice, and engaged in a compassionate and caring work. It is, thus, not surprising that, as in Germany a century ago, proponents of euthanasia utilize euphemistic language to justify assisted killing – for example, "mercy killing," "death with dignity," and the like. (The word "euthanasia" itself, of course, is euphemistic and invites a certain elasticity: it means literally "a good [or easy] death.") But as one social commentator has matter-of-factly observed, the "mercy" offered by euthanasia can only be offered by those who, logically and emotionally, hold to *a conception of the human person that is radically different* from that of traditional medicine as practiced in a "civil society"; the price of accepting euthanasia's "charity" is denying that humans have any *inherent worth* apart from their productivity or utility.[103] Citing Walker Percy, he accurately recounts the pattern of recent human history: such "tenderness" leads inevitably to the gas chambers. And, in fact, "mercy killing" and "compassionate death" for the terminally ill over time *will* come to include other categories of human beings – those deemed socially "useless" or "unproductive" as well.[104] It needs emphasizing that the "compassion" that leads to mercy killing is the first step toward a society in which the integrity of *all life* is abandoned. *But even that first step started somewhere.*[105]

***

In the previous chapter, I argued for the unity and integrity of justice and love. Where these two "cardinal" virtues are perceived to be standing in tension or working in opposition, the results in terms of social and public policy are disastrous. Where, however, their unity, symbiosis, and concordant relationship is preserved, society is less susceptible to ethical distortion and perversion, whether these perversions be rooted in soft-headed sentimentalism, hard-headed retributivism, demeaning paternalism, or unbridled and unprincipled materialism.

This volume is not about euthanasia; it is about religion. But the linkage between the two is moral law, human dignity, and our response to the suffering of others. What's more, this chapter's tragic tale of suffering – a suffering caused by the incursion of the euthanatic impulse in German thinking a century ago – was not intended to be mere historical narrative. It is meant to be illustrative. The fear of suffering and the frustration we feel when we cannot restore to health those whom we love, in some respects, is analogous to *the sense of fear – or paralysis – that we experience when we attempt to stand up and speak out for the rights of others and religious freedom.* Even when we take for granted most of the freedoms, we've grown up with, and even when the freedoms of those living in Western societies are infinitely greater than those of persecuted minorities around the world, we nevertheless are inclined to *shrink back in fear.* We fear taking up unpopular but virtuous causes. We fear confronting people who disagree with us. We fear confronting employers or institutions which are far bigger than us. And we fear confronting the political powers and cultural mechanisms that, at bottom, seem to control our lives. But, at the most basic level, *we fear engaging in moral discourse*, and I surely grant that some of these fears are quite understandable. After all, no one wishes to be branded as "hate-filled," "bigoted," and "intolerant," even when that accusation is patently false and intended to keep our point of view *removed from the public sphere.* Alas, the days of fearing others, the days of worrying about what others think of us, the days of fearing being labeled "judgmental" – these days are past. At least, they *should* be past.

Permit me explicitly to state the assumption that has buttressed my argument in the present chapter. If we refuse – if we *fear* – to stand and act on behalf of those who stand in need, both at home and abroad, then it can be said that we are neither a *charitable* nor a *just* people. Nor can it be said that we any longer inhabit a "civil society"; rather, in truth we have become an *uncivil* society. This is to say, we are (a) a society in which duties are regularly trumped by so-called rights, (b) a society in which all perceive themselves as "victims," and (c) a society in which personal rights (so-called), rooted neither in justice nor in charity but in *autonomy*, always and everywhere trump kindhearted action and benevolence.

In the end, an inconvenient question presses to the fore: do we have the moral fiber not only to *acknowledge* the most fundamental of freedoms, that sacred right of conscience, but also, in that light, to *defend* that "first" freedom on behalf of those who are grossly suffering by virtue of having their most basic freedoms denied? After all, around the world religious freedom is in *serious trouble.* This state of affairs requires that we defend human beings' place in the cosmos, regardless of whether we are theists or a-theists.

Notes

1 *Veritatis Splendor* no. 101. The encyclical is accessible at http://w2.vatican.va/content/john-paul-ii/en/encyclicals/documents/hf_jp-ii_enc_06081993_veritatis-splendor.html.

2 Stéphane Courtois, Nicolas Werth, Jean-Louis Panné, Andrzej Paczkowski, Karel Bartošek, and Jean-Louis Margolin, *The Black Book of Communism: Crimes Terror, Repression*, trans. Jonathan Murphy and Mark Kramer (Cambridge: Harvard University Press, 1999).

3 Robert Conquest, *Reflections on a Ravaged Century* (New York: W.W. Norton, 2001).
4 See Chapter 1, n. 117.
5 I refer here, foremost, to the Netherlands and Belgium.
6 Tom L. Beauchamp, "The Failure of Theories of Personhood," *Kennedy Institute of Ethics Journal* 9, no. 4 (1999): 309.
7 The Kennedy Institute of Ethics, "Forty-Five Years of Leadership in Ethics for a Complex World," accessible at https://kennedyinstitute.georgetown.edu/.
8 At the very least, the Institute might more seriously consider the authoritative documents that are a part of its own Catholic tradition, beginning with the *Catechism of the Catholic Church*. See esp. the *Catechism*'s treatment of human personhood found in nos. 27, 306–308, 342–343, 355–368, 1700–1709, 1730–1761, 1930, and 1934–1935. And let it be said that I write as a Protestant.
9 Michael J. Perry, *Human Rights in the Constitutional Law of the United States* (Cambridge and New York: Cambridge university Press, 2013), 9–18.
10 For a thoughtfully written legal and political history of events leading up to the UDHR, see Mary Ann Glendon, *A World Made New: Eleanor Roosevelt and the Universal Declaration of Human Rights* (New York: Random House, 2001)
11 W. Michael Reisman, "Through or Despite Governments: Differentiated Responsibilities in Human Rights Programs," *Iowa Law Review* 72 (1987): 391–2. Reisman is cited at length by Perry (see n. 9).
12 Calls for euthanasia in the 1930s were by no means restricted to Germany. As historian Robert Proctor has documented, a growing number of British physicians were advocates, and the *British Medical Journal* by 1935 "carried on a lively debate over this question" (*Racial Hygiene: Medicine under the Nazis* [Cambridge and London: Harvard University Press, 1988], 179–80; cf. also 285). Not unrelated is the fact that many elements of eugenics were being advanced in the United States, England, France, Scandinavia, and the Soviet Union during the 1930s. In fact, according to Proctor: "In 1914 eugenics was taught in 44 American colleges and universities; by 1928 the number had grown to 376" (400, n. 11). In other words, in roughly three-quarters of American colleges and universities, this was being taught.
13 What writer Hugh Gregory Gallagher rather succinctly stated as the essence of Darwinian thinking a century ago – genetic determinism – could well be applied to our own day, minus the "politically incorrect" language: "The eugenicists and Darwinists, for all their pretensions, made no distinctions within the fitness category. Crooks and prostitutes, the blind, the paralyzed, the retarded, all were degenerate, all were unfit. These were people with weak genes. The degeneracy of their character, as well as the flawed nature of their bodies, was seen to be inherited" (*By Trust Betrayed: Patients, Physicians, and the License to Kill in the Third Reich*, rev. ed. [Arlington: Vandamere Press, 1995], 50).
14 While the literature is voluminous, one of the best resource for understanding not only the indispensable role that Hitler's assistants played in propping up the Third Reich but also the psychology of totalitarianism as it was played out ethically in their individual lives is Guido Knopp's *Hitlers Helfer* (München: Wilhelm Goldmann Verlag, 1996). Unfortunately, the book remains untranslated from the German, even when it has been the source of cinematic reproduction.
15 Alexander Mitscherlich and Fred Mielke), *Doctors of Infamy: The Story of Nazi Medical Crimes* (New York: Henry Schuman, 1949).
16 Robert Jay Lifton, *The Nazi Doctors: Medical Killing and the Psychology of Genocide* (New York: Basic Books, 1986).
17 Proctor, *Racial Hygiene* (see n. 12).
18 Michael Burleigh, *Death and Deliverance: "Euthanasia" in Germany ca. 1900–1945* (Cambridge: Cambridge University Press, 1994).

19 Wesley J. Smith, *Forced Exit: The Slippery Slope from Assisted Suicide to Legalized Murder* (New York: Times Books, 1997), and more recently, *Culture of Death: The Assault on Medical Ethics in America* (San Francisco: Encounter Books, 2000).
20 It is telling that National Socialist leaders commonly referred to the phenomenon of National Socialism as "applied biology." An example of this in the literature is Fritz Lenz, *Menschliche Auslese und Rassenhygiene* (München: Beck, 1931), which remains untranslated from the German. (The title of this volume translates to "Human Selection and Race-Based Health.") Significantly, the 1931 version of Lenz's book was the *third* edition already.
21 Proctor, *Racial Hygiene*, 20.
22 Ibid.
23 The Weimar Republic corresponds to the period extending from 1919, the year of the German constitutional assembly at Weimar, and 1933, when the Republic was dissolved with Hitler becoming chancellor.
24 Hans-Ludwig Siemen, *Menschen Bleiben auf der Strecke: Psychiatrie zwischen Reform und Nationalisozialismus* (Gütersloh: Gütersloher Verlag, 1987), 29–30.
25 This is Burleigh's calculation (*Death and Deliverance*, 11).
26 Bonhoeffer's address was published in the *Allgemeine Zeitschrift für Psychiatrie* 76 (1920/21); the citation is from p. 600 (an English translation of which appears in Burleigh, *Death and Deliverance*, 11–12).
27 Burleigh, *Death and Deliverance*, 12.
28 Literally, the translation of the German is "life unworthy of living."
29 This is the view of historians Proctor, *Racial Hygiene*, 177–222 (= Chapter 7, "The Destruction of 'Lives Not Worth Living'"), and Burleigh, *Death and Deliverance*, 12–13.
30 Daniel Gasman, The *Scientific Origins of National Socialism: Social Darwinism in Ernest Haeckel and the German Monist League* (New York: American Elsevier Pub. Co., 1971), 150.
31 Ibid.
32 This was part of an exchange that was published in Wilhelm Börner, "Euthanasie," *Das monistische Jahrhundert* 2 (1913): 251–4. An English translation of this text appears in Burleigh, *Death and Deliverance*, 14.
33 English-language assessments of Jost can be found in Lifton, *The Nazi Doctors*, 46, and Burleigh, *Death and Deliverance*, 12–15, with a more thorough untranslated examination in Klaus Dörner, "Nationalsozialismus und Lebensvernichtung," *Vierteljahrhefte für Zeitgeschichte* 15 (1967): 121–52.
34 What constitutes a "juridical authority" is unclear.
35 What constitutes a "specialist" in this case is unclear.
36 Note here the emphasis on utility and particularly the patient's ability to work.
37 Notice that a sphere of protection for the killing is provided both before and after the act.
38 This rough "draft" was originally published in *Das monistische Jahrhundert* 2 (1913): 170–1. A written translation appears in Burleigh, *Death and Deliverance*, 13–14.
39 Karl Binding and Alfred Hoche, *Die Freigabe der Vernichtung lebensunwerten Freigabe* (Leipzig: Felix Meiner Verlag, 1920).
40 This is the shared view of numerous commentators – among them: American Holocaust historian Lifton, *The Nazi Doctors*, 46–8; German historian Christian Pross, "Nazi Doctors, German Medicine, and Historical Truth," in George Annas and Michael A. Brodin, eds., *The Nazi Doctors and the Nuremberg Code* (Oxford and New York: Oxford University Press, 1992), 40; American historian Proctor, *Racial Hygiene*, 177–80; British historian Burleigh, *Death and Deliverance*, 15–21; writer Gallagher, *By Trust Betrayed*, 60; and writer/legal expert Smith, *Forced Exit*, 73–5.

41 Proctor, *Racial Hygiene*, 178.
42 The expression "life unworthy of living" occurs regularly throughout *Freigabe* and is never qualified or questioned; see, e.g., pp. 24, 51 and 53.
43 German: *einer Todkranker oder tödlich Verwundete* (*Freigabe*, 24).
44 Binding and Hoche, *Freigabe*, 24–5.
45 Ibid., 25.
46 In a remarkable comment confined to a footnote, Binding insinuates that death would prevent the "mentally dead" person or "idiot" from having to endure the shame of being a public spectacle and mistreatment that results from other people's verbal abuse. He writes, "The life of such poor people is an unending invitation to die" (my translation of the statement, "*Das Leben solcher Armen isst ein ewiges Spiessrutenlaufen*," ibid.,).
47 These individuals Binding calls *die unrettbar Kranken*, "the hopelessly ill" (e.g., *Freigabe*, 34).
48 My own commentary on the Binding-Hoche book is based on the German original, but for the benefit of the reader I locate most (though not all) of the citations in the English translation of *Freigabe* that appeared in the journal *Issues in Law & Medicine* 5, no. 2 (1992): 231–65. Where the journal's translation is weak or misses particular nuances of the authors' language, I take liberties, for the sake of accuracy. The team of translators who prepared the journal's text of *Freigabe* consisted of three individuals, one of whom received his medical degree from the Johann Wolfgang von Goethe University of Frankfurt in 1925, where he attended lectures in neurology and psychiatry by co-author Hoche.
49 Ibid., 231–2.
50 Ibid., 232.
51 Ibid., 233.
52 Ibid., 233, 237.
53 Binding acknowledges that in 1885 he had written from the opposite viewpoint, arguing that assisted death should remain illegal or *verboten* (*Freigabe*, 19, n. 32). However, Binding's sole objection to the legality of suicide is the possible loss of potentially valuable members of society.
54 Ibid., 236–7.
55 Ibid., 241.
56 Ibid., 240.
57 Ibid., emphasis present.
58 Ibid., 241.
59 Ibid., 246.
60 Ibid., 252.
61 Ibid., 246.
62 Ibid.
63 Ibid.
64 Ibid., 246–7.
65 Ibid., 248, emphasis added.
66 Ibid., 251.
67 Ibid., 252.
68 Ibid.
69 Ibid.
70 Ibid.
71 Ibid. The authors use several German words to speak therapeutically and euphemistically of the patient's death. The term here in the text is *Erlösung*, which can be translated "solution," "deliverance," or "release."
72 Ibid., 254.
73 Ibid.
74 Ibid.
75 Ibid., 255.

76 Ibid., 256.
77 Ibid.
78 Ibid.
79 Ibid., 257.
80 Ibid.
81 Ibid., 257–8.
82 Ibid., 258.
83 Ibid., 260.
84 Ibid., 260–1.
85 Ibid., 261, 262.
86 Ibid., 265.
87 Ibid., 261.
88 Ibid., 262.
89 *The New York Times*(October 8, 1933), p. 1, cited in Gallagher, *By Trust Betrayed*, 62.
90 Cited in the foreword to Mitscherlich, *Doctors of Infamy*, ix–x.
91 Ibid., x–xi.
92 Leon Kass, in a personal interview with author Wesley Smith, cited in Smith, *Culture of Death*, 9.
93 "RMS" stands for *Reichsmarks*. The *Reichsmark* was established as official German currency in 1924.
94 Adolf Dorner, ed., *Mathematik im Dienste der nationalpolitischen Erziehung mit Anwendungsbeispielen aus Volkswissenschaft, Geläendekunde und Naurwissenschaft* (Frankfurt am Main: Fischer, 1935), 42. An English translation of the title would be as follows: "Mathematics in the Service of National Political Education with Examples Drawn from Social Science, Folk Art and Natural Science." An English translation of the aforementioned citation, with the title untranslated, appears in Burleigh, *Death and Deliverance*, ix. Proctor, *Racial Hygiene*, 183–5, also has reproduced several "mathematics" questions from the Dorner book.
95 This is Exhibit 39T-1021, Heidelberger Dokumente, Roll 18, Item 000–12–463 of the National Archives, Washington, DC. It indicates that organized euthanasia was being performed on adults during the wartime.
96 Proctor, "Nazi Doctors, Racial Medicine, and Human Experimentation," 24; see also Proctor, *Racial Hygiene*, 184–5.
97 Ibid.
98 See Proctor, *Racial Hygiene*, 179–89.
99 Cardinal John O'Connor, "A Cardinal's Chilling Warning," *New Covenant* (May 1989): 23–4.
100 "Always to Care, Never to Kill," *First Things* (February 1992): 45–7, also accessible at www.firstthings.com/article/1992/02/006-always-to-care-never-to-kill
101 Ibid.
102 Ibid.
103 Richard Rotondi, "Killing as Caring: The False Charity of Euthanasia," *Orthodoxy Today*, accessible at www.orthodoxytoday.org/articles/RotondiEuthanasia.php.
104 Ibid., citing Walker Percy, *The Thanatos Syndrome* (New York: Farrar, Straus, Giroux, 1987), esp. 358–62.
105 The fact that palliative care and pain-management today have advanced greatly, rendering the standard arguments for assisted suicide almost useless, is beyond the scope of argument. It does suggest, however, that activists for euthanasia are interested in more than mere suffering due to pain.

8 Conclusion

Dignity, depravity, and moral law

Robert P. George, the McCormick Professor of Jurisprudence at Princeton University, has argued that any healthy or decent society – what I have been calling "civil society" – will rest on three pillars for its life and sustenance. These "non-negotiables," according to George, are respect for human personhood with its intrinsic dignity, the institution of the family (what George calls "the original ministry of health, education and welfare"[1]), and a reasonably just system of law and government. Although family, law, and government are beyond the scope of this volume, the first pillar, human dignity, has been an important theme. In fact, it is not inaccurate to contend that the health of families and the status of law and government will both mirror a *proper or deficient* view of the human person.[2] Whether my reader will grant that proposition is another question, but that is an argument for another day.

As Chapter 7 was meant to illustrate, any society or culture that does not ascribe to the human person an intrinsic worth – a worth that extends from the womb to end-of life issues and governs all ethical and bioethical matters in between – in time will come to view human beings as mere instruments to other ends, and hence expendable. In that scenario, life for some – and indeed *the life of some* – becomes *lebensunwert*, which is to say, simply not worthy of living. But also part of my argument in the previous chapter was the assumption that such attitudes toward human personhood do not suddenly appear overnight and out of nowhere; they are tolerated, and then in time they are *cultivated.*

At this point, permit me to state categorically, and in no uncertain terms, what has been implicit throughout the book. Issues of religious freedom are an important indication or measurement – a sign, if you will – of our understanding of human nature. And permit me once more to "connect the dots": a society in which people are assisted toward death, for whatever reason, is *well past* the place of wrestling with issues of religious freedom. At that point, the "sacred rights of conscience" have disappeared and no longer have any meaning whatsoever. All that is left is the material realm and political power, both of which will be used *against* and not *for* the human person. In such a society, people do not flourish; they are repressed and oppressed. In such a society, not moral law but dictatorial law is supreme.

But let us rehearse the relationship between human dignity, religious freedom, and natural moral law one final time. Respect of the human person, with its commitment to human dignity, does not derive from cultural or political institutions – even relatively "sound" institutions – *per se*. Rather,

> it requires a cultural ethos in which people *act from conviction to treat one another as human beings should be treated*: with respect, civility, justice. The best legal and political institutions ever devised are of little value where selfishness, contempt for others, dishonesty, injustice and other types of immorality and irresponsibility flourish.[3]

Liberty is both a necessary prerequisite for and the result of human flourishing. Of course, here I refer not to the "liberty" that typically means the unencumbered, autonomous self of Western culture – a *liberty unto license*, if you will, which at base is rank nihilism. Rather, I am referring to a basic freedom with eminently social implications that is necessary for human flourishing – the freedom to believe and act in accordance with one's deepest moral convictions. Let us call it religious freedom, the "first freedom." Any intrusion into this sort of liberty must be qualified and justified. And that intrusion is justified *only* when and where it is based on some objective good, which in turn yields the fruit of good for others and for the individual. If, on the other hand, the state or the political authority fails to acknowledge that understanding of "liberty," it commits a wrong – an injustice – that undermines human well-being and flourishing.[4] Because governmental institutions, at least in relatively free nations, themselves are constituted by people who are moral agents (whether for better or for worse) and who (hopefully) are motivated by a sense of moral obligation to better the lives of *others*, we are back at square one. *What does it mean to be human?* Alas, how we view human personhood is *everything*.

Buttressing my argument in this book is the view that, apart from the natural law, morality, and law are fluid at best. That is, as a transcendent source of morality, the natural law exists beyond autonomous individuals and individual cultures. As noted in earlier chapters, it is a law that we do not create but which we know through reason's intuitive powers and are constrained to obey. Such a metaphysical starting-point, of course, places the "natural lawyer" in opposition to what many professional ethicists today would advance. We cite again Jonathan Glover, who denies the intrinsic wrongness of certain types of killing, inclusive of infanticide, and has argued for a humanly constructed "morality." "The prospects of reviving belief in a moral law are dim," Glover insists. "Morality could be abandoned, or *it can be re-created*. It may survive in a more defensible form when seen to be a *human creation. We can shape it* to serve people's needs and interests."[5] "Creating" something new according to people's "needs and interests," will Glover's proposal make us more or less humane?

Notice here the clashing of two views of moral reality. On the one hand is the time-tested tradition of wisdom and natural law, extending from ancients to "post-moderns," by which standards of right and wrong, justice and injustice, acceptable and unacceptable are not fluid or alterable according to human fancy and the imposition of power. On the other hand, we find the fairly recent denial of moral common ground by professional ethicists, philosophers, and behavioral theorists. According to these authorities, non-fluid moral law and fixed points of ethical reference are illusory; "morality" is to be constructed according to "people's needs and interests."

But as University of Texas philosopher J. Budziszewski and others in the natural law tradition have argued with considerable persuasion, there *is* a common moral ground. There *are* moral truths that are common to all human beings.[6] And the name of that common moral ground is the natural law, the law "written on the heart," in the words of one ancient writer.[7] Stated differently and in negative terms, not everything that is "legal" or culturally permissible is morally permissible and just. As evidence, think not only of culturally specific forms of behavior or ritual such as burning widows on funeral pyres, female genital mutilation, cannibalistic tendencies, or human sacrifice but also of *universally proscribed* forms of behavior such as murder, thievery, dishonesty, incest, and defrauding others. This wider moral framework goes by the name of *natural* law because it corresponds to our fundamental *nature*, to human design, to the way in which we are created and how we function as moral agents. Here, however, we must be clear about we do *not* mean by "nature." Natural law does not refer to mere habit or inclination or custom, since all of these can be shaped, compromised, or ignored, for good or for ill. Nor is it dependent on social contract and agreement. Nor does it issue from mere biology, inasmuch as human instincts and desires may or may not be beneficial, serving the "good," and morally sound. In fact, very often the moral sense will necessarily *counter* the biological instinct, for the good of both others and ourselves. (Just ask any parent.) And we call it natural *law* because it is *universally binding* and because it serves as a *guide* for all human beings in moral matters. In truth, as moral creatures we should perhaps be troubled more by the common moral ground shared by diverse cultures around the globe than by their differences. In sum, then, natural law asks what is the end or goal of human nature and how laws can assist humans in fulfilling that end.[8]

Moral law, as we have attempted to show in previous chapters, is *pre-legal* and *pre-political* in its nature. Recall the German example: positive law had been coopted, and this over a period of decades. Of note is the fact that this coopting process was guided primarily (though not exclusively) by legal minds, psychiatrists, and those working in medical science. Eventual resistance to Nazi tyranny, and later reflective responses to that tyranny by the nations, had recourse to only one foundation: a higher moral law. Positive law *per se* lacks any binding force, any sense of enduring moral obligation. What's more, the question of whether something might be right or wrong, just or unjust, is meaningless to the positivist, who gauges moral matters according to a materialist and utilitarian ethic. For the utilitarian positivist, not what is morally right but what accords with *the will to power* or with *the majority* is lodged at the heart of legal and political decisions.[9] It is for this reason that universal declarations on human rights followed on the heels of WWII's conclusion, in the awareness that there are human moral obligations that are *universal* in scope and *binding* in character. Moral obligations simply *cannot exist* apart from the reality of a higher moral law. Insofar as laws have an ethical aim or end, law and morality may not be separated.[10]

Democratic tyranny

But perhaps the reader is skeptical. Does anyone *really* care about natural law? Does *anyone* care about human dignity issues? Who *really* cares about issues of fundamental liberty? And *why* care about the relationship between natural law, human dignity, and religious freedom? After all, to ask such questions is to be decidedly out of step with the times. I confess: such very well may be the case. But to counter "soft" forms of "totalitarianism," which are emerging in Western societies, and to sound the alarm against majoritarian forms of "tyranny," as Tocqueville warned against 180 years removed, might rather be "what the doctor ordered." In his important 1993 encyclical *Evangelium Vitae*, noted in an earlier chapter, John Paul II cautions in the Tocquevillian spirit against "idolizing" democracy to the point of "making it a substitute for morality or a panacea for immorality."[11] This he understands as symptomatic of our day, at the heart of which lies the ethical relativism which characterizes much of present-day culture:

> There are those who consider such relativism an essential condition of democracy, inasmuch as it alone is held to guarantee tolerance, mutual respect between people and acceptance of the decisions of the majority, whereas moral norms considered to be objective and binding are held to lead to authoritarianism and intolerance.[12]

In its essence, John Paul remind us, "democracy is a 'system' and as such is a means and not an end." This means that "[i]ts 'moral' value is not automatic, but depends on conformity to the moral law to which it, like every other form of human behavior, must be subject: in other words, its morality depends on the morality of the ends which it pursues and of the means which it employs."[13]

Is it possible that *both* forms of tyranny – harder forms in overtly totalitarian states where minorities currently are being violently persecuted *and* softer forms in the secular West where moral norms are eschewed and religious freedom issues are beginning to coagulate – need our vigilance? When basic human freedoms – at the heart of which stands religious freedom – are being threatened or in danger of vanishing, we must have the courage to help create an open and frank cultural dialogue. This is true particularly in a time when "a reductive secularism which would delegitimize the Church's participation in public debate about the issues which are determining the future of American society" needs to be countered.[14] When, for example, enacted laws require people to do what is unjust or morally wrong, not only do citizens *not* have to obey them, but they are required, morally speaking, to *disobey* them.[15] Now is such a time, I would maintain. Perhaps a bit of recent history, in light of the previous chapter, is useful before I conclude.

In the year 1938, German legal theorist Heinrich Rommen (1897–1967) fled Nazi Germany, landing in the United States where he would eventually teach from 1953 until 1967 (at Georgetown University). Rommen's story is instructive. During the volatile years of the post-Weimar Republic, Rommen wrote *Der Staat in katholischen Gedankenwelt* (1935) and *Die ewige Wiederkehr des Naturrechts* (1936).[16] In the latter work (translated literally "The Eternal Return of the Natural Law"), Rommen traces the natural law tradition from its legacy in Greco-Roman culture through the age of scholasticism and its turning point in the thought of Hugo Grotius to the age of rationalism and its eventual displacement by legal positivism. Rommen concludes with what he calls "the reappearance" of natural law thought in more recent times.[17] This renaissance "has coincided with a return to a doctrine of materialist values in ethics."[18] But despite all appearances, he insists, "the rise and spread of contemporary totalitarianism do not invalidate the contention that a distinct revival of natural law is occurring."[19] In fact, modern forms of totalitarianism have "revitalized in its victims and its adversaries the idea of natural law."[20] The reason? Resistance to any form of totalitarianism, in which the end results of positivism appear as ethical and intellectual nihilism, must "look for support beyond any mere national tradition" and "base itself on something superior to history, race, class, scientific method, and the like."[21] In response to the typical and tragic totalitarian disposition of *law equals will*, Rommen well observes, "How seldom the theorists and practitioners of totalitarianism mention reason, and how frequently they glory in the triumph of the will!"[22]

Before his flight to the United States in 1938, it should be remembered, Rommen had been imprisoned by the Nazis because of his political and legal writings. Commentating on Rommen's legacy and what this might mean for future generations, natural law theorist Russell Hittinger writes that every generation "finds a new reason for the study of natural law."[23] And "[f]or Rommen and many others of his generation, totalitarianism provided that occasion."[24] For as Rommen believed, "When one of the relativist theories is made the basis of a totalitarian state, man is stirred to free himself from the pessimistic resignation that characterizes these relativist theories and to return to his principles."[25] One might even argue that people are stirred by softer forms of "totalitarianism" as well – forms that are shaped predominantly by materialistic or majoritarian tyranny.

But what precipitates this process – in *any* society – of moral degeneration? For both Rommen and Hittinger, part of the problem is the illusion that our legal and political institutions are "a sufficient bulwark against government by raw power – as though a system of positive law takes care of itself, requiring only the superintendence of certified professionals."[26] Typically forgotten is the fact that "legal institutions themselves can be made the object of the non-legal power struggle."[27]Indeed, periods of natural law recovery do seem to be triggered by periods of social upheaval. In the West, they are evidenced by two noteworthy developments: the post-WWII universal human rights declarations and, in the United States, by reactions to racial segregation and discrimination. (Thus, for example, Martin Luther King Jr.'s "Letter from a Birmingham Jail," which is rich in its dependence on natural law language and concepts.)[28]

These periods of social upheaval and cultural degeneration confront us with deeper questions – unavoidable questions – that any "civil society" sooner or later must confront. What is human dignity? What is justice? What does it mean to pursue truth? In what do human dignity and justice inhere? Why is law important? From whence does law derive its authority? Again, let us be very forthright about the implications: if law and justice and moral "truths" are arbitrary – that is, if they are social and cultural constructions to be created or modified or discarded – then "good" and "evil," "just" and "unjust" disappear. They become malleable, fashioned at will by those in power, and society (as we've known it) collapses.

But justice, which is the foundation of law, and moral "truths" are *not* arbitrary. They are *not* social and cultural constructions to be created or modified or discarded. And *all* citizens – indeed, atheists, theists, and all types of citizens in between – can be exceedingly glad for this reality. The natural law, as we have insisted, in its essence is pre-legal and pre-political. For this reason, it is antecedent to *any* exercise of political or legal or institutional power. Human rights cannot be conferred upon the individual by the state or by positive law, since these basic rights are valid absolutely and universally, whether or not a particular regime acknowledges them. When the state or positive law removes or abolishes these rights, it renders itself illegitimate insofar as justice is the foundation of all law and of any legitimate government. By themselves, positive and civil law cannot obligate and move human beings toward the deepest levels of moral obligation. In fact, they can negate or work *against* what moral law has inscribed in the hearts of human beings.

Because I have stressed throughout the book the "pre-political" and antecedent nature of the natural law, natural rights, and religious freedom, the reader might conclude that I have a low view of politics and political engagement. Quite the contrary. Before entering the university classroom full-time, I did public-policy research in our nation's capital in the realm of criminal justice. Those years, I confess, forever changed my view of politics and public engagement (for the better). Politics remains a part of the moral universe, as Heinrich Rommen insisted with great forcefulness. For this reason, it is inadequate merely to view politics as the technique or skill of acquiring and subsequently holding on to power through skilled manipulation and exploitation of other human beings. Politics, rather, should be seen as "the great architectonic art by which men build the institutions and protective forms of their individual and communal life for a more perfect realization of the good life."[29] Perfect? By no means. But "more perfect" in the sense of *flawed and needing improvement*? By all means.

The public nature of religious conviction

Serious religious conviction – and I write as a confessional Christian – always has a conspicuously public dimension. Because of this commitment – to public witness and to public principle – it may be useful to consider briefly two prevalent but misguided modes of thinking about religion and political engagement. Former Director of the Center for Religion and Society at Roanoke College Robert Benne describes these as the "separatist" and "fusionist" fallacies.[30] A word of caution about both is in order.

The first common distortion is to divorce religion and politics by claiming or requiring that they have nothing to do with each other. Notice that this separationism is produced by *both* militant secularists and the ardently religious, and in both crude and sophisticated forms. Its fruit is what the late Richard John Neuhaus called the "naked public square," wherein public life is tightly sealed off from religious presence and religious action.[31] Whether wittingly or unwittingly, these individuals and groups, in their distaste for religion becoming a public influence, tend to confuse the interaction of religion and politics with the "separation of church and state." In the end, however, to conflate the two is to corrupt both.

Most of the objections to the role of religion in political life, in Benne's view, amount to a "selective separationism" that invariably is opposed to a politically active "conservative" religion, frequently stigmatized as "fundamentalism." In fact, "selective separationists" are so bothered by conservatives' influence that they seem utterly blind to the ongoing and *pervasive* role of "liberal" religion's influence on political life. And when they rail against public religion, it is always the so-called religious right bogeyman receiving the brunt of their criticism.

While one form of separationism seeks to keep religion and politics separate because of its fear of religion, another type – "classical separationism" – operates on the assumption of politics' corrosive effect on religion. Given their optimism about the Church and thoroughgoing pessimism about the world, its representatives invariably take the pacifistic elements of the "Sermon on the Mount" as the key to Christian belief and activity. Because the world is full of violence, and politics is based on coercion by the state, there can be no compromise. Either the believer is devoted to "peace" or he must participate in a violent public sphere; there is no reconciling these two elements.

This form of separationism, alluded to in Chapter 6, continues to flourish among Anabaptist types (for example, Mennonites and Brethren) as well as in the thinking of theologians like John Howard Yoder and Stanley Hauerwas. Whatever the salutary features it might possess, Benne views this form of sectarianism as deficient precisely because it gives up on the world and, in its non-engagement, denies God's sovereignty over history in its practice (when not its theology).[32] The mainstream of the historic Christian faith, however, rejects this sectarian posture. From the standpoint of Christian theology, there can be no realm of human existence in which the presence and the commands of the Creator are *not* found and mediated. To participate actively in the affairs of men and nation is to cooperate with the divine care of the world as stewards.

The second distortion of the relationship between religion and politics is to bring them so closely together that they become fused. Fusion creates politicized religion or theological politics; in either arrangement, religion and politics are both corroded. Benne understands Nazism and Communism as bastardized and utopians versions of this fusion, in contrast to the more intentional theocratic model by which a particular party might be associated closely with faith and the divine purpose. And, of course, Islam, is thoroughly – and intentionally – theocratic; for Muslims, any division between God and "Caesar" would be nothing short of blasphemous.

In the U.S. context, given the flurry of shrill warnings against "theocracy" over the last 10 to 15 years, one would guess that massive religious oppression exists in America. (I have in mind such over-heated titles as *The Theocons*, *American Theocracy*, *Wayward Christian Soldiers*, *American Fascists: The Christian Right and the War on America*, *Kingdom Coming: The Rise of Christian Nationalism*, and *Religion, Politics, and the Christian Right: Post-9/11 Powers in American Empire*.) Diatribes like these, for Benne, are not only unconvincing but also downright dishonest. To call them "unconvincing" and "dishonest," I would even argue, is being charitable.

At the same time, Benne is not insensitive to the theocratic temptation. Christians are surely aware of those episodes in history, at least in Western history, when religion attempted to wield political power, thereby violating one of its essential principles – namely, that the Church is given the *persuasive* power of the Word and *not* the coercive power of the sword. Three classical traditions – Catholic, Lutheran, and Reformed – have theologies that clarify this important distinction, recognizing a tentative dualism (though not separation) between religious belief and the world.

In full agreement with Benne, I would suggest that the constructive task of properly construing the relationship between religion and politics is embodied in an "Augustinian realism." That is, we affirm particular theological *essentials* that necessarily inform political life. For the religious believer, this is done in the realization, noted earlier in the book, that we have two legitimate citizenships – the "city of man" and the "city of God"; the one, it needs reiterating, need not cancel out the other. Among the "essentials" belonging to an "Augustinian realism" would be the following: the wedding of justice and charity, the conviction that human nature is *both* dignified *and* depraved, the importance of a *tranquillitas ordinis* (a justly ordered peace) that must characterize the social order, the awareness of a qualitative difference between divine and human activity, and the motivation of religious faith – if it is authentic – to serve others.[33]

In his writing, Benne is quick to acknowledge that applying religious beliefs to social-cultural challenges and to matters of social and public policy is complex and rarely clear. Moreover, sound public policy is notoriously difficult to craft, given the give-and-take of the political process. Nevertheless, policy *must* be crafted, and *someone* must do the crafting. Hence, religiously minded citizens play a significant role in the shaping of responsible statecraft, which translates into both domestic social policy and foreign policy. Religious believers, it goes without saying, will need to find the appropriate "language" that will effectively communicate their values in the public sphere in ways that are meaningful to non-believers.

Of course, there will always be different *modes* of engaging in political activity and working in the public sphere. For some, it will be indirect, with an ethical focus on "character" and "conscience." For others, more direct modes may be intended. There will be occasions when religious believers will need to assume a more "prophetic" stance on particular issues, recognizing a moral obligation to protest a particular political ideology or policy prescription. This may mean, for example, extreme socio-cultural developments such as Nazism, apartheid in South Africa, or genocide in various nations. But it may take the form of countering totalitarian consumerism in Western societies, or the one-to-two million abortions that occur every year in the United States,[34] or attempts in Western societies to transmute the natural family in the name of "human rights" and "discrimination." Difficult as persuasion and confrontation are in our day, religious believers must have the courage to "translate" their convictions in the public arena. They can effectively address important policy issues not only through political activity and established NGOs but also through church agencies, service organizations, and similar mediating institutions that have a social, educational, or charitable trajectory. One need only think of the "hospital"[35] as a culture-shaping institution, which more often than not arose out of religious conviction and tough-minded charity.

A proper construal of religious freedom

Given the tendency toward disenchantment among many younger adults (at least in the in American context) – and I write on the heels of the supremely contentious 2016 U.S. Presidential election – I must reiterate the wisdom of Robert Benne's caution. Neither fusion nor separation is acceptable as a political option for citizens who are morally serious. Politics and political activity are a natural – and important – part of human culture, even when they are not the *only* part of our existence and when they do not define *ultimate* meaning in our lives. What's more, any measure of political participation in the wider public arena cannot rest on neat and tidy once-for-all or one-size-fits-all solutions. We will need to agonize over how best to respond to human need, and the level of that human need will, in the context of some issues (for example, the persecution of religious minorities), seem beyond our ability to respond. Regardless of the manner in which we contribute to the public sphere, our deepest convictions must be packaged and presented in fresh ways with the emergence of every new generation and in light of new moral and geopolitical challenges – challenges that are indeed daunting.

The main function of politics, at bottom, is "to establish an order and unity of cooperation among free persons and free associations" so as to more effectively realize "the common good under the rule of law."[36] Rommen, I think, is correct: "Through the natural law alone can we solve the crucial political problem of the legitimacy of power and the duty of free persons to obey."[37] This is only because within the soul of every human being there resides the requirement – indeed the demands – that law must be anchored in morality. Otherwise, society cannot be just, and the most basic of freedoms will evaporate.

Religious liberty is not only about our ability to worship freely (although it entails that). As expressed in the 2012 document produced by U.S. Conference of Catholic Bishops' Ad Hoc Committee for Religious Liberty, "Our First, Most Cherished Liberty: A Statement on Religious Liberty,"

> It is about whether we [religious believers] can make our contribution to the common good of all Americans. Can we do the good works our faith calls us to do, without having to compromise that very same faith? Without religious liberty properly understood, all Americans suffer, deprived of the essential contribution in education, health care, feeding the hungry, civil rights, and social services that religious Americans make every day, both here at home and overseas. What is at stake is whether America will continue to have a free, creative, and robust civil society – or whether the state alone will determine who gets to contribute to the common good, and how they get to do it. Religious believers are part of American civil society, which includes neighbors helping each other, community associations, fraternal service clubs, sports leagues, and youth groups. All these Americans make their contribution to our common life, and they do not need the permission of the government to do so. Restrictions on religious liberty are an attack on civil society and the American genius for voluntary associations.[38]

For those of us living in the United States, religious freedom is our cultural heritage, our most cherished freedom. It is the "first freedom" because "if we are not free in our conscience and our practice of religion, all other freedoms are fragile. If citizens are not free in their own consciences, how can they be free in relation to others, or to the state?"[39] And if our obligations and duties to the Creator are impeded, or even worse, suppressed by political and legal authority, then we are no longer "a land of the free" and "*a beacon of hope for the world.*"[40]

What has become abundantly clear in the twenty-first century is that threats to human dignity – to the sanctity of human life – are *necessarily* threats to religious freedom, and vice versa. There exists an organic union between the two; where the one suffers – whether in the wider global context or in Western societies – the other suffers as well. And difficult as it is in our day for citizens of Western nations to agree on *anything*, certainly we should be able to agree that overt and at times violent persecution of "religious" minorities, regardless of their creed, is morally intolerable, indefensible, and needing a principled response. John L. Allen Jr., senior Vatican analyst for CNN, has framed the matter quite well: "In terms of both secular politics and Christian doctrine," those who suffer for their faith today "represent a wide range of instincts. Simply because people understand themselves to be religious believers does not mean that they cease to be citizens, or stop having their own opinions on political questions."[41] For this reason, it is imperative that people of good will ponder with utmost sobriety the moral-philosophical underpinnings of religious freedom, implicit in the natural law, which express themselves through the "cardinal" virtues of justice and charity. Embodied in what we call a "Golden Rule" ethic, these virtues, when wed together, impel us in "neighbor-love" toward those who are oppressed and who stand in dire need by virtue of having their most basic freedoms removed.

Recall an important implication of the "Good Samaritan" model. This embodiment of "neighbor-love" will be open to cross religious, ethnic, and cultural boundaries in order to help those who stand in dire need. This, then, is the moral "first principle" of the natural law – doing good and preventing evil – and it will not be satisfied until we are advocates for the "sacred rights of conscience," whether at home or abroad.

Notes

1 Robert P. George, "Common Principles, Common Foes," in Robert P. George, ed., *Conscience and Its Enemies: Confronting the Dogmas of Liberal Secularism* (Wilmington: ISI Books, 2013), 5.
2 Based on the natural law, the family as a basic social unit as well as its basis, namely, marriage, are antecedent to the state; they are pre-political.
3 George, "Common Principles, Common Foes," 5, emphasis added.
4 David F. Forte, "Family, Nurture, and Liberty," in David F. Forte, ed., *Natural Law and Contemporary Public Policy* (Washington, DC: Georgetown University, 1998), 79–106, has helpfully developed the implications of the state and human nurture in a compelling way.
5 Jonathan Glover, *Humanity: A Moral History of the Twentieth Century* (New Haven: Yale University Press, 2000), 41. For Glover's views as they inform beginning-of-life and life-enhancement issues, see also *Causing Death and Saving Lives* (New York: Penguin, 1977).
6 J. Budziszewski, *What We Can't Not Know: A Guide* (Dallas: Spence, 2003), esp. 3–16. See as well his *Line Through the Heart: Natural Law as Fact, Theory, and Sign of Contradiction* (Wilmington: ISI Books, 2011) and *Written on the Heart: The Case for Natural Law* (Downers Grove: InterVarsity, 1997). While the last two decades have been witness to numerous works on the natural law,

in addition to Budziszewski, representative are Jesse Covington, Bryan McGraw and Micah Watson, eds., *Natural Law and Evangelical Political Thought* (Lanham and Plymouth, UK: Lexington Books, 2013); Owen Anderson, *The Natural Moral Law: The Good After Modernity* (Cambridge and New York: Cambridge University Press, 2012); John Finnis, *Natural Law and Natural Rights*, 2nd ed. (Oxford and New York: Oxford University Press, 2011); Robert C. Baker, ed., *Natural Law: A Lutheran Reappraisal* (St. Louis: Concordia, 2011); David VanDrunen, *Natural Law and the Two Kingdoms* (Grand Rapids and Cambridge, UK: Eerdmans, 2010);J. Daryl Charles, *Retrieving the Natural Law: A Return to Moral First Things* (Critical Issues in Bioethics; Grand Rapids and Cambridge, UK: Eerdmans, 2008); Matthew Levering, *Biblical Natural Law: A Theocentric and Teleological Approach* (Oxford and New York: Oxford University Press, 2008); Stephen J. Grabill, *Rediscovering the Natural Law in Reformed Theological Ethics* (Grand Rapids and Cambridge, UK: Eerdmans, 2006); Jean Porter, *Nature as Reason: A Thomistic Theory of the Natural Law* (Grand Rapids and Cambridge, UK: Eerdmans, 2005); Howard P. Kainz, *Natural Law: An Introduction and Re-Examination* (Peru: Open Court, 2004); Russell Hittinger, *The First Grace: Rediscovering the Natural Law in a Post-Christian World* (Wilmington: ISI Books, 2003); Russell Hittinger, *Natural Law and Divine Law: Reclaiming the Tradition for Christian Ethics* (Grand Rapids and Cambridge, UK: Eerdmans, 1999); Nigel Biggar and Rufus Blacks, eds., *The Revival of Natural Law: Philosophical, Theological, and Ethical Responses to the Finnis-Grisez School* (Aldershot, UK and Burlington: Ashgate, 2000); Robert P. George, *In Defense of Natural Law* (Oxford: Clarendon, 1999); Robert P. George, *Natural Law Theory: Contemporary Essays* (Oxford: Clarendon, 1994); Charles E. Rice and David F. Forte, ed., *Natural Law and Contemporary Public Policy* (Washington, DC: Georgetown University Press, 1998); David Novak, *Natural Law in Judaism* (Cambridge and New York: Cambridge University Press, 1998); and Michael Cromartie, ed., *A Preserving Grace: Protestants, Catholics, and Natural Law* (Grand Rapids and Washington, DC: Eerdmans and Ethics & Public Policy Center, 1997).

7 St. Paul in Romans 2:14–15.

8 So, Forte, 84.

9 In both of the major twentieth-century totalitarianisms – Nazism and Communism – society was organized and engineered along positivist lines.

10 Few have argued this linkage with greater force than Heinrich A. Rommen, *The Natural Law: A Study in Legal and Social History and Philosophy*, trans. Thomas R. Hanley (Indianapolis: Liberty Fund, 1998), 16–89.

11 John Paul II, *Evangelium Vitae* (1995) no. 70, accessible at http://w2.vatican.va/content/john-paul-ii/en/encyclicals/documents/hf_jp-ii_enc_25031995_evangelium-vitae.html.

12 Ibid.

13 Ibid.

14 So, Benedict XVI, *Ad limina* (2012), an address to be the U.S. Conference of Catholic Bishops (January 19, 2012), accessible at http://w2.vatican.va/content/benedict-xvi/en/speeches/2012/january/documents/hf_ben-xvi_spe_20120119_bishops-usa.html.

15 As famously declared by Thomas Aquinas, *lex iniqua lex non est* ("*an unjust law is not a law*") (*Summa Theologica* I-II Q. 95, a. 2). Aquinas, of course, was not the first to insist on this. We find it argued in Aristotle (*Politics* III.6 [1279a8]) and Augustine (*On Free Choice of the Will* I.5) as well.

16 Heinrich A. Rommen, *Die ewige Wiederkehr des Naturrechts* (Leipzig: Verlag Jakob Hegner, 1936); the revised edition was published by Herder in 1947.

17 Rommen, *The Natural Law*, 119–38. One can certainly speak of a "renewal" of natural law thinking in the 1940s, as evidenced by international declarations

concerning human rights. This recovery of natural law was chiefly a Catholic phenomenon, evidenced in the writings of people like Rommen, Jacque Maritain, Yves Simon, and John Courtney Murray.

18 Ibid., 133.
19 Ibid.
20 Ibid.
21 Ibid.
22 Ibid., 234.
23 Russell Hittinger, "Introduction," in Heinrich A. Rommen, ed., *The Natural Law: A Study in Legal and Social History and Philosophy*(trans. Thomas R. Hanley; Indianapolis: Liberty Fund, 1998), xii.
24 Ibid.
25 Heinrich A. Rommen, *The State in Catholic Thought: A Treatise in Political Philosophy* (St. Louis: Herder, 1945), 48, cited by Hittinger, ibid.
26 Hittinger, ibid.
27 Rommen, *The State in Catholic Thought*, 212, cited in Hittinger, ibid.
28 Martin Luther King, Jr., "Letter from a Birmingham Jail" (April 16, 1963), accessible at https://kinginstitute.stanford.edu/king-papers/documents/letter-birmingham-jail.
29 Rommen, *The Natural Law*, 235.
30 See Robert Benne, *Good and Bad Ways to Think about Religion and Politics* (Grand Rapids: Eerdmans, 2010).
31 Richard John Neuhaus, *The Naked Public Square: Religion and Democracy in America* (Grand Rapids: Eerdmans, 1984).
32 This is true even when Yoderians and Hauerwasians vehemently deny this charge.
33 Few have developed the implications of "Augustinian realism" as extensively – and as thoughtfully – as Jean Bethke Elshtain. See her *Augustine and the Limits of Politics* (Notre Dame: University of Notre Dame Press, 1995).
34 Let us be frank: morally speaking, "choice" begins *before* a child is conceived, not afterward.
35 In this vein, note the common etymological root of "hospital" and "hospice."
36 *Rommen, The Natural Law*, 235.
37 Ibid., 236.
38 www.ortv.org/pdf_documents/Our_First_Most_Cherished_Liberty,%204-12-2012.pdf.
39 Ibid.
40 Ibid.
41 John L. Allen Jr., *The Global War on Christians: Dispatches from the Front Lines of Anti-Christian Persecution* (New York: Image, 2013), 239. For Allen, the global war on Christians and their faith in our day is "the greatest story never told" (243).

Bibliography

Ahlstrom, Sydney E. *A Religious History of the American People*. New Haven: Yale University Press, 1972.

Allen, Brooke. *Moral Minority: Our Skeptical Founding Fathers*. Chicago: Ivan R. Dee, 2006.

Allen, Christopher. *Islamophobia*. Burlington: Ashgate, 2010.

Allen, John L., Jr. *The Global War on Christians: Dispatches from the Front Lines of Anti-Christian Persecution*. New York: Image, 2013.

Allen, William B., ed. *George Washington: A Collection*. Indianapolis: Liberty, 1988.

Alley, Robert S., ed. *James Madison on Religious Liberty*. Buffalo: Prometheus, 1985.

"Always to Care, Never to Kill." *First Things* (February 1992): 45–7. Accessible at www.firstthings.com/article/1992/02/006-always-to-care-never-to-kill.

Anderson, Owen. *The Natural Moral Law: The Good After Modernity*. Cambridge: Cambridge University Press, 2012.

Anscombe, E.M.B. "War and Murder." In M.M. Wakin, ed., *War, Morality, and the Military Profession*. Boulder: Westview, 1979. Pp. 285–98.

Aquinas, Thomas. *Commentary on the Nicomachean Ethics*. 2 vols. Trans. C.I. Litzinger. Chicago: Regnery, 1964.

———. *On Charity (De Caritate)*. Trans. Lottie H. Kendzierski. Milwaukee: Marquette University Press, 1984.

———. *Summa Theologica*. Trans. Fathers of the English Dominican Province. New York: Benziger Bros., 1947.

Aristotle. *Nicomachean Ethics*, 3rd ed. Trans. Martin Ostwald. New York: Palgrave Macmillan, 1986.

———. *Politics*. Trans. C.D.C. Reeve. Indianapolis: Hackett, 1998.

Arkes, Hadley. *First Things: An Inquiry into the First Principles of Morals and Justice*. Princeton: Princeton University Press, 1986.

Attarian, John. "In Dispraise of Tolerance, Sensitivity and Compassion." *The Social Critic* (Spring 1998): 14–23.

Audi, Robert and Nicholas Wolterstorff. *Religion in the Public Square: The Place of Religious Convictions in Public Debate*. Point/Counterpoint. Lanham: Rowman & Littlefield, 1997.

Augustine, St. *City of God*. Trans. Henry Bettenson. London: Penguin, 2003.

———. *Epistle 138 ("To Marcellinus")*. Reproduced in E.M. Atkins and R.J. Dodaro, eds., *Augustine: Political Writings*. Cambridge Texts in the History of Political Thought. Cambridge: Cambridge University Press, 2001. Pp. 30–42.

———. Epistle 155 ("To Macedonius"). In *Letters*. Vol. 3. Trans. Wilfrid Parsons. Washington, DC: The Catholic University of America Press, 1964. Pp. 305–18.

———. "On the Morals of the Catholic Church." In *Nicene and Post-Nicene Fathers*. I/IV, ed. Philip Schaff. Grand Rapids: Eerdmans, 1956. Pp. 41–63.

Baker, Robert C., ed. *Natural Law: A Lutheran Reappraisal*. St. Louis: Concordia, 2011.

Bakewell, Charles M. *Source Book in Ancient Philosophy*. New York: Scribner, 1907.

Barrett, David B. and Todd Johnson. "Quantifying Alternate Futures of Religion and Religions." *Futures* 36, no. 9 (2004): 447–60.

Barth, Karl. *The Church and the War*. New York: Palgrave Macmillan, 1944.

———. *Church DogmaticsII/1*. Trans. Geoffrey W. Bromiley. Edinburgh: T. & T. Clark, 1961.

———. *Protestant Theology in the Nineteenth Century: Its Background and History*. Rev. ed. London: SCM, 2001.

Bayle, Pierre. *Pensées diverses sur la comète*. In Elizabeth Labrousse, ed., *Vol. 3 Oeuvres diverses*. 5 vols. Hildesheim: Georg Olms, 1965–1970.

Beauchamp, Tom L. "The Failure of Theories of Personhood." *Kennedy Institute of Ethics Journal* 9, no. 4 (1999): 309–24.

Benedict XVI. *Ad limina* (2012). Accessible at http://w2.vatican.va/content/benedict-xvi/en/speeches/2012/january/documents/hf_ben-xvi_spe_20120119_bishops-usa.html.

———. *Address to the General Assembly of the United Nations* (April 18, 2008). Accessible at http://w2.vatican.va/content/benedict-xvi/en/speeches/2008/april/documents/hf_ben-xvi_spe_20080418_un-visit.html.

———. *Caritas in Veritate* (2009). Accessible at http://w2.vatican.va/content/benedict-xvi/en/encyclicals/documents/hf_ben-xvi_enc_20090629_caritas-in-veritate.html.

———. *Religious Freedom, the Path to Peace* (2011). Accessible at http://w2.vatican.va/content/benedict-xvi/en/messages/peace/documents/hf_ben-xvi_mes_20101208_xliv-world-day-peace.html.

———. *Truth and Tolerance: Christian Belief and World Religions*. Trans. Henry Taylor. San Francisco: Ignatius, 2004.

Benne, Robert. *Good and Bad Ways to Think About Religion and Politics*. Grand Rapids: Eerdmans, 2010.

Berger, Peter L. "Afterword." In James Davison Hunter and Os Guinness, eds., *Articles of Faith, Articles of Peace: The Religious Liberty Clauses and the American Public Philosophy*. Washington, DC: Brookings Institution, 1990. Pp. 114–21.

———. "The Desecularization of the World: A Global Overview." In Peter L. Berger, ed., *The Desecularization of the World: Resurgent Religion and World Politics*. Washington, DC and Grand Rapids: Ethics & Public Policy Center and Eerdmans, 1999. Pp. 1–18.

Berman, Morris. *The Twilight of American Culture*. New York: W.W. Norton, 2000.

Bidinotto, Robert James. "Crime and Moral Retribution." In Robert James Bidinotto, ed., *Criminal Justice? The Legal System Versus Individual Responsibility*. Irvington-on-the-Hudson: Foundation for Economic Education, Inc., 1994. Pp. 181–200.

Biggar, Nigel. *In Defence of War*. Oxford: Oxford University Press, 2013.

———. "Saving the Secular: The Public Vocation of Moral Theology." *Journal of Religious Ethics* 37, no. 1 (2009): 159–78.

Biggar, Nigel and Rufus Blacks, eds. *The Revival of Natural Law: Philosophical, Theological, and Ethical Responses to the Finnis-Grisez School*. Aldershot: Ashgate, 2000.

Binding, Karl and Alfred Hoche. *Die Freigabe der Vernichtung lebensunwerten Freigabe*. Leipzig: Felix Meiner Verlag, 1920.

Bloom, Allan. *The Closing of the American Mind: How Higher Education Has Failed Democracy and Impoverished the Souls of Today's Students*. New York: Simon & Schuster, 1987.

Börner, Wilhelm. "Euthanasie." *Das monistische Jahrhundert* 2 (1913): 251–4.

Braaten, Carl E. "Protestants and Natural Law." *First Things* 19 (January 1992): 20–6.

Braaten, Carl E. and Robert W. Jenson, eds. *The Two Cities of God: The Church's Responsibility for the Earthly City*. Grand Rapids: Eerdmans, 1997.

British Pregnancy Advisory Service. *UK: New Guidance for Pharmacists Retains 'Conscience Clause.'* (March 29, 2010). Accessible at www.reproductivereview.org/index.php/rr/article/724.

Brunner, Emil. *Justice and the Social Order*. New York: Harper & Bros., 1945.

Brunner, Emil and Karl Barth. *Natural Theology*. Trans. Peter Fraenkel. London: Jeffrey Bless/Centenary Press, 1946.

Budziszewski, J. "The Illusion of Moral Neutrality." *First Things* (August/September 1993): 32–7.

———. *The Line Through the Heart: Natural Law as Fact, Theory, and Sign of Contradiction*. Wilmington: ISI Books, 2011.

———. *The Revenge of Conscience: Politics and the Fall of Man*. Dallas: Spence,1999.

———. *True Tolerance: Liberalism and the Necessity of Judgment*. New Brunswick: Transaction, 1992.

———. *What We Can't Not Know: A Guide*. Dallas: Spence, 2003.

———. *Written on the Heart: The Case for Natural Law*. Downers Grove: InterVarsity Press,1997.

Burleigh, Michael. *Death and Deliverance: "Euthanasia" in Germany ca. 1900–1945*. Cambridge: Cambridge University Press, 1994.

Butler, Jon, Grant Wacker and Randall Balmer. *Religion in American Life: A Short History*. New York: Oxford University Press, 2003. Pp. 1–162.

Calhoun, Craig J., Mark Juergensmeyer, and Jonathan VanAntwerpen, eds. *Rethinking Secularism*. Oxford: Oxford University Press, 2011.

Calvin, John. *Institutes of the Christian Religion*. Trans. Henry Beveridge. Grand Rapids: Eerdmans, 1957.

Carlson-Thies, Stanley. "Religious Freedom: The Cornerstone of Strong Social Architecture (Part One)." *Comment* (May 31, 2013). Accessible at www.cardus.ca/comment/article/3974/religious-freedom-the-cornerstone-of-strong-social-architecture-part-one/.

Carter, Stephen L. *God's Name in Vain: The Wrongs and Rights of Religion in Politics*. New York: Basic Books, 2000.

Catechism of the Catholic Church. Washington, DC: United States Catholic Conference, 1994. English trans. Accessible at www.vatican.va/archive/ENG0015/_INDEX.HTM.

Ceaser, James W. *Designing a Polity: America's Constitution in Theory and Practice*. Lanham: Rowman & Littlefield, 2011.

Chaplin, Jonathan. "Rejecting Neutrality, Respecting Diversity: From 'Liberal Pluralism' to Christian Pluralism." *Christian Scholars Review* 35, no. 2 (Winter 2006): 143–75.

Charles, J. Daryl. "Burying the Wrong Corpse: Evangelicals and Natural Law." In Jesse Covington, Bryan McGraw and Micah Watson, eds., *Natural Law and Evangelical Political Thought*. Lanham: Lexington Books, 2013. Pp. 3–34.
———. "Capital Crime and Punishment: Reflections on Violating Human Sanctity." *Touchstone* 15, no. 2 (September 2002): 19–26.
———. "Do Not Suppose that I Have Come: The Ethic of the Sermon on the Mount Reconsidered." *Southwestern Journal of Theology* 46, no. 3 (2004): 47–70.
———. "Engaging the (Neo)Pagan Mind." *Trinity Journal* 16, (1995): 47–62.
———. "The Ethics of Humanitarian Intervention." In Jonathan Chaplin and Robert Joustra, eds., *God and Global Order: The Power of Religion in American Foreign Policy*. Waco: Baylor University Press, 2010. Pp. 145–69.
———. "The Moral Underpinnings of Just Retribution: Justice and Charity in Symbiosis." *Providence: A Journal of Christianity and American Foreign Policy* 3 (Spring 2016): 5–16.
———. "Outrageous Atrocity or Moral Imperative? The Ethics of Capital Punishment." *Studies in Christian Ethics* (Fall 1993): 1–14.
———. "Pacifists, Patriots, or Both? Second Thoughts on Pre-Constantinian Attitudes Toward Soldiering and War." *Logos: A Journal of Catholic Thought and Culture* 13, no. 2 (2010): 17–55.
———. "Passionately Seeking the Truth: Unpunctual Protestant Reflections on *Fides et Ratio*." *Pro Ecclesia* 11, no. 2 (Spring 2002): 133–45.
———. *Retrieving the Natural Law: A Return to Moral First Things*. Critical Issues in Bioethics. Grand Rapids: Eerdmans, 2008.
———. *The Unformed Conscience of Evangelicalism: Recovering the Church's Moral Vision*. Downers Grove: InterVarsity Press, 2002.
Charles, J. Daryl and Timothy J. Demy. *War, Peace, and Christianity: Questions and Answers from a Just-War Perspective*. Wheaton: Crossway, 2010.
Church, Forrest. *So Help Me God: The Founding Fathers and the First Great Battle over Church and State*. Orlando: Harcourt, 2007.
Ci, Jiwei. *The Two Faces of Justice*. Cambridge: Harvard University Press, 2006.
Cicero. *Cicero, On the Laws*. Trans. Clinton W. Keyes. Loeb Classical Library. Cambridge: Harvard University Press, 1928.
———. *On the Republic*. Trans. Clinton W. Keyes. Loeb Classical Library. Cambridge: Harvard University Press, 1928.
Clair, Joseph. "Wolterstorff on Love and Justice: An Augustinian Response." *Journal of Religious Ethics* 41, no. 1 (March 2013): 138–67.
Clouser, Roy. *The Myth of Religious Neutrality: An Essay on the Hidden Role of Religious Belief in Theories*. Notre Dame: University of Notre Dame Press, 1991.
Conot, Robert. *Justice at Nuremberg*. New York: Palgrave Macmillan, 1983.
Conquest, Robert. *Reflections on a Ravaged Century*. New York: W.W. Norton, 2000.
Conyers, A.J. *The Long Truce: How Toleration Made the World Safe for Power and Profit*. Dallas: Spence, 2001.
Corey, David D. and J. Daryl Charles. *The Just War Tradition: An Introduction*. Wilmington: ISI Books, 2012.
Courtois, Stéphane, Nicolas Werth, Jean-Louis Panné, Andrzej Paczkowski, Karel Bartošek and Jean-Louis Margolin. *The Black Book of Communism: Crimes, Terror, Repression*. Trans. Jonathan Murphy and Mark Kramer. Cambridge: Harvard University Press, 1999.
Covington, Jesse, Bryan McGraw and Micah Watson, eds. *Natural Law and Evangelical Political Thought*. Lanham: Lexington Books, 2013.

Crocker, David A. "Retribution and Reconciliation." *Philosophy and Public Policy* 20, no. 1 (2000): 1–6.
Cromartie, Michael, ed. *A Preserving Grace: Protestants, Catholics, and Natural Law*. Grand Rapids and Washington, DC: Eerdmans and Ethics & Public Policy Center, 1997.
Curry, Thomas J. *The First Freedoms: Church and State in America to the Passage of the First Amendment*. Oxford: Oxford University Press, 1986.
Deficiencies of the Confederation. George Washington to John Jay (August 1, 1786). Accessible at http://press-pubs.uchicago.edu/founders/print_documents/v1ch5s11.html.
Dignitatis Humanae (1965). Declaration on Religious Freedom of the Second Vatican Ecumenical Council. Accessible at www.vatican.va/archive/hist_councils/ii_vatican_council/documents/vat-ii_decl_19651207_dignitatis-humanae_en.html.
Dolezal, James E. *God Without Parts: Divine Simplicity and the Metaphysics of God's Absoluteness*. Eugene: Pickwick Publications, 2011.
Dorner, Adolf, ed. *Mathematik im Dienste der nationalpolitischen Erziehung mit Anwendungsbeispielen aus Volkswissenschaft, Geläendekunde und Naurwissenschaft*. Frankfurt am Main: Fischer, 1935.
Dörner, Klaus. "Nationalsozialismus und Lebensvernichtung." *Vierteljahrhefte für Zeitgeschichte* 15, (1967): 121–52.
Dreisbach, Daniel L. "The Bible and the Political Culture of the American Founding." In Daniel L. Dreisbach and Mark David Hall, eds., *Faith and the Founders of the American Republic*. Oxford: Oxford University Press, 2014. Pp. 152–9.
———. "Defining and Testing the Prohibition on Religious Establishments in the Early Republic." In T. Jeremy Gunn and John Witte, Jr., eds., *No Establishment of Religion: America's Original Contribution to Religious Liberty*. Oxford: Oxford University Press, 2012. Pp. 252–3.
———. "Famous Founders and Forgotten Founders: What's the Difference, and Does the Difference Matter?" In Daniel L. Dreisbach, Mark David Hall and Jeffry H. Morrison, eds., *The Forgotten Founders on Religion and Public Life*. Notre Dame: University of Notre Dame Press, 2009. Pp. 17–21.
———, ed. *Religion and Politics in the Early Republic: Jasper Adams and the Church-State Debate*. Lexington: University Press of Kentucky, 1996.
———. *Thomas Jefferson and the Wall of Separation Between Church and State*. New York: New York University, 2002.
Dreisbach, Daniel L. and Mark David Hall, eds. *Faith and the Founders of the American Republic*. Oxford: Oxford University Press, 2014.
———. eds. *The Sacred Rights of Conscience: Selected Readings on Religious Liberty and Church-State Relations in the American Founding*. Indianapolis: Liberty Fund, 2009.
Dreisbach, Daniel L., Mark David Hall and Jeffry H. Morrison, eds. *The Forgotten Founders on Religion and Public Life*. Notre Dame: University of Notre Dame Press, 2009.
———. eds. *The Founders on God and Government*. Lanham: Rowman & Littlefield, 2004.
Dworkin, Ronald. *Freedom's Law: The Moral Reading of the American Constitution*. Cambridge: Harvard University Press, 1999.
———. *Life's Dominion: An Argument About Abortion, Euthanasia, and Individual Freedom*. New York: A.A. Knopf, 1993.
———. *Taking Rights Seriously*. Cambridge: Harvard University Press, 1987.

Ellul, Jacques. *The Theological Foundation of Law*. Trans. Marguerite Wieser. New York: Seabury Press, 1969.
———. *To Will and to Do*. Trans. C. Edward Hopkin. Philadelphia: Pilgrim Press, 1969.
Elshtain, Jean Bethke. *Augustine and the Limits of Politics*. Notre Dame: University of Notre Dame Press, 1995.
———. "How Should We Talk?" *Case Western Reserve Law Review* 49, no. 4 (1999): 731–46.
———. "Just War and an Ethics of Responsibility." In Eric Patterson, ed., *Ethics Beyond War's End*. Washington, DC: Georgetown University Press, 2012. Pp. 123–44.
———. *Women and War*. Rev. ed. Chicago: University of Chicago Press, 1995.
Emon, Anver M., Matthew Levering and David Novak. *Natural Law: A Jewish, Christian, and Muslim Trialogue*. Oxford: Oxford University Press, 2014.
Ernst, Carl W., ed. *Islamophobia in America: The Anatomy of Intolerance*. New York: Palgrave Macmillan, 2013.
Esbeck, Carl H. "A Typology of Church-State Relations in Current American Thought." In Luis E. Lugo, ed., *Religion, Public Life, and the American Polity*. Knoxville: University of Tennessee Press, 1994. Pp. 3–35.
Esposito, John L. and Ibrahim Kalin, eds. *The Challenge of Pluralism in the 21st Century*. Oxford: Oxford University Press, 2011.
Evans, C. Stephen. *Kierkegaard's Ethic of Love: Divine Commands and Moral Obligations*. Oxford: Oxford University Press, 2004.
The Federalist Papers. Accessible at www.let.rug.nl/usa/documents/1786-1800/the-federalist-papers/.
Ferreira, M. Jaime. *Love's Grateful Striving*. Oxford: Oxford University Press, 2001.
Finnis, John. *Natural Law and Natural Rights*. 2nd ed. Oxford: Oxford University Press, 2011.
Fitzpatrick, John C., ed. "George Washington to John Jay," (August 1, 1786). In *The Writings of George Washington from the Original Manuscript Sources, 1745–1799*. 39 vols. Washington, DC: Government Printing Office, 1931–44. Accessible at http://press-pubs.uchicago.edu/founders/print_documents/v1ch5s11.html.
Ford, Paul Leicester, ed. *The Autobiography of Thomas Jefferson, 1743–1790*. Philadelphia: University of Pennsylvania Press, 2005.
Ford, Paul Leicester and George Haven Putnam, eds. *Autobiography of Thomas Jefferson, 1743–1790*. New York: Putnam's Sons, 1914.
Ford, Worthington Chauncey, ed. *Journals of the Continental Congress, 1774–1789*. 34 vols. New York: Johnson Reprint Corp., 1968.
Forster, Greg. *John Locke's Politics of Moral Consensus*. Cambridge: Cambridge University Press, 2005.
Forte, David F., ed. *Natural Law and Public Policy*. Washington, DC: Georgetown University,1998.
Franck, Matthew J. "Two Tales of Freedom: Getting the Origins of Religious Liberty Right Matters." *Touchstone* (July/August 2016): 19–26.
Gallagher, Hugh Gregory. *By Trust Betrayed: Patients, Physicians, and the License to Kill in the Third Reich*. Rev. ed. Arlington: Vandamere Press, 1995.
Gasman, Daniel. *The Scientific Origins of National Socialism: Social Darwinism in Ernest Haeckel and the German Monist League*. New York: American Elsevier Pub. Co., 1971.
Gaudium et Spes (1965). Pastoral Constitution on the Church in the Modern World. Accessible at www.vatican.va/archive/hist_councils/ii_vatican_council/documents/vat-ii_const_19651207_gaudium-et-spes_en.html.

Gaustad, Edwin S. *Liberty of Conscience: Roger Williams in America*. Grand Rapids: Eerdmans,1991.

———. *Neither King nor Prelate: Religion and the New Nation 1776–1826*. Grand Rapids: Eerdmans, 1993.

Gaustad, Edwin S. and Leigh E. Schmidt. *The Religious History of America*. Rev. ed. New York: HarperCollins, 2002.

Gelernter, David. "The Irreducibly Religious Character of Human Dignity." In *Human Dignity and Bioethics: Essays Commissioned by the President's Council on Bioethics*. Washington, DC: President's Council on Bioethics, 2008. Pp. 387–405.

George, Robert P. *Conscience and Its Enemies: Confronting the Dogmas of Liberal Secularism*. Wilmington: ISI Books, 2013.

———. *In Defense of Natural Law*. Oxford: Clarendon, 1999.

———. "Law, Democracy and Moral Disagreement." In *In Defense of Natural Law*. Oxford: Clarendon, 1999. Pp. 315–34.

———, ed. *Natural Law, Liberalism, and Morality*. Oxford: Clarendon, 1996.

———. *Natural Law Theory: Contemporary Essays*. Oxford: Clarendon, 1994.

———. "'Same-Sex Marriage' and 'Moral Neutrality.'" In Robert P. George, ed., *The Clash of Orthodoxies: Law, Religion, and Morality in Crisis*. Wilmington: ISI Books, 2001. Pp. 75–89.

George Washington to James Madison (May 5, 1789). Accessible at http://founders.archives.gov/documents/Washington/05-02-02-0157.

Gerson, Michael and Peter Wehner. *City of Man: Religion and Politics in a New Era*. Chicago: Moody, 2010.

Gill, Anthony. *The Political Origins of Religious Liberty*. Cambridge: Cambridge University Press, 2008.

Glendon, Mary Ann. *Rights Talk: The Impoverishment of Political Discourse*. New York: Free Press, 1991.

———. *A World Made New: Eleanor Roosevelt and the Universal Declaration of Human Rights*. New York: Random House, 2001.

Glover, Jonathan. *Humanity: A Moral History of the Twentieth Century*. New Haven: Yale University Press, 2000.

Goldstone, Richard. "Healing Wounded People." *The Washington Post* (February 2, 1997), C4.

Gorski, Philip S. and Ates Altinordu. "After Secularization?" *Annual Review of Sociology* 34, (2008): 55–85.

Gorski, Philip S., David Kyuman Kim, John Torpey, and Jonathan VanAntwerpen, eds. *The Post-Secular in Question: Religion in Contemporary Society*. New York: New York University Press, 2012.

Grabill, Stephen J. *Rediscovering the Natural Law in Reformed Theological Ethics*. Grand Rapids: Eerdmans, 2006.

Green, Steven K. *Inventing a Christian America: The Myth of the Religious Founding*. Oxford: Oxford University Press, 2015.

———. *The Second Disestablishment: Church and State in Nineteenth-Century America*. New York: Oxford University Press, 2010.

Grenz, Stanley. *Isaac Backus, Puritan and Baptist: His Place in History, His Thought and Their Implications for Modern Baptist Theology*. Macon: Mercer University Press, 1983.

Grim, Brian J. and Roger Finke. "International Religion Indexes: Government Regulation, Government Favoritism, and Social Regulation of Religion." *Interdisciplinary Journal of Research on Religion* 2, (2006). Accessible at www.religjournal.com/pdf/ijrr02001.pdf.

———. *The Price of Freedom Denied: Religious Persecution and Conflict in the Twenty-First Century*. Cambridge: Cambridge University Press, 2011.
Grotius, Hugo. *The Rights of War and Peace*. 3 vols., ed. and trans. Richard Tuck and Jean Barbeyrac. Indianapolis: Liberty Fund, 2005.
Gunn, T. Jeremy. "The Separation of Church and State Versus Religion in the Public Square." In T. Jeremy Gunn and John Witte, Jr., eds., *No Establishment of Religion: America's Original Contribution to Religious Liberty*. Oxford: Oxford University Press, 2012. Pp. 28–9.
Gutman, Amy and Dennis Thompson. *Democracy and Disagreement: Why Moral Conflict Cannot Be Avoided in Politics, and What Should Be Done About It*. Cambridge: Harvard University Press, 1996.
Habermas, Jürgen. *Dialektik der Säkularisierung: Über Vernunft und Religion*. Freiburg am Breisgau and Basel: Herder Verlag, 2005.
———."Religion in the Public Sphere." *European Journal of Philosophy* 14, (2006):1–25.
———. *Zwischen Naturalismus und Religion: Philosophische Aufsätze*. Frankfurt am Main: Suhrkamp Verlag, 2005.
Habermas, Jürgen and Joseph Ratzinger (Pope Benedict XVI). *The Dialectics of Secularization: On Reason and Religion*, ed. Florian Schuller. Trans. Brian McNeil. San Francisco: Ignatius, 2006.
Hall, Mark David. "Jefferson Walls and Madisonian Lines: The Supreme Court's Use of History in Religion Clause Cases." *Oregon Law Review* 85, (2006): 568–9.
———. *Roger Sherman and the Creation of the American Republic*. Oxford: Oxford University Press, 2013.
———. "The Sacred Rights of Conscience: America's Founders on Church and State." *Oregon Humanities* (Fall/Winter 2005): 40–6.
———. "*Vindiciae, Contra Tyrannos*: The Influence of the Reformed Tradition in the American Founding." In Daniel L. Dreisbach and Mark David Hall, eds., *Faith and the Founders of the American Republic*. Oxford: Oxford University Press, 2014. Pp. 34–52.
Hamburger, Philip. *Separation of Church and State*. Cambridge: Harvard University Press, 2002.
Hauerwas, Stanley. *The Peaceable Kingdom: A Primer in Christian Ethics*. Notre Dame: University of Notre Dame Press, 1983.
———. *Truthfulness and Tragedy: Further Investigations in Christian Ethics*. Notre Dame: University of Notre Dame Press, 1977.
———. *Unleashing the Scripture: Freeing the Bible from Captivity to America*. Nashville: Abingdon, 1993.
———. "Why the 'Sectarian Temptation' Is a Misrepresentation: A Response to James Gustafson (1988)." In John Berman and Michael Cartwright, eds., *The Hauerwas Reader*. Durham: Duke University Press, 2001. Pp. 90–110.
Hays, Richard B. *The Moral Vision of the New Testament: Community, Cross New Creation. A Contemporary Introduction to New Testament Ethics*. San Francisco: HarperCollins, 1996.
Hertzke, Allen. *Religious Freedom in America: Constitutional Roots and Contemporary Challenges*. Norman: University of Oklahoma Press, 2015.
Hittinger, Russell. *The First Grace: Rediscovering the Natural Law in a Post-Christian World*, 2nd ed. Wilmington: ISI Books, 2007.
———. *Natural Law and Divine Law: Reclaiming the Tradition for Christian Ethics*. Grand Rapids: Eerdmans, 1999.

Holmes, David L. *The Faiths of the Founding Fathers*. Oxford: Oxford University Press, 2006.

Hooker, Richard. *Of the Laws of Ecclesiastical Polity*, ed. John Keble, R.W. Church and Francis Paget. 3 vols. Oxford: Clarendon, 1888.

Huntington, Samuel P. *The Third Wave: Democratization in the Late Twentieth Century*. Norman: University of Oklahoma Press, 1991.

Hurd, Elizabeth Shakman. *Beyond Religious Freedom: The New Global Politics of Religion*. Princeton: Princeton University Press, 2015.

Hutson, James H. *Forgotten Features of the Founding: The Recovery of Religious Themes in the Early American Republic*. Lanham: Lexington Books, 2003.

———, ed. *Religion and the New Republic*. Lanham: Rowman & Littlefield, 2000.

"In Defense of Religious Freedom: A Statement by Evangelicals and Catholics Together." *First Things* (March 2012). Accessible at www.firstthings.com/article/2012/03/in-defense-of-religious-freedom.

Jackson, Timothy P. *Love Disconsoled: Meditations on Christian Charity*. Cambridge: Cambridge University Press, 1999.

———. *Political Agape: Christian Love and Liberal Democracy*. Grand Rapids: Eerdmans, 2015.

———. *The Priority of Love: Christian Charity and Social Justice*. Princeton: Princeton University Press, 2003.

Jefferson, Thomas. *Light and Liberty: Reflections on the Pursuit of Happiness*, ed. Eric S. Petersen. New York: The Modern Library, 2004.

Jensen, Steven J. *Knowing the Natural Law: From Precepts and Inclinations to Deriving Oughts*. Washington, DC: The Catholic University of American Press, 2015.

John Paul II. *Evangelium Vitae* (1995). Accessible at http://w2.vatican.va/content/john-paul-ii/en/encyclicals/documents/hf_jp-ii_enc_25031995_evangelium-vitae.html.

———. *Fides et Ratio* (1998). Accessible at https://w2.vatican.va/content/john-paul-ii/en/encyclicals/documents/hf_jp-ii_enc_14091998_fides-et-ratio.html.

———. "John Paul II on the American Experiment." *First Things* 82 (April 1998): 36–7. Accessible at www.firstthings.com/article/1998/04/john-paul-ii-on-the-american-experiment.

———. *Veritatis Splendor* (1993). Accessible at http://w2.vatican.va/content/john-paul-ii/en/encyclicals/documents/hf_jp-ii_enc_06081993_veritatis-splendor.html.

Johnson, James Turner. "Humanitarian Intervention, Christian Ethical Reasoning, and the Just War Idea." In Luis E. Lugo, ed., *Sovereignty at the Crossroads? Morality and International Politics in the Post-Cold War Era*. Lanham: Rowman & Littlefield, 1996. Pp. 127–43.

———. "Moral Responsibility After Conflict." In Eric Patterson, ed., *Ethics Beyond War's End*. Washington, DC: Georgetown University Press, 2012. Pp. 17–33.

Johnson, Todd. *Christian Martyrdom: A Global Demographic Assessment* (2012). Accessible at https://icl.nd.edu/assets/84231/the_demographics_of_christian_martyrdom_todd_johnson.pdf.

Juergensmeyer, Mark. "Beyond Words and War: The Global Future of Religion." *Journal of the American Academy of Religion* 78, no. 4 (2010): 882–95.

Kainz, Howard P. *Natural Law: An Introduction and Re-Examination*. Peru: Open Court, 2004.

Keenan, James F. *Moral Wisdom*. Lanham: Rowman & Littlefield, 2004.

Kidd, Thomas S. *God of Liberty: A Religious History of the American Revolution*. New York: Basic Books, 2010.

———. *The Great Awakening: The Roots of Evangelical Christianity in Colonial America*. New Haven: Yale University Press, 2007.
Kierkegaard, Søren. *Eighteen Upbuilding Discourses*. Trans. Howard V. and Edna H. Hong. Princeton: Princeton University Press, 1990.
———. *Works of Love*, ed. and trans. Howard V. and Edna H. Hong. New York: Harper & Row, 1962.
Kincheloe, Joe L., Shirley R. Steinberg and Christopher Darius Stonebanks, eds. *Teaching Against Islamophobia*. New York: Peter Lang, 2010.
Klugman, Jeni. *Social and Economic Policies to Prevent Complex Humanitarian Emergencies: Lessons from Experience*. Helsinki: United Nations University, World Institute for Development of Economics Research, 1999. Pp. 1–30.
Knopp, Guido. *Hitlers Helfer*. München: Wilhelm Goldmann Verlag, 1996.
Kopelman, Loretta M. "Female Circumcision/Genital Mutilation and Ethical Relativism." In Paul K. Moser and Thomas L. Carson, eds., *Moral Relativism: A Reader*. New York: Oxford University Press, 2001. Pp. 307–25.
Kosmin, Barry A. and Seymour P. Lachman. *One Nation Under God: Religion in Contemporary American Society*. New York: Crown Publishers, 1993.
Kotkin, Joel. "California's State Religion." *The Orange County Register* (June 19, 2016). Accessible at www.ocregister.com/articles/state-719782-climate-religious.html.
Kowalski, Gary. *Revolutionary Spirits: The Enlightened Faith of America's Founding Fathers*. New York: Blue Bridge, 2008.
Kumar, Deepa. *Islamophobia and the Politics of Empire*. Chicago: Haymarket Books, 2012.
Kundnani, Arun. *The Muslims Are Coming! Islamophobia, Extremism, and the Domestic War*. London: Verso, 2014.
Kuyper, Abraham. *Lectures on Calvinism*. Rev. ed. Grand Rapids: Eerdmans, 1987.
Lambert, Frank. *The Founding Fathers and the Place of Religion in America*. Princeton: Princeton University Press, 2003.
Lash, Kurt T. "The Second Adoption of the Establishment Clause: The Rise of the Non-establishment Principle." *Arizona State Law Journal* 27, (1995): 1085–1154.
Lean, Nathan. *The Islamophobia Industry: How the Right Manufactures Fear of Muslims*. London: Pluto Press, 2012.
LeBeau, Brian F. *Religion in America to 1865*. Washington Square: New York University Press, 2000.
Lee, Patrick. "Personhood, Dignity, Suicide, and Euthanasia." *National Catholic Bioethics Quarterly* (Autumn 2001): 329–43.
Lehmann, Paul. "Toward a Protestant Analysis of the Ethical Problem." *Journal of Religion* 24, no. 1 (January 1944): 1–16.
Leiter, Brian. *Why Tolerate Religion?* Princeton: Princeton University Press, 2013.
Leithart, Peter J. "Pluralism's Pride." *Touchstone* (September 2005): 15–17.
Lenz, Fritz. *Menschliche Auslese und Rassenhygiene*. München: Beck, 1931.
Lewis, C.S. "The Conditions for a Just War." In Walter Hooper, ed., *God in the Dock: Essays on Theology and Ethics*. Grand Rapids: Eerdmans, 1970. Pp. 363–65 [originally published in Theology 38, no. 227 (1939): 373–4.
———. "The Humanitarian Theory of Punishment." In Walter Hooper, ed., *God in the Dock: Essay on Theology and Ethics*. Grand Rapids: Eerdmans, 1970. Pp. 287–300.
———. *Mere Christianity*. Rev. ed. New York: Palgrave Macmillan, 1960.
Lifton, Robert Jay. *The Nazi Doctors: Medical Killing and the Psychology of Genocide*. New York: Basic Books, 1986.

Lindsay, Thomas. "James Madison on Religion and Politics: Rhetoric and Reality." *American Political Science Review* 85, no. 4 (December 1991): 1321–37.

Locke, John. *An Essay on Toleration*. Reproduced in Mark A. Goldie, ed., *Political Essays*. Cambridge Texts in the History of Political Thought. Cambridge: Cambridge University Press, 1997. Pp. 134–59.

———. *Questions Concerning the Law of Nature*, eds. Robert H. Horwitz, Jenny Strauss Clay and Diskin Clay Ithaca: Cornell University Press, 1990.

———. *Second Treatise of Government* (1690). Accessible at www.constitution.org/jl/2ndtr02.htm.

———. *Two Treatises of Government*, ed. Peter Laslett. New York: Cambridge University Press, 1960.

Lonergan, Bernard. *Insight: A Study of Human Understanding*, ed. Frederick E. Crowe and Robert M. Doran. Toronto: University of Toronto Press, 1992.

Luther, Martin. *Luther's Works*, Vol. 40, ed. Conrad Bergendoff. Philadelphia: Fortress Press, 1958.

———. *Luther's Works*, Vol. 54, ed. T.G. Tappert. Philadelphia: Fortress Press, 1967.

MacIntyre, Alasdair. *After Virtue: A Study in Moral Theory*. Notre Dame: University of Notre Dame Press, 1981.

———. *Whose Justice? Which Rationality?* Notre Dame: University of Notre Dame Press, 1988.

Macklin, Ruth. "Dignity Is a Useless Concept." *British Medical Journal* 327, (December 18, 2003): 1419–20.

———. "Universality of the Nuremberg Code." In George J. Annas and Michael A. Grodin, eds., *The Nazi Doctors and the Nuremberg Code: Human Rights in Human Experimentation*. New York: Oxford University Press, 1992. Pp. 240–57.

Madison, James. *Letters and Other Writings of James Madison*. 4 vols. Philadelphia: J.B. Lippincott, 1865.

———. *Memorial and Remonstrance Against Religious Assessments* (1785). Accessible at https://founders.archives.gov/documents/Madison/01-08-02-0163.

Maritain, Jacques. *The Things that Are Caesar's*. Trans. James F. Scanlan. New York: C. Scribner's Sons, 1930.

Marshall, Ellen Ott. *Christians in the Public Square: Faith that Transforms Politics*. Nashville: Abingdon, 2008.

Marshall, John. *John Locke: Resistance, Religion and Responsibility*. Cambridge: Cambridge University Press, 1994.

———. *John Locke, Toleration and Early Enlightenment Culture: Religious Intolerance and Arguments for Religious Toleration in Early Modern and "Early Enlightenment" Europe*. Cambridge Studies in Early Modern British History. Cambridge: Cambridge University Press, 2006.

Marshall, Paul A. *Religious Freedom in the World*. Lanham: Rowman & Littlefield, 2008.

———. "Why Religious Freedom Must Be a Top Priority." *Cardus* (November 24, 2011). Accessible at www.cardus.ca/policy/article/2992/.

Marshall, Paul A., Lela Gilbert and Nina Shea. *Persecuted: The Global Assault on Christians*. Nashville: Thomas Nelson, 2013.

Martin, Troy. "The Christian's Obligation Not to Forgive." *The Expository Times* 108, no. 12 (September 1997): 360–2.

Martin, Troy and Avis Clendenen. *Forgiveness: Finding Freedom Through Reconciliation*. New York: Crossroad Publishing Co., 2002.

May, William E. "The Sanctity of Human Life." In William Bentley Ball, ed., *In Search of a National Morality: A Manifesto for Evangelicals and Catholics*. Grand Rapids and San Francisco: Baker and Ignatius, 1992. Pp. 103–11.

McClay, Wilfred M. *A Student's Guide to History*. 3rd ed. Wilmington: ISI Books, 2003.

McConnell, Michael W. "Establishment at the Founding." In T. Jeremy Gunn and John Witte, Jr., eds., *No Establishment of Religion: America's Original Contribution to Religious Liberty*. Oxford: Oxford University Press, 2012. Pp. 45–69.

McDonald, Kim A. "A Primatologist Examines the Biological Basis for Ethical Behavior in Humans." *Chronicle of Higher Education* (March 15, 1996): A10–11.

McGrath, Alister E. "The Challenge of Pluralism for the Contemporary Christian Church." *Journal of the Evangelical Theological Society* 35, no. 3 (1992): 361–73.

———. *A Passion for Truth*. Downers Grove: InterVarsity Press, 1996.

McLean, Edward B. *Common Truths: New Perspectives on Natural Law*. Wilmington: ISI Books, 2000.

McLoughlin, William Gerald, ed. *Isaac Backus on Church, State, and Calvinism*. Cambridge: Harvard University Press, 1968.

McWilliams, Wilson Carey. "The Bible in the American Political Tradition." In Myron J. Aronoff, ed., *Religion and Politics*. Political Anthropology Series 3. New Brunswick: Transaction Books, 1984. Pp. 11–45.

———. "Protestant Prudence and Natural Rights." In Patrick J. Deneen and Susan J. McWilliams, eds., *Redeeming Democracy in America*. Lawrence: University Press of Kansas, 2011. Pp. 55–71.

Melanchthon, Philip. *The "Loci Communes" of Philip Melanchthon*, ed. and trans. Charles L. Hill. Boston: Meador, 1944.

Messner, Thomas. "From Culture Wars to Conscience Wars: Emerging Threats to Conscience." *Backgrounder* #2543 (April 13, 2011). Accessible at www.heritage.org/research/reports/2011/04/from-culture-wars-to-conscience-wars-emerging-threats-to-conscience.

Meyerson, Michael I. *Endowed by Our Creator: The Birth of Religious Freedom in America*. New Haven: Yale University Press, 2012.

Mill, John Stuart. *On Liberty*, ed. Alburey Castell. New York: Appleton-Century-Crofts, 1947.

Miller, Donald E. and John H. Yoder. "Does Natural Law Provide a Basis for Christian Witness to the State? A Symposium." *Brethren Life and Thought* 7, (1962): 8–22.

Miller, Nicholas P. *The Religious Roots of the First Amendment: Dissenting Protestants and the Separation of Church and State*. Oxford: Oxford University Press, 2012.

Miller, Perry. *Roger Williams: His Contribution to the American Tradition*. Indianapolis: Bobbs-Merrill, 1953.

Miller, William Lee. *The First Liberty: America's Foundation in Religious Freedom*. Washington, DC: Georgetown University Press, 2003.

———. "The Moral Project of the American Founders." In James Davison Hunter and Os Guinness, eds., *Articles of Faith, Articles of Peace: The Religious Liberty Clauses and the American Public Philosophy*. Washington, DC: Brookings Institution, 1990. Pp. 17–39.

Mitscherlich, Alexander and Fred Mielke. *Doctors of Infamy: The Story of Nazi Medical Crimes*. New York: Henry Schuman, 1949.

Morgan, Edmund S. *Roger Williams: The Church and the State*. New York: W.W. Norton, 1967.

Morgenthau, Hans J. "The Influence of Reinhold Niebuhr in American Political Life and Thought." In Harold R. Langdon, ed., *Reinhold Niebuhr: A Prophetic Voice in Our Time*. Greenwich: Seabury, 1962. Pp. 97–116.

Morris, Robert B. "The Judeo-Christian Foundation of the American Political System." In Robert S. Alley, ed., *James Madison on Religious Liberty*. Buffalo: Prometheus, 1985. Pp. 109–14.

Morrison, Jeffry H. *John Witherspoon and the Founding of the American Republic*. Notre Dame: University of Notre Dame Press, 2007.

———. "John Witherspoon's Revolutionary Religion." In Daniel L. Dreisbach, Mark David Hall and Jeffry H. Morrison, eds., *The Founders on God and Government*. Lanham: Rowman & Littlefield, 2004. Pp. 117–46.

Mott, Stephen Charles. *Biblical Ethics and Social Change*. 2nd ed. Oxford: Oxford University Press, 2011.

Muñoz, Vincent Phillip. *God and the Founders*. New York: Cambridge University Press, 2009.

Murray, John Courtney. *We Hold These Truths: Catholics Reflections on the American Proposition*. New York: Sheed and Ward, 1960.

Myers, Peter C. *Our Only Star and Compass: Locke and the Struggle for Political Rationality*. Lanham: Rowman & Littlefield, 1998.

Nardin, Terry. "The Moral Basis of Humanitarian Intervention." *Ethics & International Affairs*16, no. 1 (2002): 57–70.

Neuhaus, Richard John. *American Babylon: Notes of a Christian Exile*. New York: Basic Books, 2009.

———. *The Naked Public Square*. Grand Rapids: Eerdmans, 1984.

Newbigin, Lesslie. *The Gospel in a Pluralist Society*. Grand Rapids: Eerdmans, 1989.

Niebuhr, Reinhold. "Augustine's Political Realism." In Reinhold Niebuhr, *Christian Realism and Political Problems*. New York: Scribner's, 1953. Pp. 119–47.

———. *Christianity and Power Politics*. New York: Scribner's, 1940.

———. "The Ethic of Jesus and the Social Problem." In D.B. Robertson, ed., *Love and Justice: Selections from the Shorter Writings of Reinhold Niebuhr*. Louisville: Westminster John Knox Press, 1992. Pp. 29–40.

———. *An Interpretation of Christian Ethics*. Repr. New York: Meridian, 1956.

———. *Moral Man and Immoral Society*. New York: Scribner's, 1960.

———. *The Nature and Destiny of Man*. Vol. 1. New York: Scribner's, 1943.

———. "Why the Church Is Not Pacifist." In Reinhold Niebuhr, *Christianity and Power Politics*. New York: Charles Scribner's, 1940. Pp. 1–32.

Nietzsche, Friedrich. *On the Genealogy of Morals*. Trans. Walter Kaufmann and R.J. Hollingdale. New York: Vintage, 1989.

Norris, Pippa and Ronald Inglehart. *Sacred and Secular: Religion and Politics Worldwide*. Cambridge: Cambridge University Press, 2004.

Novak, David. *Natural Law in Judaism*. Cambridge: Cambridge University Press, 1998.

———. "Privacy." In David F. Forte, ed., *Natural Law and Contemporary Public Policy*. Washington, DC: Georgetown University Press, 1998. Pp. 13–28.

Novak, Michael. "Awakening from Nihilism: The Templeton Prize Address." *First Things* 45, (August–September 1994): 18–22.

———. *No One Sees God: The Dark Night of Atheists and Believers*. New York: Doubleday, 2008.

———. *On Two Wings: Humble Faith and Common Sense at the American Founding*. San Francisco: Encounter Books, 2002.
———. *The Universal Hunger for Liberty: Why the Clash of Civilizations Is Not Inevitable*. New York: Basic Books, 2004.
Nygren, Anders. *Agape and Eros*. Trans. Philip S. Watson. London: SPCK, 1953.
O'Connor, Cardinal John. "A Cardinal's Chilling Warning." *New Covenant* (May 1989): 23–4.
O'Donovan, Oliver. *Resurrection and Moral Order: An Outline for Evangelical Ethics*. Grand Rapids: Eerdmans, 1986.
Orwell, Sonia and Ian Angus, eds. *Collected Essays, Journalism and Letters of George Orwell–Vol. 1: An Age Like This, 1920–1940*. New York: Penguin, 1970.
Outka, Gene. *Agape: An Ethical Analysis*. New Haven: Yale University Press, 1972.
Pangle, Thomas L. *The Spirit of Modern Republicanism: The Moral Vision of the American Founders and the Philosophy of Locke*. Chicago: University of Chicago Press, 1988.
The Papers of Thomas Jefferson, vol. 18, 4 November 1790–24 January 1791, ed. Julian P. Boyd. Princeton: Princeton University Press, 1971. Pp. 131–135.
Pellegrino, Edmund D. "The Lived Experience of Human Dignity." In *Human Dignity and Bioethics: Essays Commissioned by the President's Council on Bioethics*. Washington, DC: President's Council on Bioethics, 2006. Pp. 503–39.
Pennings, Ray. "The Secular Democracy and Its Victims." *The Cardus Daily* (June 19, 2014). Accessible at www.convivium.ca/articles/the-secular-democracy-and-its-victims.
Perry, Michael J. *Human Rights in the Constitutional Law of the United States*. Cambridge: Cambridge University Press, 2013.
———. *Under God? Religious Faith and Liberal Democracy*. Cambridge: Cambridge University Press, 2003.
Peterson, Merrill D., ed. *Thomas Jefferson: Writings*. New York: Library of America, 1984.
Peterson, Merrill D. and Robert C. Vaughan, eds. *The Virginia Statute for Religious Freedom: Its Evolution and Consequences for American History*. Cambridge: Cambridge University Press, 1988.
Pew Research Religion and Public Life Project, "Rising Tide of Restrictions on Religion," (September 2013). Accessible at www.pewforum.org/2012/09/20/rising-tide-of-restrictions-on-religion-findings.
Pierson, George W. *Tocqueville in America*. Baltimore: Johns Hopkins University Press, 1996.
Pinker, Steven. "The Stupidity of Dignity." *The New Republic* (May 28, 2008). Accessible at https://newrepublic.com/article/64674/the-stupidity-dignity.
Pope, Stephen J. "Love in Contemporary Christian Ethics." *Journal of Religious Ethics* 23, no. 1 (1995): 165–97.
Porter, Jean. *Nature as Reason: A Thomistic Theory of the Natural Law*. Grand Rapids: Eerdmans, 2005.
Proctor, Robert. *Racial Hygiene: Medicine Under the Nazis*. Cambridge: Harvard University Press, 1988.
Ramsey, Paul. *Basic Christian Ethics*. New York: Scribner's, 1950.
———. "Christian Vocation and Resistance." In William Werpehowski and Stephen D. Crocco, eds., *The Essential Paul Ramsey: A Collection*. New Haven: Yale University Press, 1994. Pp. 41–59.
———. *Deeds and Rules in Christian Ethics*. New York: Scribner's, 1967.

———. *The Just War: Force and Political Responsibility*. Repr. Lanham: Rowman & Littlefield, 2002.

———. "Love and Law." In Charles W. Kegley and Robert W. Bretall, eds., *Reinhold Niebuhr: His Religious, Social and Political Thought*. New York: Palgrave Macmillan, 1961. Pp. 79–123.

Ratzinger, Joseph Cardinal (Benedict XVI). *Values in a Time of Upheaval*. Trans. Brian McNeil. New York and San Francisco: Crossroad and Ignatius, 2006.

Rauch, Jonathan. "The Great Secession." *The Atlantic* (July/August 2014). Accessible at www.theatlantic.com/magazine/archive/2014/07/the-great-secession/372288/.

Rawls, John. *Justice as Fairness: A Restatement*, ed. Erin Kelly. Cambridge: Belknap Press, 2001.

———. *Political Liberalism*. New York: Columbia University Press, 1993.

———. *A Theory of Justice*. Cambridge: Belknap Press, 1971.

Rice, Charles E. *50 Questions on the Natural Law: What It Is and Why We Need It*. Rev. ed. San Francisco: Ignatius, 1999.

Robbins, Chandler. *A Sermon. Preached Before His Excellency John Hancock Esq.: His Honor Samuel Adams Esq. Lieutenant Governour: The Honourable the Council and the Honourable Senate and House of Representatives, If the Commonwealth of Massachusetts, May 25, 1791, Being the Day of General Elections*. Boston: Thomas Adams, 1791.

Rommen, Heinrich A. *Die ewige Wiederkehr des Naturrechts*. Leipzig: Verlag Jakob Hegner, 1936.

———. *The Natural Law: A Study in Legal and Social History and Philosophy*. Trans. Thomas R. Hanley. Indianapolis: Liberty Fund, 1998.

———. *The State in Catholic Thought*. St. Louis: Herder, 1945.

Rorty, Richard. "Religion as Conversation-Stopper." *Common Knowledge* 3, no. 1 (1994): 1–6.

Rotondi, Richard. "Killing as Caring: The False Charity of Euthanasia." *Orthodoxy Today*. Accessible at www.orthodoxytoday.org/articles/RotondiEuthanasia.php.

Salzman, Philip Carl. "Anthropology: Abandon Truth All Ye Who Enter." *The Daily Caller* (July 19, 2016). Accessible at http://dailycaller.com/2016/07/19/anthropology-abandon-all-truth-ye-who-enter/.

Sandel, Michael J. "Freedom of Conscience or Freedom of Choice?" In James Davison Hunter and Os Guinness, eds., *Articles of Faith, Articles of Peace: The Religious Liberty Clauses and the American Public Philosophy*. Washington, DC: Brookings Institution, 1990. Pp. 74–92.

———. *Public Philosophy: Essays on Morality in Politics*. Cambridge: Harvard University Press, 2005.

Sarna, Jonathan D. *American Judaism: A History*. New Haven: Yale University Press, 2004.

Sayyid, S. and Abdool Karim Vakil, eds. *Thinking Through Islamophobia: Global Perspectives*. New York: Columbia University Press, 2010.

The Schleitheim Confession (1527). Accessible at www.anabaptists.org/history/the-schleitheim-confession.html.

Schlossberg, Herbert. *Idols for Destruction: The Conflict of Christian Faith and American Culture*. Rev. ed. Wheaton: Crossway, 1990.

Schulman, Adam. "Bioethics and the Question of Human Dignity." In *Human Dignity and Bioethics: Essays Commissioned by the President's Council on Bioethics*. Washington, DC: President's Council on Bioethics, 2008. Pp. 3–18.

Scott, James B., ed. Selections from Three Works of Francisco Suárez. Trans. Gladys L. Williams, Ammi Brown and John Waldron. Classics of International Law. Oxford: Clarendon, 1944.
———. *The Spanish Origin of International Law: Lectures on Francisco de Vitoria (1480–1546) and Francisco Suárez (1548–1617)*. Washington, DC: Georgetown University Press, 1929.
Sehat, David. *The Myth of American Religious Freedom*. Oxford: Oxford University Press, 2011.
Shain, Barry Alan. *The Myth of American Individualism: The Protestant Origins of American Political Thought*. Princeton: Princeton University Press, 1994.
Shortt, Rupert. *Christianophobia: A Faith Under Attack*. Grand Rapids: Eerdmans, 2012.
Siemen, Hans-Ludwig. *Menschen Bleiben auf der Strecke: Psychiatrie zwischen Reform und Nationalisozialismus*. Gütersloh: Gütersloher Verlag, 1987.
Singer, Peter. *Animal Liberation: A New Ethics for Our Treatment of Animals*. New York: Random House, 1975.
———. *Practical Ethics*. Cambridge: Cambridge University Press, 1980.
Skillen, James W. "Conclusion: The Religion Puzzle." In Luis E. Lugo, ed., *Religion, Public Life, and the American Polity*. Knoxville: University of Tennessee Press, 1994. Pp. 240–52.
———. *Recharging the American Experiment: Principled Pluralism for Genuine Civic Community*. Grand Rapids: Baker, 1994.
———."Religion and Education Policy: Where Do We Go from Here?" *Journal of Law and Politics* (Spring 1990): 503–29.
Smith, Stephen D. *The Rise and Decline of America Religious Freedom*. Cambridge: Harvard University Press, 2014.
Smith, Wesley J. *Culture of Death: The Assault on Medical Ethics in America*. San Francisco: Encounter Books, 2000.
———. *Forced Exit: The Slippery Slope from Assisted Suicide to Legalized Murder*. New York: Times Books, 1997.
Sowell, Thomas. *A Conflict of Visions: Ideological Origins of Political Struggles*. New York: Basic Books, 2002.
Spitzer, Robert J., Robin A. Berhhoft and Camille E. De Blasi. *Healing the Culture: A Commonsense Philosophy of Happiness, Freedom, and the Life Issues*. San Francisco: Ignatius, 2000.
Staloff, Darren. "Deism and the Founders." In Daniel L. Dreisbach and Mark David Hall, eds., *Faith and the Founders of the American Republic*. Oxford: Oxford University Press, 2014. Pp. 13–33.
Stetson, Brad and Joseph G. Conti. *The Truth About Tolerance: Pluralism, Diversity and the Culture Wars*. Downers Grove: InterVarsity Press, 2005.
Stevenson, William R., Jr. *Christian Love and Just War: Moral Paradox and Political Life in St. Augustine and His Interpreters*. Mercer: Mercer University Press, 1987.
Stillman, Samuel. *A Sermon Preached Before the Honorable Council, and the Honorable House of Representatives of the State*. Boston: T. and J. Fleet, 1779.
Strack, Hermann and Paul Billerbeck. *Kommentar zum Neuen Testament aus Talmud und Midrash*. München: Beck, 1922.
Strauss, Leo. *Natural Right and History*. Rev. ed. Chicago: University of Chicago Press, 1999.
Sullivan, Winnifred Fallers. *The Impossibility of Religious Freedom*. Princeton: Princeton University Press, 2005.

Sweetman, Brendan. *Why Politics Needs Religion: The Place of Religious Arguments in the Public Square*. Downers Grove: IVP Academic, 2006.

Tait, L. Gordon. *The Piety of John Witherspoon*. Louisville: Geneva Press, 2001.

Taras, Ray. *Xenophobia and Islamophobia in Europe*. Edinburgh: Edinburgh University Press, 2012.

Terheyden, Michael. *Catholic Charities Forced to Shut Down Services Around the Country*. Accessible at www.catholic.org/news/national/story.php?id=41680.

Tesón, Fernando R. "The Liberal Case for Humanitarian Intervention." In J.L. Holzgrefe and Robert O. Keohane, eds., *Humanitarian Intervention: Ethical, Legal, and Political Dilemmas*. Cambridge: Cambridge University Press, 2003. Pp. 130–74.

Thielicke, Helmut. *Theological Ethics – Vol. 1: Foundations*. Philadelphia: Fortress, 1966.

Tocquville, Alexis de. *Democracy in America*. Trans and ed. Harvey C. Mansfield and Delba Winthrop. Chicago: University of Chicago Press, 2000.

United States Conference of Catholic Bishops. *Discrimination Against Catholic Adoption Services*. Accessible at www.usccb.org/issues-and-action/religious-liberty/discrimination-against-catholic-adoption-services.cfm.

VanDrunen, David. *Natural Law and the Two Kingdoms*. Grand Rapids: Eerdmans, 2010.

Vitoria, Francisco de. "On the American Indians." Reproduced in Anthony Pagden and Jeremy Lawrance, eds., *Vitoria: Political Writings*. Cambridge Texts in the History of Political Thought. Cambridge: Cambridge University Press, 1992. Pp. 231–92.

Waal, Frans de. *Good Natured: The Origins of Right and Wrong in Humans and Other Animals*. Cambridge: Harvard University Press, 1996.

Waldman, Steven. *Founding Faith: How Our Founding Fathers Forged a Radical New Approach to Religious Liberty*. New York: Random House, 2009.

Walzer, Michael. *Just and Unjust Wars: A Moral Argument with Historical Illustration*. 4th ed. New York: Basic Books, 2006.

———. "The Politics of Rescue." In Michael Walzer, *Arguing About War*. New Haven: Yale University Press, 2004. Pp. 67–81.

Weber, Kent. "How Far Is Tolerance a Virtue?" *Regeneration Quarterly* (Winter 1996): 29–31.

Wenneman, Daryl J. *The Role of Love in the Thought of Kant and Kierkegaard*. Accessible at www.bu.edu/wcp/PapersHighly recommended/Reli/ReliWenn.htim.

Werpehowski, William and Stephen D. Crocco, eds. *The Essential Paul Ramsey: A Collection*. New Haven: Yale University Press, 1994.

West, Ellis. *The Religion Clauses of the First Amendment: Guarantees of States' Rights?* Lanham: Rowman & Littlefield, 2011.

Wiker, Benjamin D. "The Repaganization of the West." *New Oxford Review* (May 1996): 19–22.

Williams, Daniel Day. *The Spirit and the Forms of Love*. New York: Harper & Row, 1968.

Wilson, Edward O. *Sociobiology: The New Synthesis*. Cambridge: Harvard University Press, 1975.

Witte, John, Jr. "One Public Religion, Many Private Religions: John Adams and the 1780 Massachusetts Constitution." In Daniel L. Dreisbach, Mark David Hall and Jeffry H. Morrison, eds., *The Founders on God and Government*. Lanham: Rowman & Littlefield, 2004. Pp. 23–52.

Witte, John, Jr., and Joel A. Nichols. *Religion and the American Constitutional Experiment*. 3rd ed. Boulder: Westview Press, 2011.
Wojtyla, Karol. *Sign of Contradiction*. New York: Seabury Press, 1979.
Wolfe, Christopher. *Natural Law Liberalism*. Cambridge: Cambridge University Press, 2006.
Wolfe, Christopher and Robert P. George, eds. *Natural Law and Public Reason*. Washington, DC: Georgetown University Press, 2000.
Wolfson, Adam. "What Remains of Toleration?" *The Public Interest* (Winter 1999): 37–51.
Wolterstorff, Nicholas. *Justice in Love*. Grand Rapids and Cambridge, UK: Eerdmans, 2011.
———. *Justice: Rights and Wrongs*. Princeton: Princeton University Press, 2008.
Wolterstorff, Nicholas and Alvin Plantinga. "Faith and Reason: A Forum." *Books & Culture* (July–August 1999): 28–30 and 32–5.
Woolhouse, Roger. *Locke: A Biography*. Cambridge: Cambridge University Press, 2006.
Yoder, John Howard. *Karl Barth and the Problem of War*, ed. Mark Thiessen Nation. Portland: Wipf & Stock, 2003.
Zagorin, Perez. *How the Idea of Religious Toleration Came to the West*. Princeton: Princeton University Press, 2003.
Zempi, Irene and Neil Chakraborti. *Islamophobia, Victimisation, and the Veil*. Basinstoke: Palgrave Macmillan, 2014.
Zuckert, Michael P. *Launching Liberalism: On Lockean Political Philosophy*. Lawrence: University Press of Kansas, 2002.
———. *The Natural Rights Republic: Studies in the Foundation of the American Political Tradition*. Notre Dame: University of Notre Dame Press, 1997.

Index